Critical Essays on

T. S. ELIOT'S
THE WASTE LAND

CRITICAL ESSAYS
ON
AMERICAN LITERATURE

James Nagel, General Editor
Northeastern University

◆

Critical Essays on

T. S. ELIOT'S
THE WASTE LAND

◆

edited by

LOIS A. CUDDY

and

DAVID H. HIRSCH

G. K. Hall & Co.

BOSTON, MASSACHUSETTS

First published 1991.
10 9 8 7 6 5 4 3 2 1

Critical essays on T.S. Eliot's The waste land / edited by Lois A.
   Cuddy and David H. Hirsch.
        p.   cm. — (Critical essays on American literature)
      Includes bibliographical references (p.   ) and index.
      ISBN 0-8161-7302-8 (alk. paper)
      1. Eliot, T. S. (Thomas Stearns), 1888–1965. Waste land.
   I. Cuddy, Lois A.   II. Hirsch, David H.   III. Series.
   PS3509.L43W36415 1991
   821'.912—dc20   91-6423
                                                           CIP

The paper used in this publication meets the minimum requirements
of American National Standard for Information Sciences—Permanence
of Paper for Printed Library Materials, ANSI Z39.48-1984.⊗™

Printed and bound in the United States of America

Contents

♦

General Editor's Note

◆

This series seeks to anthologize the most important criticism on a wide variety of topics and writers in American literature. Our readers will find in various volumes not only a generous selection of reprinted articles and reviews but original essays, bibliographies, manuscript sections, and other materials brought to public attention for the first time. This volume, *Critical Essays on T. S. Eliot's The Waste Land,* is one of the most comprehensive collections of essays published on one of the great poems in English. It contains both a sizable gathering of early reviews and a broad selection of more modern scholarship. Among the authors of reprinted articles and reviews are Edmund Wilson, Conrad Aiken, Genevieve W. Foster, I. A. Richards, Cleanth Brooks, Richard Ellmann, and Eloise Knapp Hay. In addition to a substantial introduction by Lois A. Cuddy and David H. Hirsch, there are four original essays commissioned specifically for publication in this volume, new studies by Jewel Spears Brooker and Joseph Bentley, Russell Elliott Murphy, George Monteiro, and John T. Mayer. We are confident that this book will make a permanent and significant contribution to the study of American literature.

JAMES NAGEL

Northeastern University

Publisher's Note

◆

Producing a volume that contains both newly commissioned and reprinted material presents the publisher with the challenge of balancing the desire to achieve stylistic consistency with the need to preserve the integrity of works first published elsewhere. In the Critical Essays series, essays commissioned especially for a particular volume are edited to be consistent with G. K. Hall's house style; reprinted essays appear in the style in which they were first published, with only typographical errors corrected. Consequently, shifts in style from one essay to another are the result of our efforts to be faithful to each text as it was originally published.

Introduction

♦

LOIS A. CUDDY AND DAVID H. HIRSCH

I

Like T. S. Eliot's poetry, criticism of *The Waste Land* has moved in circles.[1] The initial responses to the poem expressed the confusion, ambivalence, and annoyance that many readers still feel today when confronting its allusional and hermeneutical complexities. When the poem first appeared in 1922, it was read as an expression of negation, futility, and despair over the emptiness of life after World War I. Only later did critics find a message of hope emerging from the despair. In the 1980s, critics have returned to a concentration on darkness and disintegration, now using the terminology of existentialism, deconstruction, and postmodernism. Recent interpretations apply the philosophical and critical theories engendered by Martin Heidegger and promulgated by Paul de Man and Jacques Derrida, among others, in an attempt to demonstrate once again the void, silence, and philosophical/linguistic negatives and "absences" that are said to pervade the poem. No other twentieth-century poem has generated such responses or provided a better index to the fluctuations of literary criticism in our time.

For this volume we have selected essays that embody the prevailing ideologies of each decade, that reflect a variety of perspectives, and that explicate the poem by employing various critical methodologies. Given the sheer volume of criticism on *The Waste Land* and the spatial limitations of this volume, the difficulties in compiling such a collection should be evident. In making our selections, we have considered what an essay contributed to interpretation of the poem at the time of its first publication, as well as the effectiveness with which the essay reflects the ideas, language, and philosophy of a significant critical movement. Thus, we have chosen to include a selection from the 1956, rather than from the later expanded, edition of Grover Smith's *T. S. Eliot's Poetry and Plays* because we feel it represents the most important scholarly directions of the early 1950s. We would have liked to include both Edmund Wilson's initial review of *The Waste Land* in 1922 and his later revised discussion of the poem in *Axel's Castle* because the 1922 version was an early breakthrough, while the later version, which contains significant modifications, gives an insight into the development of a great

1

critical mind. Together, the two pieces give not only an indication of Wilson's brilliance and resilience as a critic but of the shifting fortunes of the poem. Because the reader has ready access to *Axel's Castle,* however, we made the decision to omit it.

Some of the essays printed here have already been reproduced in earlier collections on *The Waste Land;* they are reprinted here because we feel, as in the case of Cleanth Brooks's essay, that they continue to hold a crucial position in the history of the poem. On the other hand, some essays have been included not only because they contribute to our understanding of the poem but because they are also relatively inaccessible. The essays written specifically for this volume reveal contemporary scholars' enduring tribute to Eliot's influence as well as their interest in expanding our understanding of the text. Though our selection inevitably reflects our personal tastes and individual judgments, we have nevertheless endeavored to deliver a fair representation of essays that break new ground in interpreting the poem and that significantly embody the methods and values of their own age.

In preparing this volume, we began to see *The Waste Land* emerge as a litmus test of critical biases and methodologies. Rereading these essays systematically, we were able to perceive the ways in which the poem took on different shapes to suit each reader's needs. And while Eliot himself is associated with the movement labeled New Criticism,[2] it seemed to us that Eliot's poem anticipated each succeeding critical movement, and perhaps was a catalyst for some. Clearly, no single volume could reproduce every controversial or original opinion about a poem as repeatedly analyzed as this one, but we hope that this book will accomplish its goals of informing and challenging readers, even as Eliot himself did in his own work.

II

Since its first appearance in the *Criterion* in October 1922 and its publication the following month in the *Dial* and in December in a volume (with "Notes") published by Boni and Liveright, *The Waste Land* has generated strong responses of either admiration or disdain. In 1922, Burton Rasco called it "perhaps, the finest poem of this generation; at all events it is the most significant in that it gives voice to the universal despair or resignation arising from the spiritual and economic consequences of the war. . . ."[3] Encouraging reviews of the poem came from perceptive, if ambivalent, critics and poets like Conrad Aiken, or Elinor Wylie, who felt that Eliot's "power of suggesting intolerable tragedy at the heart of the trivial or the sordid is used with a skill little less than miraculous in 'The Waste Land' "[4]; from members of the Erza Pound coterie (e.g., Gilbert Seldes); and from those commissioned to write often anonymous reviews designed to promote Eliot's popularity as a poet (e.g., Edmund Wilson). On the other hand, blistering assessments by people like N. P. Dawson and Charles Powell, who felt the poem was devoid of "meaning, plan, [or] intention" and therefore "so much waste paper,"[5] seemed to speak for the majority opinion.

Examination of the early reviews indicates that the supporters were the intellectuals and artists sensitized to new modes of expression—those willing to give themselves up to what I. A. Richards would call its "music of ideas" and to the emotion that transcended the need for precise meaning. In an unsigned piece in the *Times Literary Supplement,* a most discerning reviewer saw a Dantean correlation that would later become an important allegorical frame for many readings of Eliot's work. Calling *The Waste Land* "a great poem," the reviewer continued: "Life is neither hellish nor heavenly; it has a purgatorial quality. And since it is purgatory, deliverance is possible."[6] Gilbert Seldes, managing editor of the *Dial* from 1920 to 1923, also anticipated a mine of scholarly activity in a review that suggested Eliot's poem was an "inversion" and "complement" of James Joyce's *Ulysses.*[7] Helen McAfee, editor of the *Yale Review,* found unity in the mood and a "redeeming grace" "even in the barren ugliness of 'The Waste Land.' "[8] William Rose Benét, while put off by Eliot's "attitudinizing" and "eccentricity," found the poem deeply moving.[9] Reviewers were often remarkably forthright in acknowledging that they did not understand the poem. Yet, for some poets, like Benét and Humbert Wolfe, this was no deterrent to appreciation. For Wolfe, poetry, by its nature, may have a "beautiful and essential unintelligibility" which conveys "suggestion hiding behind the actual written work." It was enough for Wolfe that the poem ended with an unforgettable "sound of high and desolate music."[10] Hugh Ross Williamson summed up the situation nicely: "Eliot's admirers, though staunch, were slightly puzzled, but made up in enthusiasm what they lacked in understanding."[11]

However, not all readers were comfortable with the poem's "unintelligibility" or found it to be a sign of poetic genius. The reviewer for *Time,* for example, began his cutting, single-column piece, "There is a new kind of literature abroad in the land, whose only obvious fault is that no one can understand it," and ended, "It is rumored that *The Waste Land* was written as a hoax. Several of its supporters explain that that is immaterial, literature being concerned not with intentions but with results."[12] This same tone of annoyance can be heard in J. C. Squire's review, which said flatly that the "printing of the book is scarcely worthy of the Hogarth Press."[13] Others, like Louis Untermeyer, found Eliot's "pompous parade of erudition" and "the absence of an integrated design" to be formidable barriers to appreciation. Eliot's inability "to give form to formlessness," according to Untermeyer, was an unforgivable weakness in a poet.[14] So also was Eliot's use of allusions, which, for F. R. Lucas, resulted in cheap parodies and inferior imitations of the originals. According to Lucas, *The Waste Land* was a "toad."[15] Such critics showed no ambivalence in their response.

Eliot's detractors rejected his structural innovation as well as his use of allusions, which seemed irresponsibly esoteric and designed only to pander to those readers educated in the tradition in which Eliot and his friends operated.[16] Admittedly, Eliot's poetic method excluded most people from the club, particularly those readers who found comfort in the relative clarity of poets like E. A. Robinson and Robert Frost, or of Vachel Lindsey, who was a great favorite of the period. Even the poet and critic John Crowe Ransom, who recanted his attacks years later, wrote a derogatory assessment which initiated a rebuttal by Allen Tate that began the first of many such public arguments about this poem.[17] The published controversy set the new, young innovators against the conservative "Old Guard" in a battle that was called to a truce by Ransom and Tate but continues to this day among critics. Meanwhile Pound kept up his public relations campaign on behalf of Eliot during the years of personal and financial hardship; the avant garde literary community acknowledged Eliot's achievement; and the rest of the world ignored this incomprehensible poem.

For several years after the initial uproar there was little interest in *The Waste Land*—except in the artistic community—until Eliot's subsequent poetry, editorial reputation, and critical essays demanded recognition and reconsideration of his work. T. S. Eliot would not go away, and his serious readers began to offer more substantial critical analyses to justify their respect for the quality of his verse. By 1928 both I. A. Richards and R. P. Blackmur had published essays explicating the themes and style of *The Waste Land*. Such figures as E. M. Forster and Bonamy Dobrée were remarking on the suffering in the poem as well as the poem's virtues, and Thomas McGreevy wrote a brief but perceptive book calling Eliot a "genius."[18] But all this came slowly, despite such support by these and other writers, such as William Empson, Robert Graves, and George Williamson in *The Talent of T. E. Eliot* (1929). As late as 1930, when Charles Williams could not find a "clue" to the "maze" of the poem,[19] Eliot was still not considered a "major" (or even a minor) poet by most commentators on the state of the arts.

In the 1931 *Sewanee Review* John A. Clark summarized the prevalent confusion among the critics: "The status of American poetry today, as seen by many of its critics, is anything but a cause for rejoicing."[20] Poetry was criticized, he wrote, for being too "subjective," "esoteric," "facile," "reduced to the level of an aesthetic exercise, practiced by cliques and coteries"; poets were writing for each other and "reviewing each other's verse" (2). This was poetry of the intellect, with little or no emotion. Though Clark did not name any poet directly in his essay, the charges sounded strangely like those so often made against Eliot and Ezra Pound. Clark quoted numerous critics and reviewers in an essay that mentions Eliot directly only once, and very briefly, while intoning the virtues of the "new breed" of American poets: Edgar Lee Masters, Vachel Lindsey, Amy Lowell, Carl Sandburg, and Robert Frost. Even the article by W. E. Collin in the same issue of the *Sewanee Review,* on the method of T. S. Eliot as a metaphysical poet who "makes us read and think,"[21] could not counter the negative perspective expressed by Clark's opening essay.

Commentary on *The Waste Land* was also influenced by the political climate of the times. In the 1930s, Eliot's poem became a target of writers on the left. New York intellectuals sympathetic to socialism and Marxism were enraged by what Philip Rahv called Eliot's puritan "gentility" and "mock-aristocracy."[22] Rahv, one of the editors of *Partisan Review,* praised Eliot's first book of poems for its "social realism" and its sensitivity to the "profound spiritual problems . . . of modern life" and of "20th century man, who is now alone in the vast universe, destitute of the traditional human consolations of the past" (18). However, he went on to attack Eliot for subsequently reverting to "the classic bourgeois," who "must be discounted as a positive force in literature. His place is definitely with the retarders of the revolutionary urge toward the creation of a new *human* humanity" (19). Rahv considered the "swamp of mysticism and scholasticism" in Eliot's poetry to be "a double damnation" (19). Yet, despite disagreement with Eliot's philosophy, Rahv and William Phillips, co-editor of the left-leaning *Partisan Review,* "shaped their criticism by appropriating some of the central terms of T. S. Eliot's criticism."[23] Phillips wrote an essay in 1934 entitled "Sensibility and Modern Poetry," which, according to Harvey Teres, ironically borrowed Eliot's term in order "to counterpose it to the terms of the dominant reflectionist epistemology and corresponding socialist realist aesthetic of doctrinaire Marxism." Teres noted Phillips's comment on Eliot's own sensibility: "Thus Crane's *The Bridge* possesses 'the sensibility of the machine,' and *The Waste Land* 'conveys a feeling of restlessness, tension, and futility' by attempting to 'span our cultural traditions.' "[24] It would seem that even the ideologues who were in revolt against modernism's aesthetics and beliefs found T. S. Eliot's language and ideas useful as a springboard for their own theoretical formulations. Yet R. G. Collingwood realized that though the poet is the "spokesman of his community" and art is "the community's medicine for the worst disease of mind, the corruption of consciousness,"[25] *The Waste Land* did not fulfill the political expectations of many activists: "it describes an evil where no one and nothing is to blame, an evil not curable by shooting capitalists or destroying a social system, a disease which has so eaten into civilization that political remedies are about as useful as poulticing a cancer."

It was not until the 1930s that the academics became seriously involved in the explication of *The Waste Land* and added their voice to the poets and avant-garde intellectuals who had been singing the praises of the poem. The result was a greatly expanded clarification of themes, structure, and influences in the poem. The decade began with the incomprehension of Charles Williams and moved to sophisticated interpretation by way of the critical skills and scholarship of F. R. Leavis (1932),[26] Hugh Ross Williamson (1933),[27] F. O. Matthiessen (1935),[28] Stephen Spender (1936),[29] R. G. Collingwood (1938),[30] and Cleanth Brooks (1939).[31] Williamson's discussion of how Eliot wove together the Grail legend, Dante's *Inferno,* and other literary allusions showed *The Waste Land* to be "a poetic cryptogram" (81) in which "literary associations . . . are valuable chiefly as reminders of stages of culture and belief" (84). Spender added a psychological perspective by noting the primitive rituals and myths in Eliot's anthropological scheme in which is concealed a personal poem within the poem's historical evolution from ancient Rome to the present. While Spender discussed how the ancient and the modern individual and civilization are linked in Eliot's poem, Matthiessen took up the issue of the split between intellect and emotion, or thought and feeling, that had long troubled readers and attributed that conflict to the influences of Puritanism and the genteel tradition in Eliot's past. Each study added more literary sources and cultural background to the reader's knowledge until in 1939 Cleanth Brooks published the interpretation that has been central to the critical history of this poem. What had seemed to be unrelated fragments were given thematic and stylistic unity by recourse to new insights gleaned from *Ash-Wednesday,* the 1929 Dante essay, and other recent work by Eliot. The poem was now accessible even if the endless sources were still beyond reach.

Regardless of the thematic or philosophical emphasis chosen by the commentator in addressing the issues of the poem, the decade accepted conflicting opinion with relative grace, and critics did not flinch when William Butler Yeats, in his introduction to *The Oxford Book of Modern Verse* in 1936, pronounced on the primary influence of Eliot on poetry in our time. *The Waste Land* was not to be buried by hostility or indifference. Nevertheless, the emotional, autobiographical, and romantic dimensions of the poetry remained unexplored, resulting in charges that cold intellect devoid of heart put off readers who might have responded to his work.

Eliot himself played a crucial role in the criticism of his own work. In some instances his prose resulted in questionable interpretations of the poems. For example, *The Sacred Wood* (1920) led to misunderstandings about Eliot's "impersonal theory of poetry," the "escape from emotion," and the "escape from personality" that seemed to define Eliot's aesthetic and character.[32] On the other hand, his prose has also illuminated his poetry. The publication of his essay on Dante in 1929 and of his Harvard dissertation, *Knowledge and Experience in the Philosophy of F. H. Bradley,* in 1964, as well as the essays on other authors that were used by Eliot as occasions to announce his own literary theories, greatly expanded the critics' understanding of the structure, allusional style, "mythical method," and philosophy in his poems. Critics still return to Eliot's prose to support their theories, and Eliot's poetic and philosophical diction, his tendency to "wrestle / With words and meanings," encourages such interpretive diversity:

Words strain,
Crack and sometimes break, under the burden,
Under the tension, slip, slide, perish,
Decay with imprecision, will not stay in place,
Will not stay still.[33]

Little wonder that readers, looking to Eliot's prose—and poetry—for guidance, have continued to struggle.

Although the decade of the thirties ended with publication of the Brooks essay and other criticism that made new sense of Eliot's work, readers now rejected *The Waste Land* for different reasons. Europe and the United States were on the threshold of the Second World War, and Americans did not want an image of the world as a moral wasteland. The poem became all too real and, as Eliot said in "Burnt Norton," "human kind / Cannot bear very much reality." While the spiritual presence in *Ash-Wednesday,* the *Ariel Poems,* and the first Quartets may have brought comfort to some in the face of wartime terrors, people did not need a poem to remind them of a world they were struggling to deny or forget. Managing to ignore the rise of Hitler and all that it signified about human nature, Westerners held on to the illusion of traditional values, even when confronting a war that attempted to decimate whole populations by a design of cruelty and horror that makes the world of *The Waste Land* look like the Land of Oz. Refusing to recognize their own identification with figures in the poem whose "eyes failed" (1.39), people remained blind to the painful message of the poem—and to the hope held out to those who could see the difference between material and spiritual values. This was a time of forced optimism promising that the "lights would go on again all over the world," as the popular song assured us, and peace would bring prosperity and happiness. In the early 1940s, Eliot's poem did not speak to the needs of a war-ravaged world that could not accept the pessimism (and truth) of his vision.

In that atmosphere, then, *The Waste Land* was either ignored or denigrated for its lack of patriotism and for not expressing a belief in a better world. In 1944, Bernard DeVoto said of *The Waste Land:* "Here thirty concentrated lines of verse [describing the typist and the young man] render life in the modern world as a cheap inanity, love as a vulgar ritual without feeling or significance, and mankind as too unimportant to justify Mr. Eliot's hatred of Apeneck Sweeney."[34] He accused Eliot of making a "final judgment" for his generation about the value of people whom the poet vastly underestimated, for they proved during the war their "courage, fortitude, sacrifice, dedication, fellowship, willingness to die for the sake of the future" (110) in making the world safe for democracy. DeVoto, like most of his contemporaries, identified the "first-rate writers" of his time as "E. A. Robinson, Willa Cather, Stephen Vincent Benét, and Robert Frost" (117).

It was more than Eliot's dense allusional style and wasteland vision that now became the focus of negative attitudes toward this poet. Amid the prevailing patriotic fervor, Eliot's "rejection" of the United States in favor of British citizenship in 1937 associated him with disloyalty rather than with the romantic ex-patriates who indulged in lives of pleasure in Europe after the First World War. Furthermore, Eliot's former affiliation with Ezra Pound—whose Fascist propaganda and raging anti-Semitism during the Second World War resulted in both personal and professional tragedy—did not elevate Eliot in the estimation of American readers. To make matters worse in this climate of guilt by association, Eliot's lectures and essays— designed to promote the religious values that he believed would unify all human beings and cultures—were considered to be exclusionary and anti-Semitic. Critics expressed outrage toward this poet who *seemed* to be saying that anyone outside the Christian tradition was inferior; few would grant that Eliot's concept of the "tradition" included both the ancient pagan (Greek, Latin, and Eastern) and Hebraic values and ideas that were the source and foundation of Christianity and of "Western culture." Yet, according to Eliot's notion of social and anthropological evolution, every age and belief system accumulated to add up to the totality of what we are today.

In 1945, in an essay that indirectly addressed (and attempted to clarify) this issue, the poet Delmore Schwartz explained why Eliot was an "International Hero." Schwartz defined Eliot's frame of reference and associational style of thinking by noting that "the true protagonist of Eliot's poems is the heir of all the ages,"[35] for "Eliot cannot help but be concerned with the whole world and all history" (201). He went on to say:

> When [Eliot] writes of tradition and the individual talent, when he declares the necessity for the author of a consciousness of the past as far back as Homer, when he brings the reader back to Dante, the Elizabethans and Andrew Marvell, he is also speaking as the heir of all the ages.
> The emphasis on a consciousness of literature may also be misleading, for nowhere better than in Eliot can we see the difference between being merely literary and making the knowledge of literature an element in vision, that is to say, an essential part of the process of seeing anything and everything. (201–202)

Schwartz's acute sense of the unifying sensibility underlying both the literature and religion of Eliot is notable: "Hence, to be the heir of all the ages is to inherit nothing but a consciousness of how all heirlooms are rooted in the past. Dominated by the historical consciousness, the international hero finds that all beliefs affect the holding of any belief (he cannot think of Christianity without remembering Adonis); he finds that many languages affect each use of speech (*The Waste Land* concludes with a passage in four languages)" (205).

Despite Schwartz's recognition of Eliot's unifying "vision," readers saw (and still see today) a "shadow" between Eliot's "idea" of unity and the "reality" of what they called (and still do) his religious bigotry. Harvey Teres addresses this issue in terms of modernism: "Thus among some post-structuralist leftists, hegemonic New York intellectuals and hegemonic modernism are joined by the common charge of elitism. Behind this elitism [is] modernism's strong and ultimately determinate pre-disposition toward fascism, racism, anti-Semitism, and other forms of authoritarianism."[36]

Despite such negative attitudes, the 1940s saw an increasing interest in both The Waste Land and its author. With the recognition of his dramas, his criticism, and Four Quartets, Eliot's position in the literary community soared, and there was a dramatic increase in the number of discussions of Eliot's work during this decade. In 1941, Rica Brenner devoted a chapter to "Thomas Stearns Eliot" in Poets in Our Time; in 1942, Philo Buck also gave Eliot a full chapter in Directions in Contemporary Literature. In 1941, there were no articles on Eliot's work listed in the MLA Bibliography and only one book referring to Eliot; in 1950, there were 23 critical articles and books listed under Eliot's name. In 1947, B. Rajan published the first critical anthology on Eliot's work,[37] a practice that has been continued in each decade by such notable Eliot scholars as Leonard Unger (1948),[38] Neville Braybrooke (1958),[39] Hugh Kenner (1962),[40] Tambimutto and Richard March (1965),[41] Allen Tate (1966),[42] Graham Martin (1970),[43] Mildred Martin (1972),[44] A. Walton Litz (1973),[45] and Michael Grant (1982).[46] Several other critical anthologies were dedicated specifically to The Waste Land.[47] Recognition of the poem's value had come a long way since Clark's essay in 1931, as scholars in each decade have attempted to make the poem more accessible to readers willing to make an effort to study it.

Nevertheless, the poem remained a challenge. Not only the sources but Eliot's philosophy and style of thinking were intriguing scholars. Several highly regarded studies of Eliot as a thinker appeared at the end of the decade. In Genevieve Foster's Jungian reading of The Waste Land, for instance, Eliot's poem became a metaphor for the collective unconscious that Spender had only suggested. Her essay, included in this collection, became the acknowledged inspiration for Elizabeth Drew's study, T. S. Eliot, The Design of His Poetry (1949). Different yet converging ways of reading the poem were evident in two other books published in 1949. To Kristian Smidt, The Waste Land "is a criticism of life from a Christian and Hindu and Buddhist point of view . . . with the faith of them all but with a still more powerful scepticism."[48] The poem, said Smidt, is captivating not because "it describes a particular historical situation but because it describes a human soul tormented by eternal problems which the historical situations only served to actualise" (151). Helen Gardner went farther in her assessment of the poet's anguish. Gardner returned to the "sense of the abyss" in the poem.[49] She said that the poem contains no "revelation" of Power, Wisdom, Love, or redemption. Rather, "it discovers in its visions man's incapacity to achieve satisfaction, the boredom of his quotidian existence, and the horror of his ignobility. At the centre of its spiral movement there is simply 'the abyss,' 'the void' or 'the overwhelming question,' the terror of the unknown" which cannot finally be evaded (98). There is a difference, however, between the earliest responses and Dame Gardner's conclusions. In 1922, "the sense of the abyss" was linked to the destruction of civilization, the decay of values, and the loss of hope as a result of the Great War; in 1949, with the European existentialists speaking of the darkness and the futility that is human existence, *The Waste Land* was perceived as addressing the futile quest, the disappointments, the illusions, and the personal responsibilities that define the human condition: "Stripped of his illusions, his pride broken, man is left to face the final possibility" (98). Eliot's poem was once again taken as a representation both of his generation and of all humanity, but now from existential as well as cultural and personal perspectives.

The merits of *The Waste Land* and its author have been debated in every decade since the poem was published, and even the honors bestowed on Eliot in the 1940s and 1950s did not diminish the hostility in some quarters. Rossell Hope Robbins in 1951 offered a chilling assessment of this Nobel laureate: "a poet of minor achievement, emotionally sterile and with a mind coarsened by snobbery and constricted by bigotry."[50] In 1959 another virulent attack came from Arthur Davidson in a book dedicated to the poet Henry Wadsworth Longfellow, "the great American singer."[51] Though not everyone shared these views, they nevertheless represented the opinions of a substantial number of the postwar readers who were also troubled by what they took to be Eliot's coldness, elitism, and bigotry, charges that followed (and troubled) Eliot. The history of these controversies was recently reported by Robert Canary in *T. S. Eliot, The Poet and His Critics* (1982).[52] The various interpretations of such subjects as Eliot's allusional style, his sexuality, the Dantean and Joycean influences, the psycholoanalytic perspective, the classical and Eastern influences, the identity of the central "voice" and persona in the poem, and so on—all these and other elements were discussed and evaluated in Canary's impressive study. Yet, despite Canary's balanced and fair presentation, Eliot's reputation still suffers from the negative interpretations of his work and ideas.

In each decade Eliot's sources have fascinated and frustrated readers. From the first reviews that accused him of esoteric "dandyism" (Munson) and "pompous" "erudition" (Untermeyer), or praised him for the "delicious effect" of his allusions (McAfee), readers have struggled to find clues to the structural and thematic context of Eliot's sources. By 1949 scholars had made a substantial contribution to the recognition of allusions informing *The Waste Land,* despite the rejection of Eliot's intellectual "elitism" during that decade. However, it was in the 1950s with the work of Grover Smith that the significance of the allusions to the themes and "meaning" of the poem could no longer be questioned. Smith opened the decade with a study of Eliot's poems from 1909 to 1928[53] and in 1956 added the book on "Sources and

Meaning" that was expanded in 1974 and has been in print since its original publication.[54] Despite Hugh Kenner's injunction that both Eliot's notes to the poem and the sources should be discarded,[55] source studies proliferated. The influences from history, myth, Freud, jazz, popular songs, and other music (notably that of Stravinsky and Wagner) are but a few examples of the nature of critical exploration in this period that led to the lucid, narrative-style reading of the poem by George Williamson in his "Reader's Guide" to Eliot's work.[56] With the addition of each new critical insight, readers had progressed from incomprehensibility to a comforting sense of the poem's relative clarity so that by 1969, T. S. Pearce could present a rather matter-of-fact explanation of the poem's meaning:

> Once you have come to terms with the techniques of this poem, . . . it is by no means the most difficult of Eliot's poems. It has a fairly obvious development, and the images are not difficult to interpret. . . . To help us towards an understanding, we need to realise that all wars are one war, all battles one battle, all journeys one journey, all rivers one river, all rooms one room, all loves one love, indeed ultimately all people one person, so that all the specific examples of these things in the poem are in every case representative of their kind.[57]

In ten pages of narrative, Pearce concluded that the poem "is about the degeneracy of human nature" (104) and "concerns itself mainly with degraded forms of love" (105). It now sounded so simple.

Among the influences on *The Waste Land* to receive increased scrutiny in the post-World War II years were Dante and Christian thought. Thus, while some readers still made a distinction between Eliot's beliefs and the secular vision depicted in the poem, others conceived the narrative structure of the poem as the progress of the persona (or primary voice) from the *Inferno* to the *Purgatorio*. McGreevy's 1931 view of *The Waste Land*'s preoccupation "with the death and resurrection of the spirit"[58] and of Eliot's sense of "a personal order" (35) reemerged decades later in a perception of the London setting as a Dantean Hell, in the identification of references to Easter and other Christian elements, and in the attention given to allusions of descent and rebirth. Though readers realized that redemption may not be granted to the characters in this poem, there was a personal sense of possibility and hope for a rebirth of the spirit, a world redeemed from the European wasteland.[59] Furthermore, the influence of the *Four Quartets*—their acceptance of life's pain and patterns, the comfort and beauty of their lyrical rhythms, and the sense of transcendence and timelessness in the images and allusions— contributed to the recognition of an ascending spiral in Eliot's work as well as Dante's. The interest in the function of Dante in Eliot's poem has not subsided as A. C. Charity (1974),[60] Graham Hough (1975),[61] Grover Smith (1983),[62] and numerous others have expanded the question of Dantean influence in the poem. The astuteness of their insights may be illustrated by Charity's elaboration on an F. R. Leavis lecture: "I have already quoted Leavis: 'The general truth about [Eliot] is that he can contemplate the relations between men and women only with revulsion or disgust—unless with the aid of Dante.' That, by concentrating on the sexual, is too over-stated and too partial: Dante's aid . . . is called up almost whenever an encounter with an 'other' is required by pressure of an urgently confessional horror" (154). With the passage of time the gift of hindsight has offered a larger vision of the evolution of ideas in Eliot's canon. And with the peace enjoyed during the short interim between the Second World War and the Korean War, American scholars could read the *The Waste Land* in more positive and/or personal terms—if not for the poem's persona, at least for the poet and reader.

After that relatively calm climate, John Peter's 1952 article created a furor that was encouraged by Eliot himself in his public displeasure over the essay. In response to the poem's difficulty, Peter said, he intended his essay to provide "some simpler and more palpable epitome of the poem's meaning."[63] He began the essay, "It is easy to concede to *The Waste Land* the title of the most discussed poem of our age. I suspect, however, there are still many readers who feel, as I do, that the discussion has done little to make it more immediately intelligible and coherent to an unsophisticated audience" (140). Few could argue with this opening. However, it was the choice of theme— "the simplest hypothesis" (141)—that Peter assumed would elucidate the poem once and for all that Eliot, and others, found objectionable: that the poem's speaker had been " 'irretrievably' " in love with a young man who subsequently drowned, and that therefore, "the poem presents . . . a medita-tion upon this deprivation" (143). Though Peter pointed out that he allowed "the sex of the protagonist to remain ambiguous" (144), he ended his essay by declaring the poem an "impassioned history" of a friendship between two male friends and saw "the tragedy of its protagonist as personal" (164). The implications for the poet's life could hardly be ignored. Despite Peter's subsequent apology to Eliot and his offer to publish a retraction[64] and despite Eliot's second marriage, scholars were not discouraged from pursuing similar lines of inquiry. In fact, Peter's work was the acknowledged catalyst for James E. Miller's *T. S. Eliot's Personal Waste Land* (1977). By the 1970s, then, psychobiographical explorations were thriving, though the circumstantial evidence for such speculation remains inconclusive.

When Eliot died in January 1965, the eulogies were considerably differ-ent from the assessments of this poet printed in the 1920s. *Time* magazine, for example, again referred to the difficulty of *The Waste Land* but now in deferential terms: Eliot was called "one of the few major poets of a minor poetic age, and far and away the most influential man of letters of his half of the century."[65] John Ciardi, himself a poet of stature, referred to Eliot as "the last giant of a poetic age."[66] T. S. Eliot had made his place in history and in the tradition he had served with originality and distinction.

Eliot died during a decade of political and social upheaval, a period of revolution and unrest in the United States and elsewhere in the world. While many writers still rejected Eliot's erudition, style, and sense of tradition as irrelevant to the personal "Howl" expressed by Allen Ginsberg and other poets at this moment in history; while drugs replaced religion as the catalyst for mystical vision among the young (and not so young); while other readers dismissed Eliot because of his indifference to racial and gender inequities, even charging him with bigotry and misogyny; while he was being attacked by various literary factions for as many different reasons, he still touched and moved readers who heard the music of pain in the message of a poet who conceived himself as having survived the Underworld and returned—like Odysseus, Lazarus, Aeneas, and Dante—to tell the world of his knowledge.[67] The influence on young people in the 1960s was movingly recounted by Russell Murphy, editor of the *Yeats/Eliot Review,* in a paper presented at the T. S. Eliot Centennial Conference at the University of Maine in 1988. The literary establishment might still be embroiled in controversy over the poem, but to Murphy and others of that generation, *The Waste Land* had reflected their world and inspired young students to continue the quest for meaning and beauty. Furthermore, Eliot's powerful role for so many poets in our time can only be suggested by Donald Davie's tribute: "Mr. Eliot has been a presence in my life more insistently influential than any other writer whatever."[68]

With the publication in 1971 of Valerie Eliot's facsimile edition of *The Waste Land,*[69] curiosity about numerous unanswered questions again generated controversy and became the focus of critical discourse. The controversy over Ezra Pound's influence in shaping the published version of the poem took on new life. A. D. Moody acknowledged Pound's technical virtuosity but felt that Pound did not understand the poem's meaning;[70] George Steiner, on the other hand, paid tribute to Pound's "critical genius"[71] and felt "that he [Pound] understood the poem better than did Eliot" (138), though he admitted that the original draft was "more personal" than the poem published in 1922. The critiques ranged from Gertrude Patterson's contention that Pound's contribution was technical,[72] to Lyndall Gordon's assessment that Pound's editing altered the focus of the original manuscript and turned the spiritual content of the poem into a "cultural statement,"[73] to Richard Sheppard's skepticism about both Pound's editorial usefulness and the *Facsimile*'s value in "the laborious task of reading the poem."[74] The importance of the *Facsimile*'s appearance in print, however, is evident in the list of scholars represented as authors of the reviews. Besides those already mentioned, the list includes William Empson,[75] Bernard Bergonzi,[76] and Frank Kermode, who considered the book to be "both beautiful and absorbing" in this "publication of the most important manuscript in the history of modern poetry in English."[77] The publication of monographs on *The Waste Land* reveals not only the continued academic dedication to the study of this poem but also the importance of the *Facsimile* to some of the readings.[78]

Not only did the published manuscript arouse further debate about technical matters and the meaning intended by Eliot (and Pound); the *Facsimile* edition fomented further discord over biographical speculations that were sometimes uncomplimentary and, according to Valerie Eliot and others, often inaccurate. This issue was discussed in an interview with Mrs. Eliot conducted by Timothy Wilson in 1972:

> We talked about the problems of a biography of T. S. Eliot, an issue raised by Robert Sencourt's *Memoir,* recently published—and widely criticized. Any attempt at biography—and several publishers have blindly commissioned authors to try their hand—which is not officially sanctioned, and therefore does not have access to the papers and letters, is bound to be inaccurate. The problem facing Mrs. Eliot is that the only way to prevent gossipy biographical fragments appearing is for her, as sole literary executor of the estate, to commission an official biography; but she is expressly bound by a memorandum to Eliot's will "neither to facilitate nor countenance any biography of me."[79]

Thus, Eliot's desire that the poetry rather than the poet be the focus of attention has denied critics access to materials that might answer many important questions, and has consequently intensified curiosity and speculation even to the present day. An unfortunate aspect of Eliot's position is that in this interview Mrs. Eliot's anecdotes and memories presented "a different side of the poet" (46), one that is in fact human and well worth knowing. Now, with her 1988 edition of the first volume of the poet's letters,[80] Mrs. Eliot may again feel required to confront the question of a commissioned biography.

The 1970s witnessed an expansion of the critical methodologies and orientations applied to *The Waste Land* as well as a return to questions raised early in its publication. The linking of Eliot's poem with Joyce's *Ulysses,* suggested in 1922 and still considered today to be the major influence on Eliot's "mythical method,"[81] was illustrated by the Fall 1972 issue of *Mosaic* whose contents were divided between essays on *Ulysses* and essays on *The Waste Land* and by Stanley Sultan's *"Ulysses," "The Waste Land,"* and *Modernism* published in 1977. Psychobiographical and Freudian analyses[82] were encouraged not only by Peter's article and James Miller's book[83] but by articles written by psychiatrists (e.g., Harry Trosman[84]) and by comments like the one that appeared in the London *Times Literary Supplement* of 10 December 1971: "[*The Waste Land*] was impelled by a hatred and fear . . . of woman as a sexual partner."[85] The ensuing controversy in the *Times Literary*

Supplement embroiled no less than I. A. Richards, who supported Eliot's right to privacy, G. Wilson Knight, who insisted that the hyacinth girl was not female, Anne Ridler, Helen Gardner, and others, mostly decrying the charge against the late poet, before the argument subsided—at least in the popular press. But not all "biographical" approaches to the poem were sensationalist. A. D. Moody, who asked that "our attention [be kept] upon the poet in the poem," read *The Waste Land* as a "rite" designed "to save the self alone from an alien world."[86] While such eminent scholars focused on the man and his pain, others looked again at the stylistic, religious, and cultural contents of the poem. Ann P. Brady, who showed how "Eliot uses structural and verbal music to heighten a sense of emotional awareness," saw Eliot's poems partly as "clear exploitions of certain theological attitudes toward reality. Woven into the philosophical fabric is the intense force of lyrical expression used to fix, to capture definitively, to concretize the elusive abstractions."[87] On the other hand, Elisabeth Schneider felt that the "central concern" of the poem is once again with "the theme of death and rebirth" while "an ideal unity of culture" provides "its methods or technique."[88]

These studies emphasizing the emotions in the poems were in stark contrast to the views that had been increasingly expressed by "scientific" critics like Steven Foster whose 1965 essay, "Relativity and *The Waste Land*," extolled the poem for being "a mathematical and symbolic scheme of forces, pressures, tensions, oscillations, and waves."[89] According to Foster, who would have astounded even the earliest reviewers who felt no emotion or heartbeat in the poem, "The poem succeeds so beautifully . . . precisely because emotion is absent and the poet never need fear being out of character; like a calculus, its design never intrudes upon his material" (88). We have now arrived at the refutation of autobiographical and cultural aspects of the poem in the interest of the poem (and poet) as machine. However, Foster's view, as subsequent studies reveal, was a minority opinion. The critical emphasis remained on the personal struggles of the poet to mediate debilitating emotion and skepticism, a conflict Virendra K. Roy called Eliot's quest to affirm and "rehabilitate" this "life without belief," or, as Cleanth Brooks had put it, " 'a system of belief known but now misdirected.' "[90] Clearly, Eliot's religious and philosophical views, his attitudes toward women, and his use of sources continued to fascinate scholars.

The 1980s extended the personal possibilities in the poem with studies by Ronald Bush, who sought to examine "the subtlest expression of the innermost self,"[91] by Grover Smith's transformation of myth, symbols, and sources,[92] and by Nancy Gish's study of the "personal center" of the poem through the narrator's memories, sense of loss, fear of sensuality and emotion, and guilt.[93] Robert L. Schwarz, using sources from the books read by Eliot before 1922, presented a "network of psychological associations" in his reading of the poem as autobiography.[94] Russell Kirk rejected the interpretation of the poem as a "gay lamentation,"[95] and instead read the poem's pain as a philosophical and orthodox quest for salvation and a penetration to "causes of a common disorder in the soul of the twentieth century" (74).

Some scholars illuminated *The Waste Land* by way of examining and defining literary and critical history. For example, Sanford Schwartz[96] and Angus Calder[97] presented Eliot's work in the historical context of modernism. Eugenia M. Gunner, in her argument for "unity" as "a guiding principle in the study of [Eliot's] art and thought,"[98] read *The Waste Land* "in one way as a poem that corrects Romantic theory and reinforces tradition" in its "effort to reintegrate the disparate endeavors and beliefs found in Western literature" (99–100).

Another aspect of Eliot's work that has its own critical tradition is the relation of Eliot's work to his Indic studies. Though there are too many publications to list here, the range of Indian perspectives can be illustrated by two examples. A. N. Dwivedi looked at Indian sources as the basis of the spiritualism that informs the poem.[99] However, S. B. Srivastava perceived "an archetypal design resembling Dante's" and concluded, "Eliot in his patterns of imagery has composed the *Divine Comedy* of this century," with the end of *The Waste Land* being Purgatorial in its images.[100] Cleo McNelly Kearns has offered us the most comprehensive and inclusive study of the Indic and Western confluence in Eliot's work to date: "At all times, the juxtaposition of these very different concepts and of the different cultural contexts from which they came gave dimensions to Eliot's work that were subtle and pervasive and that affected the form as well as the matter of his poetry."[101] With this work, any question about the extent of Indic influence on Eliot's mind and art can be put to rest.

During the late 1970s and through the 1980s, European critical theories began to provide additional perspectives to Eliot studies. Although vestiges of the New Criticism were still evident in some of the close textual analyses still being published, many approaches to *The Waste Land* now assumed philosophical and semiotic significance beyond the existentialist and structural analyses that had earlier defined the darkness, despair, and form of the poem. Postmodernism now offered a multiplicity of methodologies that discarded the "fallacies" of the New Criticism and made critical directions inclusive and, ironically, more exclusive. Ways of reading became ways of knowing, so that the hermeneutical approaches examined the cognition of both the poet and the reader.

The new linguistic and poststructuralist approaches generated another round of essays on Eliot's poem. Varied treatments of Eliot's language may be found in articles by William Harmon,[102] Jonathan Bishop,[103] and Margaret Dickie Uroff whose essay on the "Metatext" argues that the language of the poem is the meaning.[104] The new vocabulary and concepts, borrowed from European philosophers and theoreticians by such authors as Gregory S. Jay revealed that Eliot was "a major precursor of contemporary theory."[105] But it required more than a familiarity with Eliot's work to make the criticism meaningful. The reader, coming to these texts without a grounding in the works of Ferdinand de Saussure, Claude Levi-Strauss, Jacques Derrida, and numerous other theoreticians, is not likely to come away with a firmer comprehension of *The Waste Land* or of Eliot. Learning each scholar's vocabulary has become as much a challenge to the reader as understanding the poem.

Yet it is testimony to the continuing cultural centrality of *The Waste Land* that postmodernist critics have remained preoccupied with the poem. Though the Second World War was in many ways more traumatic and more destructive than the Great War, it failed to produce a poem to equal the stature and influence of *The Waste Land,* perhaps because World War II did little more than bring to their culmination the forces of disintegration set in motion by World War I. It should come as no surprise, then, that the criticism of the seventies and eighties builds on the insights of earlier commentators, extending their insights into the present and translating their work into the theoretical and ideational terminology of postmodernism. In spite of the antihumanist thrust of postmodern criticism, the central human issues posed by the poem remain intact: Is *The Waste Land* a Christian or anti-Christian poem? Is Eliot's use of the motif of death-in-life an indication of post-Christian despair or a sign of Christian hope and a plea for the retrieval of lost faith? Does the poem assert or deny the humanist values of Western culture?

Under the influence of deconstructive philosophies, some recent critics have turned aside from the ethical and moral dimensions and implications in Eliot's poem to celebrate the negations that troubled early readers. Concentrating on Heidegger's formulation of the "negative way," Eloise Knapp Hay (1982) developed the thesis that Eliot's Christian beliefs did not appear in the poetry until after *The Waste Land.*[106] She maintained that "if we listen attentively to the negations of *The Waste Land,* they tell us much about the poem that was missed when it was read from the affirmative point of view brought to it by its early defenders and admirers."[107] Using Heideggerian negation as the methodological scaffolding for her approach to the poem, Hay conceived *The Waste Land* as "an expression of horror at the panorama of anarchy and futility within the poet's mind as well as outside in the modern world" (67). Although Hay arrived at this reading of the poem from a Heideggerian perspective, Edmund Wilson, writing from a humanist perspective, had pointed out as early as 1922 that "the Waste Land is only the hero's arid soul and the intolerable world about him."[108] Also in the deconstructive vein, Ruth Nevo insisted that we cannot find a "key" to the poem because there is none. In her essay, *"The Waste Land:* Ur-Text of Deconstruction," Nevo briefly summarized the reasons why the poem is a "Deconstructionist Manifesto,"[109] the quintessential Derridean "text" (459): the poem has "no one point of view, no single style, idiom, register, or recurrent and therefore linking linguistic device," no "dominant speaking or projecting persona, . . . overall subject matter, . . .

argument, . . . myth, . . . theme, . . . conventional poetic features such as meter, rhyme, stanza, . . . [or] formal pattern in any classical sense"; the poem "is totally, radically nonintegrative and antidiscursive, its parts connected by neither causes, effects, parallelism, nor antithesis" (455). "It is an apogee of fragmentation and discontinuity, referring, if at all, only to itself. But this self that it is is constituted by what it is not, its presence is made up of absences, its gaps and ellipses are the fountainheads of its significance, its disorder its order"; the symbols "refuse to symbolize" and instead "explode and proliferate . . . turn themselves inside out, diffuse their meanings, and collapse back again into disarticulated images" (456). We assume that the author intended this essay to be a serious deconstructive reading; however, it may also be read as a parody of deconstructionist methodology.

Although a knowledge of philosophical and critical theories of the twentieth century now often substitutes for the allusional background once required of Eliot's readers, both theory and allusions may be necessary. For example, following the "hermeneutical loop" designated by Brooker and Bentley in an essay included in this collection, the reader is led on a cognitive journey to see in a new way how the text of this poem reveals the inadequacy not only of symbols but of interpretation itself. Including the reader in Eliot's "practice of leading his readers through interpretative exercises before circling them back to a newly demythologized text," Brooker and Bentley offer no positive or consoling conclusions. One can hardly argue against such a persuasive and enlightening approach to the poem, yet some readers might well enjoy the comfort of earlier interpretations when "meanings" were suggested, both for this poem and for our world.

Recent commentators have attempted to deconstruct the criticism of the poem as well as the poem itself, thereby generating a new round of controversies. For example, in his extremely dense essay, "Repetition in *The Waste Land:* A Phenomenological De-struction" (1979), William Spanos concludes that "*The Waste Land* is not essentially a Modernist poem. It is not, that is, an 'ironic' work in the New Critical or Richardsian sense of a formal—a finished, inclusive auto-telic, and self referential—whole."[110] Using a Derridean vocabulary that is as exclusivist as the myriad allusions for which Eliot has been consistently criticized, Spanos described *The Waste Land* as "a poem 'grounded' in differ*a*nce, an open-ended poem the 'occasional measure' of which, like the measure of the protagonist's experience engages an interested—a care-ful—reader as *inter esse,* as being-in-the-world" (265). Many of the early readers of the poem, like Cleanth Brooks, have long granted the poem's open-endedness; Brooks wrote in 1939 that "The symbols resist complete equation with a simple meaning,"[111] but he differs from the deconstructionists in believing that there *is* "meaning" in the poem.

In an effort to define the differences between earlier readings and their own contemporary philosophical approaches, critics inevitably have addressed those essays that must be marginalized to achieve a theoretical reorientation. Even when his name is not explicitly mentioned, Cleanth Brooks often remains a presence in contemporary commentaries on the poem. Harriet Davidson's non-Christian, "Heideggerian-hermeneutic" reading (1985) desacralized Brooks's perception of the poem as a description of the shift from "physical to spiritual sterility," in its "theme of the attractiveness of death, or of the difficulty in rousing oneself from the death in life in which the people of the waste land live."[112] Davidson presented *The Waste Land* as a poem "full of anxiety about death and generation, and aching with desire for a separation from our limitation and finitude. . . . Throughout the poem, the worst horror is reserved for the barren, changeless environments devoid of a human life of pain and death." Like Brooks, Davidson responded to the motif of "spiritual sterility" and "death-in-life," but in keeping with the Heideggerian project, she expressed these motifs in a language that avoided "logocentric" implications of redemption and salvation.

True to their Heideggerian origins, deconstructionist critics dwell in what Martin Buber once described as a "strange room of the spirit [in which] we feel a game is being played whose rules we learn as we advance." As a consequence, deconstructionist critics tend to be concerned with "Being" rather than with human existence (with *Sein* rather than *Dasein*). In contrast to this perspective, John Xiros Cooper (1987), writing from a viewpoint much resembling that of DeVoto in 1944, made the cultural, ethical, and moral implications of the poem the central issue. He developed the argument that Eliot was a "conservative reactionary" dwelling among the "ultra-refined liberals of the Bloomsbury Group," and that one goal of his writing was to jolt his "enlightened" audience by showing them "the brutal face of the social world they had helped bring about."[113] Cooper cited the anti-Semitic comments in *After Strange Gods* and made the plausible point that while Eliot knew these comments would have been acceptable to the original audience for whom they were intended at the University of Virginia, he also knew they would not be "acceptable to liberal sensitivities elsewhere, especially as the fate of the Jews in Germany in the thirties was beginning to enter liberal consciousness" (24). Cooper's observation permits us to observe that although Eliot shared many of the ugly prejudices of his time, he was (unlike Pound) also sensitive enough to reexamine those prejudices in the light of new facts.

Contemporary scholars help us to see the poem freshly, not only by calling attention to aspects of the poem we may not have noticed, but by reexamining the philosophical constructs and value systems that inform the poem. We may not agree with Cooper, for example, but he makes us think about the poem from a refreshing human perspective, continually raising questions that call for a response. He is not an admirer of everything Eliot says in the poem, but he forces us to see it once again as a living work of art. So too do Jewel Brooker and Joseph Bentley, George Monteiro, Russell Murphy, and John Mayer offer new perspectives in essays written for this volume.

Contemporary critical theories, then, have transformed our response to *The Waste Land* and simultaneously returned us to ideas introduced in the '20s, '30s, and '40s. Echoes of Philip Rahv and William Phillips sound loudly in the Marxism of Terry Eagleton. The thematic emptiness of an earlier time has become the conceptual and structural "absences" discussed in essays based on the work of Heidegger and other philosophical theorists. The themes of despair and emptiness are now located not only in the words but in the spaces of the poem. The quest toward a higher, more positive goal is now defined as a "negative way," and meaning is no longer simply interpretation but a hermeneutic enterprise. The unity that was the goal of the New Criticism has been reversed by deconstruction. The understanding that eluded readers in the early decades of this poem's history—meaning that readers knew must be inherent in the poem but a meaning for which they had no key—has become the absence of anything to understand. From entirely different directions, this view sounds remarkably similar to some of the reviews of the poem in 1922 and 1923.

And so we go on reading *The Waste Land,* each in his or her own way, and wonder what the next cycle of critical theory will make of this poem, of its author, and of literary criticism. For *The Waste Land* and its critical history have been one with our civilization, mirroring our intellectual and emotional responses to life and, at the same time, generating new ways of seeing and being. It has been a rich collaboration.

Notes

1. Lois A. Cuddy, "Circles of Progress in T. S. Eliot's Poetry: *Ash-Wednesday* as a Model," in *T. S. Eliot: A Voice Descanting—Centenary Essays,"* ed. Shyamal Bagchee (London: Macmillan, 1990).

2. Hazard Adams and Leroy Searle, *Critical Theory Since 1965* (Tallahassee: Florida State University Press, 1986), 5.

3. Burton Rasco, "Review of *The Waste Land,"* *New York Tribune,* 5 November 1922, part 5, p. 8.

4. Elinor Wylie, "Mr. Eliot's Slug-Horn," *New York Evening Post, The Literary Review,* 20 January 1923, p. 396.

5. Charles Powell, "Review," *Manchester Guardian,* 31 October 1923, p. 7.

6. Unsigned review of *The Waste Land, Times Literary Supplement,* 26 October 1922, p. 690.

7. Gilbert Seldes, "T. S. Eliot," *Nation* 115 (6 December 1922); rpt. Michael Grant, ed., *T. S. Eliot, The Critical Heritage,* I (London: Routledge & Kegan Paul, 1982), 616.

8. Helen McAfee, "The Literature of Disillusion," *Atlantic* 133 (August 1923): 227.

9. William Rose Benét, "Among the New Books. Poetry Ad Lib," *Yale Review* 13 (October 1923): 161–62.

10. Humbert Wolfe, "Waste Land and Waste Paper," *Weekly Westminster,* 17 November 1923; rpt. Michael Grant, ed. *The Critical Heritage,* I (London: Routledge & Kegan Paul, 1982), 200–203.

11. Hugh Ross Williamson, *The Poetry of T. S. Eliot* (New York: G. P. Putnam's Sons, 1933), 78.

12. Anonymous review, *Time,* 3 March 1923, p. 12.

13. J. C. Squire, "Eliot's Failure to Communicate," *London Mercury,* October 1923; rpt. Michael Grant, ed., *The Critical Heritage,* I (London: Routledge & Kegan Paul, 1982), 191–92.

14. Louis Untermeyer, "Disillusion vs. Dogma," *Freeman* 6 (17 January 1923): 453.

15. F. L. Lucas, "Review," *New Statesman* 22 (3 November 1923): 116–18.

16. Gorham B. Munson, "The Esotericism of T. S. Eliot," *1924* (1 July 1924); rpt. Michael Grant, ed., *The Critical Heritage,* I (London: Routledge & Kegan Paul, 1982), 203–212.

17. John Crowe Ransom, "Waste Lands," *New York Evening Post, The Literary Review,* 14 July 1923, pp. 825–26; Allen Tate, "Waste Lands," ibid., 4 August 1923, p. 886; John Crowe Ransom, "Mr. Ransom Replies," ibid., 11 August 1923, p. 902.

18. Thomas McGreevy, *Thomas Stearns Eliot* (London: Chatto & Windus, 1931), 35.

19. Charles Williams, *Poetry at Present* (1930), quoted by John Peter, "A New Interpretation of *The Waste Land,"* *Essays in Criticism* 19 (April 1969): 142.

20. John A. Clark, "Confusion Among the Critics," *Sewanee Review* 39 (January–March 1931): 1.

21. W. E. Collin, "T. S. Eliot," ibid., 13.

22. Philip Rahv, "T. S. Eliot," *Fantasy* 2 (Winter 1932): 17–20.

23. Harvey Teres, "Marxism and the Politics of Modernism: *Partisan Review*'s Eliotic Leftism," paper presented at the T. S. Eliot Centenary Conference, University of New Hampshire, Durham, N. H. (April 1988).

24. William Phillips, "Sensibility and Modern Poetry," *Dynamo,* Summer 1934, p. 22, as quoted by Harvey Teres, ibid.

25. R. G. Collingwood, *The Principles of Art* (1938); rpt. in *A Collection of Critical Essays on "The Waste Land,"* ed. Jay Martin (Englewood Cliffs, N.J.: Prentice-Hall, 1968), 51.

26. F. R. Leavis, *New Bearings in English Poetry* (London: Chatto & Windus, 1932).

27. Hugh Ross Williamson, *The Poetry of T. S. Eliot* (New York: G. P. Putnam's Sons, 1933).

28. F. O. Matthiessen, *The Achievement of T. S. Eliot* (Boston: Houghton Mifflin, 1935).

29. Stephen Spender, *The Destructive Element* (Boston: Houghton Mifflin, 1936).

30. R. G. Collingwood, *The Principles of Art* (Oxford: Clarendon Press, 1938).

31. Cleanth Brooks, *Modern Poetry and the Tradition* (Chapel Hill, N.C.: University of North Carolina Press, 1939).

32. T. S. Eliot, "Tradition and the Individual Talent," *The Sacred Wood* (1920; rpt. London: Methuen, 1960), 53, 58.

33. T. S. Eliot, *The Complete Poems and Plays, 1909–1950* (New York: Harcourt, Brace & World, 1952), 125, 121.

34. Bernard DeVoto, *The Literary Fallacy* (Boston: Little Brown, 1944), 108.

35. Delmore Schwartz, "T. S. Eliot as the International Hero," *Partisan Review* 12 (Spring 1945): 200.

36. Harvey Teres, "Marxism and the Politics of Modernism: *Partisan Review*'s Eliotic Leftism." See also Cynthia Ozick, "T. S. Eliot at 101," *New Yorker* 20 November 1989, p. 119–154, for an example of a recent commentary on Eliot's ideas and attitudes.

37. B. Rajan, ed., *T. S. Eliot, A Study of His Writings by Several Hands* (London: Dennis Dobson, 1947).

38. Leonard Unger, ed., *T. S. Eliot: A Selected Critique* (New York: Rinehart & Company, 1948).

39. Neville Braybrooke, ed., *T. S. Eliot: A Symposium for His Seventieth Birthday* (1958; rpt. New York: Books for Libraries Press, 1968).

40. Hugh Kenner, ed., *T. S. Eliot: A Collection of Critical Essays* (Englewood Cliffs, N.J.: Prentice-Hall, 1962).

41. Tambimuttu and Richard March, eds., *T. S. Eliot* (London: Frank Cass & Co., 1965).

42. Allen Tate, ed., *T. S. Eliot, The Man and His Work* (New York: Delacorte Press, 1966).

43. Graham Martin, ed., *Eliot in Perspective: A Symposium* (London: Macmillan, 1970).

44. Mildred Martin, ed., *A Half-Century of Eliot Criticism* (London: Kaye & Ward, 1972).

45. A. Walton Litz, ed., *Eliot in His Time* (Princeton, N.J.: Princeton University Press, 1973).

46. Michael Grant, ed., *The Critical Heritage*, I (London: Routledge & Kegan Paul, 1982).

47. For example, A. D. Moody, ed., *"The Waste Land" in Different Voices* (New York: St. Martin's Press, 1974); Jay Martin, ed., *A Collection of Critical Essays on "The Waste Land"* (Englewood Cliffs, N.J.: Prentice-Hall, 1968); and Charles B. Cox and Arnold Hinchliffe, eds., *T. S. Eliot, "The Waste Land": A Casebook* (London: Macmillan, 1968).

48. Kristian Smidt, *Poetry and Belief in the Work of T. S. Eliot* (London: Routledge & Kegan Paul, 1949), 149.

49. Helen Gardner, *The Art of T. S. Eliot* (London: The Cresset Press, 1949), 84.

50. Rossell Hope Robbins, *The T. S. Eliot Myth* (New York: Henry Schuman, 1951), 169.

51. Arthur Davidson, Preface, *The Eliot Enigma, A Critical Examination of "The Waste Land"* (London: Arthur Davidson, 1959).

52. Robert Canary, *T. S. Eliot, The Poet and His Critics* (Chicago: American Library Association, 1982).

53. Grover Smith, *The Poems of T. S. Eliot 1909–1928: A Study in Symbols and Sources* (Ann Arbor: University of Michigan Press, 1950).

54. Grover Smith, *T. S. Eliot's Poetry and Plays: A Study in Sources and Meaning* (Chicago: University of Chicago Press, 1956; 2nd enlarged ed., 1974).

55. Hugh Kenner, *The Invisible Poet: T. S. Eliot* (New York: Ivan Obolensky, 1959).

56. George Williamson, *A Reader's Guide to T. S. Eliot* (New York: Noonday Press, 1955).

57. T. S. Pearce, *T. S. Eliot* (New York: Arco, 1969), 95.

58. Thomas McGreevy, *Thomas Stearns Eliot* (London: Chatto & Windus, 1931).

59. Northrop Frye, *T. S. Eliot* (New York: Grove Press, 1963). See also D. E. S. Maxwell, *The Poetry of T. S. Eliot* (London: Routledge and Kegan Paul, 1961), 141, for the importance of "the slight signs of faith" in the poem.

60. A. C. Charity, "The Dantean Recognitions," in *"The Waste Land" in Different Voices,* ed. A. D. Moody (New York: St. Martin's Press, 1974), 154.

61. Graham Hough, "Dante and Eliot," *Critical Quarterly* 16 (Winter 1974): 293–306.

62. Grover Smith, *The Waste Land* (London: George Allen & Unwin, 1983).

63. John Peter, "A New Interpretation of *The Waste Land,*" *Essays in Criticism,* July 1952; rpt. in *Essays in Criticism* 19 (April 1969): 140.

64. John Peter, "Postscript" to "A New Interpretation of *The Waste Land,*" *Essays in Criticism* 19 (April 1969): 165.

65. "T. S. Eliot: He knew the anguish of the marrow, the ague of the skeleton," *Time,* 15 January 1965, p. 86.

66. John Ciardi, "Thomas Stearns Eliot: 1888–1965," *Saturday Review* 48 (23 January 1965): 35.

67. Lois A. Cuddy, "T. S. Eliot's Classicism: A Study in Allusional Method and De-

sign," *T. S. Eliot Annual*, I, ed. Shyamal Bagchee (Atlantic Highlands, N.J.: Humanities Press International, 1989).

68. Donald Davie, "Eliot in One Poet's Life," in *"The Waste Land" in Different Voices*, ed. A. D. Moody (New York: St. Martin's Press, 1974), 221.

69. T. S. Eliot, *"The Waste Land," A Facsimile and Transcript of the Original Drafts Including the Annotations of Ezra Pound*, ed. and introduced by Valerie Eliot (New York: Harcourt Brace Jovanovich, 1971).

70. A. D. Moody, "Broken Images / Voices Singing," *Cambridge Quarterly* 6 (1972): 45–58.

71. George Steiner, "The Cruellest Months," *New Yorker*, 22 April 1972, p. 137.

72. Gertrude Patterson, "*The Waste Land* in the Making," *Critical Quarterly* 14 (Autumn 1972): 269–83.

73. Lyndall Gordon, "*The Waste Land* Manuscript," *American Literature* 45 (January 1974): 569.

74. Richard Sheppard, "Review Essay: Cultivating the Waste Land," *Journal of European Studies* 2 (1972): 189.

75. William Empson, "My God Man There's Bears On It," *Essays in Criticism* 22 (October 1972): 417–29.

76. Bernard Bergonzi, "Maps of the Waste Land," *Encounter* 38 (April 1972): 81–83.

77. Frank Kermode, "Rhythmical Grumblings," *Atlantic* 229 (January 1972): 89–92.

78. See, for example, Herbert Knust, *Wagner, the King, and "The Waste Land"* (University Park: Pennsylvania State University Press, 1967); M. C. Bradbrook, *T. S. Eliot: The Making of "The Waste Land"* (Harlow, Essex: Longman Group, 1972); A. Balachandra Rajan, *The Overwhelming Question* (Toronto: University of Toronto Press, 1976); Marianne Thormahlen, *"The Waste Land": A Fragmentary Wholeness* (Lund: Gleerup, 1978); Grover Smith, *The Waste Land* (London: George Allen & Unwin, 1983); Nancy K. Gish, *"The Waste Land": A Poem of Memory and Desire* (Boston: Twayne Publishers, 1988); Robert L. Schwarz, *Broken Images: A Study of "The Waste Land"* (Lewisburg: Bucknell University Press, 1988).

79. Timothy Wilson, "Wife of the Father of *The Waste Land*," *Esquire* 77 (May 1972): 46.

80. Valerie Eliot, ed., *The Letters of T. S. Eliot, Volume I, 1898–1922* (New York: Harcourt Brace Jovanovich, 1988).

81. Cf. Lois A. Cuddy, "Eliot's Classicism: A Study in Allusional Method and Design," *T. S. Eliot Annual*, I, ed. Shyamal Bagchee (Atlantic Highlands, N.J.: Humanities Press International, 1989).

82. George Whiteside, "T. S. Eliot: The Psychobiographical Approach," *Southern Review* 6 (March 1973): 3–26.

83. James E. Miller, Jr., *T. S. Eliot's Personal Waste Land: Exorcism of the Demons* (University Park: Pennsylvania State University Press, 1977).

84. Harry Trosman, "T. S. Eliot and *The Waste Land:* Psychopathological Antecedents and Transformations," *Archives of General Psychiatry* 30 (May 1974): 709–717.

85. Quoted by James E. Miller, Jr., in *T. S. Eliot's Personal Waste Land: Exorcism of the Demons* (University Park: Pennsylvania State University Press, 1977), 15.

86. A. D. Moody, *Thomas Stearns Eliot* (Cambridge: Cambridge University Press, 1979), 79, 111; see also George T. Wright, *The Poet in the Poem* (Berkeley: University of California Press, 1960).

87. Ann P. Brady, *Lyricism in the Poetry of T. S. Eliot* (Port Washington, N.Y.: Kennikat Press, 1978), 32, 98.

88. Elisabeth Schneider, *T. S. Eliot, The Pattern in the Carpet* (Berkeley: University of California Press, 1975), 65, 64.

89. Steven Foster, "Relativity and *The Waste Land:* A Postulate," *Texas Studies in Literature and Language* 7 (Spring 1965): 86.

90. Virendra K. Roy, *T. S. Eliot, Quest for Belief* (Delhi: Ajanta Publications, 1979), 157.

91. Ronald Bush, *T. S. Eliot, A Study in Character and Style* (New York: Oxford University Press, 1983), ix.

92. Grover Smith, *The Waste Land* (London: George Allen & Unwin, 1983).

93. Nancy K. Gish, *"The Waste Land": A Poem of Memory and Desire* (Boston: Twayne Publishers, 1988).

94. Robert L. Schwarz, *Broken Images: A Study of "The Waste Land"* (Lewisburg, Pa.: Bucknell University Press, 1988).

95. Russell Kirk, *Eliot and His Age, T. S. Eliot's Moral Imagination in the Twentieth Century* (Peru, Ill.: Sherwood Sugden & Company, 1984; rev. ed. 1988), 431.

96. Sanford Schwartz, *The Matrix of Modernism: Pound, Eliot, and Early Twentieth-Century Thought* (Princeton, N.J.: Princeton University Press, 1985).

97. Angus Calder, *T. S. Eliot* (Atlantic Highlands, N.J.: Humanities Press International, 1987).

98. Eugenia M. Gunner, *T. S. Eliot's Romantic Dilemma* (New York: Garland Publishing, 1985).

99. A. N. Dwivedi, *T. S. Eliot's Major Poems: An Indian Interpretation* (Salzburg: Universität Salzburg, 1982).

100. S. B. Srivastava, *Imagery in T. S. Eliot's Poetry* (New Delhi: Vikas Publishing House, 1984), xii, 105ff.

101. Cleo McNelly Kearns, *T. S. Eliot and Indic Traditions, A Study in Poetry and Belief* (Cambridge: Cambridge University Press, 1987), viii.

102. William Harmon, "T. S. Eliot's Raids on the Inarticulate," *PMLA* 91 (1976): 450–59.

103. Jonathan Bishop, "A Handful of Words: The Credibility of Language in *The Waste Land*," *Texas Studies in Literature and Language* 27 (Summer 1985): 154–77.

104. Margaret Dickie Uroff, "*The Waste Land:* Metatext," *Centennial Review* 24 (1980): 148–66.

105. Gregory S. Jay, *T. S. Eliot and the Poetics of Literary History* (Baton Rouge: Louisiana State University Press, 1983), 4.

106. Cf. Lyndall Gordon, *Eliot's Early Years* (Oxford: Oxford University Press, 1977).

107. Eloise Knapp Hay, *T. S. Eliot's Negative Way* (Cambridge, Mass.: Harvard University Press, 1982), 50.

108. *Dial,* 73 (December 1922): 612.

109. Ruth Nevo, "*The Waste Land:* Ur-Text of Deconstruction," *New Literary History* 13 (Spring 1982): 454.

110. William V. Spanos, "Repetition in *The Waste Land:* A Phenomenological Destruction," *Boundary* 7 (1979): 264–65.

111. Cleanth Brooks, "*The Waste Land:* Critique of the Myth," *Modern Poetry and the Tradition* (New York: Oxford University Press, 1965), 137, 138.

112. Harriet Davidson, *T. S. Eliot and Hermeneutics* (Baton Rouge: Louisiana State University Press, 1985), 103.

113. John Xiros Cooper, *T. S. Eliot and the Politics of Voice: The Argument of "The Waste Land"* (Ann Arbor: UMI Research Press, 1987), 27, 39.

REVIEWS

◆

The Poetry of Drouth

Edmund Wilson, Jr.

Mr. T. S. Eliot's first meagre volume of twenty-four poems was dropped into the waters of contemporary verse without stirring more than a few ripples. But when two or three years had passed, it was found to stain the whole sea. Or, to change the metaphor a little, it became evident that Mr. Eliot had fished a murex up. His productions, which had originally been received as a sort of glorified *vers de société,* turned out to be unforgettable poems, which everyone was trying to rewrite. There might not be very much of him, but what there was had come somehow to seem precious and now the publication of his long poem, The Waste Land, confirms the opinion which we had begun gradually to cherish, that Mr. Eliot, with all his limitations, is one of our only authentic poets. For this new poem—which presents itself as so far his most considerable claim to eminence—not only recapitulates all his earlier and already familiar motifs, but it sounds for the first time in all their intensity, untempered by irony or disguise, the hunger for beauty and the anguish at living which lie at the bottom of all his work.

Perhaps the best point of departure for a discussion of The Waste Land is an explanation of its title. Mr. Eliot asserts that he derived this title, as well as the plan of the poem "and much of the incidental symbolism," from a book by Miss Jessie L. Weston called From Ritual to Romance. The Waste Land, it appears, is one of the many mysterious elements which have made of the Holy Grail legend a perennial puzzle of folk-lore; it is a desolate and sterile country, ruled over by an impotent king, in which not only have the crops ceased to grow and the animals to reproduce their kind, but the very human inhabitants have become unable to bear children. The renewal of the Waste Land and the healing of the "Fisher King's" wound depend somehow upon the success of the Knight who has come to find the Holy Grail.

Miss Weston, who has spent her whole life in the study of the Arthurian legends, has at last propounded a new solution for the problems presented by this strange tale. Stimulated by Frazer's Golden Bough—of which this extraordinarily interesting book is a sort of offshoot—she has attempted to explain the Fisher King as a primitive vegetable god—one of those creatures who, like Attis and Adonis, is identified with Nature herself and in the temporary loss of whose virility the drought or inclemency of the season is

Reprinted from the *Dial* 73 (December 1922): 612–16.

symbolized; and whose mock burial is a sort of earnest of his coming to life again. Such a cult, Miss Weston contends, became attached to the popular Persian religion of Mithraism and was brought north to Gaul and Britain by the Roman legionaries. When Christianity finally prevailed, Attis was driven underground and survived only as a secret cult, like the Venus of the Venusberg. The Grail legend, according to Miss Weston, had its origin in such a cult; the Lance and Grail are the sexual symbols appropriate to a fertility rite and the eerie adventure of the Chapel Perilous is the description of an initiation.

Now Mr. Eliot uses the Waste Land as the concrete image of a spiritual drouth. His poem takes place half in the real world—the world of contemporary London, and half in a haunted wilderness—the Waste Land of the mediaeval legend; but the Waste Land is only the hero's arid soul and the intolerable world about him. The water which he longs for in the twilit desert is to quench the thirst which torments him in the London dusk.—And he exists not only upon these two planes, but as if throughout the whole of human history. Miss Weston's interpretation of the Grail legend lent itself with peculiar aptness to Mr. Eliot's extraordinarily complex mind (which always finds itself looking out upon the present with the prouder eyes of the past and which loves to make its oracles as deep as the experience of the race itself by piling up stratum upon stratum of reference, as the Italian painters used to paint over one another); because she took pains to trace the Buried God not only to Attis and Adonis, but further back to the recently revealed Tammuz of the Sumerian-Babylonian civilization and to the god invited to loosen the waters in the abysmally ancient Vedic Hymns. So Mr. Eliot hears in his own parched cry the voices of all the thirsty men of the past—of the author of Ecclesiastes in majestic bitterness at life's futility, of the Children of Israel weeping for Zion by the unrefreshing rivers of Babylon, of the disciples after the Crucifixion meeting the phantom of Christ on their journey; of Buddha's renunciation of life and Dante's astonishment at the weary hordes of Hell, and of the sinister dirge with which Webster blessed the "friendless bodies of unburied men." In the centre of his poem he places the weary figure of the blind immortal prophet Tiresias, who, having been woman as well as man, has exhausted all human experience and, having "sat by Thebes below the wall and walked among the lowest of the dead," knows exactly what will happen in the London flat between the typist and the house-agent's clerk; and at its beginning the almost identical figure of the Cumaean Sibyl mentioned in Petronius, who—gifted also with extreme longevity and preserved as a sort of living mummy—when asked by little boys what she wanted, replied only "I want to die." Not only is life sterile and futile, but men have tasted its sterility and futility a thousand times before. T. S. Eliot, walking the desert of London, feels profoundly that the desert has always been there. Like Tiresias, he has sat below the wall of Thebes; like Buddha, he has seen the world as an arid conflagration; like the Sibyl, he has known everything and known everything vain.

Yet something else, too, reaches him from the past: as he wanders among the vulgarities which surround him, his soul is haunted by heroic strains of an unfading music. Sometimes it turns suddenly and shockingly into the jazz of the music-halls, sometimes it breaks in the middle of a bar and leaves its hearer with dry ears again, but still it sounds like the divine rumour of some high destiny from which he has fallen, like indestructible pride in the citizenship of some world which he never can reach. In a London boudoir, where the air is stifling with a dust of futility, he hears, as he approaches his hostess, an echo of Anthony and Cleopatra and of Aeneas coming to the house of Dido—and a painted panel above the mantel gives his mind a moment's swift release by reminding him of Milton's Paradise and of the nightingale that sang there.—Yet though it is most often things from books which refresh him, he has also a slight spring of memory. He remembers someone who came to him with wet hair and with hyacinths in her arms, and before her he was stricken senseless and dumb—"looking into the heart of light, the silence." There were rain and flowers growing then. Nothing ever grows during the action of the poem and no rain ever falls. The thunder of the final vision is "dry sterile thunder without rain." But as Gerontion in his dry rented house thinks wistfully of the young men who fought in the rain, as Prufrock longs to ride green waves and linger in the chambers of the sea, as Mr. Apollinax is imagined drawing strength from the deep-sea caves of coral islands, so in this new poem Mr. Eliot identifies water with all freedom and illumination of the soul. He drinks the rain that once fell on his youth as—to use an analogy in Mr. Eliot's own manner—Dante drank at the river of Eunoë that the old joys he had known might be remembered. But— to note also the tragic discrepancy, as Mr. Eliot always does—the draught, so far from renewing his soul and leaving him pure to rise to the stars, is only a drop absorbed in the desert; to think of it is to register its death. The memory is the dead god whom—as Hyacinth—he buries at the beginning of the poem and which—unlike his ancient prototype—is never to come to life again. Hereafter, fertility will fail; we shall see women deliberately making themselves sterile; we shall find that love has lost its life-giving power and can bring nothing but an asceticism of disgust. He is travelling in a country cracked by drouth in which he can only dream feverishly of drowning or of hearing the song of the hermit-thrush which has at least the music of water. The only reappearance of the god is as a phantom which walks beside him, the delirious hallucination of a man who is dying of thirst. In the end the dry-rotted world is crumbling about him—his own soul is falling apart. There is nothing left to prop it up but some dry stoic Sanskrit maxims and the broken sighs from the past, of singers exiled or oppressed. Like de Nerval, he is disinherited; like the poet of the Pervigilium Veneris, he is dumb; like Arnaut Daniel in Purgatory, he begs the world to raise a prayer for his torment, as he disappears in the fire.

It will be seen from this brief description that the poem is complicated; and it is actually even more complicated than I have made it appear. It is sure to be objected that Mr. Eliot has written a puzzle rather than a poem and that his work can possess no higher interest than a full-rigged ship built in a bottle. It will be said that he depends too much upon books and borrows too much from other men and that there can be no room for original quality in a poem of little more than four hundred lines which contains allusions to, parodies of, or quotations from, the Vedic Hymns, Buddha, the Psalms, Ezekiel, Ecclesiastes, Luke, Sappho, Virgil, Ovid, Petronius, the Pervigilium Veneris, St. Augustine, Dante, the Grail Legends, early English poetry, Kyd, Spenser, Shakespeare, John Day, Webster, Middleton, Milton, Goldsmith, Gérard de Nerval, Froude, Baudelaire, Verlaine, Swinburne, Wagner, The Golden Bough, Miss Weston's book, various popular ballads, and the author's own earlier poems. It has already been charged against Mr. Eliot that he does not feel enough to be a poet and that the emotions of longing and disgust which he does have belong essentially to a delayed adolescence. It has already been suggested that his distaste for the celebrated Sweeney shows a superficial mind and that if he only looked more closely into poor Sweeney he would find Eugene O'Neill's Hairy Ape; and I suppose it will be felt in connexion with this new poem that if his vulgar London girls had only been studied by Sherwood Anderson they would have presented a very different appearance. At bottom, it is sure to be said, Mr. Eliot is timid and prosaic like Mr. Prufrock; he has no capacity for life, and nothing which happens to Mr. Prufrock can be important.

Well: all these objections are founded on realities, but they are outweighed by one major fact—the fact that Mr. Eliot is a poet. It is true his poems seem the products of a constricted emotional experience and that he appears to have drawn rather heavily on books for the heat he could not derive from life. There is a certain grudging margin, to be sure, about all that Mr. Eliot writes—as if he were compensating himself for his limitations by a peevish assumption of superiority. But it is the very acuteness of his suffering from this starvation which gives such poignancy to his art. And, as I say, Mr. Eliot is a poet—that is, he feels intensely and with distinction and speaks naturally in beautiful verse—so that, no matter within what walls he lives, he belongs to the divine company. His verse is sometimes much too scrappy—he does not dwell long enough upon one idea to give it its proportionate value before passing on to the next—but these drops, though they be wrung from flint, are none the less authentic crystals. They are broken and sometimes infinitely tiny, but they are worth all the rhinestones on the market. I doubt whether there is a single other poem of equal length by a contemporary American which displays so high and so varied a mastery of English verse. The poem is—in spite of its lack of structural unity—simply one triumph after another—from the white April light of the opening and the sweet wistfulness of the nightingale passage—one of the only successful pieces of contemporary blank verse—to the shabby sadness of the Thames

Maidens, the cruel irony of Tiresias' vision, and the dry grim stony style of the descriptions of the Waste Land itself.

That is why Mr. Eliot's trivialities are more valuable than other people's epics—why Mr. Eliot's detestation of Sweeney is more precious than Mr. Sandburg's sympathy for him, and Mr. Prufrock's tea-table tragedy more important than all the passions of the New Adam—sincere and carefully expressed as these latter emotions indubitably are. That is also why, for all its complicated correspondences and its recondite references and quotations, *The Waste Land* is intelligible at first reading. It is not necessary to know anything about the Grail Legend or any but the most obvious of Mr. Eliot's allusions to feel the force of the intense emotion which the poem is intended to convey—as one cannot do, for example, with the extremely ill-focussed Eight Cantos of his imitator Mr. Ezra Pound, who presents only a bewildering mosaic with no central emotion to provide a key. In Eliot the very images and the sound of the words—even when we do not know precisely why he has chosen them—are charged with a strange poignancy which seems to bring us into the heart of the singer. And sometimes we feel that he is speaking not only for a personal distress, but for the starvation of a whole civilization—for people grinding at barren office-routine in the cells of gigantic cities, drying up their souls in eternal toil whose products never bring them profit, where their pleasures are so vulgar and so feeble that they are almost sadder than their pains. It is our whole world of strained nerves and shattered institutions, in which "some infinitely gentle, infinitely suffering thing" is somehow being done to death—in which the maiden Philomel "by the barbarous king so rudely forced" can no longer even fill the desert "with inviolable voice." It is the world in which the pursuit of grace and beauty is something which is felt to be obsolete—the reflections which reach us from the past cannot illumine so dingy a scene; that heroic prelude has ironic echoes among the streets and the drawing-rooms where we live. Yet the race of the poets—though grown rarer—is not yet quite dead: there is at least one who, as Mr. Pound says, has brought a new personal rhythm into the language and who has lent even to the words of his great predecessors a new music and a new meaning.[1]

Note

1. The Waste Land. By T. S. Eliot. 12mo. 64 pages. Boni and Liveright.

An Anatomy of Melancholy

Conrad Aiken

Mr. T. S. Eliot is one of the most individual of contemporary poets, and at the same time, anomalously, one of the most "traditional." By individual I mean that he can be, and often is (distressingly, to some), aware in his own way; as when he observes of a woman (in "Rhapsody on a Windy Night") that the door "opens on her like a grin" and that the corner of her eye "Twists like a crooked pin." Everywhere, in the very small body of his work, is similar evidence of a delicate sensibility, somewhat shrinking, somewhat injured, and always sharply itself. But also, with this capacity or necessity for being aware in his own way, Mr. Eliot has a haunting, a tyrannous awareness that there have been many other awarenesses before; and that the extent of his own awareness, and perhaps even the nature of it, is a consequence of these. He is, more than those poets, conscious of his roots. If this consciousness had not become acute in "Prufrock" or the "Portrait of a Lady," it was nevertheless probably there: and the roots were quite conspicuously French, and dated, say 1870–1900. A little later, as his sense of the past had become more pressing, it seemed that he was positively redirecting his roots—urging them to draw a morbid dramatic sharpness from Webster and Donne, a faded dry gilt of cynicism and formality from the Restoration. This search of the tomb produced "Sweeney" and "Whispers of Immortality." And finally, in *The Waste Land,* Mr. Eliot's sense of the literary past has become so overmastering as almost to constitute the motive of the work. It is as if, in conjunction with the Mr. Pound of the *Cantos,* he wanted to make a "literature of literature"—a poetry actuated not more by life itself than by poetry; as if he had concluded that the characteristic awareness of a poet of the twentieth century must inevitably, or ideally, be a very complex and very literary awareness, able to speak only, or best, in terms of the literary past, the terms which had molded its tongue. This involves a kind of idolatry of literature with which it is a little difficult to sympathize. In positing, as it seems to, that there is nothing left for literature to do but become a kind of parasitic growth on literature, a sort of mistletoe, it involves, I think, a definite astigmatism—a distortion. But the theory is interesting if only because it has colored an important and brilliant piece of work.

The Waste Land is unquestionably important, unquestionably brilliant.

Reprinted from the *New Republic* 33 (7 February 1923): 294–95.

It is important partly because its 433 lines summarize Mr. Eliot, for the moment, and demonstrate that he is an even better poet than most had thought; and partly because it embodies the theory just touched upon, the theory of the "allusive" method in poetry. *The Waste Land* is, indeed, a poem of allusion all compact. It purports to be symbolical; most of its symbols are drawn from literature or legend; and Mr. Eliot has thought it necessary to supply, in notes, a list of the many quotations, references, and translations with which it bristles. He observes candidly that the poem presents "difficulties," and requires "elucidation." This serves to raise, at once, the question whether these difficulties, in which perhaps Mr. Eliot takes a little pride, are so much the result of complexity, a fine elaborateness, as of confusion. The poem has been compared, by one reviewer, to a "full-rigged ship built in a bottle," the suggestion being that it is a perfect piece of construction. But is it a perfect piece of construction? Is the complex material mastered, and made coherent? Of, if the poem is not successful in that way, in what way *is* it successful? Has it the formal and intellectual complex unity of a microscopic *Divine Comedy;* or is its unity—supposing it to have one—of another sort?

If we leave aside for the moment all other consideration, and read the poem solely with the intention of understanding, with the aid of notes, the symbolism: of making out what it is that is symbolized, and how these symbolized feelings are brought into relation with each other and with other matters in the poem; I think we must, with reservations, and with no invidiousness, conclude that the poem is not, in any formal sense, coherent. We cannot feel that all the symbolisms belong quite inevitably where they have been put; that the order of the parts is an inevitable order; that there is anything more than a rudimentary progress from one theme to another; nor that the relation between the more symbolic parts and the less is always as definite as it should be. What we feel is that Mr. Eliot has not wholly annealed the allusive matter, has left it unabsorbed, lodged in gleaming fragments amid material alien to it. Again, there is a distinct weakness consequent on the use of allusions which may have both intellectual and emotional value for Mr. Eliot, but (even with the notes) none for us. The "Waste Land" of the Grail Legend might be a good symbol, if it were something with which we were sufficiently familiar. But it can never, even when explained, be a good symbol, simply because it has no immediate associations for us. It might, of course, be a good *theme.* In that case it would be given us. But Mr. Eliot uses it for purposes of overtone; he refers to it; and as overtone it quite clearly fails. He gives us, superbly, *a* waste land—not *the* waste land. Why, then, refer to the latter at all—if he is not, in the poem, really going to use it? Hyacinth fails in the same way. So does the Fisher King. So does the Hanged Man, which Mr. Eliot tells us he associates with Frazer's Hanged God—we take his word for it. But if the precise association is worth anything, it is worth putting into the poem; otherwise there can be no purpose in mentioning it. Why, again, Datta, Dayadhvam, Damyata? Or

Shantih? Do they not say a good deal less for us than "Give: sympathize: control" or "Peace"? Of course; but Mr. Eliot replies that he wants them not merely to mean those particular things, but also to mean them in a particular way—that is, to be remembered in connection with a Upanishad. Unfortunately, we have none of us this memory, nor can he give it to us; and in the upshot he gives us only a series of agreeable sounds which might as well have been nonsense. What we get at, and I think it is important, is that in none of these particular cases does the reference, the allusion, justify itself intrinsically, make itself felt. When we are aware of these references at all (sometimes they are unidentifiable) we are aware of them simply as something unintelligible but suggestive. When they have been explained, we are aware of the material referred to, the fact (for instance, a vegetation ceremony), as something useless for our enjoyment or understanding of the poem, something distinctly "dragged in," and only, perhaps, of interest as having suggested a pleasantly ambiguous line. For unless an allusion is made to live identifiably, to flower where transplanted, it is otiose. We admit the beauty of the implicational or allusive method; but the key to an implication should be in the implication itself, not outside of it. We admit the value of the esoteric pattern; but the pattern should disclose its secret, should not be dependent on a cypher. Mr. Eliot assumes for his allusions, and for the fact that they actually allude to something, an importance which the allusions themselves do not, as expressed, aesthetically command, nor, as explained, logically command; which is pretentious. He is a little pretentious, too, in his "plan"—*qui pourtant n'existe pas*. If it is a plan, then its principle is oddly akin to planlessness. Here and there, in the wilderness, a broken finger-post.

I enumerate these objections not, I must emphasize, in derogation of the poem, but to dispel, if possible, an illusion as to its nature. It is perhaps important to note that Mr. Eliot, with his comment on the "plan," and several critics, with their admiration of the poem's woven complexity, minister to the idea that *The Waste Land* is, precisely, a kind of epic in a walnut shell: elaborate, ordered, unfolded with a logic at every point discernible; but it is also important to note that this idea is false. With or without the notes the poem belongs rather to that symbolical order in which one may justly say that the "meaning" is not explicitly, or exactly, worked out. Mr. Eliot's net is wide, its meshes are small; and he catches a good deal more—thank heaven—than he pretends to. If space permitted one could pick out many lines and passages and parodies and quotations which do not demonstrably, in any "logical" sense, carry forward the theme, passages which unjustifiably, but happily, "expand" beyond its purpose. Thus the poem has an emotional value far clearer and richer than its arbitrary and rather unworkable logical value. One might assume that it originally consisted of a number of separate poems which have been telescoped—given a kind of forced unity. The Waste Land conception offered itself as a generous net which would, if not unify, at any rate contain these varied elements. We are aware of this superficial "binding"—we observe the anticipation and repetition of themes, motifs; "Fear death by water" anticipates the episode of Phlebas, the cry of the nightingale is repeated; but these are pretty flimsy links, and do not genuinely bind because they do not reappear naturally, but arbitrarily. This suggests, indeed, that Mr. Eliot is perhaps attempting a kind of program music in words, endeavoring to rule out "emotional accidents" by supplying his readers, in notes, with only those associations which are correct. He himself hints at the musical analogy when he observes that "In the first part of Part V three themes are employed."

I think, therefore, that the poem must be taken—most invitingly offers itself—as a brilliant and kaleidoscopic confusion; as a series of sharp, discrete, slightly related perceptions and feelings, dramatically and lyrically presented, and violently juxtaposed (for effect of dissonance), so as to give us an impression of an intensely modern, intensely literary consciousness which perceives itself to be not a unit but a chance correlation or conglomerate of mutually discolorative fragments. We are invited into a mind, a world, which is a "broken bundle of mirrors," a "heap of broken images." Isn't it that Mr. Eliot, finding it "impossible to say just what he means"—to recapitulate, to enumerate all the events and discoveries and memories that make a consciousness—has emulated the "magic lantern" that throws "the nerves in pattern on a screen"? If we perceive the poem in this light, as a series of brilliant, brief, unrelated or dimly related pictures by which a consciousness empties itself of its characteristic contents, then we also perceive that, anomalously, though the dropping out of any one picture would not in the least affect the logic or "meaning" of the whole, it would seriously detract from the value of the portrait. The "plan" of the poem would not greatly suffer, one makes bold to assert, by the elimination of "April is the cruellest month" or Phlebas, or the Thames daughters, or Sosostris or "You gave me hyacinths" or "A woman drew her long black hair out tight"; nor would it matter if it did. These things are not important parts of an important or careful intellectual pattern; but they are important parts of an important emotional ensemble. The relation between Tiresias (who is said to unify the poem, in a sense, as spectator) and the Waste Land, or Mr. Eugenides, or Hyacinth, or any other fragment, is a dim and tonal one, not exact. It will not bear analysis, it is not always operating, nor can one say with assurance, at any given point, how much it is operating. In this sense *The Waste Land* is a series of separate poems or passages, not perhaps all written at one time or with one aim, to which a spurious but happy sequence has been given. This spurious sequence has a value—it creates the necessary superficial formal unity; but it need not be stressed, as the Notes stress it. Could one not wholly rely for one's unity—as Mr. Eliot *has* largely relied—simply on the dim unity of "personality" which would underlie the retailed contents of a single consciousness? Unless one is going to carry unification very far, weave and interweave very closely, it would perhaps be as well not to unify it at all; to dispense, for example, with arbitrary repetitions.

We reach thus the conclusion that the poem succeeds—as it brilliantly does—by virtue of its incoherence, not of its plan: by virtue of its ambiguities, not of its explanations. Its incoherence is a virtue because its *donnée* is incoherence. Its rich, vivid, crowded use of implication is a virtue, as implication is always a virtue—it shimmers, it suggests, it gives the desired strangeness. But when, as often, Mr. Eliot uses an implication beautifully—conveys by means of a picture-symbol or action-symbol a feeling—we do not require to be told that he had in mind a passage in the *Encyclopedia,* or the color of his nursery wall; the information is disquieting, has a sour air of pedantry. We "accept" the poem as we would accept a powerful, melancholy tone-poem. We do not want to be told what occurs; nor is it more than mildly amusing to know what passages are, in the Straussian manner, echoes or parodies. We cannot believe that every syllable has an algebraic inevitability, nor would we wish it so. We could dispense with the French, Italian, Latin, and Hindu phrases—they are irritating. But when our reservations have all been made, we accept *The Waste Land* as one of the most moving and original poems of our time. It captures us. And we sigh, with a dubious eye on the "notes" and "plan," our bewilderment that after so fine a performance Mr. Eliot should have thought it an occasion for calling "Tullia's ape a marmosyte." Tullia's ape is good enough.

Enjoying Poor Literature

N. P. DAWSON

So many people seem to be enjoying poor books these days—as in Ethan Frome's world of nostrums—that it is becoming a little alarming. Let a book only be bad, obscure, "frank" and especially "despairing" enough, and the land becomes filled with the groans and lamentations of young men and women in veritable ecstasies of mingled joy and suffering; until book reviewers seem no longer ordinary respectable persons, doing their day's work and receiving a pay envelope, but whirling and howling dervishes, mediæval holy men beating their breasts and uttering strange incantations. Or if the critics be of milder sex, they raise their voices in imitation of the mourning Irish women in a Synge play, and keen, long and shrilly. However it is, no doubt remains that a good time is being had by all those present.

The book that has recently been enjoyed the most in this odd way, because the most despairing, is Mr. T. S. Eliot's poem, "The Waste Land." Mr. Eliot seems to be one of those Americans seeking a more civilized atmosphere abroad. He is trying London. "The Waste Land" originally appeared in a publication of which he was editor. "An obscure and amusing poem," said one of the prominent English critics—which seems slightly inadequate as contrasted with the enthusiasm of some of the higher criticism in America. Later "The Waste Land" was published in an American magazine, devoted to the higher things, and an award of $2,000 was given to Mr. Eliot for his service to letters. "The Waste Land" then appeared in a thin volume, with about thirty small pages of poem to half that number of explanatory notes. Whereupon the storm broke! A number of reviewers and critics were shaken to their depths—to their depths, if the meaning is clear—by the poem; and perhaps more particularly by the awe-inspiring notes. The whole episode of the reception of Mr. Eliot's poem in this country has been sufficiently hilarious to deserve to be recorded with some detail.

"The Waste Land" did strange and truly terrifying things to some of those who read it. "Let me be frank," wrote one of the most distinguished of the critics; and he described unblushingly the "physiological phenomena" which accompanied his first reading of the poem. That he survived is a miracle:

Reprinted from *Forum* 69 (March 1923): 1371–77.

This poem sings of modern life in accents so anguished, passionate, bitter, hurt and plaintive that it tortured my emotions almost beyond endurance. . . . A mere reading of the poem induced in me such physiological phenomena as may be described as a rushing of hot, feverish blood to the head, a depressing sense of weight about the heart, moisture in the palms and eyes, tremors in the nerves, an increased rapidity of respiration—in short, the accountable and visible phenomena attending ecstasy, wonder and despair (or perhaps intimations of poignant beauty). . . .

The intimations of poignant beauty seem to have come to this particular critic through the lines that have already been sung from sea to sea, from New York to California and back again, with many stops on the way; until the very acts of the country must know them, as Mark Twain said of "Du bist wie eine Blume."

> O the moon shone bright on Mrs. Porter
> And her daughter.
> They *wash* their feet in soda water.
> O ces voix d'enfants, chantant dans la coupole!

The concluding French line is characteristic of Mr. Eliot's erudition, and explains perhaps the intellectual affinity between him and the higher critics. "To comprehend the mood and meaning of these lines," wrote our anguished critic, "is to comprehend the mood and meaning of the whole poem." And anyone who was so careless as to read ice-cream soda-water in quoting them, instead of "just plain sodawater"—which everyone knows is good for "tired and swollen feet"—could not be expected to enjoy to the full "The Waste Land." The poem, said this reviewer, is "tragic in mood," and "akin to a dirge or a lament."

Another critic reviewed Mr. Eliot's poem under the heading "The Poetry of Drought." This threw a beam of light into the obscurity. It is easier to understand that "The Waste Land" is a poem of despair, and is indeed another agonized outcry, perhaps, against the Eighteenth Amendment and the Volstead Act such as was voiced by the Thirty Americans in their inquiry ("inquest" as someone called it) into "Civilization in the United States." In "The Waste Land" this reviewer found "the delirious hallucinations of a man who is dying of thirst." He wrote that Mr. Eliot "hears in his own parched cry the voice of all the thirsty men of the past. . . ."

With this elucidation of the poem, it became easier to see the resemblance of "The Waste Land" to a "dirge or a lament," and to know also why it is "so tragic in mood." It was natural for the poem to be enjoyed more in Prohibition America than in England. The dirge is doubtless "Yo-ho-ho, and a bottle of rum," and the lament is "Oh how dry I am!" Still further support of the dry motive of the poem may be found in the equally celebrated lines:

> Out of the window, perilously spread
> Her drying combinations, touched by the
> sun's last rays.

This lyrical use of underwear led one reviewer, less anguished than the others, to resurrect Oliver Herford's lovely line about "the short and simple flannels of the poor."

A woman critic in this choral of praise for "The Waste Land" found also authentic despair, and wrote: "I think that Mr. Eliot conceived 'The Waste Land' out of an extremity of tragic emotion and expressed it in his own voice and in the voice of other unhappy men not carefully and elaborately trained in close harmony, but coming as confused and frightening and beautiful murmur out of the bowels of the earth." This reviewer was indeed shaken to the depths by Mr. Eliot's poem; and it must be admitted that tragic emotion might well be in a poem in which a man cruelly admonishes a woman:

> You have them all out, Lil, and get a new set.

A new set of teeth, that is. But how could anyone find the men's tragic voices untrained and inharmonious when confronted by what one of the reviewers of "The Waste Land" called the "ineffable" lines:

> Good night ladies, good night, sweet ladies,
> good night, good night.

Still more ineffable, perhaps, the line would have been if had been added, "We're going to leave you now."

> Twit, twit, twit,
> Jug, jug, jug, jug. . . .

These lines have been explained as "an imitation of the sound of birds," to produce a musical effect, following the example of something in the Pervigilium Veneris, Sappho, Ecclesiastes, or we forget what it was. There is musical effect also in the following lines:

Listen to this:

> On Margate Sands
> I can connect
> Nothing with Nothing.
> The broken finger nails of dirty hands.
> My people, humble people who expect
> Nothing.
> La, la . . .

Harmony and rhythm are also in the favorite lines in the poem—judging by the frequency with which they have been quoted—which so delicately tell how the woman, after her caller has gone, like Miss Sadie Thompson in Mr. Maugham's story (and play) puts a record on the gramophone:

> She turns and looks a moment in the glass,
>> Hardly aware of her departed lover;
> Her brain allows one half-formed thought to pass:
>> "Well, now that's done; and I'm glad it's over."
> When lovely woman stoops to folly and
>> Paces about her room, alone,
> She smooths her hair with automatic hand,
>> And puts a record on the gramophone.

It may be seen by this time that Mr. Eliot, as one of the higher critics admitted, "has drawn rather heavily on books." From the author's notes, this reviewer, to facilitate the reading of the poem, listed the principal sources upon which Mr. Eliot drew to produce his poem of despair: "the Vedic Hymns, Buddha, the Psalms, Ezekiel, Ecclesiastes, Luke, Sappho, Virgil, Ovid, Petronius, the Pervigilium Veneris, St. Augustine, Dante, the Grail legends, early English poetry, Kyd, Spenser, Shakespeare, John Gay, Webster, Middleton, Milton, Goldsmith, Gerard de Nerval, Froude, Baudelaire, Verlaine, Swinburne, Wagner, the Golden Bough, Miss Weston's book, various popular ballads, and the author's own earlier poems."

In view of the fact that there are only seven hundred lines in the entire poem it is agreeable to know that the author has borrowed from some little things of his own. We can imagine Mr. Eliot's amusement in collecting all the lines and sorting them and putting them together. The game of putting words together should at least be as diverting as a picture puzzle. But the point is must the rest of us enjoy it as much as he may have enjoyed it? Are we called upon to enjoy it at all? Nothing used to be more irritating than to watch another person struggling with a picture puzzle; especially if he did not seem to be getting on very well, and it remained a good deal of a muddle. After he had finished (?) reading "Ulysses," Arnold Bennett said he felt like a general who had just put down an insurrection. Not being a general, however, he seemed to have some doubts as to whether he should have taken upon himself to put down an insurrection. "After all," said Mr. Bennett, "to comprehend 'Ulysses' is not among the recognized learned professions, and nobody should give his entire existence to the job."

So far as "The Waste Land" was concerned, there were enough generals to command, so that all the rest of us had to do was to obey. But it is not enough for some to have a general say that "The Waste Land" is "the finest poem in the English language." They want to be shown. They want at least to have a few sample lines given to them so that they may judge for themselves what all the agony is about—and whether it is time to weep or to laugh.

The author of "The Diary of a Disappointed Man," who died horribly, surely had as much reason as anyone to revel in despair and to welcome a civilization at last laid waste. But even "Barbellion" (Cummings) thought that civilization, unlike modern marriage, was ours now for better or for worse; and he wrote: "There can be no monstrous deflection in its evolution at this late period any more than we can hope to cultivate the pineal eye on top of our heads—useful as it would be in these days of æroplanes."

If we did have a pineal eye on top of our heads now, we are sure we should see the gods rocking with laughter. And who knows whether Mr. T. S. Eliot himself may not be gently rocking too? At least it is to be hoped that he will try to emulate the admirable poise of Pet Marjorie's barnyard fowl, who in the distress of seeing her progeny profaned—

> . . . was more than usually ca'm
> She did not give a single damn.

But the discouraging part of the whole matter is that after all the despair and all the dryness and the lamentations, there are writers, and plenty of them, who, like Werther's Charlotte, go on cutting the plain bread-and-butter of sane and humorous and intelligible literature. Why do they do it? Do they not know that everything has been "done," and a state of "exhaustion" has been reached in prose and verse forms which makes a demand for something new and something different—even if it is something that nobody could ever hope, or even be expected, to understand?

PUBLISHING HISTORY

◆

Notes on the Publishing History
and Text of *The Waste Land*

In 1952 William H. Marshall's comparison of the various texts of T. S. Eliot's "Gerontion" demonstrated, rather surprisingly, "that no printed edition up to the present has conformed in every detail with Eliot's full intentions."[1] Then, in 1957, Robert L. Beare's important survey showed conclusively that Eliot had indeed been neglectful of the texts of many of his plays and poems.[2] But comparatively little attention has been given to the publishing history of "The Waste Land." In a general way, the publishing history of the poem points to the important assistances given to Eliot's literary career by a number of his friends and associates, and more specifically, a survey of the texts of the poem in various typescripts and printed editions is revealing about the development of Eliot's art and about the unfastidious attention which he has given to the publication of this poem. One major handicap to the historian of the poem is the absence of the original typescript of the poem as it stood before Ezra Pound's editing. Also unavailable is a manuscript notebook containing early drafts and some unpublished poems. Both of these items have been missing since the death in 1924 of their last owner, John Quinn, the New York lawyer, book collector, art patron; they are presumed to have been destroyed years ago.

The published versions of the letters which Eliot and Pound exchanged on "The Waste Land' in 1921–22 reveal much of what is known about the poem in its earliest form.[3] Aside from his letters to Eliot, what may be Pound's first reference to the poems occurs in an unpublished letter, dated 21 Feb. 1922, to Mrs. Jeanne Robert Foster, an American art critic and intimate friend of John Quinn, one of a series of letters the indefatigable Pound wrote for the as yet unnamed "Bel Esprit" project: "Eliot produced a fine poem (19 pages) during his enforced vacation, but has since relapsed. I wish something cd. be found for him, to get him out of Lloyds bank."[4] Eliot had said in a recent letter to Pound: "Complimenti {about "The Waste Land"] appreciated, as have been excessively depressed . . . I would have sent Aeschule before but have been in bed with flu, now out but miserable."[5] Pound also

Reprinted with the permission of the author from *Papers of the Bibliographical Society of America* 58 (1964): 252–69.

talked about the poem in an outline he drew up for "Bel Esprit": "Eliot, in bank, makes £500. Too tired to write, broke down; during convalescence in Switzerland did *Waste Land,* a masterpiece; one of the most important 19 pages in English."[6] Pound mentioned the poem for the first time publicly on 30 Mar. 1922, in an article drumming up support for "Bel Esprit": "Rightly or wrongly some of us consider Eliot's employment in a bank the worst waste in contemporary literature. During his recent three months' absence due to a complete physical breakdown he produced a very important sequence of poems: one of the few things in contemporary literature to which one can ascribe permanent value. That seems a fairly clear proof of restriction of output, due to enforced waste of his time and energy in banking."[7]

It is interesting that Pound refers to "The Waste Land" here as a "sequence of poems," for Pound's letter to Eliot on 24 Dec. 1921 suggests that he saw his editing job to consist of shaping several poems into one: "If you MUST keep 'em [*i.e.,* lines eventually omitted by Eliot], put 'em at the beginning before the 'April cruelest month' The POEM ends with the 'Shantih, shantih, shantih.' . . . The thing now runs from 'April . . .' to 'shantih' without a break. That is 19 pages, and let us say the longest poem in the English langwidge. Don't try to bust all records by prolonging it three pages further."[8] At least one of the early critics felt that "The Waste Land" remained a series of poems strung together, and not very satisfactorily. Even so, the critic, Conrad Aiken, concluded generously, ". . . when our reservations have all been made, we accept *The Waste Land* as one of the most moving and original poems of our time. It captures us."[9] Eliot himself insisted on the unity of the poem when he wrote to an anthologist: ". . . 'The Waste Land' is intended to form a whole, and I should not care to have anyone read *parts* of it; and furthermore, I am opposed to anthologies in principle."[10]

Despite the short life of "Bel Esprit" and his failure to get Eliot out of Lloyd's Bank until 1925, Pound showed both zeal in advancing his disciple's career and critical acumen that together must have been almost overpowering. Eliot has written: ". . . [Pound] was ready to lay out the whole of life for anyone in whose life he was interested—a degree of direction which not all the beneficiaries deserved and which was sometimes embarrassing. Yet, though the object of his beneficence might come to chafe against it, only a man of the meanest spirit could have come to resent it. He was so passionately concerned about the works of art which he expected his protégés to produce that he sometimes tended to regard them almost impersonally, as art or literature machines to be carefully tended and oiled, for the sake of their potential output. . . . It was in 1922 [actually, 1921] that I placed before him in Paris the manuscript of a sprawling, chaotic poem called *The Waste Land* which left his hands, reduced to about half its size, in the form in which it appears in print. I should like to think that the manuscript, with the suppressed passages, had disappeared irrecoverably: yet on the other hand, I should wish the blue penciling on it to be preserved as irrefutable evidence of Pound's critical genius."[11]

Pound's poem, "Sage Homme," which Eliot once considered putting at the head of "The Waste Land," was never used. But the well-known dedication, "For Ezra Pound/ il miglior fabbro," was added in the 1925 edition of Eliot's *Poems* and retained thereafter, very likely as a token of Eliot's loyalty to his much-maligned friend and mentor. The exchange of letters between Pound and Eliot and Hugh Kenner's report on Eliot's recollections show that Eliot's debt to his "cher maître" was indeed considerable. The published Pound-Eliot letters indicate that for the most part Eliot followed Pound's advice closely. Only once, after the poem had been published in *The Criterion*, did he have second thoughts, overruling Pound's approval of the uncommon "Wherefrom" (l.80) and substituting "From which" in all later editions. The other changes made as the various editions appeared seem not to have been influenced by Pound, one way or the other.[12]

Eliot attempted to find a publisher for the poem in January 1922, as he noted in a letter to Pound: "Have writ to [Scofield] Thayer [editor of The Dial] asking what he can offer for this."[13] Oddly enough, though, Eliot seems not to have sent a copy of the poem to the United States until the summer of 1922. Thayer and Eliot had been acquainted at Milton Academy, Harvard, and Oxford, and it was through the assistance of Thayer that Eliot met the first Lady Rothermere, whose patronage enabled him to found *The Criterion*.[14] Since 1920 Eliot had written London letters for *The Dial*. Eventually Eliot's correspondence with Thayer led to an agreement, for the first American publication of the poem occurred in *The Dial* for November 1922.[15] But when Thayer saw the poem in the summer of 1922 he was somewhat disappointed by it, and earlier in the year he and Eliot had disagreed about the rate of payment for it, so the negotiations were prolonged.[16] Meanwhile Pound looked for a publisher; on 6 May 1922, he wrote to Mrs. Foster, who was associated with various periodicals in New York: "What would Vanity Fair pay Eliot for 'Waste Land'? cd. yr. friend there get in touch with T.S.E.?" Mrs. Foster had published an article on Brancusi in *Vanity Fair*, but she turned Pound's letter over to John Quinn, who was a friend of Frank Crowninshield, the editor. When no offer for the poem was made, Mrs. Foster wrote the news to Pound in Paris.[17]

In July 1922, Gilbert Seldes, managing editor of *The Dial*, took the initiative to get the poem into print. Seldes arranged a meeting in Quinn's office of Horace Liveright (the book publisher), Quinn (unofficially representing Eliot, who still had to approve any deal made), and Seldes himself. These persons agreed to the publication of the poem in *The Dial* and then in an edition by Boni and Liveright.[18] Quinn received a typescript copy of the poem, presumably from someone at *The Dial*, and almost immediately, on 31 July 1922, mailed it to Mrs. Foster, who was temporarily in Schenectady, New York. This copy, made on American paper by someone other than Eliot, but not prepared in Quinn's office, was presented to the Houghton Library at Harvard by Mrs. Foster in 1961.[19] Dr. James S. Watson, Jr., the publisher of *The Dial,* also had a typescript copy of the poem in the summer of 1922; he sent it from the Hotel Meurice, in Paris, to Thayer, in Vienna. This typescript, on Hotel Meurice stationery, is among *The Dial* papers in storage at the Worcester Art Museum in Massachusetts, but it is unavailable at present.[20] Dr. Watson no longer recalls the source of it, and no one can identify the original form from which it was made.

Seldes' expedition of Thayer's and Dr. Watson's decision to publish the poem called for placing it in *The Dial,* paying Eliot at the regular rate ($20 for each page of poetry[21]—or $260), and then presenting him *The Dial* Award for 1922, worth $2,000. Seldes also worked out the details of the Boni and Liveright edition, swelled to book length by the addition of Eliot's notes.[22] The poem appeared in the November issue, in which Pound trumpeted "Bel Esprit" (pp. 549–52), to Eliot's acute embarrassment.[23] Then, after George Saintsbury declined the job,[24] Edmund Wilson wrote in the December issue a long, favorable review that included these comments: ". . . now the publication of his long poem, The Waste Land, confirms the opinion which we began gradually to cherish, that Mr. Eliot, with all his limitations, is one of our only authentic poets. For this new poem—which presents itself as so far his most considerable claim to eminence—not only recapitulates all his earlier and already familiar motifs, but it sounds for the first time in all their intensity, untempered by irony or disguise, the hunger for beauty and the anguish at living which lie at the bottom of all his work. . . . I doubt whether there is a single other poem of equal length by a contemporary American which displays so high and so varied a mastery of English verse" (pp. 611, 615). Privately, Eliot was indignant about Wilson's review, which he felt used his achievement to disparage the work of his friend Pound.[25] Seldes himself reviewed the poem in the *Nation* for 6 Dec. 1922: "It will be interesting for those who have knowledge of another great work of our time, Mr. Joyce's 'Ulysses,' to think of the two together. That 'The Waste Land' is, in a sense, the inversion and the complement of 'Ulysses' is at least tenable. We have in 'Ulysses' the poet defeated, turning outward, savoring the ugliness which is no longer transmutable into beauty, and, in the end, homeless. We have in 'The Waste Land' some indication of the inner life of such a poet" (p. 616). In effect, Eliot's American champions put on a grand show of publicity for the poem. There is, of course, absolutely no reason to doubt the sincerity of their admiration of the poem as well as the poet. But it is worth noting that the bombshell which literary historians often say was set off by the publication of the poem in 1922 was given a booster shot by the fireworks of the ingenious staff of *The Dial*. No one was more appreciative of this help than Eliot himself. He wrote to Seldes on 27 Dec. 1922: "I am deeply aware of the honour which the Dial has bestowed upon me as well as of the financial assistance which will be a very great help at a difficult time.

May I be able to give the Dial still better work in the future!" And on 21 Sept. 1922, he wrote to Quinn, approving the publishing scheme worked out by Quinn, Seldes, and Liveright:

> I am quite overwhelmed by your letter, by all that you have done for me, by the results that have been effected, and by your endless kindness. . . . Of course, I am entirely satisified with the arrangements that you have made. It is exactly what I should have liked; only I did not see how it could be done, if it was to be done at all, without calling upon you once more, which, after all you had already accomplished, I was absolutely determined not to do. I also felt that it would be in the nature of asking a favour from Liveright, and also I was loath to ask you to do this on my behalf. I gather that Liveright is quite satisfied that the arrangement will be ultimately to his advantage, and certainly the "Dial" have behaved very handsomely.
>
> My only regret (which may seem in the circumstances either ungracious or hypocritical) is that this [*Dial*] award should come to me before it had been given to Pound. I feel that he deserves the recognition much more than I do, certainly "for his services to Letters," and I feel that I ought to have been made to wait until after he had received this public testimony.[26]

"The Waste Land" was first published in England, where it appeared in the October 1922, or initial number of *The Criterion,* edited anonymously by T. S. Eliot. Tentative arrangements for publishing the poem in England as well as in the United States seem to have been made early, for Pound could write on 9 July: "Eliot's *Waste Land* is I think the justification of the 'movement' of our modern experiment, since 1900. It shd. be published this year."[27] Eliot was scrupulous about separating the English and American periodical versions of the poem, for his letters to Quinn on 21 Sept. and Seldes on 12 Nov. 1922 reveal that in order to prevent competition with the November *Dial* the first issue of *The Criterion* was not made readily available to American subscribers. A postscript in the letter to Seldes notes that by 12 Nov. the first issue of *The Criterion* had been sold out. Oddly enough, in view of his ideas about the unity of the poem, Eliot once considered publishing the poem in two parts, divided between the first two issues of *The Criterion.* His reason for this was that in view of his anonymous editorship, his critical essays should not appear in the early issues, and thus the poem should be stretched to provide his only signed contributions.[28]

The first edition in book form (Boni and Liveright's) appeared on 15 Dec. 1922, in New York.[29] According to Pound, the publication of the notes in this edition was "purely fortuitous": "Liveright wanted a longer volume and the notes were the only available matter."[30] The requirements of the book may have altered Eliot's original plan: "I had at first intended only to put down all the references for my quotations, with a view to spiking the guns of critics of my earlier poems who had accused me of plagiarism. Then, when it came to print *The Waste Land* as a book . . . it was discovered that the poem was inconveniently short, so I set to work to expand the notes, in order to provide a few more pages of printed matter, with the result that they became the remarkable exposition of bogus scholarship that is still on view to-day. I have sometimes thought of getting rid of these notes; but now they can never be unstuck. They have had almost greater popularity than the poem itself. . . . I am penitent . . . because my notes stimulated the wrong kind of interest among seekers of sources . . . It was just, no doubt, that I should pay tribute to the work of Miss Jesse Weston; but I regret having sent so many inquirers off on a wild goose chase after Tarot Cards and the Holy Grail."[31] It is certain, however, that the notes were in existence before the publication of the poem in *The Dial*. Selden wrote to Dr. Watson on 31 Aug. 1922: "We must assume that Eliot O.K.'s publication in *The Dial* without the notes . . . which are exceedingly interesting and add much to the poem, but don't become interested in them because we simply cannot have them."[32] According to the plan of Seldes, Liveright, and Quinn, the notes were to be withheld from *The Dial* in order to make the book more attractive.

Roger Fry seems to have instigated Eliot's glosses, for according to Clive Bell, he urged Eliot "to elucidate the text of *The Waste Land* with explanatory notes."[33] Mr. Eliot has confirmed this: "It may be as Mr. Clive Bell says that it was Roger Fry who suggested that I should do notes to the poem. I remember reading the poem aloud to Leonard and Virginia Woolf before they ever read it and I know that the notes were added and were of such length as the poem by itself seemed hardly long enough for book form."[34] In view of their mutual friendship and interest in each other's work, it is hardly necessary to speculate about the influence the Woolfs had on Eliot's poetry. Leonard Woolf has said that he "had a hand in converting its author from an American to an English poet,"[35] and this may be true in more than one way, since Eliot's *Poems, 1919*, and *The Waste Land, 1923*, were printed by hand at the Woolfs' Hogarth Press.

Both Mr. Woolf and Mr. Eliot have commented on the circumstances of the first English edition in book form. According to the latter: "I think it would probably have been very difficult to find a commercial publisher for the poem in 1922 or 1923. I am certain that Miss Harriett Weaver [patroness of Joyce and backer of the Egoist Press] would have published the poem, but I am pretty sure she had gone out of business by that date. I had already . . . taken a set of seven or so short poems to Leonard Woolf which he published as a booklet bound in one or another of Roger Fry's papers."[36] Mr. Woolf has described the publishing venture as the work of amateurs; "No one in 1920 would have published *The Waste Land*. We started the Hogarth Press in 1917 as a hobby; really the hobby was printing. It was only casually that we published what we printed at first and we suggested to Eliot that we should print and publish poems of his. We first published the book called *Poems* [1919] and then *The Waste Land*. The above explains why we printed the book with our own hands."[37] By publishing Eliot's poems the Woolfs made a gesture of faith in his work and also helped strengthen his position in England during a crucial period. Today, when the Hogarth Press of "The Waste Land" is a collector's item, every copy necessarily being an "association copy," it is difficult to imagine that Eliot ever had trouble finding a publisher, or that when he found one, a small edition of about 460 copies, selling at 4s. 6d. each and published on 12 Sept. 1923,[38] was still in print a year or so later. Pound did a great deal to publicize Eliot's work, especially among the critics and patrons of literature; as he wrote to Mrs. Foster on 11 Oct. 1922, about the American publications: "I shall try to place a whoop for the pome THE 'Waste Land' as soon as it is in print." But the Woolfs' timely assistance in actually making Eliot's work available to the English reading public should never be overlooked.[39]

The Hogarth Press edition of "The Waste Land" is hardly a masterpiece of printing, and its text contains a number of errors. The fault must have been due to the skill rather than the will of the participants, however, for Leonard Woolf is quite positive: "Mr. Eliot certainly read the proofs."[40] Eliot himself later corrected by hand three errors in presentation copies; in the Harvard copy, presented "to Mother from Tom. 14.ix.23," *under* (l.62) is corrected to *over,* the reading of all other editions; *coloured* (l. 96) to *carven* (*carven* was never printed, for *carvëd* appears in all other editions; in the Hogarth Press edition *coloured* obviously was transferred from the preceding line); and *Macmillan* (p. 29, heading to the notes) to *Cambridge Univ. Press,* the reading of the 1925 and all later editions."[41] But several other errors in this edition remained uncorrected, even in the hand-marked copies.

Eventually the Woolfs had to give up the hand printing they began in 1917, for the Hogarth Press became so successful that it was no longer a "private press." Even some of the earliest of their productions were reprinted by a commercial printer when the demand far exceeded the capacity of the Woolfs' hand press,[42] but such was not the case with Eliot's *Poems,* about two hundred copies printed,[43] or with *The Waste Land.* With these volumes the chief problem was merely completing the hand printing, the slowness of which delayed the publication of the Hogarth Press *Waste Land* until almost nine months after the Boni and Liveright edition came out in New York. On 24 June 1923, Virginia Woolf wrote from Hogarth House to a friend recovering from scarlet fever in a hospital: "We've had a desperate afternoon printing, and I'm more in need of the love of my friends than you are. All the 14 pt. quads have been dissed into the 12 pt. boxes! Proof taking has been made impossible, and Eliot's poem delayed a whole week. I'm sure you'll see that this is much more worth crying over than the pox and the fever and the measles all in one. . . . Leonard is still trying to take proofs in the basement. I have cheered myself up by writing to you, so please don't say that I've plunged you into despair, as another invalid did the other day, when I cheered myself up by writing to her."[44] The Woolfs bound the volume themselves, using three different labels on the front cover.[45] Their personal involvement in the routine of publishing was noticed by the poet and future publisher John Lehmann when he joined the Press in 1930; according to him, even at that time Virginia Woolf tied parcels and put labels on packages when rush orders came in,[46] and Leonard Woolf remained in some ways a private printer: "In fact I learned the essentials of publishing in the most agreeable way possible: from a man who had created his own business, had never allowed it to grow so big that it fell into departments sealed off from one another, and who saw it all as much from the point of view of an author and amateur printer as of someone who had to make his living by it."[47] The Woolfs must have been proud of their edition of "The Waste Land," for it was listed with their "books published" long after supplies of it were exhausted.[48]

Of the four editions of "The Waste Land" in 1922–23, that of Boni and Liveright has the most accurate text and is the closest to recent editions of the poem. It cannot be considered the standard text, however, for changes were made later in both the poem and the notes. Most of these changes were typographical, most of no significance, but a few were substantive. In evaluating the apparently insignificant changes in punctuation that occur in the various editions of the poem, one should keep in mind Eliot's remarks on punctuation in a letter to Quinn: "I see reason in your objection to my punctuation, but I hold that the line itself punctuates, and the addition of a comma, in many places, seems to me to over-emphasize the arrest. That is because I always pause at the end of a line in reading verse, while perhaps you do not."[49] A report on all the changes in punctuation as the poem was reprinted is an undertaking too large for this paper, but it can be said that Eliot's carelessness in seeing editions through the press is by no means proof that he was uninterested in fine pointing.

An unexpected development in regard to the text occurred in 1960, when Eliot prepared an autograph fair copy to be sold at auction for the benefit of the London Library, which Eliot served as President. After l. 137 he added, "(The ivory men make company between us)," which Eliot said "was in the original draft but for some reason or other was omitted from the published text. It came back to my mind when I was making the copy."[50] This recollection certainly did not detract from the value of the manuscript, which sold at Christie's on 22 June 1960 for £2,800.[51] The 1960 manuscript, now in the Humanities Research Center of the University of Texas, "does not follow in exact detail the punctuation, spelling, or capitalization of any of the published versions of *The Waste Land*,"[52] and its "new" line is not canonized by inclusion in the signed, limited edition of the poem printed at the Officina Bodoni and published by Faber and Faber in 1961. About this edition, Mr. Eliot says: "I think that it may be taken that the recent limited edition is the standard text. I have made one or two corrections in the notes in that edition and Mr. Mardersteig, the publisher [*i.e.*, printer] of that limited edition, suggested corrections in the quotations from Dante based on a more authentic text than the one I had used before."[53] The 1961 edition is a tastefully produced volume containing only the obvious misprint "dampg round" for "damp ground" (l. 193); it is generally close to the Boni and Liveright edition as later corrected; and it is, according to Mr. Eliot, the standard text. The principal objections that one can make to it concern the small number of copies (300), the high price (10 guineas), and the omission of consecutive line numbers for reasons of typographical elegance, the notes being renumbered according to the lines on each page.

The 1963 Faber and Faber edition of *Collected Poems 1909–1962* reprints almost all of the changes in *1961*. It does not include the attribution of the epigraph, "PETRONIUS.SATIRICON," and contains some minor misprints: *piante* for *pianto* (note on l. 64), *p. 306* for *p. 346, senxi* for *senti'* (note on l. 411). It does not always follow *1961* in respect to punctuation, typographical conventions, and spacing, notably in the following places: *speak. Speak. for speak? Speak* (l. 112); *directors;* for *directors*—(l. 180); spaces before ll. 187, 203, no space before l. 206 (the reverse in *1961*); *Et* for *Et,* (l. 202); *spar.* for *spar* (l. 272); paragraph indentations in Section V (not found in *1961*). The text in the 1963 Harcourt, Brace & World edition of *Collected Poems 1909–1962,* which does not incorporate the changes made in *1961,* is interesting only for straightening out for the first time the misnumbering of ll. 351–end in the text and the misnumbering of the notes in this part of the poem.[54]

The added line in the 1960 manuscript turns out to be an early reject, for aside from this manuscript, it appears only in the 20-page typescript copy presented to Harvard by Mrs. Foster. The Harvard typescript copy clearly was never used by a printer for any edition. The line numbering and certain mechanical characteristics suggest that it and its original were prepared by a professional typist.[55] It antedates all the printed versions of the poem and possibly the only other extant typescripts, the one now among *The Dial* papers, and the one now in the library of John Hayward, editorial director of *The Book Collector.* About the latter Mr. Hayward says: "My typescript was not the printer's copy. It is authenticated in Eliot's hand 'an early pre-publication typing by myself.' Although his inscription goes on to say that 'it may have been the printer's copy for the *Criterion,'* it is clear that it was not in fact the printer's copy. I would infer that it was the penultimate copy from an earlier draft before the copy text was finally typed out. . . . None of the [major] variants in [the Harvard typescript copy] is present. Apart from a number of small and relatively trivial alterations of single words, the only curiosity is the omission (due to an obvious copying slip . . . [*i.e., sight transference*]) of lines 400–409."[56] None of the extant typescripts contains the notes first printed in the Boni and Liveright edition. Even though the Harvard typescript is a copy-of-a-copy-of-a-copy, it would appear to be fairly close to the missing original typescript version (after Pound's editing) and possibly derives from the first copy Eliot sent to the United States in 1922. At any rate, when Quinn received it, for the second time an unpublished

Eliot work passed through his hands: in 1917 Quinn had sent along to an American publisher the typescript of Eliot's *Ezra Pound: His Metric and Poetry,* Eliot's first book of criticism.[57]

Some of the readings peculiar to the Harvard typescript copy are of considerable interest.[58] Ll. 105–06, which in the typescript read

> staring forms
> Leaned, staring, hushing the room enclosed.

were changed to

> staring forms
> Leaned out, leaning, hushing the room enclosed.

The image thus becomes more kinaesthetic. L. 115 was changed from

> I think we met first in rats' alley.

to

> I think we are in rats' alley

clearly less accusing and perhaps more desperate. Ll. 124–25 were shortened from

> I remember
> The hyacinth garden. Those are pearls that were his eyes.

to

> I remember
> Those are pearls that were his eyes.

But the effect is to make more difficult the link between ll. 35–42, 46–48, and Section IV, "Death by Water," and this difficulty seems to have led some critics astray. Perhaps Eliot felt that the line after 137 was too obvious at this point:

> The ivory men make company between us

(the 1960 parentheses are not present here) but the line did pick up the imagery of l. 86 and perhaps led toward ll. 263–65. The change in l. 149 of "theres many another will,' to "there's others will, I said," seems to tighten up the dialogue. Two other differences in this copy could be mere typing errors: l. 143, "done" typed as 'did," and l. 150, "Oh is" typed as "Is." In l. 430 "de la" instead of "a la" agrees only with the *Criterion* version. Aside from a few spelling errors, the other variants in the Harvard copy concern typographical conventions or punctuation.

The variants in the Harvard copy make the disappearance of the first autograph typescript especially tantalizing. After giving his copy to Mrs. Foster in July, Quinn bought this autograph typescript from Eliot in the fall of 1922 for £100.[59] On 21 Sept. 1922, Eliot wrote to Quinn from London:

> In the manuscript of "The Waste Land" which I am sending you, you will see the evidences of his [Pound's] work, and I think that this manuscript is worth preserving in its present form solely for the reason that it is the only evidence of the difference which his criticism has made to this poem. I am glad that you, at least, will have the opportunity of judging this for yourself. Naturally, I hope that the portions which I have suppressed will never appear in print, and in sending them to you I am sending the only copies of these parts.
>
> I have gathered together all of the manuscript in existence. The leather bound notebook is one which I started in 1909 and in which I entered all my work of that time as I wrote it, so that it is the only original manuscript (barring, of course, rough scraps and notes which were destroyed at the time) in existence. You will find a great many sets of verse which have never been printed and which I am sure you will agree never ought to be printed, and, in putting them in your hands, I beg you fervently to keep them to yourself and see that they never are printed.
>
> I do not think that this manuscript is of any great value, especially as the large part is really typescript for which no manuscript, except scattered lines, ever existed.[60]

That the "manuscript" of "The Waste Land" was a typescript is explained by the fact that when Eliot was in the Harvard Graduate School (1911–14), he strained one hand while rowing in a single shell and thereafter used a typewriter for composing.[61] These Eliot papers have been missing since Quinn's death. Mrs. Foster, who arranged Quinn's literary papers and correspondence in 1924, never saw the first autograph typescript or the notebook.[62] Quinn may have taken Eliot's letter to heart and secretly destroyed them. But there is reason for supposing that they were stolen from Quinn's collection during his final illness or shortly after his death, and that they have been destroyed.[63]

Eliot seems not to have read the proofs of *The Dial* version of the poem but was pleased by the printing. As editor he must have read the proofs of the first issue of the *Criterion,* and he is known to have done so for the Boni and Liveright[64] and Hogarth Press editions. Although he was still to make some changes in the text, in the fall of 1922 Eliot's attitude toward the poem that was becoming the most famous of the twentieth century was surprisingly offhand. On 12. Nov, he wrote to Seldes, "Nov. no [of *The Dial*] just received. Poem admirably printed. I see some remarks by you which I find very flattering. But I find this poem as far behind me as Prufrock now: my present ideas are very different." It is hardly unexpected, then, though still disconcerting, that Eliot did not bother to incorporate the changes of *1961* in the 1963 Harcourt, Brace & World edition of his *Collected Poems*.[65]

Notes

1. "The Text of T. S. Eliot's 'Gerontion,' " *SB* 4 (1951–52), 214.
2. "Notes on the Text of T. S. Eliot: Variants from Russell Square,' *SB* 9 (1957), 21–49.
3. See D. D. Paige, ed., *The Letters of Ezra Pound* (New York, 1950), pp. 169–72. Hugh Kenner, *The Invisible Poet: T. S. Eliot* (New York, 1959), pp. 145–52, has surveyed the "Ur-Waste Land" as Eliot remembers it. As early as 9 May 1921, Eliot reported to Quinn that he had "a long poem in mind and partly on paper . . ." (typescript of letter in the Quinn Collection, New York Public Library).
4. This letter and two others to Mrs. Foster are quoted with the kind permission of Mrs. Dorothy Pound and Mr. William Jackson, Director, The Houghton Library, Harvard University. According to the "Bel Esprit" plan, each of thirty contributors was to give £30 annually to a deserving writer, the first of which was to be Eliot. Eliot later refused any money from this source, and "Bel Esprit" came to an end. (See further Donald Gallup, *A Bibliography of Ezra Pound* (London, 1963), pp. 379–80.)
5. *The Letters of Ezra Pound*, p. 171.
6. *Ibid.*, p. 173 (from a typescript copy, dated 18 Mar. 1922, sent to William Carlos Williams).
7. "Credit and the Fine Arts," *The New Age*, 30 Mar. 1922, pp. 284–85.
8. *The Letters of Ezra Pound*, p. 169. *Cf.* Pound's phrase, "a series of poems," quoted by Hugh Kenner, pp. 145–46.
9. Review in *The New Republic*, 33 (7 Feb. 1923), 295. Aiken had been the intermediary who in 1914, after some unsuccessful peddling on his own, gave the typescript of Eliot's "Prufrock" to Pound, who got it published in Harriet Monroe's *Poetry* (Conrad Aiken, letter to the editor, *Times Literary Supplement*, 3 June 1960, p. 353).
10. Quoted in *An Exhibition of Manuscripts and First Editions of T. S. Eliot* (Austin, 1961), p. 10.
11. T. S. Eliot, "Ezra Pound," *Ezra Pound: A Collection of Critical Essays*, ed. Walter Sutton (Englewood Cliffs, N.J., 1963), pp. 18–19.
12. Eliot let pass what may have been an oversight of Pound's. In the first of the published letters between Pound and Eliot on the poem, Pound said, "I doubt if Conrad is weighty enough to stand the citation" (*The Letters of Ezra Pound*, p. 169). Hugh Kenner (p. 145) learned from Eliot that Pound referred to Eliot's quotation as "The horror! The horror!" from *Heart of Darkness*. As Pound suggested, Eliot removed the quotation. But Pound apparently was unaware that the words in ll. 268–70 of "The Waste Land" were derived from the first page of *Heart of Darkness* (pointed out by Kenner, p. 145, and rediscovered by John Frederick Nims, "Greatness in Moderation," *Saturday Review*, 19 Oct. 1963, p. 26), and that the various passages in the poem concerning the Thames are strongly reminiscent of the first few pages of Conrad's novel.
13. *The Letters of Ezra Pound*, p. 171.
14. Miss Pamela Barker, formerly secretary to Mr. Eliot, letter to the author, dated 9 Sept. 1963.
15. This phase in the history of the poem was first surveyed by William Wasserstrom,

"T. S. Eliot and *The Dial*," *SR* LXX (Jan.–Mar. 1962), 81–92, and again in *The Time of the Dial* (Syracuse, 1963), pp. 102–05.

16. For information about these matters I am indebted to Professor Nicholas Joost, who has had access to *The Dial* papers and who has been generous in answering my questions. His book on *The Dial* is expected to appear in 1964.

17. Mrs. Jeanne Robert Foster, letter to the author, dated 9 Sept. 1963.

18. Mr. Gilbert Seldes, letters to the author, dated 25 Sept. and 3 Nov. 1963.

19. Mrs. Foster is certain that the copy was not made in Quinn's office, and that Quinn received it only shortly before mailing it to her (letter to the author, dated 9 Sept. 1963). The conclusions about the paper and the typist were reported to me by Mr. John Hayward in a letter dated 3 Sept. 1963, and confirmed by Mr. William A. Jackson (who once showed Eliot the typescript copy), in a letter dated 16 Sept. 1963. See also *The Houghton Library Report of Accessions for the Year 1961–62* (Cambridge, 1962), pp. 45–46.

20. For information about this typescript I am indebted to Professor Joost.

21. William Wasserstrom, *A Dial Miscellany* (Syracuse, 1963), p. xiv.

22. *The Dial* did not pay for the edition but instead took 350 copies, out of the 1,000 numbered copies printed, and used them as an offer in a subscription campaign. See further William Wasserstrom, *The Time of the Dial,* pp. 103–04.

23. Public response to "Bel Esprit," especially in the newspapers, often was unfavorable. In the Feb. 1923, issue of *The Dial,* the editor had to defend Eliot's *Dial* Award against the charges of those opposed to "Bel Esprit." By May 1923, Pound had been fired as Paris correspondent of *The Dial*.

24. See further William Wasserstrom, *The Time of the Dial,* p. 104.

25. Eliot wrote to Seldes: "While I wish to express my appreciation of Mr. Wilson's praise, as well as of your own, there is one point in Mr. Wilson's article to which I must strongly take exception. I do very much object to be made use of by anyone for the purpose of disparaging the work of Ezra Pound. I am infinitely in his debt as a poet, as well as a personal friend, and I do resent being praised at his expense. Besides, what Mr. Wilson said of him was most unfair. I sincerely consider Ezra Pound to be the most important living poet in the English language. And you will see that in view of my great debt to him in literature it is most painful to me to have such comments made. I should like Mr. Wilson also to know this, if possible." (Letter dated 27 Dec. 1922; this letter and one other are quoted with the kind permission of Mr. Eliot and Mr. Seldes.) Evidently Edmund Wilson learned of Eliot's opinion, and when he wrote about Eliot's work in *Axel's Castle,* he greatly modified his remarks about the relative positions of Pound and Eliot, even though he continued to prefer Eliot's work.

26. Typescript of the letter in the Quinn Collection, New York Public Library. This letter and others to Quinn are quoted with the kind permission of Mr. Eliot and the Library.

27. *The Letters of Ezra Pound,* p. 180.

28. See further Eliot's letter to Quinn, 21 Sept. 1922, a typescript of which is in the Quinn Collection, New York Public Library.

29. Donald Gallup, *T. S. Eliot: A Bibliography* (New York, 1953), p. 7.

30. *We Moderns* (New York, 1940), cited by Gallup, p. 7.

31. T. S. Eliot, "The Frontiers of Criticism," *On Poetry and Poets* (London, 1957), pp. 109–10.

32. Quoted by William Wasserstrom, *The Time of the Dial,* p. 104.

33. Clive Bell, *Old Friends* (New York, 1957), p. 119.

34. Letter to the author, 26 June 1963. Quoted with the kind permission of Mr. Eliot.

35. *Sowing* (London, 1960), p. 52.

36. Letter to the author, 26 June 1963.

37. Letter to the author, 5 Dec. 1962. Quoted with the kind permission of Mr. Woolf.

38. Gallup, p. 8.

39. Among the consequences of the Hogarth Press edition were a review (not laudatory)

in *The Times Literary Supplement,* 20 Sept. 1923, p. 616, and a review (unfavorable) by Clive Bell in *The Nation and Athenæum,* 22 Sept. 1923, pp. 772–73.

40. Letter to the author, 5 Dec. 1962.

41. These manuscript corrections were first noted by Robert L. Beare, "Notes on the Text of T. S. Eliot: Variants from Russell Square," *Studies in Bibliography* 9, 21–49.

42. See further B. J. Kirkpatrick, *A Bibliography of Virginia Woolf* (London, 1957), pp. 7–8.

43. Gallup, p. 4.

44. Quoted by Clive Bell, pp. 104, 107.

45. Leonard Woolf, letter to the author, 5 Dec. 1962; and Gallup, p. 8.

46. *The Open Night* (New York, 1952), p. 23.

47. *The Whispering Gallery* (New York, 1955), p. 168.

48. *Ibid.,* p. 167.

49. From the typescript of a letter, 9 May 1921, in the Quinn Collection, New York Public Library.

50. *An Exhibition of Manuscripts and First Editions of T. S. Eliot,* p. 5.

51. "Good Causes," *The Times Literary Supplement,* 1 July 1960, p. 424.

52. *An Exhibition of Manuscripts and First Editions of T. S. Eliot,* p. 5.

53. Letter to the author, 26 June 1963.

54. This error in numbering seems to have been noticed first by Hugh Kenner, p. 151.

55. John Quinn's possession of a copy of the poem in the summer of 1922, before publication anywhere, requires a slight revision of one of Aline B. Saarinen's anecdotes about Quinn: "One morning in 1922 he received from T. S. Eliot a first copy of *The Waste Land.* He summoned a lovely lady [Mrs. Foster] with a melodious voice to read the lengthy poem to him while he shaved. Thereafter, he could recite it without an error. . . . She [Mrs. Foster] was an American, with burnished golden hair, black eyes and a lilting voice, who had written several volumes of verse, had been on the staffs at *Review of Reviews* and the *Transatlantic Review,* and was an intimate of the Yeats circle in New York and the 'lttie magazine' group in Paris." (*The Proud Possessors,* New York, 1958, pp. 208, 225. On Mrs. Foster and Quinn, see also Ford Madox Ford, *It Was the Nightingale,* Philadelphia, 1933, p. 298.) The typescript copy did not come from Eliot, but Mrs. Foster has confirmed that it is the copy of the poem mentioned in the anecdote.

56. Letter to the author, 16 Aug. 1963. Quoted with the kind permission of Mr. Hayward.

57. See further my short article, "John Quinn and T. S. Eliot's First Book of Criticism,' *PBSA,* 56 (Second Quarter, 1962), 259–65, and *The Houghton Library Report of Accessions for the Year 1961–62,* pp. 45–46. Eliot wrote to Quinn on 9 July 1919: "It is quite obvious that, without you, I should never get published in America at all." (From the typescript in the Quinn Collection, New York Public Library.)

58. They are quoted here with the kind permission of Mr. Eliot and Mr. William A. Jackson.

59. John Hayward, letter to the author, 3 Sept. 1963.

60. From the typescript of this letter in the Quinn Collection, New York Public Library. For telling me about this letter I am indebted to Professor Ben L. Reid, who is presently writing a biography of Quinn.

61. Miss Pamela Barker, letter to the author, 9 Sept. 1963.

62. Mrs. Foster, letters to the author and interview, Dec. 1963.

63. Informed of this probable theft, Eliot has commented: "I cannot feel altogether sorry that this [typescript] and the notebook have disappeared. The unpublished poems in the notebook were not worth publishing, and there was a great deal of superfluous matter in "The Waste Land" which Pound very rightly deleted. Indeed, the poem in the form in which it

finally appeared owes more to Pound's surgery than anyone can realise" (letter to the author, dated 3 April 1964, quoted with the kind permission of Mr. Eliot).

64. T. S. Eliot, letter to Gilbert Seldes, 12 Nov. 1922.

65. Daniel Woodward wanted the following note added to his published essay: in the early 1960s, when I was engaged on this article, the New York Public Library possessed the original manuscript of "The Waste Land," which it had acquired in 1958. That possession was kept secret from all scholars, even from those—like me—who did some of their work among the John Quinn papers in the NYPL. Today one can forgive but not easily forget such indifference to the success or failure of scholarly investigations.

The Hidden Years of the *Waste Land* Manuscript

JAMES TORRENS, S. J.

EMERGENCE OF THE *WASTE LAND* MANUSCRIPT

For fifty years Pound's exact role in making *The Waste Land* cohere was a matter of mere armchair speculation. Things changed drastically with the emergence of the original at the New York Public Library in 1968. Literary journalism at this time focused, of course, upon the question, Where had *The Waste Land* been? Valerie Eliot's edition cast some light on the answer, and people mostly were satisfied. But it is possible now to reconstruct the history of the manuscript more accurately, thanks to firsthand testimony from Dr. Thomas Francis Conroy, M.D., in whose house the manuscripts reposed during much of that time.

The key player in the *The Waste Land* story was, of course, John Quinn, the corporation lawyer in New York City, generous sponsor of contemporary art (for example, the Armory Show in 1913), patron of artists, such as Jack Yeats and "Old Man Yeats" (who was his unfailing Sunday dinner guest) and Gwen John, and liberal benefactor of Joseph Conrad, Joyce, "Willie" Yeats, Ford Madox Ford, and, with unfailing patience, Ezra Pound. It was John Quinn who, at Pound's urging, arranged for *The Waste Land* to appear in *The Dial* magazine concurrently with its separate publication by Boni and Liveright. And he was the mysterious benefactor behind the $2,000 *Dial* award to the poem's author. Eliot, encumbered by doctor bills and other expenses, was immediately relieved. How could he thank Quinn? Quinn, an avid collector of modern artists, had been anxious to buy the *Waste Land* typescript, as well as a composition book of Eliot's which contained the original of "The Love Song of J. Alfred Prufrock" plus other early poems.

Eliot would not take money for these manuscripts, but in October of 1922 gratefully mailed Quinn the 54 pages of *The Waste Land,* including unused parts and loosely associated or earlier material, plus the "Prufrock" composition book. They reached Quinn in January of 1923 but disappeared shortly thereafter, along with an enormous quantity of other literary correspondence, when Quinn died in July of 1924. *The Waste Land,* first draft, was thought to have been irretrievably lost, or destroyed. This strange conviction

Reprinted with permission from the *Santa Clara Review* 76 (1989): 36–42; copyright by Santa Clara University.

became fixed among critics and scholars, including Donald Gallup, the great Eliot bibliographer, so that no effort was made by anyone, no detective work undertaken, to test out the contrary.

Meanwhile the two Eliot documents spent a long time in storage and then accompanied a domestic move from New York City to San Mateo, California. In August of either 1952 or 1953 they were sitting on an open shelf when a San Francisco bibliophile, John Alger Flick, came to 50 West Bellevue Street in San Mateo to house sit for Dr. and Mrs. Thomas F. Conroy. While in the house, Mr. Flick got to thumbing a slipcover on one of their shelves, and made a discovery:

> The manuscript which caught my eye as it stood on the Conroys' living room bookshelf was a gray cloth, hard-cover, bound schoolboy's composition book. Upon curiously opening it, it was inscribed Gallipoli with a 1915 date, and was full of early Eliot poems in his, to me, well known handwriting (since Eliot was one of the few modern first editions I became addicted to).

The owners were not unaware of what they held, but it was the book-lover Flick who galvanized them to action. The Conroys, under the spur of John Flick's discovery and anxious to dispose of the boxes of rare papers that overcrowded their house, decided to turn over the Quinn materials to the repository he himself had desired for them, the New York Public Library. There, for another twelve years, they stayed in the keeping of Dr. John D. Gordon, curator of the Berg Collection, "until the appropriate time," as he cryptically explained to Robert Hill, custodian of The Manuscript Room. The story of the intervening, or hidden, years was eventually told, with the following detail, by Dr. Conroy.

TESTIMONY OF DR. CONROY

[Personal testimony about the history of the *Waste Land* manuscript, as first given by Thomas Francis Conroy, M.D., during the Gleason Library Symposium, "Islands of Light," University of San Francisco, August 6, 1977, and then expanded, with some corrections, between Christmas week, 1986, and April 1987.]

They say that truth is more vivid, more interesting than fiction. So with John Quinn. He was a self-made man, became a corporation lawyer, a very successful one, and all the money he made he spent pretty much. What he didn't spend on his mistresses he spent on, first, books, and became a great bibliophile; then he became interested in art and assembled the largest collection in America of what was then called modern art, meaning the

School of Paris. Quinn ultimately sold his library in 1923 in order to raise money to buy more pictures. He wanted, he loved pictures.

When Quinn died in 1924, in July, only one picture was bequeathed, and that was to the Louvre; it was "The Circus" by Seurat. At the time it was given, it was the only Seurat in France in a public museum. All the rest of the pictures, with the exception of some few of lesser note given to his sister, had to be sold—at a song, I might say. He had 58 Picassos, and some 20 of those and 15 other pictures went for less than $20,000. One heir of Quinn's was the National Bank of Commerce; a vice-president is known to have said that, in regard to this non-representational new work, the bank feels a certain embarrassment and would like to have the pictures sold and the estate closed.

It was thought by many that *The Waste Land* was either lost, destroyed, or what you will. It was not. It went to Quinn's sister, Julia Quinn Anderson. She kept it; she was the testamentary heir. She got what was coming from what pictures were sold, which wasn't very much, but it was at least significant; and she had some books and this manuscript along with a few others, plus an enormous Quinn correspondence, consisting of about 30,000 letters.

Quinn dictated all of his correspondence after the main meal on Sunday afternoon. He had two secretaries, one for artistic and literary concerns, and one for his legal work. Quinn, who sometimes showed himself difficult, with little tolerance for people of slow intelligence, was a brilliant lawyer. His handling of the Botany Mills Case set the terms for trading-with-the-enemy law as it is now recognized internationally. At his death he left 24 letter-press books, each containing up to a thousand pages of his own copied letters, transferred under pressure to onion-skin paper. And his incoming correspondence was of comparable bulk.

Julia Anderson kept all this material stored in rough packing boxes in Morgan and Company Warehouse in New York City. The apartment she, her husband, and her daughter shared was far from large enough to hold them. Julia Anderson died in 1934; they passed to her daughter Mary, who left them there. I only came into this picture late, in November of 1940 when I first met Mary Quinn Anderson at a dinner party. I at that time was doing some post-graduate work in New York. We became engaged in March, 1941, and were married in June of the same year. Jeanne Robert Foster, an intimate of Quinn's later years, highly literate and intelligent, had analyzed the material when it came into Julia's possession; a selection of letters was published at the time.

I completed my work at New York Hospital-Cornell Medical Center, then came the army, after which I returned to the Medical Center. It was in early March of 1947 that we moved to Palo Alto, and then, more permanently, in October of 1948, to San Mateo. We were pretty broke, and I was quite busy starting a practice. We had a platform storage-area in our two-car garage where all the correspondence went. Some books also were in a solid case, which I unpacked, shelving the books in my house. Amongst them, in a gray-blue slipcase, was the manuscript for *The Waste Land,* along with the "Prufrock." Although John Flick stated that only the "Prufrock" was there, he was a bit in error regarding the way *The Waste Land* and the "Prufrock" were kept. They were both in the same slipcover. I was able to tell Valerie Eliot that so far as anyone knew the two poems had reached Quinn at the same time, in the same outer cover. The address facing of the original package had been kept with the poems, and was placed with them in the slipcover, which Quinn had made in New York. This procedure was always followed by Quinn. The slipcover was later sent on to Dr. Gordan along with the microfilm. What happened to the slip cover and the wrapper segment I have never known, inasmuch as Valerie apparently did not receive either item.

So there it was, the pair of Eliot originals, and we said, we'll do something about that. It may be hard to believe that, up to the time of our moving, which was in 1947, my wife had really not been importuned for information. At no time, so far as my wife and I know, did T. S. Eliot ever attempt to find out where *The Waste Land* manuscript was. He knew that Quinn had left only one heir, and that all he needed was to make inquiries to find her, and he never did.

We also had this enormous correspondence. We had packing boxes full; and I said, "My God, we've got to do something. We don't have room to store trunks." I asked, "What's inside?" I didn't even know. Mary said, "They're letters." Well, gradually, then, over the ensuing fifteen years, I found it was a grand jumble of letters, and the only thing I contributed was merely to inventory the letters. We easily concluded that all of the correspondence should be together. Mary naturally wanted it where it meant so much to Quinn, and that was the New York Public Library. This was easily settled through Robert Hill, director of The Manuscript Room, which is now called the Manuscript and Rare Book Division. I packaged the Quinn Correspondence in several segments and began to send them east early in July of 1962. So the Library had received them by late August. The formal acknowledgements "drifted" in from the Library as they completed their inventories. In fact the formal acceptances came in annual installments for tax purposes. The Library had agreed that the material was to be available only to Ben Reid until sometime in early 1968. Public announcement was made at the dedication of the John Quinn Collection in late October, 1968.

So we found ourselves, when we first arrived, also with this special item, the Eliot slipcover, and momentarily it stayed there. Then a very dear couple with their young children came down to house sit one summer, John and Beatrice Flick. John is a bibliophile. At that time I had a hobby, which was making scale-model trains. We had built a den. I had a cabinet arrangement, so I could have these trains and still talk to my wife; when we went away. I locked this up, because two young children were coming down.

It was later that winter that we were at the Flicks' and John chided me. He said, "Frank, you locked up your toys," as he called them, "and the manuscript of *The Waste Land* is on your shelf." John kept the confidence because we said, "John, we must make a decision, we know." We asked him momentarily not to say anything, and he never did, as far as I know.

Well, then, several months after arranging for the transfer of the letters with Robert Hill, we contacted him about the Eliots. What was most appropriate to be done? Hill said that they too should be with the Quinn things in the New York Library, but more properly in the Berg Collection. And he told us, you don't need to give the Eliot documents, gratis, because the Berg Collection at the New York Public Library has lots of money to buy things they want. Why don't you contact Gordan [Dr. John D. Gordan, Curator]?" This we did, and Gordan said, "By all means." That was what happened to it. We went through a lot of soul-searching, I'll tell you; it was not on the spur of the moment, and the money part of it was really incidental. But they said, "My lord, you might just as well take some money, because they're going to use it for something." And so we did, an installment in 1958 and the second half, $9,000, in 1959. We knew it would be in safe hands, and were sure that very shortly the announcement would be made, and the whole matter would be settled and out of our hands.

No announcement was made. We wrote, we contacted our close friends at the Library, particularly Bob Hill, keeper of manuscripts. He said, "I'm embarrassed. We all are. And yet Gordan is adamant; he's waiting for what he called 'the appropriate time.' " We had turned over all rights. We had agreed to one thing—that there was to be no copy made of any part of *The Waste Land*. And that was it. We did have a microfilm made in spring of 1958 in Mountain View, at the request of Dr. Gordan, as the first step in the exchange; but we had agreed to make only one, and to turn it over to them with the manuscripts.

So as a matter of honor we felt that we couldn't say anything. Since the donation of the letters was known, we were importuned constantly about *The Waste Land*. My Mary said, "What can I say?" And I said, "What can we say? We don't want to deny it emphatically." Bob Hill suggested the answer that Mary eventually used: "I do not have it. I am deeply sorry I cannot help you in the quest." Then finally T. S. Eliot died in 1965. Immediately thereafter an emissary was sent by the Library with a microfilm of the copy to Valerie Eliot. As to Dr. Gordan's reason for holding back the news of the Eliot manuscripts, Hill thought that Gordan didn't want to open a hornet's nest. Gordan sensed that to publicize the documents would have been embarrassing to Eliot. It would have opened up a can of worms.

Valerie Eliot, as you know, brought out the definitive edition, showing Pound's corrections. It was the thought of those in whom we confided, including the biographer of John Quinn, Ben Reid, Professor of English at Holyoke College, who used to spend months with us going over all the material, that Pound had made so many changes in *The Waste Land* that there should be two names to that title, to that authorship. I leave that with you scholars. After that time I had some very nice correspondence with Valerie. She expressed no resentment at what had happened. Whether we did the right thing we'll never know. But at least those are the facts of what really happened.

CRITICISM

◆

The Poetry of T. S. Eliot

I. A. RICHARDS

We too readily forget that, unless something is very wrong with our civilisation, we should be producing three equal poets at least for every poet of high rank in our great-great-grandfathers' day. Something must indeed be wrong; and since Mr. Eliot is one of the very few poets that current conditions have not overcome, the difficulties which he has faced, and the cognate difficulties which his readers encounter, repay study.

Mr. Eliot's poetry has occasioned an unusual amount of irritated or enthusiastic bewilderment. The bewilderment has several sources. The most formidable is the unobtrusiveness, in some cases the absence, of any coherent intellectual thread upon which the items of the poem are strung. A reader of "Gerontion," of "Preludes," or of "The Waste Land" may, if he will, after repeated readings, introduce such a thread. Another reader after much effort may fail to contrive one. But in either case energy will have been misapplied. For the items are united by the accord, contrast, and interaction of their emotional effects, not by an intellectual scheme that analysis must work out. The value lies in the unified response which this interaction creates in the right reader. The only intellectual activity required takes place in the realisation of the separate items. We can, of course, make a "rationalisation" of the whole experience, as we can of any experience. If we do, we are adding something which does not belong to the poem. Such a logical scheme is, at best, a scaffolding that vanishes when the poem is constructed. But we have so built into our nervous systems a demand for intellectual coherence, even in poetry, that we find a difficulty in doing without it.

This point may be misunderstood, for the charge most usually brought against Mr. Eliot's poetry is that it is overintellectualised. One reason for this is his use of allusion. A reader who in one short poem picks up allusions to *The Aspern Papers, Othello,* "A Toccata of Galuppi's," Marston, *The Phœnix and the Turtle, Antony and Cleopatra* (twice), "The Extasie," *Macbeth, The Merchant of Venice,* and Ruskin feels that his wits are being unusually well exercised. He may easily leap to the conclusion that the basis of the poem is in wit also. But this would be a mistake. These things come in, not that the reader may be ingenious or admire the writer's erudition (this last accusation has tempted several critics to disgrace themselves), but for the sake of the emo-

Reprinted from *Principles of Literary Criticism* (1925), by permission of Harcourt, Brace, Jovanovich, Inc.

tional aura which they bring and the attitudes they incite. Allusion in Mr. Eliot's hands is a technical device for compression. "The Waste Land" is the equivalent in content to an epic. Without this device twelve books would have been needed. But these allusions and the notes in which some of them are elucidated have made many a petulant reader turn down his thumb at once. Such a reader has not begun to understand what it is all about.

This objection is connected with another, that of obscurity. To quote a recent pronouncement upon "The Waste Land" from Mr. Middleton Murry: "The reader is compelled, in the mere effort to understand, to adopt an attitude of intellectual suspicion, which makes impossible the communication of feeling. The work offends against the most elementary canon of good writing: that the immediate effect should be unambiguous." Consider first this "canon." What would happen, if we pressed it, to Shakespeare's greatest sonnets, or to *Hamlet?* The truth is that very much of the best poetry is necessarily ambiguous in its immediate effect. Even the most careful and responsive reader must reread and do hard work before the poem forms itself clearly and unambiguously in his mind. An original poem, as much as a new branch of mathematics, compels the mind which receives it to grow, and this takes time. Anyone who upon reflection asserts the contrary for his own case must be either a demigod or dishonest; probably Mr. Murry was in haste. His remarks show that he has failed in his attempt to read the poem, and they reveal, in part, the reason for his failure—namely, his own overintellectual approach. To read it successfully he would have to discontinue his present self-mystifications.

The critical question in all cases is whether the poem is worth the trouble it entails. For "The Waste Land" this is considerable. There is Miss Weston's *From Ritual to Romance* to read, and its "astral" trimmings to be discarded—they have nothing to do with Mr. Eliot's poem. There is Canto xxvi of the *Purgatorio* to be studied—the relevance of the close of that canto to the whole of Mr. Eliot's work must be insisted upon. It illuminates his persistent concern with sex, the problem of our generation, as religion was the problem of the last. There is the central position of Tiresias in the poem to be puzzled out—the cryptic form of the note which Mr. Eliot writes on this point is just a little tiresome. It is a way of underlining the fact that the poem is concerned with many aspects of the one fact of sex, a hint that is perhaps neither indispensable nor entirely successful.

When all this has been done by the reader, when the materials with which the words are to clothe themselves have been collected, the poem still remains to be read. And it is easy to fail in this undertaking. An "attitude of intellectual suspicion" must certainly be abandoned. But this is not difficult to those who still know how to give their feelings precedence to their thoughts, who can accept and unify an experience without trying to catch it in an intellectual net or to squeeze out a doctrine. One form of this attempt must be mentioned. Some, misled no doubt by its origin in a Mystery, have endeavoured to give the poem a symbolical reading. But its symbols are not mystical, but emotional. They stand, that is, not for ineffable objects, but for normal human experience. The poem, in fact, is radically naturalistic; only its compression makes it appear otherwise. And in this it probably comes nearer to the original Mystery which it perpetuates than transcendentalism does.

If it were desired to label in three words the most characteristic feature of Mr. Eliot's technique, this might be done by calling his poetry a "music of ideas." The ideas are of all kinds, abstract and concrete, general and particular, and, like the musician's phrases, they are arranged, not that they may tell us something, but that their effects in us may combine into a coherent whole of feeling and attitude and produce a peculiar liberation of the will. They are there to be responded to, not to be pondered or worked out. This is, of course, a method used intermittently in very much poetry, and only an accentuation and isolation of one of its normal resources. The peculiarity of Mr. Eliot's later, more puzzling, work is his deliberate and almost exclusive employment of it. In the earlier poems this logical freedom appears only occasionally. In "The Love Song of J. Alfred Prufrock," for example, there is a patch at the beginning and another at the end, but the rest of the poem is quite straightforward. In "Gerontion," the first long poem in this manner, the air of monologue, of a stream of associations, is a kind of disguise, and the last two lines,

> Tenants of the house,
> Thoughts of a dry brain in a dry season.

are almost an excuse. The close of "A Cooking Egg" is perhaps the passage in which the technique shows itself most clearly. The reader who appreciates the emotional relevance of the title has the key to the later poems in his hand. I take Pipit to be the retired nurse of the hero of the poem, and *Views of the Oxford Colleges* to be the still treasured present which he sent her when he went up to the University. The middle section of the poem I read as a specimen of the rather withered pleasantry in which contemporary culture has culminated and beyond which it finds much difficulty in passing. The final section gives the contrast which is pressed home by the title. Even the most mature egg was new laid once. The only other title of equal significance that I can recall is Mrs. Wharton's *The Age of Innocence,* which might well be studied in this connection. "The Waste Land" and "The Hollow Men" (the most beautiful of Mr. Eliot's poems, and in the last section a new development) are purely a "music of ideas," and the pretence of a continuous thread of associations is dropped.

How this technique lends itself to misunderstandings we have seen. But many readers who have failed in the end to escape bewilderment have begun by finding on almost every line that Mr. Eliot has written—if we except certain youthful poems on American topics—that personal stamp which is the hardest thing for the craftsman to imitate and perhaps the most certain sign that the experience, good or bad, rendered in the poem is authentic. Only those unfortunate persons who are incapable of reading poetry can resist Mr. Eliot's rhythms. The poem as a whole may elude us while every fragment, as a fragment, comes victoriously home. It is difficult to believe that this is Mr. Eliot's fault rather than his reader's, because a parallel case of a poet who so constantly achieves the hardest part of his task and yet fails in the easier is not to be found. It is much more likely that we have been trying to put the fragments together on a wrong principle.

Another doubt has been expressed. Mr. Eliot repeats himself in two ways. The nightingale, Cleopatra's barge, the rats, and the smoky candle-end recur and recur. Is this a sign of a poverty of inspiration? A more plausible explanation is that this repetition is in part a consequence of the technique above described, and in part something which many writers who are not accused of poverty also show. Shelley, with his rivers, towers, and stars, Conrad, Hardy, Walt Whitman, and Dostoevski spring to mind. When a writer has found a theme or image which fixes a point of relative stability in the drift of experience, it is not to be expected that he will avoid it. Such themes are a means of orientation. And it is quite true that the central process in all Mr. Eliot's best poems is the same; the conjunction of feelings which, though superficially opposed—as squalor, for example, is opposed to grandeur—yet tend as they develop to change places and even to unite. If they do not develop far enough the intention of the poet is missed. Mr. Eliot is neither sighing after vanished glories nor holding contemporary experience up to scorn.

Both bitterness and desolation are superficial aspects of his poetry. There are those who think that he merely takes his readers into the Waste Land and leaves them there, that in his last poem he confesses his impotence to release the healing waters. The reply is that some readers find in his poetry not only a clearer, fuller realisation of their plight, the plight of a whole generation, than they find elsewhere, but also through the very energies set free in that realisation a return of the saving passion.

T. S. Eliot

R. P. Blackmur

Writing on the Tudor translations of Seneca,[1] Mr. Eliot observes that "They represent the transformation of the older form of versification into the new— consequently the transformation of language and sensibility as well. Few things that can happen to a nation are more important than the invention of a new form of verse." A few phrases and he adds this sentence: "But the Elizabethan mind, far more than the contemporary mind in any country, grew and matured through its verse rather than through its prose." It is the possibilities and implications of these statements in connexion with Eliot's own verse that this essay wishes to rehearse; and it is the attitude of mind inherent in these statements that will be examined in the discussion of Eliot's criticism.

A change in sensibility is equivalent to a change in identity, a change in soul. Sensibility is the faculty, the working habit, of the intelligence, and as such is the stress and qualification of experience. To assert, as is here intended of T. S. Eliot, that one man's poetry and criticism have been instrumental in modifying sensibility is to ascribe a very great importance to that man. A statement so dogmatic, of a man still living and writing, cannot perhaps be supported by any argument save that one which is both indefensible and immitigable—the testimony of individual experience.

But other arguments occur, of which Mr. Eliot's own critical essays is the chief. For in Mr. Eliot's work the relation of poetry to criticism is not, as so often, perfunctory; rather the effect of the one is involved in the other; because the two forms of expression spring from the same experience, differently formulated and with different adjudications.

In another part of the essay on Seneca quoted above, Mr. Eliot remarks that the critic really interested in his subject will always attempt to connect everything past with all that is contemporary; seeing everything as present. And this statement is only another indication of the attitude suggested in the first quotation; the attitude from which poetry and its criticism are free and autonomous. And that autonomy may be defined as covering the whole territory of the intelligence; so that it is the peculiar business of poetry and the other arts to qualify with form and order so much of experience as can be made intelligible. It is notable that such an attitude establishes what poetry

Reprinted from *Hound & Horn* 1 (1928): 187–210.

is not, more than it determines what it shall be. It is not thought, nor theology, nor science. What it is depends on the courage and genius of the practitioner, and on the nature of the sensibility which he creates or with which he is supplied. And what he creates will be largely in the collaboration which he compels on the past and on the present.

Our age decries the intelligence as it works in terms of poetry; giving all that is intelligible to science; and in some quarters even tries to force poetry to become scientific. Much of what we feel is in terms of what we vaguely call "science," and being *felt* in that realm persists in vagueness. Any effort towards defining those feelings in poetry—by the use of new forms, new manipulations of substance—is exceedingly important, and, if only the effort can be removed from the isolation of the very few, should have the enormous consequence of an adequate sensibility. This labour is Mr. Eliot's business; and there is none other so wholly devoted to it.

Poetry is various, like religion or philosophy; and all three claim a lien on reality. In the same sense that the validity of a philosophy or of a religion depends on its bias, the validity of poetry depends on the degree in which it lacks bias. That is, insomuch as the object is made present and *felt* in itself, the bias becomes negligible and disappears. It is the object more than the interpretation that counts; or in other words, by stretching language a little, the object is the interpretation; whatever, being perceived, is worked into a frame of words is at once object and interpretation. Hence poetry is either true, or aside from the possibility of truth in the dialectic kind; which position is more tenable is a matter of temperament for poet as well as critic. Poetry makes no assertions about its contents; it is them. At the other extreme, poetry may not deal with intuitions in their simplest state, as essences; because it would then deny itself, losing the principles of order and freedom. By elimination, I have been saying that poetry is moved by the intelligence primarily; and by the intelligence within limits which guarantee the greater freedom and variety, the more rigidly they have been defined. It may tend, however, towards either intuition or intellect, and will employ both faculties when grounded in or associated with intelligence. Mr. Eliot's poems are an extreme illustration of the presence of intelligence making good poetry, when if the accent had been shifted towards the pure tone of specious intuition or towards the abstract schemes of the intellect, the same poems would have been bad poetry.

The *Waste Land* being presumably Eliot's most "ambitious" engine it is the most profitable example to analyze from this point of view. This is the point of view of the intelligence as it seizes the qualities of things—and thus something of their being—into an order and form which themselves so persist by the laws of contrast and context as to be, somehow, durable and sensible apart from their origins and apart from the poet who conceived them.

However clear the "structure," the scaffolding, of this poem may have been in Eliot's mind, for us it need be only a vague presence, felt now and then as a pressure, a poise, or a pointing finger. Take for example the Tarot pack of cards, which contain in microcosm the cycle of any life. One word of their history is enough;[2] and the reader will be able to catch something of the references to the various cards as they appear later in the poem. He must know that they were themselves a scheme to cover *any* life. But Mr. Eliot cannot content himself or his readers with giving the inference of an intellect or a certainty of the intuition. He presents a séance: Madame Sosostris, famous clairvoyante, had a wicked pack of cards, had a bad cold, was nevertheless the wisest woman in Europe. Madame speaks; it is true she speaks much less than one would like to hear, but enough to place her, to make her tangible, give her position as a myth: and the myth exerts, to the retentive mind, influence over the "structure" of the whole poem. But Madame is more than that; she is a compound of fraud, insight, and chicanery; she is a person; she is a contrast with Tiresias, and at once upholds him.

On the other hand, Tiresias does not at all depend on Madame Sosostris, or any one else, for the peculiar power of his being; he is the freest and most central figure in the poem. He is chosen primarily because the nature of his experience (which has left him "throbbing between two lives") makes him supremely the factor of intelligence, of consummate qualitative sensibility. He is the hero most appropriate to the spirit entered among the perilous experiments of the soul; which is precisely the spirit of this poem. Consider his attributes: he has the most intimate knowledge, by private comparison, of male and female love; he is blind; and he is that soothsayer with the fullest sanction of the gods. A man also who has walked among the lowest of the dead.

Leaving aside the possibility of Mr. Eliot himself being the dramatis persona, it is reasonable to assume the mask of Tiresias being present at the doings of these verses and, by his presence as much as his comments upon them, holding them together. In other words, for the purposes of the poem, Eliot and Tiresias are identified, and are the sensibility of the poem.

There is a further, but subsidiary, analogue between Tiresias, the Fisher King, the Hanged God, and the (supposedly) drowned king in the quotations from the *Tempest*. By subsidiary I mean loose and obscure; something vaguely, nevertheless surely, apprehended—like the foreknowledge of rain, or dawn. Mr. Eliot, if I am not mistaken, has intentionally not distinguished too clearly between the disabled king, the wasteland, and the questing knight or hero of the Grail Legends, which he employs here; conceiving these perhaps as but analogues of the one soul. That is, the more the relation of the poem to the legend is considered, the more it appears that Mr. Eliot has purposely confused its elements; so that it becomes a constant ceremony of life and death, a "vegetation ritual"[3] of the soul in an agony of consciousness. The order is simultaneous in intention and only successive because of the exigencies of language. There is a constant attempt to heap everything up into one image, one feeling, one emotion, and sometimes one word.[4] The five parts into which the poem is enumerated are each the same thing essentially but with differing concrete forms. And each section separately subdivides itself into contrasted celebrations of the one theme.

This theme may be stated severally. Like the Tarot cards the poem is a mirror for any life; only it is a life posed dramatically in a series of events, not merely indicated in a scheme, either of cards or theology. The main idea, or attitude, is that found in the legend of the Holy Grail and in the story of Adonis. In a moment, a day, a season, or a generation, there is death and resurrection—for the spirit, the body, and the world about us; each cycle is complete. And each event in a given cycle implies its accompaniment; each looks into the heart of light: the silence. The terms or events of each is known multitudinously; many have been described in poetry and religion.

The story of the Grail, as Miss Weston expounds it in *From Ritual to Romance,* is simply such a cycle. There is a wasteland ruled by a debilitated and impotent king. Either the illness of the king wasted the land, or drought and war, in wasting the land, have affected the king. The young hero, by asking the right questions and performing the right deeds, becomes himself king and rejuvenates the land. The legend also involves the young hero in three sorts of initiation—into the origins of life, or sex, into the horrors of physical death, and into the consummation of life which is the knowledge of god. The king in certain forms of the legend is called the fisher king; fish and the act of fishing are very common and very ancient life-symbols, so that the fisher king would be king of life, and in fact a god—but a god who dies, replacing himself with a new outward form. Like Adonis and Attis, of whom his myth is a later version, in his life, death, and reincarnation he repeats the drama of daily life and of the secret soul. He is especially important as a death-myth; hence his great usefulness in poetry. Death is the punctuation, perspective, and most excellent background for life: it is the most variously applicable myth, whether of a god or of the land, that man has made to set off and illustrate his thoughts and behaviour. It has the merit that under the right persuasion it is the most immediate and inexplicable or, on the other hand, the most objective and intelligible of all frames for the movement of things. As we are sentient, we are rank with death's weeds.

In Mr. Eliot's *Waste Land,* as in the original, the fisher king has considerable significance, influence, and direction. He is not so vivid nor so great a figure as Tiresias, but his presence is nevertheless constantly felt; though it is hard to say always where, since according to the appended note, all the men and women in the poem are one. There is a danger in too much precision in these matters; for example, any statement as to how much of the first half of Part V refers to Christ would be, without the author's corroboration, subject to error. Christ is only one of the slain gods, and all the slain gods are in some sense one. As has already been said, the order of this poem is simultaneous in everything except fact.

Enough ought in a vague way to have been given of the kind of use to which Mr. Eliot has put anthropology and literature. He has imported figures from history and legend, has borrowed, giving them a new significance, many remarkable lines from older poetry: not to make a picture of history or an outline of literature but to give point and form to an individual "experiment of the soul." A line of poetry or a figure from history is chosen to enforce again in a new context the whole area of feeling and experience to which it was, for those already familiar, the key. And proceeding a little, the poem itself seizes a situation, is itself a key—to what, depends on the reader's knowledge and temper.

Keeping these considerations in mind and remembering the last phrase of the epigraph: "I wish to die," the *Waste Land* has as much of an explanation as a poem may require: which is not an explanation at all, but the appropriate group of facts and feelings existing in the plane of "thought" most nearly parallel to the plane of the poem. You can set up a sensibility for poetry, and you can create poetry as the object of sensibility, but you can explain neither: for both poetry and sensibility are the residua of qualities—a field where comparison may establish only the contrasting, and analysis isolate the individual; as in that other field we call real life. The rest, our fiction that we understand one another and one another's poetry, is convention; and convention when it is alive—that is to say, intelligent—is the most daring form the imagination takes.

It is worth repeating that the conventions of Mr. Eliot's poetry are extremely intelligent. The *Waste Land* is neither allegory nor metaphysics in verse, nor anything at all but poetry. There is hardly an "idea" in the poem; there are feelings and images, and there is the peculiar emotion produced by these. Mr. Eliot once wrote of Henry James in this reference that he had a mind so fine that no *idea* could penetrate it, and he has recently, in a paper on Ezra Pound, spoken of images which combined a maximum of concreteness with an almost infinite suggestion. These two phrases indicate, perhaps, how the mind acts as it is intent on poetry: it may employ any other faculties you choose to mention in different realms, but it is roughly limited in poetry to something covered by these two phrases. It is the action, to repeat, of the intelligence as opposed to the intellect and to simple intuition.

It is not at all meant to imply that the intelligence will not deal with the abstract or the immediate as its material; only that it will always put the immediate in order and qualify the abstract. Further these categories are not, for the purposes of poetry, entirely distinct; things normally, that is typically, abstract may by their occasion be wholly intelligible: as the abstract ideas of love in Crashaw's *Hymn to St. Teresa,* or Keats' *Nightingale.* At the other pole, phenomena as immediate as sunshine may have the *quality* of an eternal idea. It depends wholly upon the occasion and how the data are seized. The richness of a poet is measured by the variety of the material he makes vividly intelligible; is measured in other words by the degree in which his sensibility covers the material that interests him, the degree in which the poetry is equivalent to the material.

Let us take five of Mr. Eliot's poems; examining them from this angle: *What the Thunder Said* (*Waste Land* V); *Gerontion; Hollow Men; Whispers of Immortality;* and *Prufrock,* these being as different from one another as Mr. Eliot's poems ever are.

The section of the *Waste Land* is in a way the easiest to handle because it is the most complicated; has the most nameable parts, each involving or overlapping the other. There is no "story" in any of Eliot's work and here less than anywhere. That is to say: nothing happens: a position, an emotion is defined, as has been said several times, in terms of certain images. Some images are facts about things, some are feelings; others are possibilities of fact or soul. All are such as can exist nowhere but in poetry, in the particular poem being read.

What the Thunder Said opens with a set of images and feelings suggested by the crucifixion of Christ in the minds of two of His disciples setting off for Emmaus on the day of the resurrection. Observe that neither Jesus, his death, or promised resurrection is once mentioned as such. Instead there is "the torchlight red on sweaty faces" and "reverberation of thunders of spring over distant mountains." Which phrases are intended to convey much more appropriate feelings and to result much more in the right emotion than at this late day would a literal recounting of names and events; so that a general emotion, which is vague, is escaped and a particular group of feelings, which may prove "universal," is defined. Not the experience is individual, for that would be incommunicable, but the medium of experience.

Christ had not previously appeared in the poem; hence to place him there is an immediate alignment or merging of his figure with the motif of "the freeing of the waters,"[5] or resurrection of the dead land, hitherto treated variously in the poem. The notion being that the freeing of the waters is analogous to the resurrection of Christ, and having the advantage also of being the oldest recorded ritual of re-birth vegetation. Here again the images introduced are particular, are "imaginative"; as witness:

> But sound of water over a rock
> Where the hermit-thrush sings in the pine trees
> Drip drop drip drop drop drop drop.

After this appears the ghost, "the third who walks always beside you, gliding wrapt in a brown mantle, hooded." This is at once Christ, and, presumably, Tiresias, and the Hanged God.

Next there is set up the image of a possible feeling; namely that of the cycle of cities, which is powerful because of its context, and because it covers a great stretch of time. The city over the mountains—perhaps the image of all possible cities—

Cracks and reforms and bursts in the violet air
Falling towers
Jerusalem Athens Alexandria
Vienna London
Unreal.

Similarly "unreal" is the woman in the following interlude who

drew her long black hair out tight
And fiddled whisper music on those strings.

The woman is the same as in the first and second sections; she has also a likeness to the woman in *La Figlia che Piange.*

The passage about the Cemetery Perilous and the Chapel Perilous is again in the mountains; and after the reference to the initiation by death we have a "damp gust bringing rain." In this passage more than any other in the poem, the uninstructed reader would be at a loss. The atmosphere is not presented, except by a previous knowledge of the ceremony; nor, without such knowledge, does the passage fit into the poem. That the first and last lines form transition or connecting links is not enough. The symbolic possibilities of the chapel, the wind, the bones and the cock are too various: they should have been more definite, not perhaps in themselves but by reinforcement, with the purpose of making them intelligible.

The remainder of the poem proper is Mr. Eliot's version of the fable of what the thunder said. Here there are no difficulties of apprehension, nor of reference, nor of context; only the inherent difficulty of the most excellent poetry. There is a sureness, a necessity, in these lines that make them the extreme articulation of the deepest honesty. Stripped of the "poetry" there remain only three simple statements about human life. What one gives or surrenders can never be returned. The mind creates the world it knows and is prisoned in it. Order and control are the principles of wisdom, or happiness, or success. These are familiar enough observations to be quite pointless. But because they are felt and situated and made wholly intelligible concrete instances of themselves—they present a personality in the terrors of contact and of isolation, and, alternatively, are graced by the dream of communion.[6] The feelings aroused and suggested by these lines form individual emotions which do not possess names or bounding lines as do the terms "love" and "hate" for example; but they have a symbolic quality which is, though not in any frame of words, far more definite. This is a very desirable quality in poetry; because it is only poetry—and the other arts—that may possess it; and because it is a quality come by only after so great labor that but few poets have ever understood what a privilege might be taken.

For the rest, Mr. Eliot heaps up eleven lines—images, feelings—each having a bearing on the entire poem, each a key to the whole, each the sum

and articulation of much experience. The lines are disjunct, disparate, dissoci-
ate; and gain their power so. I quote the three having the most obvious
meaning without their context.

> Shall I at least set my lands in order?
> London Bridge is falling down, falling down, falling down
> These fragments have I shored against my ruins.

It may occur to some that much of what has been said here has very little to
do with Eliot's poems and even less with the criticism of them; and none is
more confused on this matter than myself. What seems important is—to
expose sufficient of the data and methods of these poems to suggest, since it
is impossible to define, the new way of feeling, the new forms for the
combination of feelings of which Mr. Eliot is the creator. It is the question of
sensibility which was raised in Mr. Eliot's own words in the first paragraph of
this paper; and I think no one will disagree with me as to its importance; for
a sensibility may be a general as well as a private possession. Its construction
is not the work of an individual; only its particular application and tone. Its
use requires that it be understood and in a sense duplicated or incorporated in
other minds. However fatal the essential character of a given sensibility may
be, it is largely accidental so far as the consciousness is concerned. It is
therefore liable to many failures at either of two extremes. It may be too
personal, meeting the material too much in the private mind of the poet; or
it may not control the material, may not qualify it personally enough.
. . . .

T. S. Eliot occupies a position in the body of poetry which may be the
more limited the more his relations are observed but which will not be
diminished, nor be well lost sight of. The taste for his poetry may be rare;
but it is perennial—from moment to moment, and no doubt from age to
age.

Great subtlety of feeling and bottomless honesty of insight into feeling
may make a remarkable philosopher or a true poet, depending on the terms
in which experience informs the intelligence. In either case, finally, the
merit, and the truth is the same. Mr. Eliot is a poet; and to describe his
poetry there is a good phrase in Santayana. Life seen in immediacy is comedy,
in perspective is tragedy, and in essence is lyric. The great feat and peculiar
quality of these poems is that they present certain perspectives of the soul
with the comic force of the immediate. That is why his levity is intense and
his ritual dramatic.[7]

But this would not be true were it not for another quality which his
poems possess—that is their astonishing purity, their extreme fidelity to
poetry and intelligence. The reason Mr. Eliot leaves aside English poetry
since the Restoration is that its inspiration is impure, and its movement in a
sense undirected and wayward; its emotions not founded on the facts of

feeling exclusively. The pure intelligence went, in letters, to the novel, and elsewhere to science.

That Mr. Eliot is a "classical" poet is obvious. The extraneous, the irrelevant—all the fraud of false invention—these are lacking. The limits have been designed perfectly for each poem, and are not the limits of competence but of mastery. And this is what limits Eliot himself; he has perhaps not risked failure enough. He has devised too economical a perfection, set himself limits too much within his means, and has never yet stretched his sensibility to its utmost. It is no apology for Eliot but an indictment of the times, to insist this may well be the fault of an age which leaves almost all the work to the poet. There is nothing rarer than the kind of intelligence to which Mr. Eliot continually testifies, and its full testimony would require only a set of conventions already existing to hold the qualities of things when they were discovered. And that this age does not provide.

.   .   .   .

Notes

1. Seneca. His Tenne Tragedies Translated into English. Edited by Thomas Newton, anno 1581. With an Introduction by T. S. Eliot. London and New York, 1927. The reference is to pp. XLIX and L.

2. The Tarot cards are a considerable mystery—both as to their history and significance. They have a triple utility—as a game of chance, as a system of fortune telling among European gypsies, and as the outward index or set of emblems of a secret mystical philosophy of life. Mr. Eliot professes ignorance on these matters and uses them as a dramatic convenience. As to their interpretation, Mr. S. Foster Damon insists that all texts must be taken with a grain of salt. A complete pack consists of four suits and twenty-two trumps; and it is in the trumps only that the initiate finds the secret of life, the other cards being added for some games. The card that Mr. Eliot makes most use of is the twelfth trump, the hanged man, which is the most interesting of all. Mr. Damon says "He is hanging by one foot upside-down from a cross (his body forms a cross above a triangle); and this was a favorite symbolic posture of Blake's throughout his work." Mr. A. E. Waite in his *Pictorial Key to the Tarot* (London, 1911, p. 116), furnishes the following description: "The gallows from which he is suspended forms a *Tau* cross, while the figure—from the position of the legs—forms a fyifot cross. There is a nimbus about the head of the seeming martyr. It should be noted (1) that the tree of sacrifice is living wood with leaves thereon; (2) that the face expresses deep enchantment; (3) that the figure, as a whole, suggests life in suspension, but life and not death." Mr. Eliot's Wheel is the Wheel of Fortune, the tenth trump. His one-eyed merchant is doubtless the Fool, trump zero. Those interested should consult Mr. Waite's book as above; Papus—*The Tarot of the Bohemians*, London, 1892, which has these italics on the title-page: *For the exclusive use of initiates;* and *Les Cartes à Jouer du XIV au XX siècle,* by d'Allemagne, Paris, 1906. All these have plentiful illustrations of the Tarot cards. .

3. Objection has been made to the kind of anthropological material used in this poem, on the ground that the particular data employed are becoming rapidly "dated" and, therefore, vapid. To which the retort is that April will always be the cruelest month. Tiresias will always have foresuffered all; that the process of birth and life and death will always equip itself with ceremony and issue in symbol and ritual.

4. As for example in lines 20–30, the image of the shadow under the red rock, and its company of death's rhetoric. It may be added in this reference that during the Aurignacian culture, kings were always buried under red rock, or lacking rock, *red clay*. Red was a general life-symbol (for which gold was a later analogue); so that its association with death is especially significant. See G. Elliot Smith's book on gold.

5. See J. L. Weston: *Ritual and Romance:* Chapter on Freeing of the Waters.

6. Another translation or interpretation of this passage would put the matter thus. God speaks in the thunder: "Da Datta." And the rest is man's answer to the God. The line "What have we given?" becomes then a rhetorical question, even an "irony." God is given back His thunder with vengeance.

7. Mr. Eliot published in two numbers of the *New Criterion* portions of a play or Agon, which carry this quality further towards the serious farce than do any of his poems. One is reminded of the remarks in his essay on Marlowe relative to the virtues of farce. Not much can be said of the fragments except that they are highly interesting and intensely amusing. The versification is colloquial, hard-boiled, and the lines issue from a definite formal paraphernalia very much Eliot's own. The verse construction is easy and simple to catch, and ought to fit a variety of subjects. But there is not yet enough to judge.

T. S. Eliot

PHILIP RAHV

The trajectory of T. S. Eliot's career describes a curve from Back Bay to Mayfair, from the puritan, moribund gentility of Beacon Street to the thin-blooded, mock-aristocracy of the Mayfair *salons*—a singularly tame performance. In another respect, however, Eliot has proven himself far more thoroughgoing and consistent. Having expatriated himself, he has severed all the ties that bound him to his native country, even going to the length of repudiating his American citizenship (it is pertinent to recall that Henry James likewise became a British citizen, but that was only a wartime *beau geste*, designed to emphasize his sympathy with the cause of the Allies). The English now claim him as one of their own, while the Americans are loth to surrender him, for, all in all, his is one of the most significant voices of the age, at the present time mainly in a negative sense. In him one experiences the whole gamut of post-war disenchantment, the entire complex of spiritual and intellectual problems that torture and stultify the creative course of modern thought. Despite the relative smallness of his literary output, Eliot has exerted an immeasurable influence on contemporary writing. But in view of his recent affiliations with all that is reactionary and sterile on the modern scene, one cannot but deplore this influence, and the best way to combat it, it seems to me, is by trying to understand how it came about. Eliot is a philosophical poet with world-important implications: hence, in analysing him one must take into consideration his socio-cultural background, with the technical-esthetic criticism of his work relegated to a secondary position.

In 1919 Eliot published a small book entitled *Poems* (expanded in 1923) and immediately it became apparent that something decisive had happened in American literature. After years and years of acquiescence a New Englander (which Eliot really is despite his nominal Middle West origin) had flaunted all the conventions of his clan and set out to flay his environment with the knout of merciless wit and acrid satire. Having saturated himself with the poetry of Laforgue and Corbiere, and in fact with the whole French Symbolist school, his was a sensibility enormously superior to the reigning "talents" in American poetry. Amy Lowell, Edgar Lee Masters and Carl Sandburg were considered *the* poets in those days, and of course the taste of

Reprinted from *Fantasy*, Winter 1932, 17–20 (as reprinted by Kraus in 1969), by permission of the General Research Division, The New York Public Library, Astor, Lenox and Tilden Foundations.

most readers was still too primitive rightly to appreciate the visions and twilights, the dawns and languors, the tears and the ice of the *Poems*. Much like Baudelaire, who depicted vile scenes with charming perversity and expressed decadent sentiments in flawless classic verse, Eliot set out, with masterly metric and superlative technical virtuosity, to tear off the mask of piety and virtue from the smug bourgeoisie of New England. The absolute rightness of each and every word, the exquisite twist and turn of the psychic visage concretized in verbal diabolics of extraordinary efficacy—all proclaimed the master. Louis Untermeyer, with his usual superficiality, threw in the phrase *vers de société,* one of the most obtuse critical judgments ever perpetrated. True, the thematic dominant could thus be characterized, but the treatment and the inherent finalities involved were universal in character. Here were no flippant Dorothy Parker smart-aleckisms, but the intense dynamism of profound revolt. In one slender volume Eliot traversed the immense distance from Sweeney, the simple philistine (who, unlike Lewis's Babbitt—a two-dimensional figure—is realized in four-dimensional terms) to Prufrock, the impotent sophisticate, and thence to the wistful lady "with four wax candles in her darkened room" and the disheartened paramour who wants to know if he has "the right to smile"; the lady is Carol Endicott grown up, the Minnesota aspirant with the grapes of *culture* turning sour in her mouth. Prufrock is the modern Hamlet incarnate, epitomizing the debility of intellectualism and excessive sensibility. He asks:

> Do I dare
> Disturb the universe?
> In a minute there is time
> For decisions and revisions which a minute will reverse.

While the *révoltés* of the twenties, the brood of Mencken, lambasted the provinciality of America and hoped for the boon of sophistication, Eliot had already perceived that here there were fundamental life-patterns involved, that certain profound spiritual problems, springing from the total complex of modern life, were confronting 20th-century man, who is now alone in the vast universe, destitute of the traditional human consolations of the past. It was not till the late twenties that American writers as a whole became conscious of the real issue. Eliot had experienced all this in his *Poems;* it was all there.

In this first book Eliot made the right beginning: in it he was grappling with reality; there was no compromise, no cowardice. Vital with genuine social substance, the *Poems* were a positive step, inasmuch as a poet cannot adumbrate a constructive world-view unless he first express his repudiation of the old. But at this stage something happened to Eliot which cut short his creative progress and shunted him back to ally himself with the very elements of society he had satirized in his first work. The ancestral complex, the

Calvinistic past, and the false evasions of the classic bourgeois had all re-asserted themselves: the demonic rebel was clipped of his wings and left to creep back into the fold: back to Beacon Street via the new-humanist local. Perhaps he had become aware of the ultimate destination his revolt was leading to, and had lost heart, being in fact too organic a part of his class to be able to make a decisive break with it? At all events, at the present time Eliot must be discounted as a positive force in literature. His place is defi-nitely with the retarders of the revolutionary urge towards the creation of a new *human* humanity.

The Waste Land was Eliot's next work of note. Commenting on it, Ernest Robert Curtius, the distinguished German critic, has said that "it breathes that despair, which is also the atmosphere of Proust and Valery": the end-of-the-world mood permeates its pages. Insofar as it condenses the values of the *Poems* it was a step forward, but in all other ways it was a retrogression, a sign of defeat. The social realism evident in the *Poems* is here largely missing. Also, its structural relationships are different from those in the antecedent work. The Symbolist tradition is merged with that of Donne and Webster, a singularly tasteless mixture. In *The Waste Land* Eliot had slipped already and fallen into the swamp of mysticism and scholasticism, a double damnation. Mysticism, which has been well defined as a "tendency to obliterate distinc-tions," robs the poem of the necessary precision, and the sinister obscurity, the arbitrary choice of allusion and evocation, render it a closed book to all but a few encyclopedic intellects. No great poet of the past has ever turned his attention solely to the intellectual elite; on the contrary, they have consis-tently attempted to broaden and augment their appeal, at the same time of course without losing depth.

Whereas Catholic critics like Thomas McGreevy contend that *The Waste Land* is a poem of death and resurrection, of conflict between the flesh and the spirit, secular critics, as is the case with Curtius, discern in it the two poles of love and death—Eros and Thanatos. Its symbolism is religious—forecasting the subsequent conversion—but not Christian, as Mr. McGreevy, who is very much concerned with the Kingdom of Heaven, likes to expound. The Holy Grail legend is composed primarily of the elements of primary magic, pre-Christian as well as extra-Christian. Essentially this poem repre-sents a flight from reality, not a solution or even an authentic examination of contemporary time, but an obfuscation. The modern world is bankrupt, but nevertheless a way out exists; a way out that requires the transference of allegiance from the idealist to the materialist world-view. Eliot failed to discover it, yet he pretends to find an outlet where there really is none.

Shortly after the publication of *The Waste Land* there followed Eliot's famous conversion to Anglo-Catholicism in religion, royalism in politics, and classicism in literature, with *Ash-Wednesday* marking his debut as a devotional poet. But in the 20th century it is as possible to be a religious poet as it is possible to be a feudal knight. And, indeed, *Ash-Wednesday,* as a poetic achievement is a gross failure. Throughout the poem Eliot refers to himself as the "aged eagle"; alas, it is all too evident that this particular eagle will fly no more. A poetry of aristocratic moods and ascetic ideas is neither possible nor desirable in an era of plebian revolt and materialist dynamics. The Monarchy, the Church and the classical tradition were the three central values of the *grand siècle*, the century of Louis XIV. But the Christianity of that century of French classicism was a diluted, spiritless thing, and Eliot looks for his in the English metaphysical poets. What he really wants is a *Rex christiannisimus*, not a worldly despot like Louis. However, these three values were a natural, casually necessary reflection of the economy of their age, and can never be transferred to the world of finance-capitalism; hence they are utterly irrelevant, and together with them the devotional lucubrations of the ex-rebel, T. S. Eliot. The age of science, the age of man's triumph over Nature, has done away with religion as a vital force, despite the back-handed God-smuggling of such pseudo-philosophers as Eddington and Jeans, who refuse to see that the indeterminacy which they have discovered pertains only to the *conceptual* world of atomic physics, and not to the real world. Thus, it becomes patent that a poet basing his emotional and cerebral processes on the dissipated force of religion will of necessity become an invalid thinker and creator—illusion-ridden, permanently unhappy and sterile.

The Waste Land: Critique of the Myth

CLEANTH BROOKS

Though much has been written on *The Waste Land,* it will not be difficult to show that most of its critics misconceive entirely the theme and the structure of the poem. There has been little or no attempt to deal with it as a unified whole. F. R. Leavis and F. O. Matthiessen have treated large sections of the poem in detail, and I am obviously indebted to both of them. I believe, however, that Leavis makes some positive errors of interpretation. I find myself in almost complete agreement with Matthiessen in his commentary on the sections which he deals with in his *Achievement of T. S. Eliot,* but the plan of his book does not allow for a complete consecutive examination of the poem.

In view of the state of criticism with regard to the poem, it is best for us to approach it frankly on the basis of its theme. I prefer, however, not to raise just here the question of how important it is for the reader to have an explicit intellectual account of the various symbols and a logical account of their relationships. It may well be that such rationalization is no more than a scaffolding to be got out of the way before we contemplate the poem itself as poem. But many readers (including myself) find the erection of such a scaffolding valuable—if not absolutely necessary—and if some readers will be tempted to lay more stress upon the scaffolding than they should, there are perhaps still more readers who, without the help of such a scaffolding, will be prevented from getting at the poem at all.

The basic symbol used, that of the waste land, is taken of course, from Miss Jessie Weston's *From Ritual to Romance.* In the legends which she treats there, the land has been blighted by a curse. The crops do not grow and the animals cannot reproduce. The plight of the land is summed up by, and connected with, the plight of the lord of the land, the Fisher King, who has been rendered impotent by maiming or sickness. The curse can be removed only by the appearance of a knight who will ask the meanings of the various symbols which are displayed to him in the castle. The shift in meaning from physical to spiritual sterility is easily made, and was, as a matter of fact, made in certain of the legends. As Eliot has pointed out, a knowledge of this symbolism is essential for an understanding of the poem.

Of hardly less importance to the reader, however, is a knowledge of Eliot's basic method. *The Waste Land* is built on a major contrast—a device which is a favorite of Eliot's and is to be found in many of his poems, particularly his later poems. The contrast is between two kinds of life and two kinds of death. Life devoid of meaning is death; sacrifice, even the sacrificial death, may be life-giving, an awakening to life. The poem occupies itself to a great extent with this paradox, and with a number of variations upon it.

Eliot has stated the matter quite explicitly himself in one of him essays. In his "Baudelaire" he says:

> One aphorism which has been especially noticed is the following: *la volupté unique et suprême de l'amour gît dans la certitude de faire le mal.* This means, I think, that Baudelaire has perceived that what distinguishes the relations of man and woman from the copulation of beasts is the knowledge of Good and Evil (of *moral* Good and Evil which are not natural Good and Bad or puritan Right and Wrong). Having an imperfect, vague romantic conception of Good, he was at least able to understand that the sexual act as evil is more dignified, less boring, than as the natural, "life-giving," cheery automatism of the modern world. . . . So far as we are human, what we do must be either evil or good; so far as we do evil or good, we are human; and it is better, in a paradoxical way, to do evil than to do nothing: at least, *we exist* [italics mine].

The last statement is highly important for an understanding of *The Waste Land.* The fact that men have lost the knowledge of good and evil keeps them from being alive, and is the justification for viewing the modern waste land as a realm in which the inhabitants do not even exist.

This theme is stated in the quotation which prefaces the poem. The Sybil says: "I wish to die." Her statement has several possible interpretations. For one thing, she is saying what the people who inhabit the waste land are saying. But she may also be saying what the speaker of "The Journey of the Magi" says: ". . . this Birth was / Hard and bitter agony for us, like Death, our death / . . . I should be glad of another death."

I

The first section of "The Burial of the Dead" develops the theme of the attractiveness of death, or of the difficulty in rousing oneself from the death in life in which the people of the waste land live. Men are afraid to live in reality. April, the month of rebirth, is not the most joyful season but the cruelest. Winter at least kept us warm in forgetful snow. The idea is one which Eliot has stressed elsewhere. Earlier in "Gerontion" he had written

> In the juvescence of the year
> Came Christ the tiger
> ....
> The tiger springs in the new year. Us he devours. . . .

More lately, in *Murder in the Cathedral,* he has the chorus say

> We do not wish anything to happen.
> Seven years we have lived quietly,
> Succeeded in avoiding notice,
> Living and partly living.

And in another passage: "Now I fear disturbance of the quiet seasons." Men dislike to be roused from their death-in-life.

The first part of "The Burial of the Dead" introduces this theme through a sort of reverie on the part of the protagonist—a reverie in which speculation on life glides off into memory of an actual conversation in the Hofgarten and back into speculation again. The function of the conversation is to establish the class and character of the protagonist. The reverie is resumed with line 19.

> What are the roots that clutch, what branches grow
> Out of this stony rubbish? . . . .

The protagonist answers for himself:

> Son of man,
> You cannot say, or guess, for you know only
> A heap of broken images, where the sun beats,
> And the dead tree gives no shelter, the cricket no relief,
> And the dry stone no sound of water.

In this passage there are references to Ezekiel and to Ecclesiastes, and these references indicate what it is that men no longer know: The passage referred to in Ezekiel 2, pictures a world thoroughly secularized:

1. And he said unto me, Son of man, stand upon thy feet, and I will speak unto thee.
2. And the spirit entered into me when he spake unto me, and set me upon my feet, that I heard him that spake unto me.
3. And he said unto me, Son of man, I send thee to the children of Israel, to a rebellious nation that hath rebelled against me: they and their fathers have transgressed against me, even unto this very day.

Other passages from Ezekiel are relevant to the poem, Chapter 37 in particular, which describes Ezekiel's waste land, where the prophet, in his vision of the valley of dry bones, contemplates the "burial of the dead" and is asked: "Son of man, can these bones live? And I answered, O Lord God, thou knowest. 4. Again he said unto me, Prophesy over these bones, and say unto them, O ye dry bones, hear the word of the Lord."

One of Ezekiel's prophecies was that Jerusalem would be conquered and the people led away into the Babylonian captivity. That captivity is alluded to in Section III of *The Waste Land,* line 182, where the Thames becomes the "waters of Leman."

The passage from Ecclesiastes 12, alluded to in Eliot's notes, describes the same sort of waste land:

> 1. Remember now thy Creator in the days of thy youth, while the evil days come not, nor the years draw nigh, when thou shalt say, I have no pleasure in them;
> 2. While the sun, or the light, or the moon, or the stars, be not darkened, nor the clouds return after the rain:
> 3. In the day when the keepers of the house shall tremble, and the strong men shall bow themselves, and the grinders cease because they are few, and those that look out of the windows be darkened,
> 4. And the doors shall be shut in the streets, when the sound of the grinding is low, and he shall rise up at the voice of the bird, and all the daughters of musick shall be brought low:
> 5. Also when they shall be afraid of that which is high, and fears shall be in the way, and the almond tree shall flourish, and the grasshopper shall be a burden, *and desire shall fail* [italics mine]: because man goeth to his long home, and the mourners go about the streets:
> 6. Or ever the silver cord be loosed, or the golden bowl be broken, or the pitcher be broken at the fountain, or the wheel broken at the cistern.
> 7. Then shall the dust return to the earth as it was: and the spirit shall return unto God who gave it.
> 8. Vanity of vanities, saith the Preacher; all is vanity.

A reference to this passage is also evidently made in the nightmare vision of Section V of the poem.

The next section of "The Burial of the Dead," which begins with the scrap of song quoted from Wagner (perhaps another item in the reverie of the protagonist), states the opposite half of the paradox which underlies the poem: namely, that life at its highest moments of meaning and intensity resembles death. The song from Act I of Wagner's *Tristan und Isolde,* "*Frisch weht der Wind,*" is sung in the opera by a young sailor aboard the ship which is bringing Isolde to Cornwall. The "*Irisch kind*" of the song does not properly apply to Isolde at all. The song is merely one of happy and naïve love. It brings to the mind of the protagonist an experience of love—the vision of the hyacinth girl as she came back from the hyacinth garden. The poet says

> . . . my eyes failed, I was neither
> Living nor dead, and I knew nothing,
> Looking into the heart of light, the silence.

The line which immediately follows this passage, *"Oed' und leer das Meer,"* seems at first to be simply an extention of the last figure: that is, "Empty and wide the sea [of silence]." But the line, as a matter of fact, makes an ironic contrast: for the line, as it occurs in Act III of the opera, is the reply of the watcher who reports to the wounded Tristan that Isolde's ship is nowhere in sight; the sea is empty. And, though the *"Irisch kind"* of the first quotation is not Isolde, the reader familiar with the opera will apply it to Isolde when he comes to the line *"Oed' und leer das Meer."* For the question in the song is in essence Tristan's question in Act III: "My Irish child, where dwellest thou?" The two quotations from the opera which frame the ecstasy-of-love passage thus take on a new meaning in the altered context. In the first, love is happy; the boat rushes on with a fair wind behind it. In the second, love is absent; the sea is wide and empty. And the last quotation reminds us that even love cannot exist in the waste land.

The next passage, that in which Madame Sosostris figures, calls for further reference to Miss Weston's book. As Miss Weston has shown, the Tarot cards were originally used to determine the event of highest importance to the people, the rising of the waters. Madame Sosostris has fallen a long way from the high function of her predecessors. She is engaged merely in vulgar fortune-telling—is merely one item in a generally vulgar civilization. But the symbols of the Tarot pack are still unchanged. The various characters are still inscribed on the cards, and she is reading in reality (though she does not know it) the fortune of the protagonist. She finds that his card is that of the drowned Phoenician Sailor, and so she warns him against death by water, not realizing any more than do the other inhabitants of the modern waste land that the way into life may be by death itself. The drowned Phoenician Sailor is a type of the fertility god whose image was thrown into the sea annually as a symbol of the death of summer. As for the other figures in the pack: Belladonna, the Lady of the Rocks, is woman in the waste land. The man with three staves, Eliot says he associates rather arbitrarily with the Fisher King. The term "arbitrarily" indicates that we are not to attempt to find a logical connection here. (It may be interesting to point out, however, that Eliot seems to have given, in a later poem, his reason for making the association. In "The Hollow Men" he writes, speaking as one of the Hollow Men:

> Let me also wear
> Such deliberate disguises
> Rat's coat, crowskin, crossed staves
> In a field
> Behaving as the wind behaves.

The figure is that of a scarecrow, fit symbol of the man who possesses no reality, and fit type of the Fisher King, the maimed, impotent king who ruled over the waste land of the legend. The man with three staves in the deck of cards may thus have appealed to the poet as an appropriate figure to which to assign the function of the Fisher King, although the process of identification was too difficult to expect the reader to follow and although knowledge of the process was not necessary to an understanding of the poem.)

The Hanged Man, who represents the hanged god of Frazer (including the Christ), Eliot states in a note, is associated with the hooded figure who appears in "What the Thunder Said." That he is hooded accounts for Madame Sosostris's inability to see him; or rather, here again the palaver of the modern fortune-teller is turned to new and important account by the poet's shifting the reference into a new and serious context. The Wheel and the one-eyed merchant will be discussed later.

After the Madame Sosostris passage, Eliot proceeds to complicate his symbols for the sterility and unreality of the modern waste land by associating it with Baudelaire's *"fourmillante cité"* and with Dante's Limbo. The passages already quoted from Eliot's essay on Baudelaire will indicate one of the reasons why Baudelaire's lines are evoked here. In Baudelaire's city, dream and reality seem to mix, and it is interesting that Eliot in "The Hollow Men" refers to this same realm of death-in-life as "death's dream kingdom" in contradistinction to "death's other kingdom."

The references to Dante are most important. The line, "I had not thought death had undone so many," is taken from the third Canto of the *Inferno;* the line, "Sighs, short and infrequent, were exhaled," from the Fourth Canto. Mr. Matthiessen has already pointed out that the Third Canto deals with Dante's Limbo, which is occupied by those who on earth had "lived without praise or blame." They share this abode with the angels "who were not rebels, nor were faithful to God, but were for themselves." They exemplify almost perfectly the secular attitude which dominates the modern world. Their grief, according to Dante, arises from the fact that they "have no hope of death; and their blind life is so debased, that they are envious of every other lot." But though they may not hope for death, Dante calls them "these wretches who never were alive." The people described in the Fourth Canto are those who lived virtuously but who died before the proclamation of the Gospel—they are the unbaptized. They form the second of the two classes of people who inhabit the modern waste land: those who are secularized and those who have no knowledge of the faith. Without a faith their life is in reality a death. To repeat the sentence from Eliot previously quoted: "So far as we do evil or good, we are human; and it is better, in a paradoxical way, to do evil than to do nothing: at least, we exist."

The Dante and Baudelaire references, then, come to the same thing as the allusion to the waste land of the medieval legends; and these various allusions, drawn from widely differing sources, enrich the comment on the modern city so that it becomes "unreal" on a number of levels: as seen through "the brown fog of a winter dawn"; as the medieval waste land and Dante's Limbo and Baudelaire's Paris are unreal.

The reference to Stetson stresses again the connection between the modern London of the poem and Dante's hell. After the statement, "I could never have believed death had undone so many," follow the words, "After I had distinguished some among them, I saw and knew the shade of him who made, through cowardice, the great refusal." The protagonist, like Dante, sees among the inhabitants of the contemporary waste land one whom he recognizes. (The name "Stetson" I take to have no ulterior significance. It is merely an ordinary name such as might be borne by the friend one might see in a crowd in a great city.) Mylae, as Mr. Matthiessen has pointed out, is the name of a battle between the Romans and the Carthaginians in the Punic War. The Punic War was a trade war—might be considered a rather close parallel to our late war. At any rate, it is plain that Eliot in having the protagonist address the friend in a London street as one who was with him in the Punic War rather than as one who was with him in the World War is making the point that all the wars are one war; all experience, one experience. As Eliot put the idea in *Murder in the Cathedral:*

> We do not know very much of the future
> Except that from generation to generation
> The same things happen again and again

I am not sure that Leavis and Matthiessen are correct in inferring that the line, "That corpse you planted last year in your garden," refers to the attempt to bury a memory. But whether or not this is true, the line certainly refers also to the buried god of the old fertility rites. It also is to be linked with the earlier passage—"What are the roots that clutch, what branches grow," etc. This allusion to the buried god will account for the ironical, almost taunting tone of the passage. The burial of the dead is now a sterile planting—without hope. But the advice to "keep the Dog far hence," in spite of the tone, is, I believe, well taken and serious. The passage in Webster goes as follows

> But keep the wolf far thence, that's foe to men.
> For with his nails he'll dig them up again.

Why does Eliot turn the wolf into a dog? And why does he reverse the point of importance from the animal's normal hostility to men to its friendliness? If, as some critics have suggested, he is merely interested in making a reference to Webster's darkest play, why alter the line? I am inclined to take the Dog (the capital letter is Eliot's) as Humanitarianism* and the related philosophies which, in their concern for man, extirpate the supernatural—dig up the corpse of the buried god and thus prevent the rebirth of life. For the general idea, see Eliot's essay, "The Humanism of Irving Babbitt."

The last line of "The Burial of the Dead"—"You! hypocrite lecteur!—mon semblable,—mon frère!" the quotation from Baudelaire, completes the universalization of Stetson begun by the reference to Mylae. Stetson is every man including the reader and Mr. Eliot himself.

II

If "The Burial of the Dead" gives the general abstract statement of the situation, the second part of *The Waste Land,* "A Game of Chess," gives a more concrete illustration. The easiest contrast in this section—and one which may easily blind the casual reader to a continued emphasis on the contrast between the two kinds of life, or the two kinds of death, already commented on—is the contrast between life in a rich and magnificent setting, and life in the low and vulgar setting of a London pub. But both scenes, however antithetical they may appear superficially, are scenes taken from the contemporary waste land. In both of them life has lost its meaning.

I am particularly indebted to Mr. Allen Tate's comment on the first part of this section. To quote from him, "The woman . . . is, I believe, the symbol of man at the present time. He is surrounded by the grandeurs of the past, but he does not participate in them; they don't sustain him." And to quote from another section of his commentary: "The rich experience of the great tradition depicted in the room receives a violent shock in contrast with a game that symbolizes the inhuman abstraction of the modern mind." Life has no meaning; history has no meaning; there is no answer to the question: "What shall we ever do?" The only thing that has meaning is the abstract game which they are to play, a game in which the meaning is assigned and arbitrary, meaning by convention only—in short, a game of chess.

This interpretation will account in part for the pointed reference to Cleopatra in the first lines of the section. But there is, I believe, a further reason for the poet's having compared the lady to Cleopatra. The queen in Shakespeare's drama—"Age cannot wither her, nor custom stale / Her infinite variety"—is perhaps the extreme exponent of love for love's sake, the

---

*The reference is perhaps more general still: it may include Naturalism and Science in the popular conception as the new magic which will enable man to conquer his environment completely.

feminine member of the pair of lovers who threw away an empire for love. But the infinite variety of the life of the woman in "A Game of Chess" *has* been staled. There is indeed no variety at all, and love simply does not exist. The function of the sudden change in the description of the carvings and paintings in the room from the heroic and magnificent to "and other withered stumps of time" is obvious. But the reference to Philomela is particularly important, for Philomela, it seems to me, is one of the major symbols of the poem.

Miss Weston points out (in *The Quest of the Holy Grail*) that a section of one of the Grail manuscripts, which is apparently intended to be a gloss on the Grail story, tells how the court of the rich Fisher King was withdrawn from the knowledge of men when certain of the maidens who frequented the shrine were raped and had their golden cups taken from them. The curse on the land follows from this act. Miss Weston conjectures that this may be a statement, in the form of a parable, of the violation of the older mysteries which were probably once celebrated openly, but were later forced underground. Whether or not Mr. Eliot noticed this passage or intends a reference, the violation of a woman makes a very good symbol of the process of secularization. John Crowe Ransom makes the point very neatly for us in *God Without Thunder*. Love is the aesthetic of sex; lust is the science. Love implies a deferring of the satisfaction of the desire; it implies a certain asceticism and a ritual. Lust drives forward urgently and scientifically to the immediate extirpation of the desire. Our contemporary waste land is in large part the result of our scientific attitude—of our complete secularization. Needless to say, lust defeats its own ends. The portrayal of "the change of Philomel, by the barbarous king" is a fitting commentary on the scene which it ornaments. The waste land of the legend came in this way; the modern waste land has come in this way.

This view is corroborated by the change of tense to which Edmund Wilson has called attention: "And still she *cried,* and still the world *pursues* [italics mine]." Apparently the "world" partakes in the barbarous king's action, and still partakes in that action.

To "dirty ears" the nightingale's song is not that which filled all the desert with inviolable voice—it is "jug, jug." Edmund Wilson has pointed out that the rendition of the bird's song here represents not merely the Elizabethans' neutral notation of the bird's song, but carries associations of the ugly and coarse. The passage is one, therefore, of many instances of Eliot's device of using something which in one context is innocent but in another context becomes loaded with a special meaning.

The Philomela passage has another importance, however. It if is a commentary on how the waste land became waste, it also repeats the theme of the death which is the door to life, the theme of the dying god. The raped woman becomes transformed through suffering into the nightingale: through the violation comes the "inviolable voice." The thesis that suffering is action, and that out of suffering comes poetry is a favorite one of Eliot's. For example, "Shakespeare, too, was occupied with the struggle—which alone constitutes life for a poet—to transmute his personal and private agonies into something rich and strange, something universal and impersonal." Consider also his statement with reference to Baudelaire: "Indeed, in his way of suffering is already a kind of presence of the supernatural and of the superhuman. He rejects always the purely natural and the purely human: in other words, he is neither 'naturalist' nor 'humanist.' " The theme of the life which is death is stated specifically in the conversation between the man and the woman. She asks the question, "Are you alive, or not?" Compare the Dante references in "The Burial of the Dead." (She also asks, "Is there nothing in your head?" He is one of the Hollow Men—"Headpiece filled with straw.") These people, as people living in the waste land, know nothing, see nothing, do not even live.

But the protagonist, after this reflection that in the waste land of modern life even death is sterile—"I think we are in rats' alley / Where the dead men lost their bones"—remembers a death that was transformed into something rich and strange, the death described in the song from *The Tempest*—"Those are pearls that were his eyes."

The reference to this section of *The Tempest* is, like the Philomela reference, one of Eliot's major symbols. A general comment on it is therefore appropriate here, for we are to meet with it twice more in later sections of the poem. The song, one remembers, was sung by Ariel in luring Ferdinand, Prince of Naples, on to meet Miranda, and thus to find love, and through this love to effect the regeneration and deliverance of all the people on the island. Ferdinand, hearing the song, says:

> The ditty does remember my drowned father.
> This is no mortal business, nor no sound
> That the earth owes . . .

The allusion is an extremely interesting example of the device of Eliot's already commented upon, that of taking an item from one context and shifting it into another in which it assumes a new and powerful meaning. The description of a death which is a portal into a realm of the rich and strange—a death which becomes a sort of birth—assumes in the mind of the protagonist an association with that of the drowned god whose effigy was thrown into the water as a symbol of the death of the fruitful powers of nature but which was taken out of the water as a symbol of the revivified god. (See *From Ritual to Romance*.) The passage therefore represents the perfect antithesis to the passage in "The Burial of the Dead": "That corpse you planted last year in your garden," etc. It also, as we have already pointed out, finds its antithesis in the sterile and unfruitful death "in rats' alley" just commented upon. (We shall find that this contrast between the death in rats' alley and the death in *The Tempest* is made again in "The Fire Sermon.")

We have yet to treat the relation of the title of the second section, "A Game of Chess," to Middleton's play *Women Beware Women,* from which the game of chess is taken. In the play, the game is used as a device to keep the widow occupied while her daughter-in-law is being seduced. The seduction amounts almost to a rape, and in a *double entendre,* the rape is actually described in terms of the game. We have one more connection with the Philomela symbol, therefore. The abstract game is being used in the contemporary waste land, as in the play, to cover up a rape and is a description of the rape itself.

In the latter part of "A Game of Chess" we are given a picture of spiritual emptiness, but this time, at the other end of the social scale, as reflected in the talk between two cockney women in a London pub. (It is perhaps unnecessary to comment on the relation of their talk about abortion to the theme of sterility and the waste land.)

The account here is straightforward enough, and the only matter which calls for comment is the line spoken by Ophelia in *Hamlet,* which ends the passage. Ophelia, too, was very much concerned about love, the theme of conversation between the women in the pub. As a matter of fact, she was in very much the same position as that of the woman who has been the topic of conversation between the two ladies whom we have just heard. And her poetry, like Philomela's, had come out of suffering. We are probably to look for the relevance of the allusion to her here rather than in an easy satiric contrast between Elizabethan glories and modern sordidness. After all, Eliot's criticism of the present world is not merely the sentimental one that this happens to be the twentieth century after Christ and not the seventeenth.

III

"The Fire Sermon" makes much use of several of the symbols already developed. The fire is the sterile burning of lust, and the section is a sermon, although a sermon by example only. This section of the poem also contains some of the most easily apprehended uses of literary allusion. The poem opens on a vision of the modern river. In Spenser's "Prothalamion" the scene described is also a river scene at London, and it is dominated by nymphs and their paramours, and the nymphs are preparing for a wedding. The contrast between Spenser's scene and its twentieth-century equivalent is jarring. The paramours are now "the loitering heirs of city directors," and, as for the nuptials of Spenser's Elizabethan maidens, in the stanzas which follow we learn a great deal about those. At the end of the section the speech of the third of the Thames-nymphs summarizes the whole matter for us.

The waters of the Thames are also associated with those of Leman—the poet in the contemporary waste land is in a sort of Babylonian Captivity.

The castle of the Fisher King was always located on the banks of a river or on the seashore. The title "Fisher King," Miss Weston shows, originates from the use of the fish as a fertility or life symbol. This meaning, however, was often forgotten, and so his title in many of the later Grail romances is accounted for by describing the king as fishing. Eliot uses the reference to fishing for reverse effect. The reference to fishing is part of the realistic detail of the scene—"While I was fishing in the dull canal." But to the reader who knows the Weston references, the reference is to that of the Fisher King of the Grail legends. The protagonist is the maimed and impotent king of the legends.

Eliot proceeds now to tie the waste-land symbol to that of *The Tempest* by quoting one of the lines spoken by Ferdinand, Prince of Naples, which occurs just before Ariel's song, "Full Fathom Five," is heard. But he alters *The Tempest* passage somewhat, writing not, "Weeping again the king my father's wreck," but

> Musing upon the king my brother's wreck
> And on the king my father's death before him.

It is possible that the alteration has been made to bring the account taken from *The Tempest* into accord with the situation in the Percival stories. In Wolfram von Eschenbach's *Parzival,* for instance, Trevrezent, the hermit, is the brother of the Fisher King, Anfortas. He tells Parzival, "His name all men know as Anfortas, and I weep for him evermore." Their father, Frimutel, is dead.

The protagonist in the poem, then, imagines himself not only in the situation of Ferdinand in *The Tempest* but also in that of one of the characters in the Grail legend; and the wreck, to be applied literally in the first instance, applies metaphorically in the second.

After the lines from *The Tempest,* appears again the image of a sterile death from which no life comes, the bones, "rattled by the rat's foot only, year to year." (The collocation of this figure with the vision of the death by water in Ariel's song has already been commented on. The lines quoted from *The Tempest* come just before the song.)

The allusion to Marvell's "To His Coy Mistress" is of course one of the easiest allusions in the poem. Instead of "Time's winged chariot" the poet hears "the sound of horns and motors" of contemporary London. But the passage has been further complicated. The reference has been combined with an allusion to Day's "Parliament of Bees." "Time's winged chariot" of Marvell has not only been changed to the modern automobile; Day's "sound of horns and hunting" has changed to the horns of the motors. And Actaeon will not be brought face to face with Diana, goddess of chastity; Sweeney, type of the vulgar bourgeois, is to be brought to Mrs. Porter, hardly a type of chastity. The reference in the ballad to the feet "washed in soda water" reminds the poet ironically of another sort of foot-washing, the sound of the children singing in the dome heard at the ceremony of the foot-washing which precedes the restoration of the wounded Anfortas (the Fisher King) by Parzival and the taking away of the curse from the waste land. The quotation thus completes the allusion to the Fisher King commenced in line 189— "While I was fishing in the dull canal."

The pure song of the children also reminds the poet of the song of the nightingale which we have heard in "The Game of Chess." The recapitulation of symbols is continued with a repetition of "Unreal city" and with the reference to the one-eyed merchant.

Mr. Eugenides, the Smyrna merchant, is the one-eyed merchant mentioned by Madame Sosostris. The fact that the merchant is one-eyed apparently means, in Madame Sosostris' speech, no more than that the merchant's face on the card is shown in profile. But Eliot applies the term to Mr. Eugenides for a totally different effect. The defect corresponds somewhat to Madame Sosostris' bad cold. He is a rather battered representative of the fertility cults: the prophet, the *seer,* with only one eye.

The Syrian merchants, we learn from Miss Weston's book, were, along with slaves and soldiers, the principal carriers of the mysteries which lie at the core of the Grail legends. But in the modern world we find both the representatives of the Tarot divining and the mystery cults in decay. What he carries on his back and what the fortune-teller is forbidden to see is evidently the knowledge of the mysteries (although Mr. Eugenides himself is hardly likely to be more aware of it than Madame Sosostris is aware of the importance of her function). Mr. Eugenides, in terms of his former function, ought to be inviting the protagonist into the esoteric cult which holds the secret of life, but on the realistc surface of the poem, in his invitation to "a weekend at the Metropole" he is really inviting him to a homosexual debauch. The homosexuality is "secret" and now a "cult" but a very different cult from that which Mr. Eugenides ought to represent. The end of the new cult is not life but, ironically, sterility.

In the modern waste land, however, even the relation between man and woman is also sterile. The incident between the typist and the carbuncular young man is a picture of "love" so exclusively and practically pursued that it is not love at all. The tragic chorus to the scene is Tiresias, into whom perhaps Mr. Eugenides may be said to modulate, Tiresias, the historical "expert" on the relation between the sexes.

The fact that Tiresias is made the commentator serves a further irony. In *Oedipus Rex,* it is Tiresias who recognizes that the curse which has come upon the Theban land has been caused by the sinful sexual relationship of Oedipus and Jocasta. But Oedipus' sin has been committed in ignorance, and knowledge of it brings horror and remorse. The essential horror of the act which Tiresias witnesses in the poem is that it is not regarded as a sin at all—is perfectly casual, is merely the copulation of beasts.

The reminiscence of the lines from Goldsmith's song in the description of the young woman's actions after the departure of her lover gives concretely and ironically the utter break-down of traditional standards.

It is the music of her gramophone which the protagonist hears "creep by" him "on the waters." Far from the music which Ferdinand heard bringing him to Miranda and love, it is, one is tempted to think, the music of "O O O O that Shakespeherian Rag."

But the protagonist says that he can *sometimes* hear "the pleasant whining of a mandoline." Significantly enough, it is the music of the fishmen (the fish again as a life symbol) and it comes from beside a church (though—if this is not to rely too much on Eliot's note—the church has been marked for destruction). Life on Lower Thames Street, if not on the Strand, still has meaning as it cannot have meaning for either the typist or the rich woman of "A Game of Chess."

The song of the Thames-daughters brings us back to the opening section of "The Fire Sermon" again, and once more we have to do with the river and the river-nymphs. Indeed, the typist incident is framed by the two river-nymph scenes.

The connection of the river-nymphs with the Rhine-daughters of Wagner's *Götterdämerung* is easily made. In the passage in Wagner's opera (to which Eliot refers in his note), the opening of Act III, the Rhine-daughters bewail the loss of the beauty of the Rhine occasioned by the theft of the gold, and then beg Siegfried to give them back the Ring made from this gold, finally threatening him with death if he does not give it up. Like the Thames-daughters they too have been violated; and like the maidens mentioned in the Grail legend, the violation has brought a curse on gods and men. The first of the songs depicts the modern river, soiled with oil and tar. (Compare also with the description of the river in the first part of "The Fire Sermon.") The second song depicts the Elizabethan river, also evoked in the first part of "The Fire Sermon." (Leicester and Elizabeth ride upon it in a barge of state. Incidentally, Spenser's "Prothalamion" from which quotation is made in the first part of "The Fire Sermon" mentions Leicester as having formerly lived in the house which forms the setting of the poem.)

In this second song there is also a definite allusion to the passage in *Antony and Cleopatra* already referred to in the opening line of "A Game of Chess."

> Beating oars
> The stern was formed
> A gilded shell

And if we still have any doubt of the allusion, Eliot's note on the passage with its reference to the "barge" and "poop" should settle the matter. We have already commented on the earlier allusion to Cleopatra as the prime example of love for love's sake. The symbol bears something of the same meaning here, and the note which Eliot supplies does something to reinforce the "Cleopatra" aspect of Elizabeth. Elizabeth in the presence of the Spaniard De Quadra, though negotiations were going on for a Spanish marriage, "went so far that Lord Robert at last said, as I [De Quadra was a bishop] was on the spot there was no reason why they should not be married if the queen pleased." The passage has a sort of double function. It reinforces the general contrast between Elizabethan magnificence and modern sordidness: in the Elizabethan age love for love's sake has some meaning and therefore some magnificence. But the passage gives something of an opposed effect too: the same sterile love, emptiness of love, obtained in this period too: Elizabeth and the typist are alike as well as different. (One of the reasons for the frequent allusion to Elizabethan poetry in this and the preceding section of the poem may be the fact that with the English Renaissance the old set of supernatural sanctions had begun to break up. See Eliot's various essays on Shakespeare and the Elizabethan dramatists.)

The third Thames-daughter's song depicts another sordid "love" affair, and unites the themes of the first two songs. It begins "Trams and *dusty* trees." With it we are definitely in the waste land again. Pia, whose words she echoes in saying "Highbury bore me. Richmond and Kew / Undid me" was in Purgatory and had hope. The woman speaking here has no hope—she too is in the Inferno: "I can connect / Nothing with nothing." She has just completed, floating down the river in the canoe, what Eliot has described in *Murder in the Cathedral* as

> . . . the effortless journey, to the empty land
> ....
> Where those who were men can no longer turn the mind
> To distraction, delusion, escape into dream, pretence
> Where the soul is no longer deceived, for there are no objects, no tones,
> No colours, no forms to distract, to divert the soul
> From seeing itself, foully united forever, nothing with nothing,
> Not what we call death, but what beyond death is not death, . . .

Now, "on Margate Sands," like the Hollow Men, she stands "on this beach of the tumid river."

The songs of the three Thames-daughters, as a matter of fact, epitomize this whole section of the poem. With reference to the quotations from St. Augustine and Buddha at the end of "The Fire Sermon" Eliot states that "the collocation of these two representatives of eastern and western asceticism, as the culmination of this part of the poem, is not an accident."

It is certainly not an accident. The moral of all the incidents which we have been witnessing is that there must be an asceticism—something to check the drive of desire. The wisdom of the East and the West comes to the same thing on this point. Moreover, the imagery which both St. Augustine and Buddha use for lust is fire. What we have witnessed in the various scenes of "The Fire Sermon" is the sterile burning of lust. Modern man, freed from all restraints, in his cultivation of experience for experience's sake burns, but not with a "hard and gemlike flame." One ought not to pound the point home in this fashion, but to see that the imagery of this section of the poem furnishes illustrations leading up to the Fire Sermon is the necessary requirement for feeling the force of the brief allusions here at the end to Buddha and St. Augustine.

IV

Whatever the specific meaning of the symbols, the general function of the section "Death by Water" is readily apparent. The section forms a contrast with "The Fire Sermon" which precedes it—a contrast between the symbolism of fire and that of water. Also readily apparent is its force as a symbol of surrender and relief through surrender.

Some specific connections can be made, however. The drowned Phoenician Sailor recalls the drowned god of the fertility cults. Miss Weston tells that each year at Alexandria an effigy of the head of the god was thrown into the water as a symbol of the death of the powers of nature, and that this head was carried by the current to Byblos where it was taken out of the water exhibited as a symbol of the reborn god.

Moreover, the Phoenician Sailor is a merchant—"Forgot . . . the profit and loss." The vision of the drowned sailor gives a statement of the message which the Syrian merchants originally brought to Britain and which the Smyrna merchant, unconsciously and by ironical negatives, has brought. One of Eliot's notes states that the "merchant . . . melts into the Phoenician Sailor, and the latter is not wholly distinct from Ferdinand Prince of Naples." The death by water would seem to be equated with the death described in Ariel's song in *The Tempest*. There is a definite difference in the tone of the description of this death—"A current under sea / Picked his bones in whispers," as compared with the "other" death—"bones cast in a little low dry garret, / Rattled by the rat's foot only, year to year."

Further than this it would not be safe to go, but one may point out that whirling (the whirlpool here, the Wheel of Madame Sosostris' palaver) is one of Eliot's symbols frequently used in other poems (*Ash Wednesday*, "Gerontion," *Murder in the Cathedral*, and "Burnt Norton") to denote the temporal world. And I may point out, supplying the italics myself, the following passage from *Ash Wednesday*:

> Although I do not hope to *turn* again
> ....
> Wavering between the *profit and the loss*
> In this brief transit where the dreams cross
> The dreamcrossed twilight *between birth and dying*

At least, with a kind of hindsight, one may suggest that "Death by Water" gives an instance of the conquest of death and time, the "perpetual recurrence of determined seasons," the "world of spring and autumn, birth and dying" through death itself.

V

The reference to the "torchlight red on sweaty faces" and to the "frosty silence in the gardens" obviously associates Christ in Gethsemane with the other hanged gods. The god has now died, and in referring to this, the basic theme finds another strong restatement:

> He who was living is now dead
> We who were living are now dying
> With a little patience

The poet does not say "We who *are* living." It is "We who *were* living." It is the death-in-life of Dante's Limbo. Life in the full sense has been lost.

The passage on the sterility of the waste land and the lack of water provides for the introduction later of two highly important passages:

> There is not even silence in the mountains
> But dry sterile thunder without rain—

lines which look forward to the introduction later of "what the thunder said" when the thunder, no longer sterile, but bringing rain, speaks.

The second of these passages is, "There is not even solitude in the mountains," which looks forward to the reference to the Journey to Emmaus theme a few lines later: "Who is the third who walks always beside you?" The god has returned, has risen, but the travelers cannot tell whether it is really he, or mere illusion induced by their delirium.

The parallelism between the "hooded figure" who "walks always beside you," and the "hooded hordes" is another instance of the sort of parallelism that is really a contrast. In the first case, the figure is indistinct because spiritual; in the second, the hooded hordes are indistinct because completely *unspiritual*—they are the people of the waste land—

> Shape without form, shade without colour,
> Paralysed force, gesture without motion—

to take two lines fròm "The Hollow Men," where the people of the waste land once more appear. Or to take another line from the same poem, perhaps their hoods are the "deliberate disguises" which the Hollow Men, the people of the waste land, wear.

Eliot, as his notes tell us, has particularly connected the description here with the "decay of the eastern Europe." The hordes represent, then, the general waste land of the modern world with a special application to the breakup of Eastern Europe, the region with which the fertility cults were especially connected and in which today the traditional values are thoroughly discredited. The cities, Jerusalem, Athens, Alexandria, Vienna, like the London of the first section of the poem, are "unreal," and for the same reason.

The passage which immediately follows develops the unreality into nightmare, but it is a nightmare vision which is something more than an extension of the passage beginning, "What is the city over the mountains"—in it appear other figures from earlier in the poem: the lady of "A Game of Chess," who, surrounded by the glory of history and art, sees no meaning in either and threatens to rush out into the street "With my hair down, so," has here let down her hair and fiddles "whisper music on those strings." One remembers in "A Game of Chess" that it was the woman's hair that spoke:

> . . . her hair
> Spread out in fiery points
> Glowed into words, then would be savagely still.

The hair has been immemorially a symbol of fertility, and Miss Weston and Frazer mention sacrifices of hair in order to aid the fertility god.

As we have pointed out earlier, this passage is also to be connected with the twelfth chapter of Ecclesiastes. The doors "of mudcracked houses" and the cisterns in this passage are to be found in Ecclesiastes, and the woman fiddling music from her hair is one of "the daughers of musick" brought low. The towers and bells from the Elizabeth and Leicester passage of "The Fire Sermon" also appear here, but the towers are upside down, and the bells, far from pealing for an actual occasion or ringing the hours, are "reminiscent." The civilization is breaking up.

The "violet light" also deserves comment. In "The Fire Sermon" it is twice mentioned as the "violet hour," and there it has little more than a physical meaning. It is a description of the hour of twilight. Here it indicates the twilight of the civilization, but it is perhaps something more. Violet is one of the liturgical colors of the Church. It symbolizes repentance and it is the color of baptism. The visit to the Perilous Chapel, according to Miss Weston, was an initiation—that is, a baptism. In the nightmare vision, the bats wear baby faces.

The horror built up in this passage is a proper preparation for the passage on the Perilous Chapel which follows it. The journey has not been merely an agonized walk in the desert, though it is that; nor is it merely the journey after the god has died and hope has been lost; it is also the journey to the Perilous Chapel of the Grail story. In Miss Weston's account, the Chapel was part of the ritual, and was filled with horrors to test the candidate's courage. In some stories the perilous cemetery is also mentioned. Eliot has used both: "Over the tumbled graves, about the chapel." In many of the Grail stories the Chapel was haunted by demons.

The cock in the folk-lore of many people is regarded as the bird whose voice chases away the powers of evil. It is significant that it is after his crow that the flash of lightning comes and the "damp gust / Bringing rain." It is just possible that the cock has a connection also with *The Tempest* symbols. The first song which Ariel sings to Ferdinand as he sits "Weeping again the king my father's wreck" ends

> The strain of strutting chanticleer,
> Cry, cock-a-doodle-doo.

The next stanza is the "Full Fathom Five" song which Eliot has used as a vision of life gained through death. If this relation holds, here we have an extreme instance of an allusion, in itself innocent, forced into serious meaning through transference to a new context.

As Miss Weston has shown, the fertility cults go back to a very early period and are recorded in Sanscrit legends. Eliot has been continually, in the poem, linking up the Christian doctrine with the beliefs of as many peoples as he can. Here he goes back to the very beginnings of Aryan culture, and tells the rest of the story of the rain's coming, not in terms of the setting already developed but in its earliest form. The passage is thus a perfect parallel in method to the passage in "The Burial of the Dead":

> You who were with me in the ships *at Mylae!*
> That corpse you planted *last year* in your garden . . .

The use of Sanscrit in what the thunder says is thus accounted for. In addition, there is of course a more obvious reason for casting what the thunder said into Sanscrit here: onomatopoeia.

The comments on the three statements of the thunder imply an acceptance of them. The protagonists answers the first question, "What have we given?" with the statement:

> The awful daring of a moment's surrender
> Which an age of prudence can never retract
> By this, and this only, we have existed.

Here the larger meaning is stated in terms which imply the sexual meaning. Man cannot be absolutely self-regarding. Even the propagation of the race— even mere "existence"—calls for such a surrender. Living calls for—see the passage already quoted from Eliot's essay on Baudelaire—belief in something more than "life."

The comment on *aayadhvam* (sympathize) is obviously connected with the foregoing passage. The surrender to something outside the self is an attempt (whether on the sexual level or some other) to transcend one's essential isolation. The passage gathers up the symbols previously developed in the poem just as the foregoing passage reflects, though with a different implication, the numerous references to sex made earlier in the poem. For example, the woman in the first part of "A Game of Chess" has also heard the key turn in the door, and confirms her prison by thinking of the key:

> Speak to me. Why do you never speak. Speak.
> What are you thinking of? What thinking? What?
> I never know what you are thinking. Think.

The third statement made by the thunder, *damyata* (control), follows the condition necessary for control, sympathy. The figure of the boat catches up the figure of control already given in "Death by Water"—"O you who turn the wheel and look to windward"—and from "The Burial of the Dead" the figure of happy love in which the ship rushes on with a fair wind behind it: *"Frisch weht der Wind . . ."*

I cannot accept Mr. Leavis' interpretation of the passage, "I sat upon the shore / Fishing, with the arid plain behind me," as meaning that the poem "exhibits no progression." The comment upon what the thunder says would indicate, if other passages did not, that the poem does "not end where it began." It is true that the protagonist does not witness a revival of the waste land; but there are two important relationships involved in his case: a personal one as well as a general one. If secularization has destroyed, or is likely to destroy, modern civilization, the protagonist still has a private obligation to fulfill. Even if the civilization is breaking up—"London Bridge is falling down falling down falling down"—there remains the personal obligation: "Shall I at least set my lands in order?" Consider in this connection the last sentences of Eliot's "Thoughts After Lambeth": "The World is trying the experiment of attempting to form a civilized but non-Christian mentality. The experiment will fail; but we must be very patient in awaiting its collapse; meanwhile redeeming the time: so that the Faith may be preserved alive through the dark ages before us; to renew and rebuild civilization, and save the World from suicide."

The bundle of quotations with which the poem ends has a very definite relation to the general theme of the poem and to several of the major symbols used in the poem. Before Arnaut leaps back into the refining fire of Purgatory with joy he says: "I am Arnaut who weep and go singing; contrite I see my past folly, and joyful I see before me the day I hope for. Now I pray you by that virtue which guides you to the summit of the stair, at times be mindful of my pain." This theme is carried forward by the quotation from *Pervigilium Veneris:* "When shall I be like the swallow." The allusion is also connected with the Philomela symbol. (Eliot's note on the passage indicates this clearly.) The sister of Philomela was changed into a swallow as Philomela was changed into a nightingale. The protagonist is asking therefore when shall the spring, the time of love, return, but also when will he be reborn out of his sufferings, and—with the special meaning which the symbol takes on from the preceding Dante quotation and from the earlier contexts already discussed—he is asking what is asked at the end of one of the minor poems: "When will Time flow away."

The quotation from "El Desdichado," as Edmund Wilson has pointed out, indicates that the protagonist of the poem has been disinherited, robbed of his tradition. The ruined tower is perhaps also the Perilous Chapel, "only the wind's home," and it is also the whole tradition in decay. The protagonist resolves to claim his tradition and rehabilitate it.

The quotation from *The Spanish Tragedy*—"Why then Ile fit you. Hieronymo's mad againe"—is perhaps the most puzzling of all these quotations. It means, I believe, this: The protagonist's acceptance of what is in reality the deepest truth will seem to the present world mere madness. ("And still she cried . . . 'Jug Jug' to dirty ears.") Hieronymo in the play, like Hamlet, was "mad" for a purpose. The protagonist is conscious of the interpretation which will be placed on the words which follow—words which will seem to many apparently meaningless babble, but which contain the oldest and most permanent truth of the race:

Datta. Dayadhvam. Damyata.

Quotation of the whole context from which the line is taken confirms this interpretation. Hieronymo, asked to write a play for the court's entertainment, replies:

Why then, I'll fit you; say no more.
When I was young, I gave my mind
And plied myself to fruitless poetry;
Which though it profit the professor naught
Yet it is passing pleasing to the world.

He sees that the play will give him the opportunity he has been seeking to avenge his son's murder. Like Hieronymo, the protagonist in the poem has found his theme; what he is about to perform is not "fruitless."

After this repetition of what the thunder said comes the benediction:

Shantih Shantih Shantih

The foregoing account of *The Waste Land* is, of course, not to be substituted for the poem itself. Moreover, it certainly is not to be considered as representing *the method by which the poem was composed*. Much which the prose expositor must represent as though it had been consciously contrived obviously was arrived at unconsciously and concretely.

The account given above is a statement merely of the "prose meaning," and bears the same relation to the poem as does the "prose meaning" of any other poem. But one need not perhaps apologize for setting forth such a statement explicitly, for *The Waste Land* has been almost consistently misinterpreted since its first publication. Even a critic so acute as Edmund Wilson has seen the poem as essentially a statement of despair and disillusionment, and his account sums up the stock interpretation of the poem. Indeed, the phrase, "the poetry of drouth," has become a cliché of left-wing criticism. It is such a misrepresentation of *The Waste Land* as this which allows Eda Lou Walton to entitle an essay on contemporary poetry, "Death in the Desert"; or which causes Waldo Frank to misconceive of Eliot's whole position and personality. But more than the meaning of one poem is at stake. If *The Waste Land* is not a world-weary cry of despair or a sighing after the vanished glories of the past, then not only the popular interpretation of the poem will have to be altered but also the general interpretations of post-War poetry which begin with such a misinterpretation as a premise.

Such misinterpretations involve also misconceptions of Eliot's technique. Eliot's basic method may be said to have passed relatively unnoticed. The popular view of the method used in *The Waste Land* may be described as follows: Eliot makes use of ironic contrasts between the glorious past and the sordid present—the crashing irony of

But at my back from time to time I hear
The sound of horns and motors, which shall bring
Sweeney to Mrs. Porter in the spring.

But this is to take the irony of the poem at the most superficial level, and to neglect the other dimensions in which it operates. And it is to neglect what are essentially more important aspects of his method. Moreover, it is to overemphasize the difference between the method employed by Eliot in this poem and that employed by him in later poems.

The basic method used in *The Waste Land* may be described as the application of the principle of complexity. The poet works in terms of surface parallelisms which in reality make ironical contrasts, and in terms of surface contrasts which in reality constitute parallelisms. (The second group sets up effects which may be described as the obverse of irony.) The two aspects taken together give the effect of chaotic experience ordered into a new whole, though the realistic surface of experience is faithfully retained. The complexity of the experience is not violated by the apparent forcing upon it of a predetermined scheme.

The fortune-telling of "The Burial of the Dead" will illustrate the general method very satisfactorily. On the surface of the poem the poet reproduces the patter of the charlatan, Madame Sosostris, and there is the surface irony: the contrast between the original use of the Tarot cards and the use made by Madame Sosostris. But each of the details (justified realistically in the palaver of the fortune-teller) assumes a new meaning in the general context of the poem. There is then, in addition to the surface irony, something of a Sophoclean irony too, and the "fortune-telling," which is taken ironically by a twentieth-century audience, becomes *true* as the poem develops—true in a sense in which Madame Sosostris herself does not think it true. The surface irony is thus reversed and becomes an irony on a deeper level. The items of her speech have only one reference in terms of the context of her speech: the "man with three staves," the "one-eyed merchant," the "crowds of people, walking round in a ring," etc. But transferred to other contexts they become loaded with special meanings. To sum up, all the central symbols of the poem head up here; but here, in the only section in which they are explicitly bound together, the binding is slight and accidental. The deeper lines of association only emerge in terms of the total context as the poem develops—and this is, of course, exactly the effect which the poet intends.

This transference of items from an "innocent" context into a context in which they become charged and transformed in meaning will acount for many of the literary allusions in the poem. For example, the "change of Philomel" is merely one of the items in the decorative detail in the room in the opening of "A Game of Chess." But the violent change of tense—"And still she cried, and still the world pursues"—makes it a comment upon, and a symbol of, the modern world. And further allusions to it through the course of the poem gradually equate it with the general theme of the poem. The allusions to *The Tempest* display the same method. The parallelism between Dante's Hell and the waste land of the Grail legends is fairly close; even the equation of Baudelaire's Paris to the waste land is fairly obvious. But the parallelism between the death by drowning in *The Tempest* and the death of the fertility god is, on the surface, merely accidental, and the first allusion to Ariel's song is merely an irrelevant and random association of the stream-of-consciousness:

> Is your card, the drowned Phoenician Sailor,
> (Those are pearls that were his eyes. Look!)

And on its second appearance in "A Game of Chess" it is still only an item in the protagonist's abstracted reverie. Even the association of *The Tempest* symbol with the Grail legends in the lines

> While I was fishing in the dull canal
> ....
> Musing upon the king my brother's wreck

and in the passage which follows is ironical merely. But the associations have been established, even though they may seem to be made in ironic mockery, and when we come to the passage, "Death by Water," with its change of tone, they assert themselves positively. We have a sense of revelation out of material apparently accidentally thrown together. I have called the effect the obverse of irony, for the method, like that of irony, is indirect, though the effect is positive rather than negative.

The melting of the characters into each other is, of course, an aspect of this general process. Elizabeth and the girl born at Highbury both ride on the Thames, one in the barge of state, the other supine in a narrow canoe, and they are both Thames-nymphs who are violated and thus are like the Rhine-nymphs who have also been violated, etc. With the characters as with the other symbols, the surface relationships may be accidental and apparently trivial and they may be made either ironically or through random association or in hallucination, but in the total context of the poem the deeper relationships are revealed. The effect is a sense of the oneness of experience, and of the unity of all periods, and with this, a sense that the general theme of the poem is true. But the theme has not been imposed— it has been revealed.

This complication of parallelisms and contrasts makes, of course, for ambiguity, but the ambiguity, in part, resides in the poet's fidelity to the complexity of experience. The symbols resist complete equation with a simple meaning. To take an example, "rock" throughout the poem seems to be one of the "desert" symbols. For example, the "dry stone" gives "no sound of water"; woman in the waste land is "the Lady of the Rocks," and most pointed of all, there is the long delirium passage in "What the Thunder Said": "Here is no water but only rock," etc. So much for its general meaning, but in "The Burial of the Dead" occur the lines

> Only
> There is shadow under this red rock,
> (Come in under the shadow of this red rock).

Rock here is a place of refuge. (Moreover, there may also be a reference to the Grail symbolism. In *Parzival,* the Grail is a stone: "And this stone all men call the grail . . . As children the Grail doth call them, 'neath its shadow they wax and grow.") The paradox, life through death, penetrates the symbol itself.

To take an even clearer case of this paradoxical use of symbols, consider the lines which occur in the hyacinth girl passage. The vision gives obviously a sense of the richness and beauty of life. It is a moment of ecstasy (the basic imagery is obviously sexual); but the moment in its intensity is like death. The protagonist looks in that moment into the "heart of light, the silence," and so looks into—not richness—but blankness: he is neither "living nor dead." The symbol of life stands also for a kind of death. This duality of function may, of course, extend to a whole passage. For example, consider:

> Where fishmen lounge at noon: where the walls
> Of Magnus Martyr hold
> Inexplicable splendour of Ionian white and gold.

The function of the passage is to indicate the poverty into which religion has fallen: the splendid church now surrounded by the poorer districts. But the passage has an opposed effect also: the fishmen in the "public bar in Lower Thames Street" next to the church have a meaningful life which has been largely lost to the secularlized upper and middle classes.

The poem would undoubtedly be "clearer" if every symbol had a single, unequivocal meaning; but the poem would be thinner, and less honest. For the poet has not been content to develop a didactic allegory in which the symbols are two-dimensional items adding up directly to the sum of the general scheme. They represent dramatized instances of the theme, embodying in their own nature the fundamental paradox of the theme.

We shall better understand why the form of the poem is right and inevitable if we compare Eliot's theme to Dante's and to Spenser's. Eliot's theme is not the statement of a faith held and agreed upon (Dante's *Divine Comedy*) nor is it the projection of a "new" system of beliefs (Spenser's *Faerie Queene*). Eliot's theme is the rehabilitation of a system of beliefs, known but now discredited. Dante did not have to "prove" his statement; he could assume it and move within it about a poet's business. Eliot does not care, like Spenser, to force the didacticism. He prefers to stick to the poet's business. But, unlike Dante, he cannot assume acceptance of the statement. A direct approach is calculated to elicit powerful "stock responses" which will prevent the poem's being *read* at all. Consequently, the only method is to work by indirection. The Christian material is at the center, but the poet never deals with it directly. The theme of resurrection is made on the surface in terms of the fertility rites; the words which the thunder speaks are Sanscrit words.

We have been speaking as if the poet were a strategist trying to win acceptance from a hostile audience. But of course this is true only in a sense. The poet himself is audience as well as speaker; we state the problem more exactly if we state it in terms of the poet's integrity rather than in terms of his strategy. He is so much a man of his own age that he can indicate his attitude toward the Christian tradition without falsity only in terms of the difficulties of a rehabilitation; and he is so much a poet and so little a propagandist that he can be sincere only as he presents his theme concretely and dramatically.

To put the matter in still other terms: the Christian terminology is for the poet a mass of clichés. However "true" he may feel the terms to be, he is still sensitive to the fact that they operate superficially as clichés, and his method of necessity must be a process of bringing them to life again. The method adopted in *The Waste Land* is thus violent and radical, but thoroughly necessary. For the renewing and vitalizing of symbols which have been crusted over with a distorting familiarity demands the type of organization which we have already commented on in discussing particular passages: the statement of surface similarities which are ironically revealed to be dissimilarities, and the association of apparently obvious dissimilarities which culminates in a later realization that the dissimilarities are only superficial—that the chains of likeness are in reality fundamental. In this way the statement of beliefs emerges *through* confusion and cynicism—not in spite of them.

The Archetypal Imagery of T. S. Eliot

Genevieve W. Foster

"Dichten heisst, hinter Worten das Urwort erklingen lassen." These words of Gerhardt Hauptmann are quoted by C. G. Jung in his essay "On the Relation of Analytical Psychology to Poetic Art,"[1] as illustration of the poet's sense of tapping a deeper level of the psyche than that which is called into play in everyday thought and action. This lower level of psychic activity (Jung explains), that of the collective or racial unconscious, contains the inherited potentiality of mental images that are the psychic counterpart of the instincts. "In itself the collective unconscious cannot be said to exist at all; that is to say, it is nothing but a possibility, that possibility in fact which from primordial time has been handed down to us in the definite form of mnemic images, or expressed in anatomical formations in the very structure of the brain. It does not yield innate ideas, but inborn possibilities of ideas, which also set definite bounds to the most daring phantasy. It provides categories of phantasy-activity, ideas *a priori* as it were, the existence of which cannot be ascertained except by experience."[2] This theory is not peculiar to Jung, being in fact rather prevalent in our time. "I began certain studies and experiences," says Yeats, describing his activities in the year 1887, "that were to convince me that images well up before the mind's eye from a deeper source than conscious or subconscious memory."[3] Jung, however, has given the idea its scientific formulation. For these ideas *a priori* of the collective unconscious, Jung employs the term "primoridal image," borrowed from Jacob Burckhardt, or "archetype" as used by St. Augustine.[4] The peculiar gift of the poet, or of the artist in any field, is his ability to make contact with the deeper level of the psyche and to present in his work one of these primordial images. The particular image that is chosen will depend on the unconscious need of the poet and of the society for which he writes. "Therein lies the social importance of art; it is constantly at work educating the spirit of the age, since it brings to birth those forms in which the age is most lacking. Recoiling from the unsatisfying present, the yearning of the artist reaches out to that primordial image in the unconsious which is best fitted to compensate the insufficiency and one-sidedness of the spirit of the age. The artist seizes this image, and in the work of raising it from deepest uncon-sciousness he brings it into relation with conscious values, thereby transform-

Reprinted by permission of the Modern Language Association of America from *PMLA*, 1945, 567–85.

ing its shape, until it can be accepted by his contemporaries according to their powers."[5] In this view the artist is the cultural leader indispensable to any social change. "What was the significance of realism and naturalism to their age? What was the meaning of romanticism, or Hellenism? They were tendencies of art which brought to the surface that unconscious element of which the contemporary mental atmosphere had most need. The artist as educator of his time—much could be said about that today."[6]

It is not so difficult a matter to trace the rise of the compensating image in the poetry of a past period. There is a unique interest, however, in examining the work of one's own time for the same purpose. The chances of accuracy are lessened, to be sure, by a view that is so close to the subject, but the contemporary image, to the extent that it is understood, has relevance to unsolved contemporary problems, and hence has a kind of meaning for the contemporary mind that historical imagery cannot have. The work of many writers of our time embodies the search for a new image and a new value, and occasionally the reader seems able to trace that value as it emerges. A group of the poems of T. S. Eliot exhibits both the search and the rising image with peculiar clarity. *The Waste Land, The Hollow Men,* and *Ash-Wednesday,* written over a period of approximately ten years, describe the quest. In another group of poems, chronologically overlapping the first—*Journey of the Magi, A Song for Simeon, Marina,* and *Triumphal March*—the image sought in the first group seems gradually to be apprehended. The four poems recently collected under the title *Four Quartets* exhibit an increasingly clear realization of the value in question. It is of the first two groups of these poems, those describing the search and the early realization of the value, that I wish now to write. Lest the discussion that follows should seem fantastic or arbitrary to academic readers, I should like to explain that I am merely attempting what I believe to be an ordinary Jungian interpretation of certain of Eliot's images. It seems to me that this method, or something like it, can be applied very usefully to that part of contemporary literature that is written largely from the unconscious level and that deals in images and imaginative patterns and leaves the task of intellectual formulation to the reader.

The general substance of *The Waste Land* is much clearer to the reader than it was twenty years ago.[7] Parts I to III consist of a series of episodes and comments unconnected except by their common theme. The reading is difficult because all exposition is omitted; the reader must use his intuition to determine when one episode ends and another begins, who the characters are and what their relation is to one another, and what the significance is of the episodes taken as a group. In this last task he is given considerable guidance by the author's notes. The episodes chosen involve characters drawn from various classes in England and on the Continent at the time of writing—that is, in the years just before 1922. The poem is, then, a criticism of post-war European society. But in the note on Tiresias, who appears in line 218 of the poem, Eliot implies that the poem is at the same time an exposition of the state of mind of an individual: "Just as the one-eyed merchant, seller of currants, melts into the Phoenician Sailor, and the latter is not wholly distinct from Ferdinand Prince of Naples, so all the women are one woman, and the two sexes meet in Tiresias."[8] This is to say that the poem is to be taken at once subjectively and objectively. Although it deals with the ills of a society, it is also the expression of a single protagonist, various facets of whose character are represented by the different men and women of the poem. This necessity for interpreting simultaneously in two modes makes an unusual demand on readers accustomed to look for a single "meaning" in a poem,[9] but it is familiar enough to those acquainted with Jung's distinction between the objective and subjective modes of interpreting dreams. "I call every interpretation in which the dream symbols are treated as representations of real objects an interpretation on the objective plane. In contrast to this is the interpretation which refers back to the dreamer himself every part of the dream, as, for instance, all the personalities who take part in it. This is interpretation on the subjective plane."[10]

The Grail legend, via Miss Weston's now famous book *From Ritual to Romance*[11] and with some contributions from Frazer's *Golden Bough,* furnishes the basic imagery of the poem. The waste land to which the Grail knight must travel symbolizes thus the condition both of a single individual and of the civilization in which he lives. Because of the illness of the king of the country, the rain will not fall; therefore the crops do not grow, and the cattle and the people do not reproduce; all life is at a standstill. If some modern Parzifal could achieve the vision of the Grail, he would restore the king to health, and the land to fertility. The poem is the record of a quest for the essential vision. In this earth-water symbolism, earth stands for material reality, or conscious life; water for the psychological or spiritual values of the unconscious—or, in an older terminology, of the imagination. Water is a constant symbol for the unconscious in mythology and folk-lore, as well as in dream-language.[12] It is clear from Eliot's individual episodes that the earth-water imagery has its usual meaning here. The characters, whatever their situation in life, are caught up in material reality and can make no contact with the imagination. The two psychological realms co-exist but they do not interpenetrate. The tourists, the young couple, and the crowd flowing over London Bridge of Part I, the neurotic lady and the two gossips of Part II, and the typist and the clerk of Part III, all are leading essentially aimless and barren lives. The point is made sharp by the sudden allusions to other times—ancient Greece, or the England of Elizabeth—when the conscious life was permeated with the imagination and accordingly had a significance now lost. For instance, the luxurious apartment of the neurasthenic lady described in Part II contains a picture showing "the change of Philomel," and for a moment we are transported to the world of the ancients where myth and reality were intermingled. Then, as we are brought back from past to present, the tone shifts with the tense, within a single sentence, from poetry to ugly actuality:

> Yet there the nightingale
> Filled all the desert with inviolable voice
> And still she cried, and still the world pursues,
> "Jug Jug" to dirty ears.

If the rain could fall, if the qualities of the unconscious could enter into everyday affairs, life would become fruitful again. Instead the unconscious is felt to be simply a menace. "Fear death by water," says the fortune-teller in Part I.

The poem has been so frequently interpreted that the briefest summary of the first three parts will suffice.[13] The first seven lines of Part I are a commentary of the poet's on the cruelty of springtime, which brings new life to all nature, but not to man. These lines introduce the first episode (ll. 8–18), in which a group of tourists in Germany have coffee together, and the chatter of an idle woman dominates the conversation. Another comment of the author's follows (ll. 19–30), in which, in language drawn from Ezekiel and Ecclesiastes, he laments the barrenness of the life just described. A four-line love-song borrowed from *Tristan and Isolde* introduces the second episode, a scene between a young man and girl (ll. 35–42), in which the criticism of society implied in the first episode is sharpened and individualized. The problem is the failure of relationship. The man and the girl are together; she is lovely, but the feeling between them fails because his attention is turned inward:

> I could not
> Speak, and my eyes failed, I was neither
> Living nor dead, and I knew nothing,
> Looking into the heart of light, the silence.
> *Oed' und leer das Meer.*

In the third episode (ll. 43–59) an unnamed character visits a fortune-teller, and the cards of the Tarot pack which she uses serve to introduce the important characters of the poem[14]—the Phoenician Sailor, who is drowned in Part IV of the poem; the man with three staves, who corresponds to the Fisher King; and the one-eyed merchant, who apears in Part III. There is also "Belladonna, the Lady of the Rocks, The lady of situations," who seems not to appear again in the poem except as a presiding deity (unless she is represented by the typist in Part III), but who is destined to appear, transformed, in much of Eliot's later work. The fourth episode (ll. 60–75) shows us the crowd moving over London Bridge, a crowd of the living dead. Among them the poet spies an acquaintance, a man whose name is Stetson, but whose relation to the author is timeless ("You who were with me in the ships at Mylae!") and he directs to him a curious question:

> "That corpse you planted last year in your garden,
> "Has it begun to sprout? Will it bloom this year?
> "Or has the sudden frost disturbed its bed?
> "Oh keep the Dog far hence, that's friend to men,
> "Or with his nails he'll dig it up again!"

The Dog, Eliot explains in a note, is the dog-star, which heralds the rising of the waters of the Nile and brings fertility to the land. The timeless companion knows the burial place of that which is dead, that which is lost; the dead might be resurrected; and resurrection is to be both hoped and feared. The poet turns upon the reader: this is your problem as well as mine: "You, hypocrite lecteur!—mon semblable,—mon frère!"

Part II of the poem consists of only two episodes, and these have a common theme, the failure of human relationship in our civilization. . . . In Part III, the season has changed to autumn, and the scene is the Thames, the Thames of Spenser's *Prothalamion,* the Thames of the river-nymphs. But, it develops in one of those characterstic transitions from past to present, these are different nymphs, city nymphs . . . . An adequate discussion of Sweeney would occupy a whole essay. It may be enough, however, to say that he is a character with whom Eliot is much occupied in other poems, among others the unfinished *Sweeney Agonistes,* and that he is a hearty and vulgar person who seems to act as foil and counterpart to the intellectual and academic author. He serves here somewhat the same purpose that Bloom serves in *Ulysses* as counterpart to Stephen. In Yeats' terminology he represents the "anti-self" ("most like me, being . . . my double, And . . . of all imaginable things the most unlike"), while Jung would probably call him the "shadow," the representative of those psychic potentialities that are not a part of the conscious personality.[15] Hence he appears here in the poem as a symbol of hope, for he is necessary to the achievement of wholeness. Of Mrs. Porter, Sweeney's lady friend, we know nothing except that she washes her feet in soda water—but perhaps the less said of her the better. We are briefly reminded again of the song of the nightingale, and the next episode introduces "Mr. Eugenides, the Smyrna merchant," the modern and degraded version of the ancient sea-farer of the mediterranean, of whom Phlebas the Phoenician, in Part IV, is to be the true type. The next episode (ll. 215–56) recounts the meeting between the typist and the clerk, which, according to Eliot's note, is the real substance of the poem. Here again the theme is the absence of true psychological relationship. The clerk's chief emotion is vanity, the typist's is boredom; in truth they care nothing for each other and hence the affair between them is absolutely sterile, void of real values. The encounter is witnessed by the blind seer Tiresias, who possesses the wisdom of all times and all places:

> I who have sat at Thebes below the wall
> And walked among the lowest of the dead.

After a brief transition in which the author speaks in the first person comes the song of the three Thames-daughers (ll. 266–306), patterned on that of Wagner's Rhine-daughters, in which the contrast between past and present is again made sharp. The next few lines (307–311), borrowed from the Fire Sermon of the Buddha and the *Confessions* of St. Augustine, introduce the theme of fire for the first time in the poem. The tone is one of despair and (it may be) of readiness for sacrifice. The two allusions taken together indicate a turning away from the world, which is thought of as burning with sterile desire.

Part IV, entitled "Death by Water," marks a turning point in the poem. A character called Phlebas the Phoenician, who "melts into" the one-eyed merchant, seller of currants, and "is not wholly distinct from" Ferdinand Prince of Naples, falls into the water and is drowned.

. . . .

> Gentile or Jew
> O you who turn the wheel and look to windward,
> Consider Phlebas, who was once handsome and tall as you.

Taking this on the subjective plane, we must say that a component of the writer's personality has been submerged in the unconscious. From the lines at the beginning of Part V, however, this death is seen to be not a simple calamity, but something in the nature of a sacrifice. The opening imagery suggests the moment immediately after crucifixion of Christ, and—as we are assured by the reference to Frazer's *Golden Bough*—the deaths of the other sacrificed gods.

> After the torchlight red on sweaty faces
> After the frosty silence in the gardens
> After the agony in stony places
> The shouting and the crying
> Prison and palace and reverberation
> Of thunder of spring over distant mountains
> He who was living is now dead
> We who were living are now dying
> With a little patience

Shortly we are reminded of the journey to Emmaus: "Who is the third who walks always beside you?" With Part V the tone of the poem has changed.

The first three parts were made up largely of episodes taking place in reality; in Part V the imagery is strange and imaginative, with a touch of prophecy.

> What is that sound high in the air
> Murmur of maternal lamentation
> Who are those hooded hordes swarming
> Over endless plains, stumbling in the cracked earth
> Ringed by the flat horizon only?

It is as though the artist in Eliot had been drawn down into the region of the unconscious in search of a solution to the problem posed in the first three parts of the poem. "Recoiling from the unsatisfying present the yearning of the artist reaches out to that primordial image in the unconscious that is best fitted to compensate the insufficiency and one-sidedness of the spirit of the age." That image, however, is not found within the limits of the poem. The essential sacrifice has been made, but the redeeming vision has not yet been attained. The corresponding point in the Grail legend is the visit to the Chapel Perilous, where the knight sees the vision of the dead hand that puts out the altar light, and whence he barely escapes. The nature of the compensating value—the nature of the quality signified by the Grail—is, however, suggested at the end of the poem by the allusion to the Indian legend of the three words of the thunder, *Datta, Dayadhvam, Damyata*—"Give, Sympathize, Control." The thunder, the voice of God, speaks these words in the manner of an inquisition, and the poet is compelled to reply, for himself and his contemporaries, that the three commands have been virtually disobeyed. Only to the first, "Give," can he offer a small, ironic claim. We have given

> The awful daring of a moment's surrender
> Which an age of prudence can never retract—
> By this, and this only, have we existed.

To the word *Sympathize* the reply "I have heard the key/ Turn in the door and turn once only" refers us to the line in Canto XXXIII of the *Inferno*

> Ed io sentii chiavar l'uscio di sotto
> All'orribile torre.

The door is that which locks in Ugolino and his sons to perish of starvation. The word *Control* is answered in a past contrary to fact statement: "The sea was calm, your heart would have responded."

Although all the replies to the inquisition of the thunder have been in the negative, the questions themselves give a certain clue to the missing value. What is required in each case is a manifestation of human feeling—the "moment's surrender which a lifetime of prudence can never retract" is most evidently a surrender to feeling, and with "Sympathize" and "Control" the meaning becomes obvious. This feeling, indeed, has been the missing element in each of the episodes describing the barrenness of our civilization—notably in those describing the failure of the relationship between two people. "What Tiresias *sees*, in fact," the bored, meaningless encounter between the typist and the clerk, "is the substance of the poem." For the modern intellectual, feeling is what Jung designates the "inferior function," the undervalued, often repressed function the conscious development of which is an essential to psychological wholeness. As a social document the poem suggests the same unbalance in our civilization—fact and logic have a high valuation while feeling-judgments are too often dismissed as irrelevant.[16] The poem ends with the tension unresolved; the knight, still sojourning in the Chapel Perilous, has not yet come to the Grail Castle nor attained the vision of the redeeming symbol; the rain has not fallen, though all the world waits for it.

· · · · · · · · · · · · · · · · · · · ·

To translate the living myth that revelas itself in Eliot's poetry into cold intellectual concepts is in some measure to falsify it, but it seems better to make the attempt than to leave our intellectual understanding unsatisfied. We have been dealing with two major images. The first is represented in *The Waste Land* by the Grail, in *The Hollow Men* by the eyes, the rose, and the star, and in the later poems by the anima image in all its variety. Interpreted individually, this seems to represent the unconscious part of the psyche, with which the conscious ego must make and maintain contact if psychological wholeness is to be achieved. Taken socially, it represents those lost qualities of feeling and intuition so much needed in our civilization. The second image, that of the redeemer or hero, seems to represent the principle of integration ("at the still point of the turning world"), the force that can mediate conscious and unconscious, masculine and feminine, and all polar opposites. These images are not ideas, but representations of human experience. Their development throughout the poems displays that struggle for completeness of personality with which other artists and thinkers have been concerned and which, in its completer phases, Jung has called the "individuation process."[17] The primordial image offered by Eliot's poetry as answer to the "insufficiency and one-sidedness of the spirit of the age" is thus the principle of individuation.

Notes

1. *Contributions to Analytical Psychology,* translated by H. G. and Cary F. Baynes (N. Y., 1928), pp. 225–249. I shall refer to the English translations of Jung's work, which are more accessible in this country than the originals. The German version of the above essay may be found in *Seelenprobleme der Gegenwart* (Zürich, 1931).

2. *Contributions,* p. 246.

3. *Autobiography* (N. Y., 1938), p. 160.

4. For a fuller definition, see Jung's *Psychological Types,* translated by E. Godwin Baynes (N. Y., 1926), pp. 554–560.

5. *Contributions,* p. 248.

6. *Ibid.,* pp. 248–249.

7. Among the critics who have contributed to this better understanding are Edmund Wilson, in his chapter on Eliot in *Axel's Castle* (N.Y. and Toronto, 1931), Hugh Ross Williamson, in *The Poetry* of T. S. Eliot, (N. Y., 1933), F. O. Matthiessen in *The Achievement of T. S. Eliot* (Boston and N. Y., 1935), and F. R. Leavis in a chapter in *New Bearings in English Poetry* (London, 1938). To the last named I feel particularly indebted. The psychological interpretation of the poem given by M. Esther Harding in her study of the myths associated with the Magna Mater, entitled *Woman's Mysteries* (London, N. Y. and Toronto, 1935), is in general the same that I am attempting to formulate here. I am indebted to her particularly for the interpretation of a crucial passage in *The Hollow Men.*

8. Leavis' comment on this note is of interest here: "If Mr. Eliot's readers have a right to a grievance, it is that he has not given this note more salience; for it provides the clue to *The Waste Land.* It indicates plainly enough what the poem is: an effort to focus an inclusive human consciousness" (p. 95).

9. The effect produced by Eliot's ambiguity in the use of words has received attention from Mr. William Empson in *Seven Types of Ambiguity,* London, 1930 (pp. 98–101). "Two or more meanings all add to the single meaning of the author" (p. 62). We seem to be dealing here with an allied phenomenon.

10. *Two Essays on Analytical Psychology,* translated by H. G. and Cary F. Baynes (N. Y. 1928), p. 87.

11. Cambridge, 1920.

12. A discussion of this principle, as well as of the themes of sacrifice and rebirth (mentioned below), may be found in the last four chapters of Jung's *Psychology of the Unconscious,* translated by Beatrice M. Hinkle (N. Y., 1916).

13. The clearest interpretation, I believe, is that of F. O. Matthiessen. My summary of these three parts contains nothing that is very new except the digression on Sweeney.

14. Miss Weston traces the Tarot cards, like the Grail legend itself, to the Near Eastern mystery cults. Eliot was not familiar with the actual Tarot pack, however, and invented a number of cards to suit his purpose.

15. "If the repressed tendencies, the shadow as I call them, were decidedly evil, there would be no problem whatever. But the shadow is merely somewhat inferior, primitive, unadapted, and awkward; not wholly bad. It even contains inferior, childish or primitive qualities which would in a way vitalize and embellish human existence, but 'it is not done.' " (*Psychology and Religion* [New Haven, 1938], p. 94b.)

16. "The Voice of the Thunder in *Wasteland* speaks not only of the emotional problems of modern man as an individual but also of world problems in a century where the almost exclusive concern with masculine and mechanical concepts of life has well-nigh choked the springs of living water which are gifts of . . . the feminine principle of Eros." (Harding, p. 298.)

17. "Consciousness and the unconscious do not make a whole when either is suppressed or damaged by the other. If they must contend, let it be a fair fight with equal right on both sides. Both are aspects of life. Let consciousness defend its reason and its self-protective ways, and let the chaotic life of the unconscious be given a fair chance to have its own way, as much of it as we can stand. This means at once open conflict and open collaboration. Yet, paradoxially, this is presumably what human life should be. It is the old play of hammer and anvil: the suffering iron between them will in the end be shaped into an unbreakable whole, the individual." (*Integration of the Personality,* p. 27)

Memory and Desire: *The Waste Land*

Grover Smith, Jr.

I. "The Burial of the Dead"

Part I of Eliot's *The Waste Land*[1] derives its title from the majestic Anglican service for the burial of the dead. The theme of resurrection, proclaimed through Saint Paul's subtly moving assurance that "the dead shall be raised incorruptible, and we shall be changed," finds here its counterpoint in the rhythmic annual return of spring, when once more "the cruelest month" of April touches "dull roots," and memory and desire blend an old man's inert longing and lost fulfilment.[2] Tiresias, who is speaking, has been content to let winter cover him "in forgetful snow, feeding / A little life with dried tubers." In the lines of James Thomson which Eliot put to use: "Our Mother feedeth thus our little life, / That we in turn may feed her with our death."[3] Blind and spiritually embittered, Tiresias wrestles with buried emotions unwittingly revived. In his mind "the floors of memory," as in "Rhapsody on a Windy Night," are dissolved. He is borne in phantasmagoria to scenes recalling the "Dixi, custodiam" of the rites of burial. They are scenes both of joy and of agony, and in memory they reveal that consciousness is death and that truly the speaker was alive only when he could forget. The death of winter and the life of spring usurp each other.

Memory takes him from the general truth to a particular event, to another springtime, in his youth, when warm days of the resurrection season brought rain, the water of life, with sunlight, and he was beside the Starnbergersee near the city of Munich.[4] A voice of a Lithuanian girl who recounted a childhood experience of terror, exhilaration, and freedom comes back to him. Against the double happiness of her memory and his, he must now set the present reality of the loveless, arid desert within him. He thinks of Ezekiel, the "son of man," chosen to turn the Israelites in their captivity back to God, and hence of Christ, the "Son of man," whose temples, like his own, are now in ruins. In this waste land Tiresias is the Fisher King, a type of all the mighty who are fallen. It is too late for the message of Ecclesiastes, who besought men to remember God before the time of the grasshopper and the day of evil.[5] Ezekiel's solemn prophecy has been fulfilled against the

Reprinted by permission of the author from *T. S. Eliot's Poetry and Plays: A Study in Sources and Meaning* (Chicago: University of Chicago Press, 1956), 72–98. Copyright The University of Chicago Press.

unholiness of the mountains of Israel: their altars are desolate and their images are broken.[6] "For," as in Bildad's words to Job, "we are but of yesterday, and know nothing, because our days upon earth are a shadow. . . . So are the paths of all that forget God; and the hypocrite's hope shall perish. . . . He is green before the sun, and his branch shooteth forth in his garden. His roots are wrapped about the heap, and seeth the place of stones."[7] The desert nourishes no roots; the spirit of vegetation, meaning love, cannot survive; the Fisher King, like the suffering Job, is a withered plant—in the phrase of the Lord to Isaiah, "a dry tree," spiritually a eunuch.[8]

The only temporary refuge from the parching sun is a red rock, which emotionally recalls the Grail (sometimes figured as a stone) and Chrétien's castle of ladies, "la roche de Sanguin." It is an obscure symbol—altar-like and sacrificial, the rock of St. Peter, the grotto of the sibyl—which the protagonist remembers as the scene of his failure in the Grail quest, as the entrance way to an intense revelation of death:

> . . . something different from either
> Your shadow at morning striding behind you
> Or your shadow at evening rising to meet you.

The mystery is "fear in a handful of dust." Man who "fleeth as it were a shadow, and never continueth in one stay" stands face to face with his fall. There are echoes here of "The Death of Saint Narcissus," where the glow of firelight turns a gray rock red and where the poet "shows" the dead Narcissus; and of Donne's "A Lecture upon the Shadow," or of Beaumont and Fletcher's *Philaster* (Act III, scene 2), where Philaster hurls at Arethusa his angry complaint against woman:

> . . . how that foolish man,
> That reads the story of a woman's face
> And dies believing it, is lost for ever;
> How all the good you have is but a shadow,
> I' the morning with you, and at night behind you
> Past and forgotten. . . .

In some tangential way the symbol of the shadow relates to sex and to the woman with whom the quester fails. Tiresias is recollecting an incident of his past, when in his vigor he played the part not of Fisher King but of Grail knight. A kind of death occurred in a garden. Fear vanquished him; the reality of love with which the hyacinth girl confronted him was overwhelming.

In the Grail legend the sacred talismans, as Jessie L. Weston tries to demonstrate, may have been sexually symbolic. The Grail, either a cup or a dish, represented the female; the lance or spear with it, the male.[9] The goal of the quest was never ostensibly to obtain these objects but rather, by asking the proper question, to liberate the Fisher King from his distress. Indeed, so far as can be seen, the various talismans had no essential connection with the story itself; they were symbols of the life principle behind the Grail legend. Since in the romances they lost much of their original meaning and became misunderstood, they were interchanged, omitted, or described inconsistently from version to version. In *The Waste Land* Eliot avoided the ambiguities attached to the cup and lance and substituted for these things other symbols.

The memories of Tiresias as the Fisher King contain no more important event than his failure with the hyacinth girl. Whether she is the Lithuanian or not is immaterial. She is the Grail-bearer, the maiden bringing love. As in the legends, he has met her in a place of water and flowers,[10] the Hyacinth garden. The function of the Grail-bearer is dual: first, she directs the quester to the place of his initiation or blames him for his failure there; second, she appears in the castle and bears the Grail into the great hall.[11] It is she whom, if his quest is completed, he marries; she would be in Frazer's terms the consort of the wounded and resurrected god, and she universally appears in proximity to the water symbol. At his meeting with the hyacinth girl in *The Waste Land,* Tiresias as the quester has omitted to ask the indispensable question of the Grail initiation. Evidently he has merely stood agape while she, bearing the sexual symbol—the spike-shaped blossoms representing the slain god Hyacinth of *The Golden Bough*[12]—has awaited the word he cannot utter:

> —Yet when we came back, late, from the Hyacinth garden,
> Your arms full, and your hair wet, I could not
> Speak, and my eyes failed, I was neither
> Living nor dead, and I knew nothing,
> Looking into the heart of light, the silence.

Eliot diversified the pattern slightly, for the hyacinth is a male symbol, and then, too, the quester himself has given the flowers to the hyacinth girl. But the effect is the same as in the Grail narratives. The quester becomes like the King, "neither living nor dead."[13] In fact, he is the King only from this point, for Tiresias in *The Waste Land* is merely what his own folly has created.[14]

The hyacinth girl occupies the position of the "word within a word" in "Gerontion," but with a sharp difference in emphasis. She symbolizes centrality; and in her, so to speak, the spokes of the turning wheel converge, just as the wheeling procession or dance of youths and maidens in the legend turns toward the Grail. But she is not for this quester the Word through whom at length he can rest content; his search must go on until he finds the Word by some other way. For she embodies romantic love, the promise of fleshly joy. About her there hovers the kind of spiritual air that romantic poets discern in the presence of the beloved. It is perhaps not the spiritual grace which is sometimes associated with Dante's young adoration of Beatrice. But, like Dante at the beginning of the *Vita nuova,* the quester trembles. And somehow he falters in confronting her. *The Waste Land* is only repeating the old pattern of disaster which overcame the child in "Dans le Restaurant" when the big dog frightened him in the rain.[15] Still, the moment has been one of joy, bringing together the two worlds of flesh and spirit. Though attended with disappointment, it contains, transitory as it is, values proceeding from the unmoved center and cited as the sustaining hope in Eliot's later poetry.[16]

Two citations from *Tristan und Isolde* outline further the drama of love and death. In the opera Tristan, having been mortally wounded, dies before Isolde, hastening to reach him, can restore him through her powers of healing. Like the Fisher King, Tristan languishes from an injury curable only through the lovers' reunion. Of the quotations appropriated by Eliot, the first occurs at the beginning of Wagner's action, when Tristan is bringing Isolde from Ireland to Cornwall, where she is to become his uncle's bride. The song is sung by a sailor at the masthead, and though it does not refer to Isolde herself, she hearing it supposes for a moment that it does. The ship bears her to her destination, but not before she and Tristan, through a magical potion, have fallen in love. After reaching Cornwall, they meet in a garden of Mark's castle, and it is there that Melot, who has betrayed them to Mark, wounds Tristan upon a bank of flowers. After the scene in the garden—virtually equivalent to Eliot's Hyacinth-garden passage—Tristan is taken to Brittany, where he awaits Isolde's coming. As he lies wounded, a shepherd enters to report that her ship is not in sight—that the sea is waste and void, "Oed' und leer das Meer!" The desolation in this second quotation used by Eliot contrasts with the fresh breeze, a portent of happy love, in the first.[17] Just so in Eliot's poem the love and hope at the beginning shatter in bitterness as the quester fails. He receives his own wound in the garden, and, like Tiresias, he becomes blind; the hyacinth girl vanishes, but he himself lingers to meditate on his ruins.

Except for the moment in the Hyacinth garden Tiresias sees in his memories only a dreary travesty of the initiation into love. The remainder of the poem up to the second initiation into the mystery of the Chapel recounts his past wanderings through the waste land of the "Unreal City." The other characters, base imitations of the Grail actors, include Madame Sosostris, appearing immediately after the hyacinth girl as if to reinforce a contrast. Oddly, she has a masculine name. Sesostris, whose exploits are narrated by Herodotus, was a great king of Egypt in the twelfth dynasty. Eliot's acknowledged source of the name is an amusing scene in Aldous Huxley's *Crome Yellow* (1921), where the crocodilian Mr. Scogan, for a Bank Holiday charity fair, dresses up as a gypsy woman to tell fortunes and advertises himself as "Sesostris, the Sorceress of Ecbatana."[18] The episode, by contributing to the theme of female impersonation, supports Eliot's note on Tiresias. But Eliot presumably worked also from the petition for foresight in the burial service

("Lord, let me know mine end"), which with *Crome Yellow*, the sixth book of the *Aeneid*, Apollinaire's *Les Mamelles de Tirésias*, and Jessie L. Weston's references to the Tarot could have provided the substance of his synthesis.

Though Madame Sosostris is presumably not young, she partly symbolizes rebirth, for she is a "wise woman" or midwife (*sage-femme*).[19] She is a caricature of her predecessor the hyacinth girl. In her hands she holds a group of symbols identical in value with the hyacinths. Since her Tarot cards are considered Grail talismans, she is unmistakably another type of the Grail-bearer. She is a charlatan, however; her activities (even her midwifery, such as it may be) are sadly decadent and have nothing to do with the solemnity of her role in the Grail legend. But in certain versions of the myth the young Grail-bearer becomes an old witchwoman after the quester fails in his test. In Wagner the sorceress Kundry embodies Wolfram's Kondrie, the Grail-bearer as a hideous crone (the Loathly Damsel), as well as the water-lady Orgeluse, whom the Fisher King loved and in whose service he was wounded. Old or young, the Grail-bearer is not generally of her own accord hostile to the quester, whose success can restore her beauty as well as the King's virility. When in *The Waste Land* the quester fails, Madame Sosostris, occupying the sibyl's place in the initiation pattern, falls victim to a general desolation.

The Tarot pack, discussed by Jessie L. Weston, contains in its four suits—cup, lance, sword, and dish—the life-symbols found in the Grail narrative. Whether, as Jessie L. Weston contends, the designs shown on the face cards (the *atouts*) ever appeared in a calendar used for predicting the rise and fall of the Nile, the names of the four suits themselves recall the sexual talismans.[20] The twenty-two *atouts*, numbered from zero to twenty-one, are used in fortunetelling. There seems to be little evidence that the pictures on the *atouts* of the Tarot compare in antiquity with the Grail symbols. Some of the personages look like characters in particular myths, including the Grail legend, but the resemblances seem fortuitous. Among the *atouts*, Jessie L. Weston mentions only the Pope, who in the set to which she refers shows the influence of the Eastern Church, for he has a beard and holds a triple cross; and the King (otherwise the Emperor), who wears the headdress of a Russian grand duke.[21] Both of these may have been alluded to in *The Waste Land:* the former as "the man with three staves" and the latter as the archduke, mentioned near the beginning. The Tarot contains no drowned sailor or blank card; but the Wheel and the Hanged Man are authentic, though Jessie L. Weston says nothing about them. Eliot therefore had some other source for his knowledge. His one-eyed "merchant" is the Fool. He alluded also to the Tower, the High Priestess, the Moon, the Lovers, the Hermit, and the Star, which is identified by A. E. Waite, in *The Pictorial Key to the Tarot*, with Sirius, the Dog Star.[22] Belladonna, in "A Game of Chess," is perhaps the Empress.

The drowned Phoenician sailor and the Hanged Man symbolize respectively the loveless "death" ("Here, said she, / Is your card") and the potential healing or rebirth of Tiresias; but the Hanged Man, Christ who suffered and rose again, is a stranger to Madame Sosostris and to the spiritual state of the unsuccessful quester. Tiresias must go into the depths from which there is no return; he is denied the death, longed for by the sibyl, into a new life. The "crowds of people" whom Madame Sosostris sees are turning on the Wheel, the Wheel of Fortune in the Tarot, broadly interpretable as a symbol of life in the world, like the great wheel of Buddhism. These people, spiritually sterile, describe a purposeless circle. They are ironically similar to the Grail procession displaying the talismans in the legend. When they flow in a crowd over London Bridge, each man's eyes fixed before his feet like the old men's in Baudelaire's "Les Sept Vieillards," they go past the church of St. Mary Woolnoth, typifying a Grail castle which the quester of the romances would similarly have reached by crossing water. Nine o'clock strikes: the hour to start work;[23] it condemns them to the tedium of another futile day. Muted on the last stroke, the clock ends with a "dead sound."[24] They, the ordinary people of the world, inhabit an "Unreal City," the "Fourmillante cité" of Baudelaire's poem, cited in Eliot's notes. This city is also a hell, for it is inhabited on the one hand by the secular and on the other hand by the spiritually ignorant, like those characterized in the third and fourth cantos of the *Inferno*.[25]

Stetson, the modern representative of "him who from cowardice made the great refusal" (*Inferno*, III), is another counterpart to the quester. The corpse he has planted in his garden is the dead god, of whom he has knowledge, but whose life he rejects, choosing to remain a "trimmer." The sprouting of this god, the quickening of the slaughtered Osiris (the triple phallused, the man with three staves),[26] would be tantamount to a spiritual revival; but, like Marcello in Webster's *The White Devil* (Act V, scene 4), the deity lies murdered and can live again only through a power still withheld. This corpse is also Tiresias, the Fisher King, and his sprouting, as of the dead "grain" in the burial service, would effect the restoration of love destroyed by his own cowardly refusal in the Hyacinth garden. The "sudden frost" that may have disturbed the bed of the corpse is analogous to his numbing failure in the initiation. And the Dog (which has troubled many) is whatever wrenches forth the buried disgrace of the past instead of letting it send up sprigs of life. The symbols, with the levels of reference, are mixed: as the corpse is the god, its brutal disinterment would correspond to an act of sacrilege; as it is Tiresias, its exposure would repeat his incapacity in the Hyacinth garden. The Dog connotes his terror, his shame, and even, perhaps, the lusts that later sections of the poem suggest may have abused him. In the Tarot a dog accompanies the Fool (Eliot's Mr. Eugenides). Eliot's change from Webster's "wolf" adjusts the symbolism to that of "Dans le Restaurant"; it also secures an allusion to the Dog Star, the star of lust and polestar of the Phoenician navigators, to Stephen Dedalus' joke about the fox and his grandmother,[27] and, even more curiously, to the tradition of the dog and the mandrake. If the anthropomorphic mandrake, which can safely be pulled out of the ground only by means of a dog and a piece of string, was itself a god (or, as J. Rendel Harris thought, the primeval Aphrodite),[28] then it supplies a workable analogue here. The mandrake, according to Frazer's *Folk-Lore in the Old Testament,* is sown from the body of a man hanged on a gallows.[29]

There is danger lest multiplied allusions, adventitious or not, should defeat meaning. It might be wisest for a cynical critic of this passage simply to regard the Dog as himself scratching away in the poem as in a great charnel graveyard.

> "Oh keep the Dog far hence, that's friend to men,
> "Or with his nails he'll dig it up again!
> "You! hypocrite lecteur!—mon semblable,—mon frère!"

For Eliot's quotation from "Au Lecteur" in Baudelaire's *Les Fleurs du mal* was an insulting one. The second book which Eliot is known to have reviewed, James Huneker's *Egoists: A Book of Supermen* (1909), contains the statement that after reading Griswold on Poe, Baudelaire asked, "Who shall keep the curs out of the cemetery?"[30] That is a problem indeed.

II. "A Game of Chess"

The subject of Part II is sex without love, specifically within marriage, just as the subject of Part III is the same horror outside it. For people who must be continually excited and amused if they are not to be overwhelmed by boredom, sex is merely escape, and when it palls it converts marriage into tedious bondage. "A Game of Chess" reveals the working of this process in two classes of society. Having lost the hyacinth girl, the quester finds himself joined with a neurotic, shrewish woman of fashion, who is probably Belladonna, the "lady of situations."[31] She is to be contrasted chiefly with the hyacinth girl herself. Unlike Madame Sosostris, a mysterymonger who pretends to find some meaning in life, she stands merely as a symbol of lovelessness. Yet she too has something of the sibyl's role, for she has introduced the quester to the mystery of sex.

. . . .

Blindness in "A Game of Chess," as in the Hyacinth garden, correlates with silence. Eliot's own reading of Part II differentiates carefully between the shrill, rasping voice of the lady and the detached, melancholy voice of her husband. The absence of quotation marks from the man's lines probably means that in reality he does not answer at all, and only meditates his thoughts. She first begs him to speak—but, as before, he cannot speak. . . .

Afflicted with boredom, she thinks, again with unconscious irony, of rushing out and walking the street, much like the frenzied Dido in her palace at Carthage when Aeneas abandoned her.[32]

The chief symbols of this section—the sexual violation, the fiery hair, the chess game and the blindness, as well as the silence—are all more or less consonant with the Grail legend or other fertility myths. Cleanth Brooks has pointed out that the sexual violation occurs in one version of the Grail story.[33] The fiery points of the woman's hair present a Medusa-like contrast to the wet hair of the hyacinth girl; fire is here a symbol of lust; water, of love. The game of chess likewise means more than Eliot's note reveals. In the Grail romances the hero occasionally visits a chessboard castle, where he meets a water-maiden. In addition, chess has often been a symbol, notably with Elizabethan and Jacobean dramatists, for man's life and government in the world. Even putting aside the analogy between chess and the combats in ritual, one may discern in Eliot's use of the symbol a suggestion that the people in the waste land belong to a drama they do not understand, where they move like chessmen toward destinations they cannot foresee.

Blindness, as in the careers of Samson and Oedipus, symbolizes defeat and punishment, and at the same time it convicts the quester of moral inadequacy. The line from *The Tempest* foreshadows "Death by Water" and opposes to that death the regenerative "death" of Ferdinand's father, Alonso, whose eyes, according to Ariel, have been changed to pearls—there a symbol of rebirth. Indeed, Alonso has survived his shipwreck to become regenerate in the most practical sense; he repents and begs forgiveness of Prospero. The line, "Of his bones are coral made" presents the antithesis of "rats' alley / Where the dead men lost their bones," and there is no "sea change" in *The Waste Land*. The "lidless eyes," sleepless, imply the torture in which the man and woman live, waiting for the knock of death upon the door—or, it may be, for the Saviour who stands at the door and knocks.[34]

The ritual marriage, which should insure the restoration of life to the waste land, fails because the test of love has not first been passed.[35] Another side of the same picture comes in view through the second half of "A Game of Chess." The sordidness now is more candidly physical. In these lines the pawns, Bill, Lou, and May, forgathered in a pub, hear about Lil's and Albert's misfortunes: Lil, having undergone an abortion, suffers from its effects and from the loss of her teeth; Albert, like Stetson, has been away at war. The tale is several times interrupted by the proprietor, who has to close up for the night, and in his urgent "HURRY UP PLEASE ITS TIME" most of the serious tone of this passage is compressed. The cry is an ironic warning to turn from this way of life. The pub itself recalls in the context that the Grail is associated with drinking and feasting; and, indeed, some of the best recent scholars identify the Grail solely with food-producing caldrons of Celtic mythology. The key symbol in the passage, however, is abortion, which advances the theme of unfruitfulness and sterility. The final line, grotesquely echoing a popular ballad ("Merrily we roll along"), Shakespeare's Ophelia, and Laforgue's Yorick, heralds "Death by Water," the death of those condemned for lust. Yet Ophelia, "the violet girl," is essentially a symbol of betrayed innocence; she is the Grail-bearer herself after the quester's failure, but her undoing, like that of Philomel, cannot be literally applied to the hyacinth girl; it indicates rather another aspect of Tiresias' wound, as does the physical decay of Lil, with whom Ophelia is immediately identified.

Up to this point and in Part III, just as the quester is distinguishable from the Fisher King, so, too, the female characters are divisible into two categories, corresponding to the metamorphoses of the Grail-bearer: on the one side is the hyacinth girl, as Imogen, Philomel, Bianca, and Ophelia; on the other is Madame Sosostris, Belladonna, or Lil, as Cleopatra and Dido. The change, occurring when the Fisher King receives his wound, is symbolized by rape. The pertinence of the deceived maidens from literature needs no further comment. Eliot's choice of analogues to Belladonna was not altogether a happy one; neither Cleopatra nor Dido nor, later, Queen Elizabeth I is mainly associated in the popular mind with lust but rather with grandeur. Hence "A Game of Chess" seems to invite the wrong interpretation as simple nostalgia for a golden age. Eliot's Belladonna, however, like Vergil's Dido, is a temptress, a Circe or Duessa who has trapped the quester in her toils, as in Tennyson's poem Merlin is enchanted to his doom.

III. "THE FIRE SERMON"

With Part III the Grail narrative turns once more to the quester standing disconsolately beside the river, figuratively the same water as in the Tristan and Isolde passage. The season is still winter, after the summer throngs have left the Thames, from which have long departed the fertility nymphs of Spenser's "Prothalamion." The attendance of nymphs at a marriage festival reflects disgrace on casual lovers by the Thames or "by the waters of Leman," the waters now of Lake Geneva, where Eliot, Byron-like, composed the poem, and of Babylon, where the exiled Hebrews sat down and wept. The analogue of Hebrew captivity has appeared once before, in the allusions to Ezekiel, and it appears again in Part V through the wanderings in the desert, which parallel the Exodus. Before the dramatization of lust in "The Fire Sermon," the earlier themes are recapitulated. The wind blowing across the dead land recalls Ezekiel, the prophet to whom was revealed in Babylon the ultimate restoration of the twelve tribes, the scattered bones in the valley. Here the wind is no Spirit of life, but a cold blast symbolizing death, "Time's winged chariot hurrying near" in Marvell's "Coy Mistress." The blight of time upon the waste land, the spiritual death, has made this a place of fetid decay. The rattling bones of the dead bring to mind details of the "Hades" episode in Ulysses, where on the way to Paddy Dignam's funeral Mr. Bloom repeats to himself a melancholy jingle: "Rattle his bones. Over the stones. Only a pauper. Nobody owns"; and where, crawling in the cemetery, is a rat among the other tokens of corruption.[36] The subject of gas in that episode arises first as the funeral procession stops for a moment near the Dublin gasworks:

> Mr. Bloom put his head out of the window.
> —The grand canal, he said.
> Gas works.[37]

Eliot's quester chooses a spot behind the gashouse from which to fish in "the dull canal." Having long since become the Fisher King, he is seeking, so that he may be redeemed from his torment, the primitive religious symbol of the fish, synonymous with the Grail.[38]

Simultaneously he becomes identified with Ferdinand in *The Tempest* (Act I, scene 2, lines 389–91), through another echo of the meeting between Ferdinand and Ariel:

> Sitting on a bank,
> Weeping again the King my father's wreck,
> This music crept by me upon the waters.

It is once more possible (though Colin Still's book may have affected the passage) that Eliot was following James Joyce; for in the "Proteus" episode Stephen, thinking of a man who has been drowned, quotes to himself Ariel's "Full fathom five" as well as a line from "Lycidas."[39] But Eliot expanded Ferdinand's words to:

> Musing upon the king my brother's wreck
> And on the king my father's death before him.

. . . The quester is consequently in some sense about to re-enact his own father's misfortune. One may here detect the rudiments of a cyclical pattern: what happens to the father happens to the son (as in *The Family Reunion*), and, by inference, it happens to each generation of human brotherhood. This is not the world of *The Tempest*, where neither father nor son is drowned and where both survive to experience redemption—Alonso through penitence and Ferdinand through love.

Among the bones and the naked bodies of the dead,[40] the quester hears another kind of rattle, "The sound of horns and motors," heralding the prediction that in the spring the cycle of life, or rather death-in-life, will revive as Apeneck Sweeney visits Mrs. Porter. The entrance of Sweeney propels into *The Waste Land* another symbol of the rebellious flesh. He has already, like Agamemnon, suffered foully through too implicit faith in a woman, in "Sweeney among the Nightingales"; in "Sweeney Erect" he has played Theseus to the epileptic's Ariadne and, more ludicrously, Polyphemus to her Nausicaa. Presently he is to become the Cyclops again, Mr. Eugenides, the one-eyed merchant. His vernal encounter with Mrs. Porter is simply a new travesty of the scene in the Hyacinth garden; John Day's lines, which Eliot parodied, depict Actaeon's fatal meeting with Diana when he saw her bathing naked in a pool. Like the quester with the Grail-bearer, Actaeon suffered the punishment of his folly. He was turned into a stag and was pulled down and slain by his dogs, being an unlucky prototype of the waiter in "Dans le Restaurant."

. . . .

The Tarot Fool, Mr. Eugenides, well born but fallen on evil days, is a cosmopolite, speaking demotic French (not demotic Egyptian) and selling currants in London. The Smyrna question, culminating in the expulsion of the Greeks from Smyrna in 1923, was already of topical interest when *The Waste Land* was written; the merchant is from a city in turmoil, another "Unreal City," perhaps connoting the decay of the Hellenic fertility cults and the Seven Churches of Asia. The very currants of the one-eyed merchant's trade hint that the joyous grape has shriveled up in the waste land. The dried fertility symbol which he transports is equivalent to knowledge of the sacramental Grail mystery, for Jessie L. Weston points out that the cults of Attis and Mithra were spread throughout the Roman Empire partly by Syrian merchants (as well as by soldiers, of whom Albert, the consort of Lil, is a modern representative); and, undoubtedly, Mr. Eugenides, uniting Phlebas the Phoenician sailor and the Fisher King in his boat, is a type of these.[41] His invitation, supposed to be a homosexual one,[42] is a travesty of that which usually the Fisher King makes to the quester outside the Grail castle. It is prepared for by the context of the line from Verlaine.

The one-eyedness of Mr. Eugenides accords with various forms of initiation ritual or myth. Sometimes the one-eyed man is as at this point a symbol of death or winter—the monster whom the primitive hero fights in his lair. . . . Mr. Eugenides, if not the ritual fool and physician of drama, is sexually ambiguous. He corresponds, moreover, to the chief actor in Frazer's account of the ritual "ride of the beardless one"[43]—which links Mr. Eugenides with the Hanged Man and even explains partly why Mr. Eugenides is unshaven. . . .

"What Tiresias *sees*" at this point, the fornication of a clerk and a tired typist, summarizes the theme of lust in the poem, besides furnishing in the Grail pattern an episode of the quester's attempted seduction by maidens. Moreover, the act of love, debased through the absence of love into a kind of chemical reaction, implies the very opposite of the ritual prostitution in witch covens and fertility cults, where it is a symbol not of sapped but of created vitality.[44] The "young man carbuncular" is the quester himself; the food laid out in tins is a kind of Grail repast which the Loathly Damsel has prepared. The sailor home from sea (the Syrian merchant again) is the quester after he has crossed the water into the Grail castle, from which he must descend by the stairs into the infernal waste land. Tiresias recognizes in this affair the endless repetitions of vice, his own agony and his own guilt. . . .

"The Fire Sermon" is the cardinal turning point of the poem. Up to Eliot's "collocation" of St. Augustine and the Buddha, the quest to be reconciled through love and the fusion of body and spirit has reached nothing except disappointment. But asceticism is a way of reaching the terminus of union with Love itself. If what goes by the name of love can only draw one further downward into the hell of the waste land, with its seething caldrons of lust, then one must reject all burning; if one cannot be brought through love into the center, one must seek the center by another road. Yet *The Waste Land* does not realize a full victory for Tiresias, and no later work of Eliot disregards some importunate echo of love calling through flesh, even though the voice of the divine darkness becomes clearer, calling for the negation of all burning things.

IV. "DEATH BY WATER"

The death of Phlebas writes the epitaph to the experience by which the quester has failed in the garden. In one sense it resymbolizes that failure, just as the closing lines of "Dans le Restaurant" recapitulate the terror there. But inasmuch as in *The Waste Land* the inability to love signifies the ascendancy of lust, Phlebas the Phoenician, the joint incarnation of Mr. Eugenides and an unsaved Ferdinand, drowns for the same reason that the quester in another guise becomes a buried corpse. He is not resurrected, nor does the corpse sprout. Instead he is sucked into the whirlpool, and, in a manner of speaking, he has been on the whirling wheel all the time, performing the same nugatory transactions of life that obsess Hakagawa, the connoisseur of Titian, for example, and the others whose furtive pleasure it is to divide Christ "among whispers." Now it is Phlebas who disintegrates in "fractured atoms." He is still, as Buddhists say, "bound to the wheel."

> As he rose and fell
> He passed the stages of his age and youth
> Entering the whirlpool.

His drowning, against which Madame Sosostris has warned him, reenacts the rise and fall in the flower garden and the rise and decline through which, headed for death, he has passed his life; and as he dies the same movement returns, passing, in accordance with the superstition, as an instantaneous memory through his mind.[45] And yet, on an ironic level, he is like Christ; he is the sacrificial god descending into the waters. . . . But for Phlebas the

baptism is a descent followed by no emergence; his seven days have length-
ened into a fortnight; he is no Lycidas, "sunk low but mounted high," and
his eyes like those of Tiresias have not been turned to pearls. His death
resembles that in Part IV of "The Dry Salvages." If it hints also at the
physical death beyond the death-in-life of the waste land, it certainly offers
no hope of immortality, or of an escape from the wheel, but rather a lapse
into hell or the endlessly recurring avatars of suffering in the flesh. Lastly, or
perhaps more properly, first of all, Phlebas dies in the capacity of a Syrian
merchant, carrying, according to Jessie L. Weston's theory, the Grail mystery
to Britain—the merchant with his blank card.[46] The lines intone a de-
functive music, regretful and admonitory, counseling everyone who turns the
wheel, "Gentile or Jew," to renounce the traffic in worldy things and the lusts
of the flesh which sunder men from love.

V. "WHAT THE THUNDER SAID"

After the quester's wound in the garden, his immersion in the sea of lust, he
languishes in a desert; and though now he should understand that salvation
can redound from nothing and no one trapped there with him, the struggle
not to desire, to accept and not to will, still imposes agony. The ascetic way,
pointed to in "The Fire Sermon," he has not adopted. By a second initiation
in this quest he attempts to achieve peace by turning directly to religion;
but, just as love has failed because he has not affirmed it, religion fails
because he does not make the requisite denial—the denial of self permitting
an affirmation of self-discipline.

The opening lines of Part V, alluding to Gethsemane and Golgotha and
to the failure of the quester's search for love, say, in effect, that death has not
been conquered:

> He who was living is now dead
> We who were living are now dying.

The desert, like the wilderness of Sinai, contains no water, nor is there
anyone to bring forth from the rock of life such a stream as Moses summoned
with his rod. The rocks are dry like the rotten teeth of a skull. The region of
the quester's wandering is a place of torture; hence the image borrowed from
low, narrow cells of medieval dungeons.[47] In the midst of the physical waste
land, where the cicada, like the grasshopper in the twelfth chapter of Ecclesiastes, is a burden, the quester longs for even the illusion of dripping water,
for the voice of the hermit-thrush which would symbolize the Hermit of the
Grail legend and, thus, spiritual redemption. He longs for the pine trees,
sacred to Attis, the hanged god.[48] Now he is climbing up into the mountains, a place of thunder but no rain. The geographic location of this journey

is not specified; it is partly in Palestine and partly in the foothills of the Himalayas,[49] just as the spiritual quest is partly in the Western and partly in the Eastern tradition. The travelers to Emmaus also passed through a waste land of defeat. Just as, when Christ appeared to the two disciples, they did not see that He had risen, so here the protagonist's blindness prevents him, as always, from seeing that life may come through death. His own death in the garden and in the sea has been analogous to the Hanged Man's sacrifice, but it has not merged with that sacrifice itself. Tiresias is a wounded god who is not God; he can be healed only by the unfound Redeemer. Like the disciples he believes that "He who was living is now dead"; the supposition is true of himself, but not of Christ, who still walks half-seen on the other side.[50]

. . . .

The cock, crowing enigmatically in Portuguese while perched on the rooftree, is the power to disperse the darkness and the shapes that walk by night.[51] A bird of sacrifice and good omen, it symbolizes the living Spirit beyond the dead Chapel, able even now to pour rain upon the land if the quester succeeds. The sunken river and the dry foliage await the outcome of the test; the approaching rain will fall if the quester gives assent to the three commands of the thunder. But this he cannot do. The test, like that in the garden, is one of worthiness. The voice of the god Pragâpati utters in the sound of the thunder the three cryptic syllables "Da Da Da," that is, "give, sympathize, control."[52] If the quester could reply, "I have given, I have sympathized, I have controlled," he could end his vigil and achieve restoration and spiritual rebirth. But because it is no more possible to answer the question affirmatively than to have asked another question among the hyacinths, he can only fail the second initiation like the first. Thus the voice of the cock becomes an ironic symbol, for, like Peter, who three times denied his Lord before the second crowing, the quester has abandoned the Hanged Man and has held back the longed-for rain, not at this moment alone, but throughout the quest. The "freeing of the waters," the pristine object of the fertility ritual in the *Rig-Veda* to which Jessie L. Weston traces the symbolism of the Grail legend, must wait.

The quester's three negative answers deny not the self but the means to redemption; they are the wrong denials, refusals to descend and submit. They are expressed as replies to the three commands, and, since they form one of the most oblique passages in the poem, their dramatic connection is difficult to grasp. The first surely concerns the sexual blunder to which Tiresias has already confessed. The surrender has involved no acceptance of love, of the demands of life, but a yielding to lust—a choice which "an age of prudence can never retract." This alone, the craven surrender to a tyranny of the blood, has secretly dominated the quester's whole existence, though it is "not to be found in our obituaries." Joined with him in disgrace is someone else, the conjunct partner in a lust now become bondage. Whether this surrender denotes more or less than the failure in the garden, it is symbolically identical with it. The echo of Webster's *The White Devil* is to the point:

> —ô Men
> That lye upon your death-beds, and are haunted
> With howling wives, neere trust them, they'le re-marry
> Ere the worme peirce your winding sheete: ere the Spider
> Make a thinne curtaine for your Epitaphes.

The second denial, that of sympathy, has proceeded from the same cause. Like the traitor Ugolino, the speaker is shut in the horrible tower of his own loneliness, and he has also lost sympathy through his surrender to the imprisonment. The introduction of another traitor, Coriolanus, who betrayed his country and those who loved him, characterizes the quester as a renegade from his own land and traditions. The questing knight traduces the land when he fails in his initiation.

The third denial, that of control, refers to the hyacinth girl again, to Tristan and Isolde, and, ironically, to the line "My nerves are bad to-night" in "A Game of Chess." Eliot may have had in mind Arnold's "Dover Beach" and the entreaty, "Ah, love, let us be true / To one another!"—an appeal which is now unavailing, regardless of what "would have" been.

With this first and last failure the initiation concludes. The arid plain stretches behind Tiresias, who is still fishing and still wounded. He has found no love or redemption, for he has turned his back on both. . . . Meanwhile, disinherited, even as "Le Prince d'Aquitaine" in Nerval's "El Desdichado," Tiresias waits in a cruel April for his own spring to return beside the demolished tower, the Tower in the Tarot pack. This Tower, which the card calls "La Maison Dieu" ("the Hospital"), is a dismal pile of crumbling masonry, struck by a thunderbolt, with two figures, a man and a woman, hurtling from its summit. It is evidently a symbol of the shattered marriage in "A Game of Chess," the prison where the quester's surrender locked him up with Belladonna. Yet its broken ruins have not set him free; it is broken and not broken, and the surrender is irrevocable. Tiresias is alone spiritually, but not otherwise.

. . . The most obvious connection between Hieronymo and *The Waste Land* is that at the end of the tragedy the old man bites out his tongue; but Hieronymo, besides serving for another allusion to Philomel, corresponds to Tiresias in a further way. He is an inspired madman, a prophet, who oversees the destinies of the other characters and who must, like an ancient prophet, be mad in order to do so.[53] In *The Spanish Tragedy* the business of Hieronymo is to avenge the hanging of Horatio; in *The Waste Land* the business of Tiresias is to restore his youth, which, in a manner of speaking, has been slain like the Hanged Man on the tree. Hieronymo succeeds; Tiresias fails: but at least the destruction prophesied by Tiresias will also come to pass. The fragments he has shored against his own ruins fit equally well the ruins of all society; the quotation says, in essence, that you too, "mon semblable, mon frère," have your ruins: you too are the Fisher King in need of the prescribed cure. In proclaiming his madness, Tiresias is announcing that he has become a prophet to warn the crumbling world. Over against the prospect of its irremediable calamity stands the counsel of the Aryan myth, to give, sympathize, and be controlled, that all may come at length to peace.

The poem has ended with the focus again upon the present Tiresias. What his memories have dramatized is his past effort to appease the gnawing of fleshly and spiritual desire. They have summed up the crucial experiences that leave him unable to participate, through his interior life, in the April renewal of earth. Yet he has his fragments—touchstones, Matthew Arnold might have called them. Without words of hope to prop his mind Tiresias would be Empedocles on Etna; with them, attentive to their suasion, he may exorcise despair. His quest through his private waste land, the poet's quest through the poem, has achieved nothing that either fertility religion or the ascetic traditions set as a positive goal. His quest for love has failed; his quest for spiritual knowledge remains only inceptive and must still proceed, not through a mere formality of religion, but through inward conversion. But the very act of recognition, the deliberate acknowledgment of humility, points toward ultimate triumph, if not for society, nevertheless for himself. He can expect, if not the joy of Ferdinand, then at any rate the liberation of Prospero.[54]

Notes

1. Valuable commentaries on the poem include R. P. Blackmur, "T. S. Eliot," *Hound and Horn,* I (March, 1928), 187–213; Hugh Ross Williamson, *The Poetry of T. S. Eliot* (New York, 1932), pp. 78–150; F. R. Leavis, *New Bearings in English Poetry* (London, 1932), pp. 91–114; C. R. Jury, *T. S. Eliot's The Waste Land: Some Annotations* (Adelaide, 1932); Cleanth Brooks, "The Waste Land: Critique of the Myth," *Modern Poetry and The Tradition* (North Carolina, 1939), pp. 136–172; George Williamson, *A Reader's Guide to T. S. Eliot* (New York, 1953), pp. 115–54. See also H. Reid MacCallum, "*The Waste Land* after Twenty-five Years," *Here and Now,* I (December, 1947), 16–24; Eric Mesterton, *The Waste Land: Some Commentaries* (Chicago, 1943); Derek Traversi, "*The Waste Land* Revisited," *Dublin Review,* No. 443, 1948, pp. 106–23; C. M. Bowra, *The Creative Experiment* (London, 1949), pp. 159–88.

2. Cf. Charles-Louis Philippe, *Bubu of Montparnasse* (Paris, 1932), chap. 1: "A man walks carrying with him all the properties of his life, and they churn about in his head. Something he sees awakens them, something else excites them. For our flesh has retained all our memories, and we mingle them with our desires."

3. James Thomson, "To Our Ladies of Death," *The City of Dreadful Night, and Other Poems* (London, 1910), p. 148.

4. Cf. Rupert Brooke, *Letters from America* (New York, 1916), p. 174; F. O. Matthiessen, *The Achievement of T. S. Eliot* (New York, 1947), pp. 92–93.

5. Eccles. 12:5.

6. Ezek. 6:3–4.

7. Job 8:9, 13, 16–17.

8. Isa. 56:3.

9. Jessie Weston, *From Ritual to Romance* (Cambridge, 1920), pp. 62–71.

10. *Ibid.*, p. 13.

11. *Ibid.*, p. 159; W. F. Jackson Knight, *Cumaean Gates* (Oxford, 1936), p. 144.

12. Sir James Frazer, *The Golden Bough* (3d ed.; London, 1911–19), Vol. V, Book II, chap. 7.

13. Cf. Dante, *Inferno*, XXXIV, 25: "Io non morii, e non rimasi vivo." With the phrase "heart of light," cf. *Paradiso*, XII, 28: "del cor dell'una delle luci nuove."

14. Jessie L. Weston, *From Ritual to Romance*, p. 114, says that in the Grail "ritual" the Fisher King may have been an effigy, whose place the quester filled in the course of initiation. Here, as it were, the quester becomes an effigy.

15. Ross Williamson, *The Poetry of T. S. Eliot*, pp. 93–94.

16. See Leonard Unger, "T. S. Eliot's Rose Garden," Unger, pp. 374 ff.; Louis L. Martz, "The Wheel and the Point: Aspects of Imagery and Theme in Eliot's Later Poetry," Unger, pp. 444–62.

17. Brooks, Unger, p. 323.

18. Aldous Huxley, *Crome Yellow* (London, 1921), chap. 27. See my article, "The Fortuneteller in Eliot's *Waste Land*," *American Literature*, XXV (January, 1954), 490–92.

19. Pound wrote three little poems into his correspondence with Eliot about *The Waste Land;* one of them was called "Sage Homme" (*Letters 1907–1941*, ed. D. D. Paige [New York, 1950], p. 170). I suspect no direct connection here, but the conceit is amusing: Pound was the midwife for Eliot's production. Eliot wanted (perhaps not seriously) to use the two relevant "squibs" with it, but Pound overruled the idea. The third poem did not concern Eliot. It is omitted from the bowdlerized Pound *Letters*.

20. Weston, *From Ritual to Romance*, pp. 71–76.

21. *Ibid.*, p. 75.

22. A. E. Waite, *The Pictorial Key to the Tarot* (London, 1911). I have no idea whether Eliot knew this book. One must bear in mind his statement, whatever it may have meant, that he was "not familiar with the exact constitution of the Tarot pack of cards."

23. Eliot, *Poèmes 1910–1930* (Paris, 1947), p. 140. But see Elizabeth Drew, *T. S. Eliot: The Design of His Poetry* (New York, 1949), p. 73.

24. Cf. North's Plutarch (*Crassus*), as quoted by Wyndham, *Essays in Romantic Literature*, pp. 173–74: "[With their] kettle drommes, hollow within . . . they all made a noise everywhere together, and it is like a dead sounde. . . . The Romans being put in feare with this dead sounde, the Parthians straight threw the clothes and coverings from them that hid their armour. . . ." Eliot noticed the passage in his review of Wyndham.

25. Brooks, Unger, p. 325.

26. Plutarch *Isis and Osiris* xxxvi.

27. James Joyce, *Ulysses* (New York, 1934), p. 47.

28. J. Rendel Harris, *The Ascent of Olympus* (Manchester, 1917), pp. 109 ff.

29. Sir James Frazer, *Folk-Lore in the Old Testament* (London, 1919), II, 381–82.

30. James Huneker, *Egoists: A Book of Supermen* (New York, 1909), p. 67.

31. On the link between Belladonna, Leonardo da Vinci, and Walter Pater see my article, "T. S. Eliot's Lady of the Rocks," *Notes and Queries*, CXCIV (March 19, 1949), 123–25.

32. *Aeneid* iv. 589–90. Cf. Beaumont and Fletcher, *Philaster*, Act III, scene 2:

> Thou hast overthrown me once;
> Yet, if I had another Troy to lose,
> Thou, or another villain with thy looks,
> Might talk me out of it, and send me naked,
> My hair deshevelled, through the fiery streets.

But see also Rossetti's translation of *Vita nuova*, xxiii ("Canzone," stanza 4).

33. Brooks, Unger, p. 328.

34. See Rossetti, *The House of Life,* lxiii.

35. See Weston, *From Ritual to Romance,* pp. 28–30.

36. Joyce, *Ulysses,* pp. 95, 112. Observe also the phrasing used earlier by Stephen (p. 43): ". . . pretending to speak broken English as you dragged your valise, porter threepence, across the slimy pier at Newhaven."

37. *Ibid.,* p. 89; see also pp. 102, 106.

38. Weston, *From Ritual to Romance,* chap. 9.

39. Joyce, *Ulysses,* p. 50.

40. Eliot's "White bodies naked on the low damp ground" sounds like an echo of Walter Kittredge's "Tenting on the Old Camp Ground," though the rhythm recalls Vachel Lindsay. The "low dry garret" was perhaps suggested by Svidrigaïlov's garret in *Crime and Punishment,* Part VI, chap. 6.

41. See Weston, *From Ritual to Romance,* p. 160.

42. Brooks, Unger, p. 333.

43. Frazer, *The Golden Bough,* Vol. IX, chap. 8 and "Note."

44. Drew, p. 80; see Frazer, *The Golden Bough,* V, 36 ff.; VI, 264–66.

45. Cf. Rossetti, *The House of Life,* lxii.

46. See Brooks, Unger, p. 337. Cf. the phrase "to draw a blank."

47. Cf. D. H. Lawrence, *The Rainbow* (London. 1915), p. 95.

48. Frazer, *The Golden Bough,* V, 264 ff. Both the thrush and the pine trees recall Whitman's "When Lilacs Last in the Door-Yard Bloom'd."

49. Some of the imagery may have come from Kipling's *Kim,* chap. 13.

50. Cf. Whitman, "When Lilacs Last in the Door-Yard Bloom'd":
> Then with the knowledge of death as walking one side of me,
> And the thought of death close-walking the other side of me,
> And I in the middle, as with companions. . . .

The incident of the Antarctic expedition mentioned by Eliot is narrated by Sir Ernest Shackleton, *South* (London, 1919), p. 209.

51. Cf. *Hamlet,* Act I, scene 2, lines 157–64.

52. *Brihadaranyaka Upanishad,* V, 2.

53. Cf. Frazer, *The Golden Bough,* V, 77.

54. See Colin Still, *Shakespeare's Mystery Play: A Study of "The Tempest"* (London, 1921), pp. 242–48.

Unreal City

NORTHROP FRYE

The Waste Land is a vision of Europe, mainly of London, at the end of the
First World War, and is the climax of Eliot's "infernal" vision. It appeared in
1922, just before the poet had reached thirty-five, the middle of life's journey, when Dante began the *Inferno*. The setting is civilisation in the winter of
its discontent, and the images are those of the end of the natural cycle:
winter, the "brown land," ruins (including the nursery-rhyme collapse of
London Bridge and, in the notes, the proposed demolition of nineteen city
churches), and the Thames flowing to the sea. This world is physically above
ground but spiritually subterranean, a world of shadows, corpses and buried
seeds. The inhabitants live the "buried life" (a phrase from "Portrait of a
Lady") of seeds in winter: they await the spring rains resentfully, for real life
would be their death. Human beings who live like seeds, egocentrically,
cannot form a community but only an aggregate, where "Each man fixed his
eyes before his feet," imprisoned in a spiritual solitude that recalls the story
of the death of Ugolino in Dante. Such lines as "And if it rains, a closed car at
four" associate human life with its vegetative metaphors.

Dante's journey through hell begins on Good Friday evening, and he
emerges on the other side of the earth on Easter Sunday morning. Thus his
journey fits inside the three-day rhythm of the redemption, where Christ is
buried on Friday evening, descends to hell on Saturday, and rises on Sunday
morning. Similarly in the first section of *The Waste Land,* "The Burial of the
Dead," we sink into the lower world of the "unreal city," crowds streaming
into it like the damned in Dante. Here Christ appears as Isaiah's "shadow of a
rock in a weary land," before we descend to the shades below, or as the
possible power of resurrection in Ezekiel's valley of dry bones. We remain in
the underworld all through the next two sections, and then follows "Death by
Water," evidently physical death, as burial on earth symbolises the physical
life which is spiritual death. Physical death is the final judgment between the
seeds who can understand the commands of the thunder and die to a new life,
and those who merely die and are rejected, as the sterile seed is rejected by
nature. The last section repeats the image of a streaming crowd, "hooded

Reprinted by permission of the author from *T. S. Eliot* (Chicago: University of Chicago Press, 1963), 64–
71. Copyright The University of Chicago Press.

hordes swarming," an apocalypse in which the invisible presence of the risen Christ accompanies scenes of terror and chaos as the valley of dry bones becomes "an exceeding great army," as Ezekiel says.

Easter represents the end of a long period of religious symbolism in which a "dying god," a spirit representing the fertility of nature, was thought to die and rise again, usually in a three-day festival. The information about the cults of Adonis, Attis, Osiris and others collected in Frazer's *Golden Bough* is referred to by Eliot in the notes. In these rites a red or purple flower was associated with the god's blood: this appears in the hyacinths of *The Waste Land* and perhaps the "belladonna" or deadly nightshade (as well as in the dogwood and judas of "Gerontion," the lilacs of *Ash Wednesday*, and elsewhere). The death of Adonis was mourned by women representing the spirit of the earth, and the line "Murmur of maternal lamentation" associates this with the Biblical weeping of Rachel.

As later in *Four Quartets*, there is an elaborate imagery of the four elements. The cycle of water, from spring rains and the wet hair of the hyacinth girl to the Thames flowing out to sea, returning as the rains bringing new life to the parched land, is most prominent. According to Charles Lamb, Webster's "Call for the robin redbreast and the wren," and Shakespeare's "Full fathom five" are the great elegies of death by earth and water respectively in the language, and both are referred to in *The Waste Land*. In "The Fire Sermon" there is the implicit contrast between the St. Augustine and Buddha who appear at the end, seeking "the fire that refines them" (the last line of Canto 26 of the *Purgatorio*), and those who are burning in their own lusts with heat but without light. The air is hidden in the "brown fog" of a London winter; it blows freshly towards home but leaves Tristan as far away as the Ancient Mariner or Ulysses; it stirs up and confuses the perfumes of the woman in "A Game of Chess"; it is the element of the fearful apparitions and mirages of the closing scenes. The Ovidian theme of metamorphosis, associated chiefly with Philomela's transformation to a bird, runs through the poem, and modulates into the swallow of the *Pervigilium Veneris*. The dissolving and reforming of physical elements suggest that the reality of which they are an appearance is a spiritual substance, the risen Christ.

Apart from Easter, the idea of a descent into hell came to Dante from the sixth book of the Aeneid, where Aeneas enters the lower world with the aid of a "golden bough" and the Cumaean Sibyl. Another story about the Cumaean Sibyl hanging in a jar between heaven and earth and wanting only to die, a most vivid image of the "nightmare life in death" which is Eliot's theme, is told by Petronius, and forms the motto of the poem. Another, or perhaps the same, Sibyl is said to have asked the gods for as many years to live as she held grains of sand in her hand, but forgot to ask for continuous youth, in other words real life. She may be behind the phrase "fear in a handful of dust." The Sibyl is parodied in *The Waste Land* by Madame

Sosostris, with her fake Egyptian name and her "wicked pack of cards." Aeneas sees, besides Dido, the shades and a hell of torments, a further world of rebirth into new life.

Virgil in turn drew for his vision from the Odyssey, where Ulysses calls up the shades to consult Tiresias. *The Waste Land,* we are told in the notes, is a reverie of Tiresias, who has the same relation to it that Gerontion has to his poem, and whose hermaphroditic shadow-mind contains all the men and women who appear in it. Tiresias had been both a man and a woman, and was considered an authority on the pleasures of sexual intercourse from both points of view, but the production of children is beyond him, and all the sexual unions in the poem are as sterile as the waste land itself. Eliot leaves it to Pound, however, to elaborate the Odyssey scene in his first canto: *The Waste Land* is an intensely Latin poem, owing much more to Virgil and Ovid.

The contrasting figure to Tiresias is Phlebas, sailing (as we learn from "Dans le restaurant") to Britain in quest of tin, symbolising a commerce which continues in "Mr. Eugenides, the Smyrna merchant," whose "pocket full of currants" makes a startling pun on the "current" that picks the bones of Phlebas. Carthage was a Phoenician colony, the hereditary enemy of Rome (the naval battle of Mylae is referred to in passing), and from Carthage, a "cauldron of unholy loves," St. Augustine, repeating the journey of Aeneas, went to Italy to become a Christian. He later returned to become bishop of nearby Hippo, and a note left by Joyce, "Eliot: Bishop of Hippo," associates him neatly with the author of "The Hippopotamus."

In Virgil and Homer the motive for the underworld journey is to learn the future, the kind of knowledge ordinarily closed to mankind. Thus Ulysses in Homer wishes to know his personal fate, and is told that he will return home and eventually meet death from the sea, like Phlebas. A similar anxiety to know the future is gratified by Madame Sosostris, and "The Dry Salvages" later explains that a shoddy occultism pandering to man's desire to know his future is characteristic of sterile cultures. In *The Waste Land* the coming of Christianity represents the turning of Classical culture from its winter into a new spring, for the natural cycle is also associated with the cycles of civilisation. This may be one reason for the prominence of the poets, Virgil and Ovid, who were contemporary with Christ. Whatever future faces us today would, then, logically be connected with a second coming of Christ. The second coming, however, is not a future but a present event, a confronting of man with an immediate demand for self-surrender, sympathy and control, virtues which are primarily social and moral, and are preliminary to the Christian faith, hope and love. The London churches, St. Magnus Martyr, St. Mary Woolnoth, and others, stand like sentinels to testify to the presence of the risen Christ in the ruins of Europe.

Thus the underworld journey seems to be an initiation, a learning of mysteries. It is an old theory that the sixth book of the Aeneid is an allegory of initiation into Eleusinian mysteries, and a similar theory was applied to

Shakespeare's *Tempest* by Colin Still in *Shakespeare's Mystery Play,* a book mentioned in Eliot's preface to Wilson Knight's *Wheel of Fire* and published the year before *The Waste Land.* The court party in *The Tempest* make, like Aeneas and Augustine, a journey to Italy from Tunis (identified with Carthage by Gonzalo); they are thrown on an island off the Italian coast and go through an experience there which brings them to self-knowledge and repentance. Ferdinand, the hero, mourns the drowning of his father, and finds him alive after all, while in wooing Miranda he has to appease and then be reconciled with Miranda's father. In Christianity, similarly, Christ as the second Adam succeeds but also redeems the first Adam, and appeases and is reconciled with his eternal Father. This similarity between the Christian myth and the structure of comedy will meet us in the plays. The recognition scene in *The Tempest* discovers Ferdinand playing chess with Miranda, a game which ends either in checkmate, the death of the king, or in stalemate, like the two unions in the second section of *The Waste Land* which is called "A Game of Chess." Here Miranda is replaced by two female wrecks, with bad nerves and bad teeth respectively, corresponding to the spiritual and physical narcoses symbolised by burial in earth and in water. The former is a "Lady of the Rocks" who has overtones of Dido, Cleopatra, Pope's Belinda, Keats's Lamia, the Great Whore of the Bible, and other stylish vixens; the latter has no literary splendours around her except a dim recall of the drowned Ophelia. Eliot's note on his title for this section refers to two plays of Middleton and does not mention *The Tempest,* but we cannot always trust Eliot's notes.

The Tempest uses the romance theme of the prince who comes to a strange land and marries its king's daughter. In stories of the St. George and Perseus type the king is aged or suffering from a mysterious wound symbolising sexual impotence; the land he rules is therefore waste, on the principles of sympathetic magic, and it is ravaged by a sea-monster for the same reason. The hero kills the monster and succeeds to the kingdom. In the background is a nature myth of winter turning to spring, sea and snow turning to spring rain, age turning to youth, a sleeping beauty awakened by her prince charming. But if the monster *is* winter, the hero must enter and emerge from it, like Jonah in the Bible, must die himself and be reborn. There is no monster in Eliot, but there are vestiges of his open mouth in the references to "Dead mountain mouth of carious teeth" and "This decayed hole among the mountains." With the theme of death and revival the dragon-killer story merges with the dying-god story.

In some medieval versions of the same myth studied by Jessie Weston in *From Ritual to Romance,* cited by Eliot as a source for *The Waste Land,* the youthful knight comes to a waste land ruled by an aged and wounded "fisher king." Two mystical signs, a lance and a cup, are exhibited to him: had he asked their meaning the king would have been healed. Here the theme of descent and temporary death is represented by a "Chapel Perilous," an empty lighted chapel where the hero must pass a night while the lights are extinguished one by one. In the final section of *The Waste Land* the Chapel Perilous represents the underworld of death and burial, the tomb from which Christ rises. The lance and cup, originally fertility and sexual symbols, became associated with the lance of Longinus and the Holy Grail in the passion of Christ. They are to be connected also with the two red suits of the modern pack of cards, the diamond being a lance-head and the heart a chalice. Our cards are derived from a much more elaborate set, the Tarots, consulted by Madame Sosostris, which have twenty-two additional "trumps" with such names as the hanged man, the falling tower, death, the last judgment, and so on. Some of these, and others invented by Eliot, are mentioned in *The Waste Land.*

Another monster is slain by Jesus in his Easter victory over death and hell: the leviathan of the Old Testament, a sea-monster who *is* the sea, as he is death and hell, and also the devil, the serpent of Paradise, described in *The Rock* as "the great snake at the bottom of the pit of the world." In the Bible he or a similar monster is also identified with the kingdoms of tyranny, Egypt, Babylon, and the Phoenician city of Tyre. Thus the world that needs redemption is to be conceived as imprisoned in the monster's belly, whence the Messiah, following Jonah, descends to deliver it. In Christian iconography hell is often represented as an open-mouthed monster, from which Jesus emerges with the procession of the redeemed behind him, these forming a ghostly background to the final section of *The Waste Land.* The world to be redeemed is symbolically under water as well as under the earth, which gives point to the symbolism of fishing in the Gospels, and establishes a link with the "fisher king" of romance. Eliot's fisher king, sitting gloomily on the shore at the end of the poem with his "arid plain" behind him, thus corresponds to Adam, or human nature that cannot redeem itself. The progression of *bateaux ivres,* from Tristan's faraway ship to the "narrow canoe" of a girl's seduction, ending with the shipwrecked Phlebas, has the same relation to Adam that the responding boat, the symbol of the virtue of "control," has to the fisher of men who had the power to command the sea.

Why Then Ile Fit You

PHILIP R. HEADINGS

. . . The necessity to transcend one's self is a basic theme of the poem. Further, social responsibility is at the very core of the mythic and traditional elements combined in it. Eliot's social consciousness is widely documented in such essays as *The Idea of a Christian Society* and in a number of his critical writings such as the early "Tradition and the Individual Talent." That the unifying ground of the poem in the mind of the speaker has gone unnoticed by many readers is due to the poem's startlingly original form and techniques. These divergences from earlier usage are in no sense arbitrary and pointless, but highly functional; they are matters of scale and degree, not of kind.

. . . .

Many critics have written of the antitheses, the antinomies, and the contrasts in *The Waste Land.* These exist in abundance and are not just accidents of inclusion; they comprise a basic and indispensable aspect of the poem's technique, progression, and meaning. Many such polarities could be identified in the poem: universal-personal, male-female, conscious-unconscious, hope-fear, and others. But the technique of contradiction goes deeper than this in the poem's structure. Many of its symbols are involved in what I should like to call "parallelodoxes." Many of its symbols, that is, simultaneously develop in antithetical directions. The symbol of water, for instance, is already present ambiguously in line nine of the first section: The shower of rain that comes over the Starnbergersee both heralds the summer and makes the speaker run for shelter.

The absence of water and the thirst for it enter in line 24, "the dry stone [gives] no sound of water"; in line 42, *"Oed und leer das Meer"* ("Wide and empty the sea"), water is both a negative and a positive symbol: it may carry Isolde and her healing arts to the dying Tristan, but as yet it is waste and barren. The fear of death by water is first made explicit by Madame Sosotris. Both sides of this ambiguous symbol are inconspicuously present in the game of chess: "The hot water at ten. / And if it rains, a closed car at four"; and again the negative side is seen through the allusion to Ophelia, who drowned herself: "Good night, ladies, good night, sweet ladies, good night, good night."

*From *T. S. Eliot* (New York: Twayne, 1964), 50–69. Reprinted with permission of Twayne Publishers, a division of G. K. Hall & Co., Boston.

In Section III, "The Fire Sermon," the river has both positive and negative connotations, suggesting both purity and pollution, both innocence and immorality. Mrs. Porter's soda water is contrasted with the ceremonial water of the Grail chapel in Verlaine's *Parsifal.* This parallel but antithetical development is amplified in great detail throughout the poem. Death by water, which in Section I was to be feared, has become by Section IV ambiguous—suggesting both the dissolution of physical death and the promise of resurrection in the Year-god ceremonies, Christian baptism, the Easter pageant, and the other chief symbolic patterns used.

· ·

Such "parallelodoxes" are inevitable concomitants of the associative method by which the poem develops in the mind of the speaker. Its associational basis is not in ideas or images, but in total states of a complex and individual consciousness that is always aware of multiple implications. This sort of progression is implicit in the poem's entire structure, but it is easy to miss, since its recognition arises in the reader's empathic identification— "You! hypocrite lecteur!—mon semblable,—mon frère!" The requirement of this identification necessarily limits the readership of the poem, but it also allows degrees of compression and of subtle complexity probably impossible to achieve by any other structural technique. The poem is essentially dramatic, and its appreciation depends on what Francis Fergusson calls "the histrionic sensibility." But both the stage and the cast of the poem exist in the mind of the speaker. It is true that often we need to recognize the personages through whom he speaks, but always we need to recognize as well the tone and emphasis of his voice speaking through them.

DANTEAN SCHEME AND INTENT

Eliot wrote in 1935 that he wanted literature to be unconsciously rather than deliberately and defiantly Christian. This statement, of course, refers to technique as well as to content. In the same essay is expressed the view that reading does affect our moral and religious existence, and that the greatness of literature is not determined solely by literary standards: the poet's job is to present to his readers true worldy wisdom, which will lead up to other-worldly wisdom, and will be completed and fulfilled by it.[1]

Dante exerted a very strong influence on Eliot's use of the Christian tradition, and especially on his use of its rituals in *The Waste Land:* the crucifixion and resurrection; baptism; and the burial ritual and liturgy, from which the first section of the poem takes its title. (The Mass is dramatically embodied in the Earthly Paradise and Paradise sections of Dante's *Divine Comedy.* Eliot followed that lead in writing *The Rock, Murder in the Cathedral,* and especially *Ash-Wednesday.*)

The Dantean scheme and intent are central to the unity and to the proper interpretation of *The Waste Land*. The most immediately obvious borrowings from the *Divine Comedy* are seen in the "crowd flowing over London Bridge" passage of Section I and in the *"Poi s'ascose nel foco che gli affina"* quotation at the end of the poem. Dante's influence, however, permeates the whole poem, as a number of critics who compare it to Dante's *Inferno* have noted. Philo M. Buck, in his *Directions in Contemporary Literature,* wrote of the "irrelevant waste and despair that knows not its emptiness" seen in *The Waste Land,* and he further pointed out that the purpose of Dante's *Inferno* is to make unregenerate humanity see, "with no veil to obscure, the ugliness of sin. Evil must be stripped of all of its false allure and stand before the poet naked, grotesque, and unashamed, not that he may recoil at its horror and stand in judgement . . . but that he may suffer in mind and body the moral illness that is necessary before the discipline of Purgatory can be begun."[2]

This confrontation is precisely what the speaker of *The Waste Land* tries to accomplish for the wastelanders. We see in the poem not the expression of such emptiness, but rather its description. That is, the attitudes depicted are not those of the speaker, but rather states that he has recognized and transcended (as Mr. Buck goes on to point out).

Thus the speaker, by recognizing its anatomy and significance, has passed out of hell, where no psychic postures except those observed are conceivable; and he has made the difficult transition into purgation of his damning tendencies—has exercised "the good of the intellect." He is aware of the antithetical poles of the poem's symbols, aware now of the depths of its negative implications but also the height of its positive dimensions. He is aware both of "the prison" (involvement with the profitless aspects of the immediate) and of "the key." And thanks to the collocation in his mind of Buddha's "Fire Sermon," Shakespeare's *The Tempest,* the three commands of the Hindu thunder myth, Christ's resurrection, St. Augustine's reversal, the Fisher King's restoration, and the other echoes in the poem, he is aware of the means needed to complete the transformation in his psychic focus to the high felicity of a properly ordered love. Hell, then, is represented in *The Waste Land* only through images. His contemporaries and readers, to whom the speaker addresses himself, are, like him, still living; and they have yet the possibility of putting the intellect to its good and proper use.

Eliot, like Dante, tries to stimulate his reader to do so by showing first—using language to communicate to the reader's bones and muscles— the feel of inferno, and then by introducing guides from literature and tradition, both classical and contemporary, who help one understand what he has seen and felt. And just as Dante has philosophical passages in which Virgil, Statius, Marco Lombardo, Beatrice, and others explain to Dante what he has already experienced so that he will understand it, will "use the good of the intellect," Eliot occasionally in the earlier poems and much more frequently in *Ash-Wednesday* and in the *Four Quartets* has written philosophical poetry aimed at the understanding of the reader as well as at his senses—the senses whose appeal the reader must transcend in order to escape inferno. *The Waste Land,* however, omits all such explicit statements.

The speaker sees his contemporaries largely in those attitudes of soul symbolized in Dante's *Inferno* either by the trimmers—who "lived without blame, and without praise" and who are admitted neither to heaven nor the depths of hell (Dante's description of them is echoed in the lines "A crowd flowed over London Bridge, so many, / I had not thought death had undone so many")—or by the shades in Limbo who lived and died before Christianity and thus without baptism. Though they were virtuous, these latter shades occupy the first circle of Dante's hell (their description is echoed in Eliot's lines "Sighs, short and infrequent, were exhaled, / And each man fixed his eyes before his feet"). But only if Eliot's Londoners are caught by death and frozen in such attitudes of the soul will they partake of hell.

The meeting with Stetson (the reader) echoes the many passages in which Dante converses with the shades he and Virgil encounter in hell, and the Arnaut Daniel fragment at the end of the poem focuses the relevance to *The Waste Land* of the Dantean scheme. As with more borrowings in this poem than in any other, Eliot demands of his reader for full understanding a familiarity with the broad context of his borrowed line; for he hopes to send his readers on a tour through the works of literature most relevant to the paramount problems of the wastelanders.

Dante the Pilgrim meets Arnaut Daniel in the seventh and last cornice of purgatory, where the lustful are purged. As he previously ascended the stairway to this cornice with his guides, the pagan Virgil and the Christian Statius, the latter has expounded to Dante the doctrine of the development of the soul which further clarifies Marco Lombardo's discourse. Statius has linked the soul's history closely to divine love and to the reproductive processes with their sexual basis. Through this discourse, Dante has been brought to understand the mode of existence of the shades populating Dante's hell, purgatory, and heaven.

Similarly, Eliot's reader, in order to understand the workings of *The Waste Land's* imagery and structure, must become aware that the immediate scene, the "unreal city" of London, and the bodies of himself and his contemporaries are much less important than *their* souls.

Virgil's explanation of purgatory emphasizes the fact that Dante (like Eliot's readers) is still alive, and that full repentance before death can bring one to such an advanced stage of purgation as this—to the level of those in purgatory nearest their goal. For Arnaut is encountered shortly before the entrance to the Earthly Paradise at the top of Mount Purgatory. Dante has been allowed to experience these things before death, he says, through the grace of "a Lady above"—through unearned good fortune.

The shades in Cornice VII of the *Purgatorio* are divided into two groups: those who suffer for homosexual lust and those who, though their lusts were heterosexual, "followed them like brute beasts." (Both groups have also been included in *The Waste Land.*) This last conversation with a suffering shade in purgatory indicates approximately the limits beyond which, in Dante's scheme, the unChristian knowledge of Virgil cannot progress. It takes place on the narrow path where those who pass on between the flames and the cliff must go single file, alone; the nature of the progress beyond that point excludes help from outside; and it also requires the withdrawing of attachment to others or of love improperly directed toward them. And it is out of the searing flames that Arnaut addresses Dante.

This necessity of renouncing lust is also the message of Buddha's "Fire Sermon," which like the present passage is couched in fire imagery—though there the fire has only negative connotations; here it symbolizes both the burning flames of lust and the purging flames of proper love. Yet, though one must go alone to be plucked out of the first burning (lust) by the second (love), the plucking enables him to give, sympathize, and control, just as, when the two bands of shades pass in Dante's Cornice VII, each of them quickly kisses one of those in the other group and hurries on. Of this sympathy, this properly directed love, their lust formerly made them incapable.

"What Tiresias sees," "the substance of the poem" according to Eliot's often-misinterpreted note, is therefore the necessity of pure concern for one's fellow-humans without the sins of lust that violate the proper natural order and make individuals incapable of genuine love. Like Dante's Virgil, though, Tiresias in *The Waste Land* lacks the Christian dimension; and he is able to point one only so far as the earthly felicity represented in Dante's scheme by the Earthly Paradise at the top of Mount Purgatory.

When *The Waste Land* appeared in 1922, Eliot already had given frequent hints of his preoccupation with Arnaut's speech, a passage earlier emphasized in Ezra Pound's *The Spirit of Romance;* and in 1920 he had given the title *Ara Vos Prec* to a collection of his poems containing chiefly the observations of Dantean watchers of the fruits of improperly ordered love. He was later to use *"Sovegna vos"* in Part IV of *Ash-Wednesday,* and in his 1929 *Dante* book he quoted the speech both in Provençal and in English translation. Because a number of the Provençal phrases are scattered through Eliot's works, it bears repeating here:

> "Ieu sui Arnaut, que plor e vau cantan;
> consiros vei la passada folor,
> e vei jausen lo jorn, qu' esper, denan.
> Ara vos prec, per aquella valor
> que vos guida al som de l'escalina,
> sovegna vos a temps de ma dolor."
> POI S' ASCOSE NEL FOCO CHE GLI AFFINA.

("I am Arnold, who weeps and goes singing. I see in thought all the past folly. And I see with joy the day for which I hope, before me. And so I pray you, by that Virtue which leads you to the topmost of the stair—be mindful in due time of my pain." Then dived he back into that fire which refines them.)[3]

As Arnaut and his fellow shades speak to Dante, they take great care not to step outside the painful flames which are purging them. It is crucial to note that their suffering is entirely voluntary. And this is not just a point of Dante's fiction: It is Thomistic doctrine. But more importantly, it is a psychological necessity known to the medical doctor as well as to the psychologist: the patient must will his own recovery—the bit can never be removed from the horse's mouth safely until he *wants* to go in the right direction. What is involved in Dante's purgatory is not mere punishment, but the willing acceptance of the effects of misguided, defective, or excessive love which will make the sufferer aware of the improper nature of his past acts and will alter or erase his tendencies toward such acts. Thus at the top of Mount Purgatory he has achieved the regained innocence—not of ignorance but of understanding. And hence he recognizes the instant when his purgation in any one cornice of purgatory is complete, and nothing holds him back to suffer further if his own improper focus does not.

Such also is the nature of escape from Eliot's waste land; and, like Arnaut Daniel, Eliot's speaker has spoken out of the cleansing purgatorial fire only long enough to make clear to his hearers the nature of the place in which he has been met, of the ravages of lust in its most inclusive sense (the anatomy of hell), and of the process necessary to its transcendence—"Then dived he back into the fire that refines them." As Roy Battenhouse says, Eliot has in his poetry made a vocation of diving back into the fire.

. . . .

It is easy to see why Eliot denied that his poem was intended to express the disillusionment of a generation. Its message, though universal, is intensely personal; and the waste land exists in no one time or generation, but in a wrong psychic focus equally possible to all generations—and escapable, as our art reminds us, by individuals in every generation. What it is intended to express is the recognition not only of the anatomy of hell but of the necessity and promise of escape from it.

Notes

1. "Religion and Literature," *Selected Essays* (1932; rpt. New York, 1964).
2. Philo M. Buck, *Directions in Contemporary Literature* (New York, 1942), pp. 275–77.
3. "Dante," *Selected Essays*, p. 217.

T. S. Eliot Among the Prophets

FLORENCE JONES

It has been customary to cite *The Waste Land* as chief exhibit of the romantic nihilism of Eliot's youth and thereafter to trace his spiritual pilgrimage through *Ash-Wednesday* and the *Four Quartets* to the point where he can affirm the meaningfulness of what is; or, remarking Eliot's preoccupation with Time, to say, as does Claude Edmonde Magny, that at the stage of writing *The Waste Land* Eliot found Time to be the enemy and therefore "took refuge in a timeless perspective," and only later, in the *Four Quartets,* did he strive "to integrate time and its multiplicity of dimensions into the spiritual life of man, so as to make possible a true access to eternity."[1]

I

"In *The Waste Land,*" says Magny, "we are in the bleak even time before the Incarnation, before the unique, exceptional event took place, that which, moreover, the cards are unable to predict, because it is outside Time."[2] This I would contest. The theological objection is that we are *not* in the bleak, even time before the Incarnation—and neither, in a sense, were the Hebrew prophets, whose influence is, I think, paramount in Eliot's poem. Certainly the cards could not predict the event, but the prophets could and did predict it as part of the total action of God in history which they proclaimed. Furthermore, the Incarnation is not only "outside Time," but also inside Time and "in the fullness of Time." Therein lies the paradox of the event. To conduct the argument at the level of literary allusion, when Eliot talks of the Rock, we are reminded of the Rock of Israel, the God of the prophets. When he speaks of the Hanged Man, we are reminded of Christ. If ever these names had validity and meaning in the past, they have validity and meaning now and always, and their meaning becomes part of the poem. To assume that such allusions are ironic because Adonis and Osiris figure in the same poem

Reprinted with permission from *American Literature* 38 (November 1966): 285–302. Copyright 1966 by Duke University Press.

may well be as erroneous in Eliot's case as in the case of Milton or the prophet Jeremiah, who also utilized the myth and language of the fertility cults—in honor to the God of Israel.

The Yahwehist prophets harnessed the attributes of the fertility gods to the God of history: it was Yahweh who made the seasons and sent the rain and the drought. But Yahweh's purpose and personality are primarily to be seen in the dialectic of history; events in time provide the clue to reality, meaning, and identity. With respect to Mr. Magny, I suggest that this Judeo-Christian perspective in Time prevails also in Eliot's poem. The people in his wasteland suffer drought and winter as in the wasteland of the fertility cults, but the extent of their despair is that, having lost sight of the purpose behind their history, they have lost identity and the basis for hope. Their history lies in fragments around them—Athens, Rome, Phoenicia, Mylae, and the London of Elizabeth. They can connect nothing with nothing. But if only they could reconstruct the pattern where all these fragments fit, Time and Life and Death would no longer appall.

One puts Eliot and Jeremiah side by side to read of two wastelands, or perhaps they are the same: Europe in the twentieth century and Judah in the seventh century B.C. There is the same degeneration, described in terms of drought and the failure of vegetation and other vicissitudes of nature. Both speak of agony and alienation, of political instability and the deterioration of morality. There is the same authentic note of doom. Both speak of the yearning of their age to be united to its proper good, but the prophet affirms a deliverance that will come, and Eliot—so it is said—knows that deliverance has not come and will not come. The prophet proclaims that this time when God appears absent is in fact the time when he is actively exercising his judgment, winnowing, purging, and burning, in order to reclaim his people at last and restore his Creation. Can we assume that the desolation and destruction in Eliot's wasteland are unconnected with judgment? And would not the process of judgment ultimately imply a vindication of the purpose behind Creation?

I propose to treat Eliot's poem as a reworking of the themes of the prophetic writings of the Old and New Testaments. In particular, the poem invites comparison with the Book of Jeremiah, for among the abundance of images that characterizes the writing of the Hebrew prophet there run three persistent and intricate lines of imagery: those of the wasteland, the vine, and the marriage bed. Both pieces of writing lack a coherent structure, Eliot's poem being designed to give the appearance of a series of fragments, and the Book of Jeremiah being a collection of oracles in poetry and prose, spoken from time to time as political exigency and the Word of the Lord demanded, and compiled later, almost haphazardly, from various written and oral sources. The texture, on the other hand, is consistent in both cases, so that a study of the imagery provides the more useful approach.

II

Here is the prophet:

> "Judah mourns
>   and her gates languish; . . .
> Her nobles send their servants for water;
>   they come to the cisterns,
> they find no water,
>   they return with their vessels empty;
> they are ashamed and confounded
>   and cover their heads.
> Because of the ground which is dismayed,
>   since there is no rain on the land,
> the farmers are ashamed . . . ,
>   there is no grass. . . .
>   there is no herbage." (Jer. 14:2–6)[3]

Not only have the rains been withheld, but the wells and fountains are poisoned. How can this be, when the Lord God of Israel is the fountain of living water, the author of rain and dew and fruitfulness? The fountain does not run dry, but the people,

> they have forsaken me,
> the fountain of living waters,
>   and hewed out cisterns for themselves,
> broken cisterns,
>   that can hold no water. (Jer. 2:13)

> And I brought you into a plentiful land
>   to enjoy its fruits and its good things.
> But when you came in you defiled my land. . . . (Jer. 2:7)

Side by side with the image of the wasteland run the images of the vine and of the unfaithful wife:

> . . . I planted you a choice vine,
>   wholly of pure seed.
> How then have you turned degenerate
>   and become a wild vine? (Jer. 2:21)

> I remember the devotion of your youth
>   your love as a bride. . . . (Jer. 2:2)

> You have played the harlot with many lovers;
> and would you return to me?
>
> says the LORD. (Jer. 3:1)

> what do you mean that you dress in scarlet,
> that you deck yourself with ornaments of gold . . . ?
> In vain you beautify yourself.
> Your lovers despise you. . . . (Jer. 4:30)

> What right has my beloved in my house,
> when she has done vile deeds? (Jer. 11:15)

Yet God, the loving husband, persistently calls back the wife who has forfeited her right to his house.

> Return, faithless Israel. . . .
> I will not look on you in anger,
> for I am merciful. . . . (Jer. 3:12)

One can use these three images to phrase in three different ways the prophet's assertion about Israel's relationship to God:

At first God married Israel, a loving wife; in her perversity she became a harlot and adulteress. Therefore, God will divorce her, and after her chastening she shall be restored by God as his bride.[4]

At first God planted Israel a choice vine; in her perversity she grew to be a wild vine. Therefore, God will rip her out, and after her chastening she shall again be planted a choice vine.[5]

At first God made Israel a fruitful and well-watered land; in her perversity she made of herself a wasteland. Therefore, God will parch and desolate her, and after her chastening she will again become a fruitful and well-watered land.[6]

Now the personae are basically two, God and Israel. God is at the same time Israel's great enemy and her great deliverer, the inflicter of her grievous wound and her healer. In terms of the Grail legend, Israel is paradoxically both the distressed Queen and the Fisher-King whose inadequacy is the cause of the distress; and God, or his agent, is the Deliverer. Yet when the prophet talks of the marriage between God and Israel, Israel is the Queen and God the King, with this singular difference from the Grail legend—it is the King who remains the profitable partner in the marriage. He remains also the Deliverer. Whereas the part of the legend that deals with the Chapel Perilous emphasizes the testing of the Deliverer to see whether he is fit for his role, Jeremiah's emphasis lies upon the testing and refining of the one who is to be delivered, namely Israel herself.[7] The scheme is not complete, however, until to those two personae the prophet himself has been added, for he represents them both and mediates between them. On the one hand, the prophet is a leader of the people, chosen for his vocation, like Israel herself, from before the time of self-awareness.[8] Like Israel, he must be chastened when he seeks to evade his role,[9] and his tears anticipate the tears which Israel will shed when the water of grace begins its work of regeneration upon her arid heart.[10] On the other hand, the prophet is God's spokesman, whether the message be of wrath or consolation. The Word (Heb. *Dabar*) of God which he delivers from his mouth is tantamount to the Act (again, Heb. *Dabar*) of God, which effects all things. He has a part to play in the affairs of the land unparalleled by any of the Grail poets. However, the righteous king, rather than the prophet, will claim the role of God's agent and the people's champion in the days of Israel's restoration. The present king, like the Fisher-King of the Grail legend, is a "despised, broken pot, a vessel no one cares for," and "none of his offspring shall succeed in sitting on the throne of David";[11] his inadequacy indicates the parlous condition of his land and people. But in the days when Israel returns to grace she will be ruled by "the righteous Branch of David," a vital shoot sprung from what now appears to be a lifeless stump of a royal house, while the City of David, meanwhile desolate, "shall be inhabited for ever."[12] Here lies the origin of the Jewish and Christian concept of the Messiah, who is pre-eminently a king over the people whom God has reclaimed.

III

To turn then to Eliot's poem is to find oneself on surprisingly familiar ground. There is the same wasteland, the same desolate city, the same faithless woman and futile king. As for the land:

> What are the roots that clutch, what branches grow
> Out of this stony rubbish? Son of man,
> You cannot say, or guess, for you know only
> A heap of broken images, where the sun beats,
> And the dead tree gives no shelter, the cricket no relief,
> And the dry stone no sound of water. Only
> There is shadow under this red rock,
> (Come in under the shadow of this red rock),
> And I will show you something different from either
> Your shadow at morning striding behind you
> Or your shadow at evening rising to meet you;
> I will show you fear in a handful of dust.

The allusions are at once apparent. What indeed is the root that clutches and the branch that grows from stony rubbish but the Servant of God described by Deutero-Isaiah:

> For he grew up before him like a young plant,
>   and like a root out of dry ground. . . . (Is. 53:2)

And what is he but the Righteous Branch (Jer. 23:5) which would be raised up out of David? Or he might be designated as "Son of man," a title which belongs, in once sense, to any man. It was used by Ezekiel for his own designation as God's prophet and by the author of the Book of Daniel as the name of the divine hero of the apocalypse, and Christ then took it as his own peculiar title.

Similarly with the "red rock." ("Come in under the shadow of this red rock"). In the same context with the "handful of dust," it recalls the lines from Isaiah:

> Enter into the rock,
>   and hide in the dust
> from before the terror of the Lord. . . . (Is. 2:10)

Yet what rock will hide men in safety, unless the Lord himself, who is "a shelter from the storm and a shade from the heat" (Is. 25:4); "an everlasting rock" (Is. 26:4); "the Rock of your refuge" (Is. 17:10)? If the passage in Eliot's poem appears on the face of it more ominous than reassuring, there is the same ambivalent tone in the prophetic sources. In Jeremiah, God is enemy as well as saviour. So here in Isaiah: he is a "rock of stumbling" as well as the rock of refuge. The "Lord of hosts . . . let him be your dread. And he will become a sanctuary, and a stone of offence, and a rock of stumbling to both houses of Israel, a trap and a snare to the inhabitants of Jerusalem" (Is. 8:13–14). The ambivalence in the prophet's attitude comes from his knowledge that God alone controls the destiny of Israel: it is he who condemns and he who delivers from condemnation. If the people would only recognize the author of their misfortune, they would find at the same time their source of confidence and rescue. May it not be that this applies in Eliot's wasteland also?

One is led at this point to identify the "something different from either / Your shadow at morning striding behind you / Or your shadow at evening rising to meet you" (that is, to take a hint from the cadence that suggests Eccles. 12, "something to alter one's perspective from one's sense of self-sufficiency in youth, and one's sense of futility in old age"). The "something different" must surely be the fear of the Lord on the part of man, the reverence for the Creator on the part of the creature whom he has made from a "handful of dust." ("I will show you something different, . . . I will show you fear in a handful of dust.") The placing of this phrase, "handful of dust," in the passage from the poem puts it in line with "stony rubbish," "a heap of broken images," and "dry stone." These in turn recall the phrases used by the prophets to describe the arid spiritual soil of God's people Israel, given over to exploitation and idolatry: "the heap of ruins of your idols," "wilderness," "desolation," "heart of stone." Rightfully men fear God, not only because they are his creatures, but because they are wayward and unjust while he is eminently righteous, and they stand under his condemnation.

In the prophet Jeremiah sin and condemnation are described in a catalogue of woes—drought and famine, pestilence, foreign invasion, carnage, and captivity. Here in *The Waste Land* Eliot has focused on one woe to exemplify all. There is no water. Therefore, the trees are dead and the grass is dry; men are parched and women brittle. In the prophecies of Jeremiah sons and daughters are cut off in their youth, but here they cannot even be conceived. So great is the desolation of this place that the faint pushings of life are its most painful vicissitudes.

> April is the cruellest month . . . stirring
> Dull roots with spring rain.

A human situation in the poem offers a parallel, where Albert is in much the same humiliating position as the Lord God who married the virgin Israel and found her an ungrateful partner!

> It's them pills I took, to bring it off, she said.
> ....
> You *are* a proper fool, I said.
> Well, if Albert won't leave you alone, there it is, I said,
> What you get married for if you don't want children?

In Jeremiah's wasteland the showers have been withheld from Israel because she polluted the land which was her marriage bed (Jer. 3:2–3). Here in Eliot's wasteland the rain still falls in the season, and there is still some virility in men, but both rain and virility are cruelly felt, because of the recalcitrance of the land and the woman.

Along with the description of the land runs the description of the city, built like Rome and London upon a river.

> Unreal City,
> Under the brown fog of a winter dawn,
> A crowd flowed over London Bridge, so many,
> I had not thought death had undone so many.

Although the obvious influence here is Dante's, Dante himself looks back to the Hebrew concept of Sheol, which in the writings of the classical Hebrew prophets is regarded as the destiny of all men for all time. It is not yet, as in Maccabean Judaism, an eternal house of punishment specifically for the wicked, but already a place that carries its own peculiar condemnation, in that the man consigned to Sheol has lost his last chance of righteousness. The prophets rightly associate with it the terror of the Pit, the spirit of a man being hunted hence as if he were an animal. Isaiah, like Eliot, speaks of Sheol along with exile, as the destiny of a whole nation.

> Therefore my people go into exile for want of knowledge;
>> their honored men are dying of hunger,
>> and their multitude is parched with thirst.
> Therefore Sheol has enlarged its appetite . . .
>> and the nobility of Jerusalem and her multitude go
>> down, . . .
> Man is bowed down, and men are brought low,
>> and the eyes of the haughty are humbled. (Is. 5:13–15)

Eliot has continued in the same vein:

> Sighs, short and infrequent, were exhaled,
> And each man fixed his eyes before his feet.

The underlying message is the same. The prophets threaten that Jersualem shall be a city laid waste without inhabitant, all its people dead by pestilence, famine, fire, and the sword. Eliot depicts a city more horrible still, a city whose crowd is already dead in the spirit, but not yet gone beyond despair into comfortable oblivion. And yet there will be fire for that city, too. Later in "The Fire Sermon" we find

> The river's tent is broken: the last fingers of leaf
> Clutch and sink into the wet bank. The wind
> Crosses the brown land, unheard. The nymphs are departed.

The river does not often appear in the prophetic literature concerned with the fate of the City of David, but Ezekiel, envisioning the restoration of Israel and the holiness of the people reclaimed by God, has the new city built around the temple; the River of Life, issuing from below the threshold of the temple, flows from Jerusalem toward the east.

> And wherever the river goes every living creature which swarms will live, and there will be very many fish. . . . And on the banks, on both sides of the river, there will grow all kinds of trees for food. Their leaves will not wither nor their fruit fail, . . . because the water for them flows from the sanctuary. (Ezek. 47:9–12)

Ezekiel's vision is all the more wonderful because it comes to him "in the twenty-fifth year of our exile . . . in the fourteenth year after the city was conquered," after the capture, plundering, and burning of the city predicted by Jeremiah. As the iniquity of the old city is characterized by the neglect and destruction of the temple of the Lord, so the holiness of the reconstructed Jerusalem is characterized by the centrality and magnificence of the new temple, from which the River of Life issues.

The temple in Jerusalem is also called God's tent[13] because it succeeds the tent which was the house of God in the days of the wandering in the wilderness. The erection of God's tent in the royal city is a sign that God dwells and "tabernacles" with his people; indeed, the whole city, when it stands firm in its obligation and love to him, might well be called the tent of God. The conjunction of "river" and "tent" in Eliot's line is not fortuitous; it is to be found also in Isaiah when he is describing the final reconciliation of his people of Israel with the God who is their ruler and the source of their life:

> Your eyes will see Jerusalem,
>   a quiet habitation, an immovable tent,
> whose stakes will never be plucked up,
>   nor will any of its cords be broken.
> But there the LORD in majesty will be for us
>   a place of broad rivers and streams. (Is. 33:20–21)

Meanwhile, it is one of God's complaints against Jerusalem that "My tent is destoyed,/ and all my cords are broken" (Jer. 10:20; cf. 4:20), and a consequence of this that there comes

> a great commotion out of the north country
> to make the cities of Judah a desolation,
>   a lair of jackals, (Jer. 10:22)

> to make your land a waste;
>   your cities will be ruins
>   without inhabitant. (Jer. 4:7)

Does not Eliot describe the same city standing under the same condemnation, since "the river's tent is broken"? Its inhabitants, too, seem to have departed, and the last possibility of love has fled. Have they all gone into exile where they sit by the waters of Babylon and weep for their lovelessness and their separation from the thing they would have loved?

> my children have gone from me. . . .
> For the shepherds [i.e., kings] are stupid,
>   and do not inquire of the LORD;
> therefore they have not prospered,
>   and all their flock is scattered. (Jer. 10:20–21)

The Fisher-King, an unprosperous "shepherd" indeed, sits now among the ruins and laments the scattering of his flock. Or his people remain on the spot, exiled nonetheless from their true estate, and he is alone in a far-off place.

> By the waters of Leman I sat down and wept . . .

The city is a "desolation," as the prophet had said. There are no jackals there, but a rat creeps slowly through the vegetation, scuttling the bones of the dead ancestors. Rotten and decayed, the city stands as if under plague, only to be cleansed by that fire which the prophets proclaimed to be the wrath of God.

> Burning burning burning burning
> O Lord Thou pluckest me out[14]

Later still, in "What the Thunder Said," we have the city's violent destruction before the "hooded hordes swarming," or, as it might be, Jeremiah's "nation from the north."

> What is the city over the mountains
> Cracks and reforms and bursts in the violet air
> Falling towers
> Jerusalem Athens Alexandria
> Vienna London

This is the tone of the Hebrew prophets pronouncing doom upon Jerusalem, Babylon, Memphis, Tahpanhes. . . . Thus, Ezekiel against Tyre: "They shall destroy the walls of Tyre, and break down her towers; and . . . make her a bare rock" (Ezek. 26:4). And Isaiah:

> . . . The foundations of the earth tremble. . . .
> The earth staggers like a drunken man. . . . (Is. 24:18–20)

It is, for the prophet also, a time of "violet air," when

> . . . the moon will be confounded
> and the sun ashamed; (Is. 24:23)

though the Lord of hosts will reign at that time in his glory.

> And bats with baby faces in the violet light
> Whistled, and beat their wings . . .
> And upside down in air were towers
> Tolling reminiscent bells, that kept the hours
> And voices singing out of empty cisterns and exhausted
> wells.

The imagery is particularly horrible in view of Jeremiah's prediction of the slaughter of infants (now only "bats with baby faces"!), and his insistence that the people had built their own "empty cisterns," even though the living fountain had been available to them. The "exhausted wells" were, alas, "the wells of salvation" from which, in the day of restoration, we might yet draw water with joy (Is. 12:3). The destruction, which was accompanied at first by the "murmur of maternal lamentation" (cf. Is. 32:12; Jer. 4:8, 9:17 & 19), is now unsung and unwept; or at least only

> . . . the grass is singing
> Over the tumbled graves, about the chapel
> There is the empty chapel, only the wind's home. . . .
> Dry bones can harm no one.

This recalls Jeremiah in tow particulars: "They shall die of deadly diseases. They shall not be lamented" (Jer. 16:4), and "The whole valley of the dead bodies and the ashes . . . shall be sacred to the Lord" (Jer. 31:40). The hint in Jeremiah about the sacred valley of the dead bodies is expanded in a passage of Ezekiel:

> [He] set me down in the midst of the valley; it was full of bones. . . . and lo, they were very dry. And he said to me, "Son of man, can these bones live? . . . Prophesy to these bones. . . . Thus says the LORD GOD to these bones: Behold, I will cause breath to enter you, and you shall live. . . ." (Ezek. 37:1–5)

Is it true, then, as Eliot says (tongue in cheek!): "Dry bones can harm no one"? Is there not still some hope for life in the city which is "rats' alley / Where the dead men lost their bones"?

IV

After the land and the city there remain for consideration the personae of the poem, the same three whom we encounter again and again in various roles and disguises: the Woman, the Fisher-King, and the Deliverer. Here is the Woman first as a German aristocrat ("I read, much of the night, and go south in the winter"); as Madame Sosostris, famous clairvoyante, "known to be the wisest woman in Europe,/With a wicked pack of cards," known, in short, for one of the false prophets and diviners who were the abomination of Jeremiah's Jerusalem. ("For thus says the Lord of hosts. . . . Do not let your prophets and your diviners who are among you deceive you," Jer. 29:8; cf. 27:9). Eliot plays the trick on her that the Hebraic author played on Balaam, making her speak more wisely than she knows: "Fear death by water" and "I do not find the Hanged Man." Later on the Woman is a

Cleopatra *manqué*, the voluptuousness of that queen become metallic, her liveliness degenerated to neurosis:

> The Chair she sat in, like a burnished throne,
> Glowed on the marble, where the glass
> Held up by standards wrought with fruited vines
> From which a golden Cupidon peeped out

In the Lord's vineyard, which was Israel, there was no fruitful vine left, nor is there a fruitful vine in this modern wasteland unless artificially wrought; no love is left, and its place is ironically supplied by a golden cupidon. Jeremiah's image of the harlot is not far away:

> "What shall I do now? What shall I do?"
> "I shall rush out as I am, and walk the street
> "With my hair down, so. . . ."

Alas, she is too elegant and well-brought up for that, whereas the Thames maiden copulates habitually and wearily by the river where Elizabeth and Leicester once beat oars. There is the typist who surrenders perfunctorily to perfunctory embraces. Like the harlot Israel, but in her own way, she has found lovers who are her enemies and despise her (Jer. 4:30, 12:7).

> Flushed and decided, he assaults at once; . . .
> His vanity requires no response,
> And makes a welcome of indifference.

The note of compassion struck by the Hebrew prophet ("Return, O faithless Israel"), mediating between the forsaken husband and the forsaking wife, is sounded here by another prophet:

> I Tiresias, . . . throbbing between two lives,
> ....
> . . . have foresuffered all
> Enacted on this same divan or bed;

suffering for the inadequacy and disillusionment of man and woman. The impotent husband and ruler we have already met

> . . . fishing in the dull canal
> On a winter evening round behind the gashouse
> Musing upon the king my brother's wreck
> And on the king my father's death before him.

This passage recalls not only the vicissitudes of kings and princes in *The Tempest* but the prophecies of Jeremiah against the profitless dynasty of Israel.

Because those prophecies in turn recall the Messianic prophecies of the Righteous Branch of David, we are justified in seeing an element of hope in the last words that we have from the Fisher-King. Whereas previously he had had no expectations, and his people were humble people who expected nothing, now:

> Shall I at least set my lands in order? . . .
> These fragments I have shored against my ruins

"These fragments" refers not only to the ruins of the castle (*la tour abolie*), but to the people who will yet live to inherit the kingdom and its law: Datta, Dayadhvam, Damyata. They are the "remnant" spoken of by the prophets, or the "few survivors" of Isaiah.[15] If this king, "fishing with the arid plain behind him" (behind him in point of time?), were to be transposed into an Hebraic setting, it would be as Jeremiah describes it: "Behold, I am sending for many fishers, says the LORD, and they shall catch them. . . . For I will bring them back to their own land which I gave to their fathers" (Jer. 16:15–16). Meanwhile, the Fisher-King is apt to be confused with the spurious Deliverers, many of whom claim an association with the water. Thus, "the drowned Phoenician sailor," who is Phoenician presumably because the poet must suggest the Ancient Near East and the Canaanite fertility cults which the Phoenicians propagated throughout the Western world. Are Christianity and Judaism, having extinguished their rival, to become extinct in turn?

> Gentile or Jew
> O you who turn the wheel and look to windward,
> Consider Phlebas, who was once handsome and tall as you.

And will those two religions, which, in contradistinction to the fertility cults, base their case on the acts of God in history and the meaningfulness of the perspective of Time whereby his purposes are manifest, die as the Phoenician died, *entering the whirlpool?*

V

But what of the Rock? And what of the Hanged Man? It is the ninth hour, and the Hanged Man has given up the ghost, the Father having forsaken him.

> After the torchlight red on sweaty faces
> After the frosty silence in the gardens
> After the agony in stony places
> The shouting and the crying
> Prison and palace and reverberation

> Of thunder of spring over distant mountains
> He who was living is now dead
> We who were living are now dying

His promise, too, appears to have come to nothing. The one who might have delivered us from death is himself dead, and we die with him—for two wretched days.

> Sweat is dry and feet are in the sand
> If there were only water amongst the rock
> Dead mountain mouth of carious teeth that cannot spit
> Here one can neither stand nor lie nor sit
> There is not even silence in the mountains
> But dry sterile thunder without rain

But toiling in the place of torment we have the illusion (is it?) that there is another walking beside us. We are three children in the fire, and there is someone else, a fourth. ("Did we not cast three men bound into the fire? . . . I see four men loose, walking in the midst of the fire, and they are not hurt; and the appearance of the fourth is like a son of the gods," Dan. 3:24–25.) Or we are two disciples walking to Emmaus, bereft of all hope because Jesus is crucified, and yet perplexed by the rumor of the empty tomb—when Jesus himself draws near and walks with us, "gliding wrapt in a brown mantle, hooded," because as yet our eyes are kept from recognizing him.

Nor will we recognize him until we have understood the meaning of it all: that the fire and drought signified all the time not God's absence but his active judgment; that they were to destroy but also to refine and purify (*foco che gli affina*); that Death was not the end but the prelude to Resurrection. In the Gospel of Luke it is this same Journey to Emmaus where the meaning of man's distress and the action of God's providence finally become clear to the disciples who have walked with Jesus.

> "O foolish men, and slow of heart to believe all that the prophets have spoken! Was it not necessary that the Christ should suffer these things and enter into his glory?" And beginning with Moses and all the prophets, he interpreted to them in all the scriptures the things concerning himself. (Luke 24:25–27)

Only so can the writers of the New Testament describe the deliverance that God had wrought in Christ—it was the same deliverance of which "all the prophets" had spoken. The Crucifixion was the strange means by which the people living in spiritual desolation had been reunited with the source of life. Conscious of the fact that they stand in a long cultural and literary tradition, the New Testament writers rework the material of the old prophecies until they have built up an elaborate structure of quotation and allusion. Eliot, standing in the same tradition some centuries later, builds his poem in similar fashion, appealing to the record of the Old Testament and the New. After his recasting of the Crucifixion scene and his reference to the Journey to Emmaus have been given full weight, one can hardly doubt that his meaning is substantially the same. Like the writers of the Old Testament and the New, he is insisting that God is our Deliverer. It is the same wasteland and drought, the same fire and thunder (dry sterile thunder as it seemed in those first two harrowing days, but thunder that actually brought the rain long awaited), the same "day of the great slaughter, when the towers fall" and the reconciliation is effected between God and man.

If more evidence were needed, one could follow up the references at the end of the poem. Consider this description by Isaiah of Israel's present unseaworthiness:

> Your tackle hangs loose;
>   it cannot hold the mast firm in its place,
>   or keep the sail spread out. (Is. 33:23)

and the promise held out by Jeremiah for the latter days:

> I will give them a heart to know that I am the LORD; and they shall be my people and I will be their God, for they shall return to me with their whole heart. (Jer. 24:7)

Note how both passages are subsumed in Eliot's lines:

> *Damyata:* The boat responded
> Gaily, to the hand expert with sail and oar
> The sea was calm, your heart would have responded
> Gaily, when invited, beating obedient
> To controlling hands.

The tense ("would have responded") still implies an element of doubt, as if what the prophets affirm, the poet can merely speculate upon. But in the context, after we have languished "each in his prison/Thinking of the key," these lines come with a surge of release, as if Peace and Wholeness and Joy already begin to invade our hearts (the Hindu Shantih for the Hebrew Shalom). God's blessings, his sympathy and control, awaken similar capacities in his people: Datta. Dayadhvam. Damyata.

The motifs of Eliot's poem are satisfied in this passage from Isaiah:

> And he will give rain for the seed, . . . the produce of the ground . . . will be rich and plenteous. . . . And upon every lofty mountain and every high hill there will be brooks running with water, in the day of the great slaughter, when the towers fall. . . . in the day when the LORD binds up the hurt of his people, and heals the wounds inflicted by his blow. (Is. 30:23–26)

The "day" in question is the Day of the Lord, the *Yom Yahweh*, the day of judgment and vindication, of calamity and glory. It is Eliot's long winter's day, through morning, noon, and evening, when the rain finally falls upon the parched land.

Notes

1. Claude E. Magny, "A Double Note on T. S. Eliot and James Joyce," trans. Sonia Brownell, in *T. S. Eliot: Symposium,* comp. Richard March and Tambimuttu (Chicago, 1949), pp. 213, 215.
2. Magny, p. 214.
3. The biblical text used throughout is that of the Revised Standard Version.
4. See also Jer. 12:7, 13:26, 31:4.
5. See also Jer. 8:13, 12:10, 31:5.
6. See also Jer. 4:26, 12:10, 22:6, 31:12.
7. Sometimes with the imagery of smelting, as in Jer. 6:27–30; sometimes with the imagery of the potter's wheel, as in Jer. 18:1–6; usually in terms of a bushfire, Jer. 21:14, or a fire at the gates of the city, Jer. 17:27.
8. Jer. 1:5.
9. Jer. 20:7–9.
10. Jer. 9:1; cf. 9:10, 31:9.
11. Jer. 22:28–30.
12. Jer. 17:25, 23:5, 33:15.
13. See, for example, Ps. 15:1.
14. Grover Smith, Jr. in *T. S. Eliot's Poetry and Plays* (Chicago, 1956), p. 90, has noted that the symbolism of fire Eliot owes not only to Buddha and St. Augustine, but also to the Hebrew prophets. He cites Amos:

> "I overthrew some of you,
>   as when God overthrew Sodom and Gomorrah,
> and you were as a brand plucked out of the burning;
>   yet you did not return to me,"
>   says the LORD. (Amos 4:11)

The passage in Amos is only one of very many prophetic oracles that proclaim the burning of the city as a chastisement of Israel for her waywardness. See, for example, in Jeremiah 4:4, 15:14, 17:4, 17:27, 21:10, 21:12, 21:14, 32:29, 34:2, 34:22, 37:8, 38:23.

Mr. Smith, somewhat misleadingly, places his citation in a discussion of asceticism, whereas there is no such connotation in the words of the prophet; but one is apt to misread the biblical allusions if one regards the poem as primarily a reworking of the myth of the fertility cults.

15. Grover Smith calls attention to the fact that the Fisher-King (he says "Tiresias") is in a position similar to that of "King Hezekiah, hearing in his sickness the bidding of Isaiah (38:1): 'Set thine house in order: for thou shalt die, and not live' " (p. 96).

The First *Waste Land*

RICHARD ELLMANN

Lloyds' most famous bank clerk revalued the poetic currency fifty years ago. As Joyce said, *The Waste Land* ended the idea of poetry for ladies. Whether admired or detested, it became, like *Lyrical Ballads* in 1798, a traffic signal. Hart Crane's letters, for instance, testify to his prompt recognition that from that time forward his work must be to outflank Eliot's poem. Today footnotes do their worst to transform innovations into inevitabilities. After a thousand explanations, *The Waste Land* is no longer a puzzle poem, except for the puzzle of choosing among the various solutions. To be penetrable is not, however, to be predictable. The sweep and strangeness with which Eliot delineated despair resist temptations to patronize Old Possum as old hat. Particular discontinuities continue to surprise even if the idea of discontinuous form—to which Eliot never quite subscribed and which he was to forsake—is now almost as familiar as its sober counterpart. The compound of regular verse and *vers libre* still wears some of the effrontery with which in 1922 it flouted both schools. The poem retains the air of a splendid feat.

Eliot himself was inclined to poohpooh its grandeur. His chiseled comment, which F. O. Matthiessen quotes, disclaimed any intention of expressing "the disillusionment of a generation," and said that he did not like the word "generation" or have a plan to endorse anyone's "illusion of disillusion." To Theodore Spencer he remarked in humbler mood, "Various critics have done me the honour to interpret the poem in terms of criticism of the contemporary world, have considered it, indeed, as an important bit of social criticism. To me it was only the relief of a personal and wholly insignificant grouse against life. It is just a piece of rhythmical grumbling."

This statement is prominently displayed by Mrs. Valerie Eliot in her excellent decipherment and elucidation of *The Waste Land* manuscript. If it is more than an expression of her husband's genuine modesty, it appears to imply that he considered his own poem, as he considered *Hamlet,* an inadequate projection of its author's tangled emotions, a Potemkin village rather than a proper objective correlative. Yet no one will wish away the entire civilizations and cities, wars, hordes of people, religions of East and West, and exhibits from many literatures in many languages that lined the Thames in Eliot's ode to dejection. And even if London was only his state of mind at the time, the picture he paints of it is convincing. His remark to Spencer, made after a lapse of years, perhaps catches up another regret, that the poem emphasized his *Groll* at the expense of much else in his nature. It identified him with a sustained severity of tone, with pulpited (though brief) citations of Biblical and Sophoclean anguish, so that he became an Ezekiel or at least a Tiresias. (In the original version John the Divine made a Christian third among the prophets.) While Eliot did not wish to be considered merely a satirist in his earlier verse, he did not welcome either the public assumption that his poetic mantle had become a hairshirt.

In its early version *The Waste Land* was woven out of more kinds of material, and was therefore less grave and less organized. The first two sections had an overall title (each had its own title as well), "He Do the Police in Different Voices," a quotation from *Our Mutual Friend*. Dickens has the widow Higden say to her adopted child, "Sloppy is a beautiful reader of a newspaper. He do the Police in different voices." Among the many voices in the first version, Eliot placed at the very beginning a long, conversational passage describing an evening on the town, starting at "Tom's place" (a rather arch use of his own name), moving on to a brothel, and concluding with a bathetic sunrise:

> First we had a couple of feelers down at Tom's place,
> There was old Tom, boiled to the eyes, blind . . .
> —("I turned up an hour later down at Myrtle's place.
> What d'y' mean, she says, at two o'clock in the morning,
> I'm not in business here for guys like you;
> We've only had a raid last week, I've been warned
>   twice . . .
> So I got out to see the sunrise, and walked home.

This vapid prologue Eliot decided, apparently on his own, to expunge, and went straight into the now familiar beginning of the poem.

Other voices were expunged by Eliot's friend Ezra Pound, who called himself the "sage homme" (male midwife) of the poem. Pound had already published in 1920 his own elegy on a shipwrecked man, *Hugh Selwyn Mauberley*. Except in the title, the hero is unnamed, and like Eliot's protagonist, he is more an observing consciousness than a person, as he moves through salons, esthetic movements, dark thoughts of wartime deaths. But Mauberley's was an esthetic quest, and Eliot deliberately omitted this from his poem in favor of a spiritual one. (He would combine the two later in *Four Quartets*.) When Eliot was shown *Mauberley* in manuscript, he had remarked that the meaning of a section in Part II was not so clear as it might be, and Pound revised it accordingly.

Pound's criticism of *The Waste Land* was not of its meaning; he liked its despair and was indulgent of its neo-Christian hope. He dealt instead with its stylistic adequacy and freshness. For example, there was an extended, unsuc-cessful imitation of *The Rape of the Lock* at the beginning of "The Fire Sermon." It described the lady Fresca (imported to the waste land from "Gerontion" and one day to be exported to the States for the soft drink trade). Instead of making her toilet like Pope's Belinda, Fresca is going to it, like Joyce's Bloom. Pound warned Eliot that since Pope had done the couplets better, and Joyce the defecation, there was no point in another round. To this shrewd advice we are indebted for the disappearance of such lines as:

> The white-armed Fresca blinks, and yawns, and gapes,
> Aroused from dreams of love and pleasant rapes.
> Electric summons of the busy bell
> Brings brisk Amanda to destroy the spell . . .
> Leaving the bubbling beverage to cool,
> Fresca slips softly to the needful stool,
> Where the pathetic tale of Richardson
> Eases her labour till the deed is done . . .
> This ended, to the steaming bath she moves,
> Her tresses fanned by little flutt'ring Loves;
> Odours, confected by the cunning French,
> Disguise the good old hearty female stench.

. . . .

As a result of this resmithying by *il miglior fabbro,* the poem gained immensely in concentration. Yet Eliot, feeling too solemnized by it, thought of prefixing some humorous doggerel by Pound about its composition. Later, in a more resolute effort to escape the limits set by *The Waste Land,* he wrote *Fragment of an Agon,* and eventually, "somewhere the other side of despair," turned to drama.

Eliot's remark to Spencer calls *The Waste Land* a personal poem. His critical theory was that the artist should seek impersonality, but this was probably intended not so much as a nostrum as an antidote, a means to direct emotion rather than let it spill. His letters indicate that he regarded his poems as consequent upon his experiences. When a woman in Dublin (Mrs. Josephine MacNeill, from whom I heard the account) remarked that Yeats had never really felt anything, Eliot asked in consternation, "How can you say that?" *The Waste Land* compiled many of the nightmarish feelings he had suffered during the seven years from 1914 to 1921, that is, from his coming to England until his temporary collapse.

Thanks to the letters quoted in Mrs. Valerie Eliot's introduction, and to various biographical leaks, the incidents of these years begin to take shape. In 1914 Eliot, then on a travelling fellowship from Harvard, went to study for the summer at Marburg. The outbreak of war obliged him to make his way, in a less leisurely fashion than he had intended, to Oxford. There he worked at his doctoral dissertation on F. H. Bradley's *Appearance and Reality.* The year 1914–1915 proved to be pivotal. He came to three interrelated decisions.

The first was to give up the appearance of the philosopher for the reality of the poet, though he equivocated about this by continuing to write reviews for philosophical journals for some time thereafter. The second was to marry, and the third to remain in England. He was helped to all three decisions by Ezra Pound, whom he met in September 1914. Pound had come to England in 1908 and was convinced (though he changed his mind later) that this was the country most congenial to the literary life. He encouraged Eliot to marry and settle, and he read the poems that no one had been willing to publish and pronounced his verdict, that Eliot "has actually trained himself *and* modernized himself *on his own.*" Harriet Monroe, the editor of *Poetry,* must publish them, beginning with "The Love Song of J. Alfred Prufrock." It took Pound some time to bring her to the same view, and it was not until June 1915 that Eliot's first publication took place. This was also the month of his first marriage, on June 26. His wife was Vivien Haigh-Wood, and Eliot remained, like Merlin with another Vivian, under her spell, beset and possessed by her intricacies for fifteen years and more.

What the newlyweds were like is recorded by Bertrand Russell, whom Eliot had known at Harvard. In a letter of July 1915, which he quotes in his *Autobiography,* Russell wrote of dining with them: "I expected her to be terrible, from his mysteriousness; but she was not so bad. She is light, a little vulgar, adventurous, full of life—an artist I think he said, but I should have thought her an actress. He is exquisite and listless; she says she married him to stimulate him, but finds she can't do it. Obviously he married in order to be stimulated. I think she will soon be tired of him. He is ashamed of his marriage, and very grateful if one is kind to her." Vivien was to dabble in painting, fiction, and verse, her mobile aspirations an aspect of her increasing instability.

Eliot's parents did not take well to their son's doings, though they did not, as has been said by Robert Sencourt, cut him off. His father, president of the Hydraulic Press Brick Company of St. Louis, had expected his son to remain a philosopher, and his mother, though a poet herself, did not like the *vers libre* of "Prufrock" any better than the free and easy marriage. To both parents it seemed that bright hopes were being put aside for a vague profession in the company of a vague woman in a country only too distinctly at war. They asked to see the young couple, but Vivien Eliot was frightened by the perils of the crossing, perhaps also by those of the arrival. So Eliot, already feeling "a broken Coriolanus," as Prufrock felt a Hamlet *manqué,* took the ship alone in August for the momentous interview.

His parents urged him to return with his wife to a university career in the States. He refused: he would be a poet, and England provided to a better atmosphere in which to write. They urged him not to give up his dissertation when it was so near completion, and to this he consented. He parted on good enough terms to request their financial help when he got back to London, and they sent money to him handsomely, as he acknowledged—not handsomely enough, however, to release him from the necessity of very hard work. He taught for a term at the High Wycombe Grammar School, between Oxford and London, and then for two terms at Highgate Junior School. He completed his dissertation and was booked to sail on April 1, 1916, to take his oral examination at Harvard; when the crossing was cancelled, his academic gestures came to an end. In March 1917 he took the job with Lloyds Bank, in the Colonial and Foreign Department, at which he stuck for eight years.

During the early months of their marriage the Eliots were helped also by Russell, who gave them a room in his flat, an act of benevolence not without complications for all parties. Concerned for his wife's health, and fearful—it may be—that their sexual difficulties (perhaps involving psychic impotence on his part) might be a contributing factor, Eliot sent her off for a two-week holiday with Russell. The philosopher found the couple none the less devoted to each other, but noted in Mrs. Eliot a sporadic impulse to be cruel towards her husband, not with simple but with Dostoevskyan cruelty. "I am every day getting things more right between them," Russell boasted, "but I can't let them alone at present, and of course I myself get very much interested." The Dostoevskyan quality affected his imagery: "She is a person who lives on a knife-edge, and will end as a criminal or a saint—I don't know which yet. She has a perfect capacity for both."

The personal life out of which came Eliot's personal poem now began to be lived in earnest. Vivien Eliot suffered obscurely from nerves, her health was subject to frequent collapses, she complained of neuralgia, of insomnia. Her journal for January 1, 1919, records waking up with migraine, "the worst yet," and staying in bed all day without moving; on September 7, 1919, she records "bad pain in right side, very very nervous." Ezra Pound, who knew her well, was worried that the passage in The Waste Land,

"My nerves are bad to-night. Yes, bad. Stay with me.
"Speak to me. Why do you never speak? Speak.
"What are you thinking of? What thinking? What?
"I never know what you are thinking. Think."

might be too photographic. But Vivien Eliot, who offered her own comments on her husband's verse (and volunteered two excellent lines for the lowlife dialogue in "A Game of Chess"),[1] marked the same passage as "Wonderful." She relished the presentation of her symptoms in broken metre. She was less keen, however, on another line from this section, "The ivory men make company between us," and got her husband to remove it. Presumably its implications were too close to the quick of their marital difficulties. The reference may have been to Russell, whose attentions to Vivien were intended to keep the two together. Years afterwards Eliot made a fair copy of The Waste Land in his own handwriting, and reinserted the line from memory. (It should now be added to the final text.) But he had implied his feelings six months after his marriage when he wrote in a letter to Conrad Aiken, "I have lived through material for a score of long poems in the last six months."

Russell commented less sympathetically about the Eliots later, "I was fond of them both, and endeavoured to help them in their troubles until I discovered that their troubles were what they enjoyed." Eliot was capable of estimating the situation shrewdly himself. In his poem, "The Death of Saint Narcissus," which *Poetry* was to publish in 1917 and then, probably because he withdrew it as too close to the knuckle, failed to do so, and which he thought for a time of including in *The Waste Land,* Eliot wrote of his introspective saint, "his flesh was in love with the burning arrows. . . . As he embraced them his white skin surrendered itself to the redness of blood, and satisfied him." For Eliot, however, the search for suffering was not contemptible. He was remorseful about his own real or imgined feelings, he was self-sacrificing about hers, he thought that remorse and sacrifice, not to mention affection, had value. In the Grail legends which underlie *The Waste Land,* the Fisher King suffers a Dolorous Stroke that maims him sexually. In Eliot's case the Dolorous Stroke had been marriage. He was helped thereby to the poem's initial clash of images, "April is the cruellest month," as well as to hollow echoes of Spenser's *Prothalamion* ("Sweet Thames, run softly, till I end my song"). From the barren winter of his academic labors Eliot had been roused to the barren springtime of his nerve-wracked marriage. His life spread into paradox.

Other events of these years seem reflected in the poem. The war, though scarcely mentioned, exerts pressure. In places the poem may be a covert memorial to Henry Ware Eliot, the unforgiving father of the ill-adventured son. Vivien Eliot's journal records on January 8, 1919, "Cable came saying Tom's father is dead. Had to wait all day till Tom came home and then to tell him. *Most terrible.*" Eliot's first explicit statement of his intention to write a long poem comes in letters written later in this year. The references to "the king my father's death" probably derive as much from this actual death as from *The Tempest,* to which Eliot's notes evasively refer. As for the drowning of the young sailor, whether he is Ferdinand or a Phoenician, the war furnished Eliot with many examples, such as Jean Verdenal, a friend from his Sorbonne days, who was killed in the Dardanelles. (Verdenal has received the posthumous distinction of being called Eliot's lover, but in fact the rumors of homosexuality—not voiced directly in Sencourt's biography but whispered in all its corners—remain unwitnessed.) But the drowning may be as well an extrapolation of Eliot's feeling that he was now fatherless as well as rudderless. The fact that the principal speaker appears in a new guise in the last section, with its imagery of possible resurrection, suggests that the drowning is to be taken symbolically rather than literally, as the end of youth. Eliot was addicted to the portrayal of characters who had missed their chances, become old before they had really been young. So the drowned sailor, like the buried corpse, may be construed as the young Eliot, himself an experienced sailor, shipwrecked in or about *l'an trentième de son âge,* like the young Pound in the first part of *Hugh Selwyn Mauberley* or Mauberley himself later in that poem, memorialized only by an oar.

It has been thought that Eliot wrote *The Waste Land* in Switzerland while recovering from a breakdown. But much of it was written earlier, some in 1914 and some, if Conrad Aiken is to be believed, even before. A letter to John Quinn indicates that much of it was on paper in May 1921. The breakdown, or rather, the rest cure, did give Eliot enough time to fit the pieces together and add what was necessary. At the beginning of October 1921 he consulted a prominent neurologist, who advised three months away from remembering "the profit and loss" in Lloyds Bank. When the bank had agreed, Eliot went first to Margate and stayed for a month from October 11. There he reported with relief to Richard Aldington that his "nerves" came not from overwork but from an "aboulie" (Hamlet's and Prufrock's disease) "and emotional derangement which has been a lifelong affliction." But, whatever reassurance this diagnosis afforded, he resolved to consult Dr. Roger Vittoz, a psychiatrist in Lausanne. He rejoined Vivien and on November 18 went with her to Paris. It seems fairly certain that he discussed the poem at that time with Ezra Pound. In Lausanne, where he went by himself, Eliot worked on it and sent revisions to Pound and to Vivien. Some of the letters exchanged between him and Pound survive. By early January 1922 he was back in London, making final corrections. The poem was published in October.

The manuscript had its own history. In gratitude to John Quinn, the New York lawyer and patron of the arts, Eliot presented it to him. Quinn died in 1924, and most of his possessions were sold at auction; some, however, including the manuscript, were inherited by his sister. When the sister died, her daughter put many of Quinn's papers in storage. But in the early 1950's she searched among them and found the manuscript, which she then sold to the Berg Collection of the New York Public Library. The then curator enjoyed exercising seignorial rights over the collection, and kept secret the whereabouts of the manuscript. After his death its existence was divulged, and Valerie Eliot was persuaded to do her knowledgeable edition.

She did so the more readily, perhaps, because her husband had always hoped that the manuscript would turn up as evidence of Pound's critical genius. It is a classic document. No one will deny that it is weaker throughout than the final version. Pound comes off very well indeed; his importance is comparable to that of Louis Bouilhet in the history of composition of *Madame Bovary.* Yeats, who also sought and received Pound's help, described it to Lady Gregory: "To talk over a poem with him is like getting you to put a sentence into dialect. All becomes clear and natural." Pound could not be intimidated by pomposity, even Baudelairean pomposity:

> London, the swarming life you kill and breed,
> Huddled between the concrete and the sky;
> Responsive to the momentary need,
> Vibrates unconscious to its formal destiny.

Next to this he wrote "B-ll-S." (His comments appear in red ink on the printed transcription that is furnished along with photographs of the manuscript.) Pound was equally peremptory about a passage that Eliot seems to have cherished, perhaps because of childhood experiences in sailing. It was the depiction at the beginning of "Death by Water" of a long voyage, a modernizing and Americanizing of Ulysses' final voyage as given by Dante, but joined with sailing experiences of Eliot's youth:

> Kingfisher weather, with a light fair breeze,
> Full canvas, and the eight sails drawing well.
> We beat around the cape and laid our course
> From the Dry Salvages to the eastern banks.
> A porpoise snored upon the phosphorescent swell,
> A triton rang the final warning bell
> Astern, and the sea rolled, asleep.

From these lines Pound was willing to spare only

> with a light fair breeze
> We beat around the cape from the Dry Salvages.
> A porpoise snored on the swell.

All the rest was—seamanship and literature. It became clear that the whole passage might as well go, and Eliot asked humbly if he should delete Phlebas as well. But Pound was as eager to preserve the good as to expunge the bad: he insisted that Phlebas stay because of the earlier references to the drowned Phoenician sailor. With equal taste, he made almost no change in the last section of the poem, which Eliot always considered to be the best, perhaps because it led into his subsequent verse. It marked the resumption of almost continuous form.

Eliot did not bow to all his friend's revisions. Pound feared the references to London might sound like Blake, and objected specifically to the lines,

> To where Saint Mary Woolnoth kept the time,
> With a dead sound on the final stroke of nine.

Eliot wisely retained them, only changing "time" to "hours." Next to the passage,

"You gave me hyacinths first a year ago;
"They called me the hyacinth girl,"

Pound marked "Marianne," and evidently feared—though Mrs. Eliot's note indicates that he has now forgotten and denies it—that the use of quotation marks would look like an imitation of Marianne Moore. (He had warned Miss Moore of the equivalent danger of sounding like Eliot in a letter December 16, 1918.) But Eliot, for whom the moment in the Hyacinth garden had obsessional force—it was based on feelings, though not on a specific incident in his own life—made no change.

Essentially Pound could do for Eliot what Eliot could not do for himself. There was some reciprocity, not only in *Mauberley* but in the *Cantos*. When the first three of these appeared in *Poetry* in 1917, Eliot offered criticism which was followed by their being completely altered. It appears, from the revised versions, that he objected to the elaborate windup, and urged a more direct confrontation of the reader and the material. A similar theory is at work in Pound's changes in *The Waste Land*. Chiefly by excision, he enabled Eliot to tighten his form and get "an outline," as he wrote in a complimentary letter of January 24, 1922. The same letter berated himself for "always exuding my deformative secretions in my own stuff . . ." and for "going into nacre and objets d'art." Yet if this was necessity for Pound, he soon resolved to make a virtue of it, and perhaps partially in reaction to Eliot's form, he studied out means of loosening his own in the *Cantos*. The fragments which Eliot wished to shore and reconstitute Pound was willing to keep unchanged, and instead of mending consciousness, he allowed it to remain "disjunct" and its experiences to remain "intermittent." Fits and starts, "spots and dots," seemed to Pound to render reality much more closely than the outline to which he had helped his friend. He was later to feel that he had gone wrong, and made a botch instead of a work of art. Notwithstanding his doubts, the *Cantos*, with their violent upheaval of sequence and location, stand as a rival eminence to *The Waste Land* in modern verse.

Note

1. "If you don't like it you can get on with it
What you get married for if you don't want to have children"

The Waste Land Manuscript

Lyndall Gordon

The manuscript of *The Waste Land* was a hoard of fragments, accumulated slowly over seven and a half years. Only in the seventh year did the hoard assume the proportions of a major work. The earliest fragments, which go back to T. S. Eliot's last years as a student, show a different bias from the poem that emerged in the autumn and winter of 1921–22. It is curious to read *The Waste Land* in terms of the rather scrappy but emphatic vision from which it evolved and certain persistent notions that were edited or obscured only at the last moment. In order to trace the growth of *The Waste Land* through all the stages of its composition, I first grouped the fragments according to the different batches of paper Eliot used and then established a chronological order by means of a variety of clues, many of which were provided by Valerie Eliot's clear and well-annotated facsimile edition of the manuscript.[1]

At the age of twenty-six, when Eliot was still at Harvard and living in an Ash Street attic in Cambridge, Massachusetts, he wrote three visionary fragments (108–115) on the same quadruled paper, punched for filing.[2] All three are concerned with revelation and its aftermath: the attractions and problems of "turning" or conversion. Two fragments, "After the turning" and "So through the evening," foreshadow the climactic scene in the completed *Waste Land,* the dangerous initiating journey to the deserted chapel in the mountains. In the third, a voice speaks to Eliot, infusing him with divine power: "I am the Resurrection and the Life . . . ." It is easy to dismiss these earliest fragments in the manuscript as inelegant scraps Eliot sensibly discarded, but together they announce a persistent mood. In "Ash Wednesday" Eliot refers again to his "turning" towards the religious life. Other visionary, introspective poems of the 'twenties—"Doris's Dream Songs," "The Hollow Men"—seem to move so naturally out of the fragments of 1914 that, in retrospect, the witty, satiric poems Eliot wrote between 1917 and 1919 seem like a deliberate digression in his career.

Years later, Eliot told friends that he had a personal upheaval after writing "Prufrock" (1911) which altered his rather Jamesian sensibility. Eliot wrote little in the years after "Prufrock"; but a sudden batch of poems in

Reprinted with permission from *American Literature* 45 (January 1974): 557–70. Copyright 1974 by Duke University Press.

1914, including the visionary *Waste Land* fragments, suggests that the upheaval had a religious focus. In "The Burnt Dancer," "The Love Song of Saint Sebastian," "Oh little voices," and "The Little Passion: From 'An Agony in a Garret' " Eliot explores his fascination with martyrdom and the cross at the end of the path, and debates the reality of the material world.[3] None of these poems is included in *The Waste Land* manuscript but they presage *Waste Land* material. A moth's expiatory ordeal by fire and a lover's self-inflicted penance foreshadow the ordeals or Narcissus and the seducer. A withered man who has lost his spiritual energy and direction has obvious affinities with Gerontion and the shadowy hero of the completed *Waste Land.*

In the summer of 1914, Eliot moved to England and, a few months later, wrote "The Death of Saint Narcissus" while a student of philosophy at Merton College, Oxford. He wrote his first draft on paper with the watermark "Excelsior Fine British Make" (90–93), the same paper he used for "Mr. Apollinax." Both poems must have been written by January, 1915, for, on February 2, Eliot alluded to them in a letter to Pound.[4] Pound submitted the second draft (94–97) to *Poetry* in August, 1915, while Eliot was briefly in America. Evidently, this was against Eliot's wishes—he might have considered the poem too confessional—for, when he returned to London, he withdrew it from publication. With "The Death of Saint Narcissus" Eliot first introduces the desert with its hot sand and rock, ultimately glimpsed in part I and developed at length in part V of the completed *Waste Land.* Narcissus, carried away by his own beauty and his willingness to be transformed, deliberately seeks out the desert as the proper spot for a religious drama. He goes to become "a dancer to God," but to his dismay discovers no divine light, only his own flaws—his self-enthrallment, his indifference to others, his masochistic delight in the burning arrows. The ordeal leaves him dry and stained, with the taste of death in his mouth. It is crucial, I think, to see *The Waste Land,* indeed all of Eliot's subsequent work, in the context of this martyr's tale, the story of an unsuccessful saint.

No more fragments were written until some time after Eliot's marriage, in June, 1915, to an Englishwoman, Vivien Haigh-Wood. She was bright and literate and enthusiastic about her husband's poetry, but her nervous hysteria and her physical frailty—compounded by insomnia and dependence on sedatives—made her a frightening burden. Within a few months of their immediately unhappy marriage she fell seriously ill. In January, 1916, Eliot wrote to his Harvard friend Conrad Aiken that he was not writing, but had "*lived* through material for a score of long poems in the last six months" (x).

Between 1916 and 1919 Eliot wrote another batch of fragments, introducing new themes—the threatening wife, the metropolitan environment, random sexual desire. "The Death of the Duchess" (104–107) describes a couple trapped in a bedroom and unable to communicate their separate needs.[5] The wife urges her emotional claims only through the insistent strokes of her hairbrush. The husband silently longs to escape through the door. The tile suggests a sequel to "The Death of Saint Narcissus": God denies the would-be saint his chosen role, and the husband denies his wife. It is probable Eliot showed "The Death of the Duchess" to Pound by 1918. There is a joking reference, among Pound's comments on "Whispers of Immortality," to a Duchess who is outraged by Grishkin's animality.[6] The poem is the first of *The Waste Land* fragments in typescript: Eliot used his own typewriter (call it A), which he had brought with him from Harvard.[7]

"Elegy" is another confession of the emotional tensions of Eliot's first marriage (116–17).[8] Again, the "Poe-bride" is a complex of victim and demon, and again the husband would be rid of her. "Elegy," in turn, is linked with "The river sweats" (48–53), which became the finale of part III or the completed *Waste Land*. In both pieces, religious emotions are associated with remorse for a terrible wrong done to a woman or womankind. In each, sexual guilt precedes purgatorial pain. Eliot believed he might hold to the visionary power promised in "I am the Resurrection" only if the flesh were purged, burnt away by that refining fire he so often invoked. The raining flames in "The Death of Saint Narcissus" are one attempt to punish the flesh. They are followed, in "Elegy," by "God in a rolling ball of fire," and by the burning agony which follows a seducer's promiscuity on the River Thames, at Moorgate, and on Margate sands:

> Burning burning burning burning
> O Lord though pluckest me out
> O Lord thou pluckest
> burning

"Elegy" and "The river sweats" belong with a group of fragments written on small notepad sheets with an "Hieratica Bond" watermark. On the verso of "Elegy" Eliot wrote "Dirge," a fantasy of Bleistein's frightful disembodiment under the sea (118–19). The theme of death by water, like the death by fire of Narcissus and the seducer, is a drastic means of eliminating an unwanted identity. There is a similar drowning scene, involving the disembodiment and transformation of a Phoenician sailor, in "Dans le Restaurant" (1918), which was later translated with alterations and added to *The Waste Land*.[9]

It is impossible, so far, to date the Hieratica cluster exactly, but 1918 seems a reasonable guess. The earliest estimate would be the spring of 1917 when Eliot began his career as a bank clerk in the City, for there are two other Hieratica fragments clearly associated with that experience. "O City City" (36–37) reports Eliot's impression of the Billingsgate fishmarket, near Lloyd's Bank, and the white and gold Anglican church on Lower Thames Street, St. Magnus the Martyr, which he used to visit during lunch hour.[10] I think the second fragment, "London" (36–37), provides one organizing idea for *The Waste Land,* and it is rather a pity it is cut from the final draft. Briefly,

Eliot regards the swarming, ugly metropolis from the point of view of a seer haunted by intuitions of ideal possibilities. He envisions phatasmal gnomes burrowing in brick and steel and men bound upon the meaningless wheel of fortune, yet about this hellish scene there curls an "ideal meaning." In the revised version (30), Eliot explicitly contrasts the city of men with the City of God.

By 1919 Eliot had amassed a substantial hoard of private visions, fantasies, and ordeals. The earlier fragments are timeless and unlocalized; the later ones alight occasionally on specific sites of London that Eliot knew well—suburban Hampstead, where he would have visited his parents-in-law, the City, and the Thames.

The turning point between a hoard of fragments and a unified poem comes about through "Gerontion" (May, 1919). Eliot did not include "Gerontion" in the manuscript and I shall not discuss it here except to say that it introduces several new organizing ideas: the character of a religious candidate who has lost his passion, the private crisis against the backdrop of historical decline, the identification of spiritual desert and familiar urban waste.[11] Eliot saw "Gerontion" as a prelude to *The Waste Land,* but in the end submitted to Pound's advice to exclude it. Towards the end of 1919 Eliot wrote to his New York benefactor John Quinn and to his mother in Boston that he wished to write a long poem he had had in mind for some time (xvii–xviii).

Like Gerontion desperately awaiting a sign, the speaker of "Song," the next new fragment, published in April, 1921, is "waiting a touch a breath" (98–99).[12] "Song" returns to the theme of the 1914 fragments, the torment of living between two worlds. In May, Eliot wrote again to John Quinn that he had a "long poem" in mind and "partly on paper" which he wished to finish (p. xxi). There is no other evidence, as yet, that Eliot wrote anything more that spring, so I assume what was "on paper" was the old hoard of fragments.[13] The "poem" at this stage was still a personal record. Although the ground of Eliot's ordeal shifts—sometimes the domestic scene, sometimes the divine visitation, sometimes the imaginary trial by fire or water—he is always present, blighted and skeptical, hovering between the remote role of a religious candidate and a more immedaite despair.

In September, 1921, Eliot became increasingly "shaky" and was given three months' sick leave from Lloyd's Bank. On October 12 he went to Margate for rest and treatment, and ten days later moved to the Albemarle Hotel. At the Albemarle he at last had the solitude and leisure he had craved for so many years. It seems likely that it was during his three weeks there that he put together a first rudimentary draft of *The Waste Land.* Eliot ironically attached to the manuscript his hotel bill for the period October 22 to November 12. The first draft cost him approximately £16. The first week he indulged himself in the "white room." The next two weeks he spent rather more frugally in a modest room *en pension.*

Using an alternative typewriter (B), which he brought with him, and yellowish paper with a "Verona" watermark, Eliot typed his title page with what he called a "somewhat elucidative" epigraph from *Heart of Darkness:*

> Did he live his life again in every detail
> of desire, temptation, and surrender during
> the supreme moment of complete knowledge?
> He cried in a whisper at some image, at
> some vision,—he cried out twice, a cry
> that was no more than a breath—
> "The horror! The horror!"[14]

Eliot also typed two new pieces, a short lyric, "Exequy" (100–101), and, in duplicate, a larger episodic section (22–23, 26–27, 30–35, 38–47) which combines the old City and Thames fragments with satiric accounts of unappealing Londoners: Fresca, a pampered intellectual woman, Mr. Eugenides, an insinuating merchant, a wanton typist and her lover, the clerk. Eliot called the section "The Fire Sermon" because he planned to contrast these worldy types with the seducer who sacrifices his lust to purgatorial flames. As the seducer turns his back on women he recalls St. Augustine's early years, his cauldron of unholy loves, and the Buddha's fire sermon, when he urged his priests to conceive an aversion for all the impressions of the senses, to forget this world, and to live the holy life.

   Possibly, Eliot also wrote at Margate an unpreserved first draft of "Death by Water." The sea might have reminded him of his boyhood heroes, the hardy fishermen of Gloucester, Massachusetts—men who were "inhuman, clean and dignified." In the preserved fair copy Eliot identifies with the fisherman's bravado when his schooner crashes into an iceberg. He admires the fisherman's calm acceptance of personal disaster ("And if *Another* knows I know I know not"). He remembers Phlebas the sailor and his strange transformations under the sea.

   What did the Albermarle draft look like? I assume all the early fragments like "Elegy" and "I am the Resurrection" were part of the poem when it took shape at this stage, since Eliot would otherwise have had little reason to include them in the manuscript he later sent Quinn. It is impossible to guess the order of the fragments, but the issues are clear. For the most part, *The Waste Land* seems to have been originally a dirge for aspects of Eliot's identity that he had lost. Stripped of marital love in "Elegy" and "The Death of the Duchess," stripped of divine love in "The Death of Saint Narcissus," stripped of flesh in "Dirge" and "Death by Water," stripped of the right kind of fame in "Exequy," he feels fatally reduced. In "Exequy" he sees himself buried in suburbia, a would-be saint mistaken for a lover, and from his tomb there comes a great cry for sympathy: "SOVEGNA VOS AL TEMPS DE MON DOLOR" (Take thought in due time for my pain. *Purgatorio*, xxvi).

If *The Waste Land* was originally Eliot's personal dirge, it was also potentially a rebirth rite. The despair of the numerous "death" fragments is counterbalanced by the dim promise of the visionary fragments—"Song," "I am the Resurrection," "After the turning," and "So through the evening." Eliot presents his case against the material world with authority; his evidence for an alternative is flimsy. But the mere contemplation of its possibility is probably essential to his recovery. The Albemarle draft has a stronger autobiographical feeling. It stresses a suffering individual rather than a culture, an individual who is living in the dangerous space between two worlds and is unable to choose.

After Eliot left Margate, he spent a week with his wife in London, then left for a further period of recuperation in the sanatorium of Dr. Vittoz in Lausanne. While he was there Eliot shifted the emphasis of his poem from personal case history to cultural disease. Possibly, Pound influenced him in this direction. On November 18, Eliot passed through Paris and left his wife with the Pounds, who were then living there. It seems likely that Eliot showed his mentor the Albemarle draft. Pound called Eliot's next draft in Lausanne "the nineteen page version," which implies he had previously seen another. He also mentioned seeing the manuscript on more than one occasion when he wrote:

> If you must needs enquire
> Know diligent Reader
> That on each Occasion
> Ezra performed the caesarian Operation.[15]

The strongest evidence is Pound's markings of the "Verona" sheets and "Song." He marked these on two occasions: once in pencil, probably on November 18, once in ink, on Eliot's return from Lausanne early in January.[16] One wonders about Pound's verbal comments on the Albermarle draft. He must have criticized "The Death of the Duchess" because in January, after Eliot revised and expanded it, he said that "the bad nerves is O.K. as now led up to."[17] I think he also suggested that some fragments be cut because later, in the same January letter, he talked of the "remaining" superfluities at the end of the poem.

In Lausanne *The Waste Land* was greatly altered and began to take its final shape. Eliot cut "The Death of Saint Narcissus," except for a few lines, and wrote "The Burial of the Dead" (4–9) to take up the death-rebirth theme in a more general way. He cut "Elegy" and rewrote "The Death of the Duchess" as part of a larger section (10–21) where his account of his own marriage is less conspicuous between a set piece on the luxurious woman and an account of a snarling lower-class marriage. He reworked bits of "After the turning" and "So through the evening" in another new section, "What the

Thunder Said" (70–81), which takes up the theme of revelation. He kept the title page and "The Fire Sermon" and the long fisherman's ordeal. He saved "Dirge," "Exequy," and "Song," and put them at the end.

In short, the Lausanne draft removes Eliot's more autobiographical items and overlays private sorrows with an abundance of realistic contemporary scenes. If one person's experience is stressed, it is not because he is special but because he represents the weak human mass with its modest potential and meager opportunities. For the first time in his career Eliot takes his audience into his story and tries to write from the center of common cultural experience. At this point he toys with an odd title from Dickens: "He Do the Police in Different Voices." He begins to disperse the distinctive voice of the sufferer among the voices of a variety of standard cultural figures—the would-be playboy, the trapped husband, the adulteress, the resentful worker, the glib intellectual. Eliot's air of representativeness is frankly contrived, even mocking, for he never truly submerges his self. Nevertheless the new "representativeness" probably served to make the poem more popular than it would otherwise have been. Eliot still tried to keep his private search for salvation alive in "What the Thunder Said," and later told Bertrand Russell that this section alone justified the poem. Suddenly, at Lausanne, the pilgrim's journey of 1914 revived in his imagination with renewed urgency—the sunbaked twisting road, the bells and chanting voices, the revelation of a new world of reversed images. But the visionary element, so forthright in the earliest *Waste Land* fragments, is now depersonalized and even disguised. In place of the man with extraordinary powers there is now a "form" and, in a later draft, merely a bat. And instead of a voice saying plainly "I am the Resurrection," the thunder now rumbles obscure Sanskrit words.

Eliot probably took to Lausanne his own typewriter (A) and white "British Bond" typing paper, which he used for "The Burial of the Dead" and "A Game of Chess." Helen Gardner, in her essay *"The Waste Land:* Paris 1922," makes a strong case for the possibility that Eliot had no typewriter in Lausanne and that these sections were typed before he left London.[18] Grover Smith, however, points out that the name of the clairvoyant in "The Burial"—Sosostris—comes from Aldous Huxley's *Crome Yellow* and, since this was published only in November, 1921, it appears unlikely Eliot wrote the section before he was in Lausanne.[19] After Eliot finished "A Game of Chess" he kept the carbon and mailed the original typescript to his wife for her comments. Vivien Eliot wrote "wonderful wonderful" next to her husband's graphic description of the tormented couple. She also made several intelligent suggestions and comments and, on the verso of the second sheet, asked Eliot if she might have it for keeps: "Send me back this copy & let me have it" (15).

There is no doubt that in Lausanne Eliot wrote several pieces by hand on quadruled paper: "What the Thunder Said," fair copies of "Dirge" and

"Death by Water," and a rough draft of "Venus Anadyomene" (which was soon discarded along with the Fresca episode for which it was designed). Eliot used the same black ink for the two fair copies. It is hard to say why he did not type them. Perhaps Eliot wrote them at night when he would not have wished to disturb other patients by typing.[20]

The Lausanne draft consists of approximately twenty-two pages.[21] The first three sections—"The Burial of the Dead," "A Game of Chess," "The Fire Sermon"—review familiar urban life. In the second half of the poem the wandering hero moves into scenes remote from ordinary experience. His heroic expedition to the Grand Banks in "Death by Water," and his initiation near the deserted chapel in "What the Thunder Said" is followed by further ordeals in the three closing fragments of the semifinal draft, "Dirge," "Exequy," and "Song." These include his imaginative participation in Bleistein's "sea-change," his own purgatorial agony underground, and his nocturnal vigil for the divine "touch." In a sense these ordeals offer modes of release from the urban waste, and the presence of the sea in the second half of the poem suggests a new, quite different, arena.

Eliot again stopped in Paris on his way home early in January, 1922, and showed Pound his new draft. Pound cut the line "(Those are pearls that were his eyes. Look!)" from Mme. Sosostris's prophecy, whereupon Eliot—reluctant to let the transformation theme go—scribbled a new fragment on his "British Bond" paper (122–23). It elaborates on the fate of the drowned man. When all his gross flesh is washed away and the skeleton reduced to a sea-object, then pearls grow in his eye-sockets. And Eliot wonders whether then, at last, the spirit finds peace.

Pound looked critically at "Death by Water" and ordered Eliot to type it. He drew a thick line through the central "London" fragment in "The Fire Sermon," and cancelled references to churches, Michael Paternoster and St. Mary Woolnoth. He attacked the Fresca episode and Eliot cut it completely. On the verso Eliot wrote an alternative passage: "The river's tent is broken." It foretells the winter scene in London. The sky breaks into rain over the Thames, and the last leaves of autumn are washed away. An exile gloomily contemplates the forbidding city to which he must return.

Pound signified, with a green crayon, his approval of two pieces, the seducer's exploits (on which he wrote "OK echt") and the pilgrim's journey ("OK"). Either Pound or Eliot immediately typed a fair copy of "What the Thunder Said," using Pound's typewriter and double foolscap.

When Eliot returned to London he probably left this manuscript, or part of it, in Paris so that Pound might consider it further. References to minor details in their subsequent correspondence suggest that, later in January, Pound marked and mailed to Eliot an unpreserved copy of "The river's tent is broken," Vivien's typescript of "A Game of Chess" (Pound marked this a second time), and the typescript of "Death by Water," which Pound cut heavily. When Eliot offered the poem to the *Dial*, on January 20, he said it had been three times through the sieve by Pound and himself and should soon be in its final form.[22] On January 24 and a little later, Eliot got two letters from Pound with further suggestions.[23] Pound wrote that the Conrad epigraph was not "weighty enough," and Eliot dropped it. But the main force of the letters was aimed at abolishing the three final lyrics with their themes of baptismal death to the world, purgatory, and mystical experience. Pound advised Eliot repeatedly "to abolish 'em altogether." "One test," he wrote, "is whether anything would be lacking if the last three were omitted. I don't think it would. . . . The thing now runs from 'April' to 'shantih' without a break. . . . Don't try to bust all records by prolonging it three pages further." Eliot replied that he accepted the criticism "so far as understood." The "superfluities" were cut.

In the semifinal draft the cultural statement in the first half of the poem is more or less balanced by the visionary speculation in the second half. The effect of Pound's last suggestions is to curtail the second half so that cultural statement comes to dominate the poem.

After Eliot returned to London he complained to Pound that he was sick, miserable, and "excessively depressed."[24] That winter he used to meet Conrad Aiken regularly for lunch, and would confess to him—over rump steak at a pub in Cannon Street—how he would come home from work, sharpen his pencil, and then be unable to write. Yet there seemed material there, waiting. He later wrote to his mother that he had in mind a sequel to *The Waste Land,* a more optimistic poem about coming to the grail. More than anything, he wanted to give the religious ordeal back to his generation, and the dimensions of a universe in which such an ordeal belonged. In the winter of 1922 he carried Dante everywhere with him in his pocket—Dante who had surveyed that universe and written his autobiography in colossal cipher.

Eliot seemed to remain dissatisfied even after the poem was published in the *Criterion* and *Dial* in mid-October, 1922. He said *The Waste Land* seemed like something he had written long before which could no longer speak for him. "My present ideas are very different," he told Gilbert Seldes, a *Dial* editor. Quinn's reaction to the manuscript was not reassuring: "I have noted the evidence of Pound's criticisms on the poem," he wrote. "Personally I should not have cut out some of the parts that Pound advised you to cut out" (xxvi). During the 'twenties Eliot's uneasiness was confirmed by misreadings of *The Waste Land.* He was irritated to be hailed as the spokesman for that generation because, when it fastened so hungrily on his disillusion and erudition, it ignored the fact that they were subsidiary to a religious vision.

The manuscript of *The Waste Land* shows that at first Eliot made the religious vision an unmistakable priority, but that the poem underwent a radical change after he showed it to Pound. *The Waste Land* began as the purely personal record of a man who saw himself as a potential candidate for a religious life but was constrained by his own nature and distracted by domestic claims. Eliot was writing a kind of spiritual autobiography in an age that was not cordial to the genre. He decided he could reach his audience only by indirection. Like many autobiographers he compelled attention by presenting himself as a child of the times, with the result that readers overlooked the would-be saint. Eliot's strategy failed by its success, for the strategy took over the poem, and he was forced to rewrite his saint's life in more explicit terms in "Ash Wednesday" and *Four Quartets*.[25]

Notes

1. T. S. Eliot, *The Waste Land: A Facsimile and Transcript of the Original Drafts,* ed. Valerie Eliot (New York: Harcourt, 1971). The page numbers in the text refer to this edition. I should like to thank the Berg Collection, New York Public Library, for making available the original manuscript of *The Waste Land* and Eliot's "Poems," a notebook and folder of early holograph and typescript poems.

2. The paper has a "Linen Ledger" watermark (used by several paper companies in America). Valerie Eliot dates the handwriting "1914 or even earlier" (p. 130).

3. "Poems" (Berg Coll., NYPL), "The Burnt Dancer" (dated by Eliot: June, 1914), "Oh little voices," and "Saint Sebastian" were written before Eliot left America. Eliot used American paper with a "Marcus Wards" watermark. "The Little Passion" is the last poem copied into Eliot's notebook which he abandoned soon after his arrival in England in August, 1914.

4. "I understand that Priapism, Narcissism etc are not approved of . . . ." The letter is quoted in *Ezra Pound: Perspectives,* ed. Noel Stock (Chicago, 1965), pp. 110–11. Valerie Eliot reports (p. 129) that Eliot could not remember the date of "Narcissus," but it may have been early in 1915.

5. It might be possible to be more specific about the date by matching the paper with that of non-*Waste Land* manuscripts but, in the absence of other clues, the paper evidence is inconclusive. The paper matches that of an unpublished review (1916) of H.D.'s translation of choruses from *Iphegenia in Aulis* (Berg Coll.). It also matches a draft of "Gerontion," which Eliot sent to John Rodker in the summer of 1919 (David Schwab Coll., University of Virginia Library, Charlottesville). In a letter to Rodker (July 9, 1919) Eliot mentioned the prospect of another poem, about the same length as "Gerontion"; this might be "The Death of the Duchess."

6. "Poems," Berg Coll., NYPL.

7. According to Eliot, there were never any handwritten drafts of the sections in typescript, only scattered lines (letter to Quinn, Sept. 21, 1922, John Quinn Coll., Manuscript Division, NYPL). Eliot used two typewriters. The differences between them are identified by Hugh Kenner, "The Urban Apocalypse," *Eliot in His Time,* ed. A Walton Litz (Princeton, N.J., 1973), pp. 23–49. See also Grover Smith, "The Making of *The Waste Land,*" *Mosaic,* VI (Fall, 1972), 127–141. Eliot's early manuscripts and letters indicate that typewriter A was the one he brought from Boston. "The Love Song of Saint Sebastian," written at Harvard, was typed on A, as well as all Eliot's early poems through "Gerontion." A was also used for letters to Leonard Woolf, John Rodker, and John Quinn. It seems, however, Eliot had very easy access to an alternative typewriter B, which he used for letters to Virginia Woolf, for later letters to Quinn, for some *Waste Land* fragments, and for the envelope of the manuscript he finally sent Quinn. B might be an office typewriter: in one B letter to Quinn, Eliot mentions that it was dictated.

8. The form of "Elegy" suggests that it was written during Eliot's quatrain period (1917–19).

9. Mrs. Eliot dated "Dirge" 1921 (p. 131), but the first draft on Hieratica paper might have been much earlier. The theme of death by water and the name Bleistein appear in poems written in 1918 and 1919. In 1921 Eliot made a fair copy of "Dirge" on "British Bond" paper.

10. "O City City" was retained and became ll.259–265 in the final draft of *The Waste Land*.

11. At the same time as Eliot wrote "Gerontion" he reviewed *The Education of Henry Adams* for the *Athenaeum*. Eliot's use of an exemplary figure against the backdrop of historical decline perhaps owes something to Adams's mode of autobiography.

12. "Song to the Opherian" was published under the pseudonym Gus Krutsch in *The Tyro* (April, 1921). Eliot used the A typewriter and "British Bond" paper for the copy he retained for *The Waste Land*.

13. In May, Eliot also wrote a London Letter to the *Dial* which reverberates with *données* for *The Waste Land*. See A. Walton Litz, "*The Waste Land* Fifty Years After," *Eliot in His Time*, pp. 13–15.

14. Eliot eventually deleted this epigraph at Pound's suggestion in a letter written on January 24, 1922. See *Selected Letters of Ezra Pound*, ed. D. D. Paige (New York, 1971), pp. 169–170. (Paige dated this letter Dec. 24, 1921. It has been authoritatively redated by Hugh Kenner in *Eliot in His Time*, p. 44.)

15. Included in letter to Eliot (Jan. 24, 1922), ibid., p. 170.

16. The carbon copy, with Pound's marginalia in pencil, was clearly shown first. Eliot then revised the original typescript in accordance with Pound's suggestions before submitting it for further corrections.

17. To Eliot (Jan. 24, 1922), *Selected Letters*, p. 169.

18. *Eliot in His Time*, pp. 67–94.

19. "The Making of *The Waste Land*," *Mosaic*, VI (Fall, 1972), 132. It is of course possible that Huxley's manuscript was circulated among his friends and that Eliot read it prior to publication.

20. Robert Sencourt says that Eliot left the sanatorium and completed his writing at Chardonne above Vevey, but he does not cite the source of this information. See *T. S. Eliot: A Memoir* (New York, 1971), p. 105. If this is true, it may explain why Eliot did not use a typewriter for his fair copies of "Dirge" and "Death by Water."

21. Hugh Kenner and Grover Smith have suggested that there was another (now missing) typescript of *The Waste Land*, which Eliot mailed to Pound after his return to London in January, 1922. Pound wrote to Eliot on January 24 that the manuscript was now nineteen pages long. My own supposition is that the "19 pages" could easily apply to the present manuscript, to the twenty-two page Lausanne version, completed in Paris, minus the three final lyrics which, in the same letter, Pound advised Eliot to discard. The Lausanne draft consisted of:

"The Burial of the Dead" (first page cut)	2	pages
"A Game of Chess"	3	
"The Fire Sermon" (Fresca, Venus discarded)	3–4	
"The river sweats" (approved)	3	
"Death by Water" (under consideration)	4	
"What the Thunder Said"	4	
	19–20	
plus "Dirge," "Exequy," "Song" at end	3	
	22–23	

Further evidence against a missing manuscript is a letter Eliot wrote to Quinn, in September, 1922, assuring him that this manuscript—which he sent Quinn as a gift—

contained the "only copies" of discarded portions (John Quinn Coll., Manuscript Division, NYPL).

22. The letter is paraphrased by Nicholas Joost, *Scofield Thayer and "The Dial"* (Carbondale, Ill., 1964), p. 159.

23. *Selected Letters,* pp. 169–170, 171–172.

24. Letter to Pound (Jan., 1922), ibid., pp. 170–171.

25. Acknowledgment: I should like to thank A. Walton Litz and Sacvan Bercovitch for their help in preparing this article.

[From *Marxism and Literary Criticism*]

TERRY EAGLETON

Let us take a concrete literary example. A "vulgar Marxist" case about T. S. Eliot's *The Waste Land* might be that the poem is directly determined by ideological and economic factors—by the spiritual emptiness and exhaustion of bourgeois ideology which springs from that crisis of imperialist capitalism known as the First World War. This is to explain the poem as an immediate "reflection" of those conditions; but it clearly fails to take into account a whole series of "levels" which "mediate" between the text itself and capitalist economy. It says nothing, for instance, about the social situation of Eliot himself—a writer living an ambiguous relationship with English society, as an "aristocratic" American expatriate who became a glorified City clerk and yet identified deeply with the conservative-traditionalist, rather than bourgeois-commercialist, elements of English ideology. It says nothing about that ideology's more general forms—nothing of its structure, content, internal complexity, and how all these are produced by the extremely complex class relations of English society at the time. It is silent about the form and language of *The Waste Land*—about why Eliot, despite his extreme political conservatism, was an *avant-garde* poet who selected certain "progressive" experimental techniques from the history of literary forms available to him, and on what ideological basis he did this. We learn nothing from this approach about the social conditions which gave rise at the time to certain forms of "spirituality," part-Christian, part-Buddhist, which the poem draws on; or of what role a certain kind of bourgeois anthropology (Frazer) and bourgeois philosophy (F. H. Bradley's idealism) used by the poem fulfilled in the ideological formation of the period. We are unilluminated about Eliot's social position as an artist, part of a self-consciously erudite, experimental elite with particular modes of publication (the small press, the little magazine) at their disposal; or about the kind of audience which that implied, and its effect on the poem's styles and devices. We remain ignorant about the relation between the poem and the aesthetic theories associated with it—of what role that aesthetic plays in the ideology of the time, and how it shapes the construction of the poem itself.

Any complete understanding of *The Waste Land* would need to take

Reprinted from *Marxism and Literary Criticism* by Terry Eagleton, 14–17, with permission from the University of California Press, © 1976 Terry Eagleton.

these (and other) factors into account. It is not a matter of *reducing* the poem to the state of contemporary capitalism; but neither is it a matter of introducing so many judicious complications that anything as crude as capitalism may to all intents and purposes be forgotten. On the contrary: all of the elements I have enumerated (the author's class position, ideological forms and their relation to literary forms, "spirituality" and philosophy, techniques of literary production, aesthetic theory) are directly relevant to the base/superstructure model. What Marxist criticism looks for is the unique *conjuncture* of these elements which we know as *The Waste Land*. No one of these elements can be conflated with another: each has its own relative independence. *The Waste Land* can indeed be explained as a poem which springs from a crisis of bourgeois ideology, but it has no simple correspondence with that crisis or with the political and economic conditions which produced it. (As a poem, it does not of course *know itself* as a product of a particular ideological crisis, for if it did it would cease to exist. It needs to translate that crisis into "universal" terms—to grasp it as part of an unchanging human condition, shared alike by ancient Egyptians and modern man.) *The Waste Land's* relation to the real history of its time, then, is highly *mediated;* and in this it is like all works of art.

[From *T. S. Eliot's Negative Way*]

ELOISE KNAPP HAY

The contemplation of the horrid or sordid or disgusting, by an artist, is the necessary and negative aspect of the impulse toward the pursuit of beauty. But not all succeed as did Dante in expressing the complete scale from negative to positive. The negative is the more importunate.

—"Dante," 1920

INTRODUCTION

The single volume that makes up the "complete poems and plays" of T. S. Eliot presents an enormous challenge to critical theory. My proposal is that we consider this challenge under two headings, both signaled by the poetic phrase "the negative way," which James Johnson Sweeney taught us to take as the key to Eliot's culminating poem, *Four Quartets*. In my rereadings of Eliot's poems and plays, this phrase has come to have as much importance for the early works as for the late ones, though in very different senses. The two theoretical problems implicit in "the negative way" are of course the problem of *negativity* and the problem of *the way* (as path, direction, mode, method, and finally as ultimate goal). "The negative way" is an oxymoron. Is all going or making, arriving or finding—everything implicit in "way"—nullified when the word is prefixed by "negative"? Eliot's early poems focused on this tension, long before he made the Christian *via negativa* the matrix of his late poems and plays. Sometimes the early poems take both images together, as when Prufrock summons us to go a certain way with him and then takes us nowhere. Sometimes the two images of void and path are separated, as when "Gerontion," with its rhythmic denials, projects stasis with no direction but that of a "gull against the wind," or when "Lune de Miel" traces a honeymoon tour without a single negative, yet charts the perfect vacancy of the lovers' vacation. My interest has been to pursue the scope and meanings of these recurring themes, linguistically and tropologically, as developing patterns that reveal a striking design in Eliot's entire poetic corpus.

It was only in the middle of his career that Eliot arrived at the convic-

Reprinted from *T. S. Eliot's Negative Way* (Cambridge, Mass.: Harvard University Press, 1982).

tion that "the way up and the way down are the same" (as his second epigraph quoting Heraclitus reads in *Four Quartets*) and that Heraclitus's vision of cosmic order in chaos was an appropriate metaphor for the Christian "way." Tempting as it may be to read the early poems in this light, nothing could be more damaging to our understanding. Too many readings, even some of the best, have taken Eliot's early volumes and *The Waste Land* as poems already leading through death to the promise of new life—written as if under the sign of St. Augustine's words in the *Confessions* (IV, 19): "Descend that ye may ascend." Each successive reading has convinced me, to the contrary, that Eliot's poems before "Ash-Wednesday" have the opposite matrix within them. "Ascend that ye may descend" is a better interpretant of his early poetry.

Exploration of the void, either as a stasis or as a "way," was already a project of Eliot's during his philosophical studies and in his first poetry notebook, before he began to publish professionally, as Lyndall Gordon has recently shown. His resolute turn from Western forms of "affirmative" religions to the study of Buddhism and primitive religions paralleled philosophical movements in the first two decades of the twentieth century which also were probing the uses of negation.

Critics have often observed that American writers before Eliot were disposed, by the very conditions of being American, to write "deconstructively" or negatively. J. Hillis Miller considers the tendency a mark of the Protestant heritage, inherited from the Old Testament's assailing of human constructs and institutions. Terence Martin cites examples of nineteenth-century novelists who prided themselves on negative stances as a badge of Americanism. . . .

Another force directing Eliot's thought toward negativity was the German philosophical tradition as it influenced his Harvard studies (and as it had influenced the American literary heritage beginning with Emerson). Though it has not been part of my task to consider Eliot's relation to other writers in detail, a striking parallel can be found between his work and that of at least one of his contemporaries trained in this tradition. Martin Heidegger, born in Germany in 1899, believed that German Idealism was the only modern philosophy (1) to see Being as always a Transcendental and (2) to dare thinking of negation as comprehended in Being.[1] Heidegger very early gave up his commitment to Catholic theology, because he rejected a metaphysics claiming to grasp positive concepts of Being, and turned toward a metaphysical viewpoint that he described as the experience of "Being in Nothing."[2] Describing the "dread" or "anxiety" occasioned by the "withdrawal of Being" felt at various periods of history, including our own, he noted that the phenomenon of anxiety in the face of Nothingness had first become a central concern among Christian theologians, especially St. Augustine, Luther, Pascal, and Kierkegaard. Both Eliot and Heidegger began their major work listening to what Heidegger called "the soundless voice which attunes us to the horrors of the abyss [of Nothing]."[3] Like Eliot, too, Heidegger fastened on images of "the way" as the clearest expression of human experience in time. In 1959 Heidegger wrote, "I have abandoned an earlier standpoint, not so that I might adopt a different one in its place, but because even that earlier standpoint was a halting place in a thinking that is on its way. The way is what is enduring in thought."[4] But unlike Jean-Paul Sartre, a later prominent philosopher of Being and Nothingness, both Eliot and Heidegger declared that the philosophy of Humanism (man-centeredness) is not only a failure "to inquire into the relation of Being to man but is even a hindrance in the way of such inquiry," as Heidegger said in his 1946 "Letter on 'Humanism.' "[5] Eliot's view was already established in his essay "The Humanism of Irving Babbitt" in 1927. In "Burnt Norton," V, he speaks of love experienced in time as "Caught . . . / Between un-being and being," thus finding its center only in relation to another (nonhuman) center.

Heidegger differed from Eliot, however, in severely refusing to identify this Being with any name given to it by any church, preferring "now to be silent about God in the sphere of thinking."[6] While the movement of Eliot's thought was away from Unitarianism and philosophy to Catholicism and poetry, Heidegger's was away from Catholicism to a philosophy that deferred to poetry in search of expression: "To sing, truly to say worldly existence . . . means: to belong to the precinct of beings themselves. This precinct, as the very nature of language, is Being itself. To sing the song means to be present in what is present itself. It means: *Dasein,* existence."[7]

Eliot, both early and late, rejected such tendencies, as he found them in Shelley and Matthew Arnold, to make poetry a substitute for religion. His relinquishing of philosophy for poetry was nevertheless a step along the same negative way in thought expressed by Heidegger. The pure presence that Eliot described for the first time in "Marina" in 1930 exactly coincides with a statement Heidegger made in 1946 on the same subject. Eliot's Pericles asks:

> What is this face, less clear and clearer
> The pulse in the arm, less strong and stronger—
> Given or lent? more distant than stars and nearer than the eye.
>
> Whispers and small laughter betwen leaves and hurrying feet
> Under sleep, where all the waters meet

"Being," says Heidegger, "is farther away than all that is, and nevertheless is nearer to man than any thing, whether it be a rock, an animal, a work of art, a machine, an angel, or God. Being is the nearest and yet the nearest is what remains remotest from man."[8]

If Heidegger is right, the philosophical negatives that Eliot studied as a student form a separate tradition from the mystical "way" found in the Pseudo-Dionysius and the Christian mystics. We should therefore defer consideration of the mystical strain in Eliot's poetry till we meet it in *Four Quartets* and the plays, beginning with *Murder in the Cathedral*. Since Eliot's distrust of mysticism was evident in his essays (as well as in his poems on pathological saints) before 1927, I have maintained a neutral (nonreligious) use of the phrase "negative way" before discussing the later works. This neutral usage seems warranted by the prominence of the image long before he gives it a Christian emphasis in the poems. Heidegger's insistence on such a nonmystical neutral interpretation to the end of *his* life seems clear. His discussions of mankind's "waymaking" remind us that Eliot's image of "exploration" has the widest, least sectarian, basis. Thus at the end of "Little Gidding" (1942) Eliot writes:

> With the drawing of this Love and the voice of this Calling

> We shall not cease from exploration
> And the end of all our exploring
> Will be to arrive where we started
> And know the place for the first time.

And in 1946 Heidegger, answering the question "What Are Poets For?," writes:

> The venture sets free what is ventured, in such a way indeed that it sets free what is flung free into nothing other than a drawing toward the center. Drawing this way, the venture ever and always brings the ventured toward itself in this drawing. . . . The gravity of the pure forces, the unheard-of center, the pure draft, the whole draft, full Nature, Life, the venture—they are the same.

[Heidegger] seems further to echo Eliot's thought in "Language" (1950) when [he] says, "We do not aim at advancing further. All that we want is just really to get where we already are."[9]

Philosophy rather than theology directed Eliot's first steps along the negative way, and we should be wary of matching the design of his poetry with Dante's, as many readers have done. Ever since Douglas Bush spoke poetically, at the Harvard memorial service for Eliot, of *The Waste Land*, "Ash-Wednesday," and *Four Quartets* as Eliot's *Inferno*, *Purgatorio*, and *Paradiso*,[10] readers have hunted in his poetry for counterparts to Dante's descent and ascent in the *Commedia*, despite the anomalies this view creates in reading the poems before "The Hollow Men." If Eliot had been retracing Dante's design in the *Commedia*, descending into Hell inspired by a glimpse of the earthly Paradise and with a classical humanist (Virgil) for a guide, why did his *Poems* of 1920 level broadsides against the Christian legacy of Dante, and not merely against the degradations of that legacy?

Reading these poems, one may question Lyndall Gordon's conclusion that they reflect a "dream of sainthood," implicit from the earliest period.[11] If any such dream can be found reflected in the poems before 1925, it was pure nightmare. Gordon cogently argues that the extraordinary blasphemies and obscenities found in many of the early poems are examples of the "partial belief" that Eliot attributed to Baudelaire. But the argument loses some of its force when we consider that Eliot's recurrent statements on blasphemy— in 1928, 1931, and 1933—all came in the years soon after his conversion. Before that, his poems on neurotic saints and poems like "Mr. Eliot's Sunday Morning Service" testify to a powerful resistance to Christian belief, and indeed mercilessly ridicule such belief. Though he wrote in defense of preserving London churches before 1927, such an effort was hardly more in the way of Christian commitment than his support of Charles Maurras and the Action Française.[12] Eliot's essays on these subjects show him subscribing to social, political, and aesthetic programs without spiritual engagement. In fact, the papal condemnation of the Action Française in 1926—because the movement had shown itself to be politically rather than spiritually motivated— exactly coincided with the change on Eliot's own part from a spiritually uncommitted stand on Christianity to one of spiritual assent. At this point, as I shall hope to show, the contradiction between his defensive prose (defending the Christian *tradition*) and his offensive poetry (satirizing the Christian tradition) was closed. At this point he could say, as he did in 1933, "that in one's prose reflections one may be legitimately occupied with ideals, whereas in the writing of verse one can only deal with actuality."[13]

. . . .

THE WASTE LAND'S ROADWAY TO NOWHERE

The Waste Land, Eliot's first long philosophical poem, can now be read simply as it was written, as a poem of radical doubt and negation, urging that every human desire be stilled except the desire for self-surrender, for restraint, and for peace. Compared with the longing expressed in later poems for the "eyes" and the "birth," the "coming" and "the Lady" (in "The Hollow Men," the Ariel poems, and "Ash-Wednesday"), the hope held out in *The Waste Land* is a negative one. Following Hugh Kenner's recommendation, we should lay to rest the persistent error of reading *The Waste Land* as a poem in which five motifs predominate: the nightmare journey, the Chapel, the Quester, the Grail Legend, and the Fisher King.[14] The motifs are indeed introduced, as Eliot's preliminary note to his text informs us, but if (as this note says) "the plan and a good deal of the incidental symbolism of the poem were suggested by Miss Jessie L. Weston's book on the Grail legend," the plan can only have been to question, and even to propose a life without hope for, a quest, or Chapel, or Grail in the modern waste land. The themes of interior prison and nightmare city—or the "urban apocalypse" elucidated by Kenner and Eleanor Cook—make much better sense when seen as furnishing the centripetal "plan" and "symbolism," especially when one follows Cook's discussion of the disintegration of all European cities after the First World War and the poem's culminating vision of a new Carthaginian collapse, imagined from the vantage point of India's holy men.[15] A passage canceled in the manuscript momentarily suggested that the ideal city, forever unrealizable on earth, might be found (as Plato thought) "in another world," but the reference was purely sardonic. Nowhere in the poem can one find convincing allusions to *any* existence in another world, much less to St. Augustine's vision of interpenetration between the City of God and the City of Man in *this* world.[16] How, then, can one take seriously attempts to find in the poem any such quest for eternal life as the Grail legend would have to provide if it were a continuous motif—even a sardonic one?

It seems that only since Eliot's death is it possible to read his life forward—understanding *The Waste Land* as it was written, without being deflected by our knowledge of the writer's later years. Before Eliot's death the tendency was to read the poem proleptically—as if reflecting the poems of the later period. This is how Cleanth Brooks, writing the first fully elucidative essay on *The Waste Land*, read it, stressing the Grail legends, the longing for new life, rather than the purely negative aspects of the theme. Thus Brooks interpreted the Sibyl's appeal for death at the beginning of the poem as exactly parallel to the Magus's appetite for death in the Ariel poems (the Magus's, of course, filled with the pain of knowing that Christ had subjected himself to weak mortality and not knowing yet the Resurrection).[17] To make the Sibyl and the Magus parallel was to read Eliot's development backward— perhaps an irresistible temptation when the pattern in his life was so little known and when (as then in 1939) Brooks was acquainted with the man at work on *Four Quartets*, who had recently produced the celebrated *Murder in the Cathedral*. It was also irresistible, in a culture still nominally Christian, to hope that *The Waste Land* was about a world in which God was not dead. But the poem was not about such a world.

Within ten years after finishing *The Waste Land*, Eliot recognized that the poem had made him into the leader of a new "way." His own words of 1931, however, require us to read the poem as having pushed this roadway through to its end—for him. It was no Grail quest. Those who followed him into it, and stayed on it, he said in "Thoughts After Lambeth," "are now pious pilgrims, cheerfully plodding the road from nowhere to nowhere." There could be no more decisive reference to the negative way he had followed till 1922, and also to the impasse where it ended.

A good reading of *The Waste Land* must begin, then, with recognition that while it expressed Eliot's own "way" at the time, it was not intended to lay down a way for others to follow. He did not expect that his prisonhouse would have corridors connecting with everyone else's. "I dislike the word 'generation' [he said in "Thoughts After Lambeth"], which has been a talisman for the last ten years; when I wrote a poem called *The Waste Land* some of the more approving critics said that I had expressed the 'disillusionment of a generation,' which is nonsense. I may have expressed for them their own illusion of being disillusioned, but that did not form part of my intention."[18] Dismay at finding his personal, interior journey (which he later called "rhythmic grumbling") converted into a superhighway seems to have been one of the main impulses toward his discovery of a new way after 1922.

If we listen attentively to the negations of *The Waste Land,* they tell us much about the poem that was missed when it was read from the affirmative point of view brought to it by its early defenders and admirers. Ironically, it was only its detractors—among them Eliot's friend Conrad Aiken—who acknowledged its deliberate vacuity and incoherence and the life-questioning theme of this first venture into "philosophical" poetry on Eliot's part. Aiken considered its incoherence a virtue because its subject was incoherence, but this was cool comfort either to himself or to Eliot, who was outraged by Aiken's opinion that the poem was "melancholy."[19] It was far from being a *sad* poem—like the nineteenth-century poems that Eliot had criticized precisely because of their wan melancholias, based as he said on their excesses of desire over the possibilities that life can afford.[20] Neither Aiken, who found the poem disappointing, nor I. A. Richards, who was exhilarated by its rejection of all "belief," spotted the poem's focus on negation as a philosophically meditated position.

. . . .

In Part II, "A Game of Chess," the presiding *revenant* relives one of his many lives as a tormented city-dweller, first as the upper-class husband of a neurotic wife, herself a reincarnation (the images reveal) of Dido, Cleopatra, Hérodias, and Emma Bovary. We have seen such passages before (in verses on Burbank, Bleistein, and Sweeney, for instance) written all in affirmatives but signifying lives that come to nothing. It is only when the truth comes out that the negatives again recur: " 'I never know what you are thinking. Think.' "And " 'What is the wind doing?' / Nothing again nothing. / 'Do / 'You know nothing? Do you see nothing? Do you remember / 'Nothing?' " He remembers his own death: "Those are pearls that were his eyes," for surely this is the ghost of the Phoenician, wishing for a death that will *not* give him back to life, while his wife taunts him with it: "Are you alive, or not? Is there nothing in your head?"

Just before their conversation (if one can call it that, considering that the husband's answers are all unspoken) the marker of the stairway, which we have learned to expect in the early poems, recurs as a transition (from the passage evoking ladies of bygone days) to the domestic game of chess. "Footsteps shuffled on the stair" outside the boudoir where the scene is set, outside their "room enclosed"—isolated and isolating. Again the stairway signals an ascent just before plunging us into horror, crystallized in the last lines of the scene:

> And we shall play a game of chess:
> The ivory men make company between us
> Pressing lidless eyes and waiting for a knock upon the door.

The middle line, so distressing to Vivien Eliot that she called for its removal, will surely be restored eventually now that it can no longer hurt. As Eliot's widow notes, he had already restored it in 1960, thirteen years after Vivien's death.[21] The line is essential to the poem's unified vision of interior prison and exterior waste land. It also dramatizes the devastating contrast between this couple—with no children but chessmen—and the succeeding scene in a pub, where a lower-class woman tells Bill, Lou, and May about her friend Lil (dreading her husband's return from the war), who has five children and is sick from aborting her sixth—another buried corpse.

After this the third part, "The Fire Sermon," can tell us little more about loveless sexuality except the perfunctory coupling snatched in any city. Echoes of Spenser's *Epithalamion* establish the mood of the first scene—the banks of the Thames, emptied even of trash, the old river still running softly while the *revenant* hears at his back the cold blast, rattle of bones, and hellish, disembodied chuckle of a *danse macabre*. Insistent negations—evacuation and emptiness—again create the tone of solemn reflection:

> The wind
> Crosses the brown land, unheard. The nymphs are departed.
> ....
> The river bears no empty bottles, sandwich papers,
> Silk handkerchiefs, cardboard boxes, cigarette ends
> Or other testimony of summer nights. The nymphs are departed.
> And their friends, the loitering heirs of City directors;
> Departed, have left no addresses.

"The river's tent is broken," but foggy drizzle rather than Spenser's stubborn sun appears when the clouds break. Farther within the Unreal City, spring will soon bring Sweeney to his brothel, and even now on "a winter noon," Mr. Eugenides propositions the speaker for a lunch and weekend at two disreputable hotels. Like Madame Sosostris, we are forbidden to understand what mystery this Smyrna merchant may carry with his currants, but clearly the "vanished" cults are blank to him as well.

The introduction of Tiresias at this point makes a distinct transition from the first half of the poem, which dealt—however negatively—with the "normal" world of births (and abortions), marriages (sterile ones), and deaths (however doubtful in "The Burial of the Dead"), to the second half of the poem where all the Western world collapses in images of falling towers and bridges. Just before Tiresias enters in "The Fire Sermon" section, the "I" of the poem (which had been associated with the Phoenician sailor in lines 6–8) becomes associated for the first time with "the man with three staves," or the Fisher King (the two identified with each other "quite arbitrarily," as Eliot's note says). Thus in the passage just preceding Tiresias's entry we read

> A rat crept softly through the vegetation
> Dragging its slimy belly on the bank
> While I was fishing in the dull canal
> On a winter evening round behind the gashouse
> Musing on the king my brother's wreck

This last line leads me to believe that Eliot's first intention was to have the long shipwreck scene—finally reduced to the ten lines of "Death by Water"—come *before* the shift of perspective to the Fisher King and Tiresias. Since in the typescript "The Fire Sermon" (whose perspective is also that of the Buddha's fire sermon) is not assigned a part number, we are free to think it may have been Eliot's first thought for a conclusion—before he went to Lausanne and wrote "What the Thunder Said." In either case his plan would have been to end the poem with allusions from a non-Western sacred poem. By preceding "The Fire Sermon," the drowning of the Phoenician sailor would not only account for the change of narrative point of view but would also take us to the underworld of the *Odyssey,* where the sailor Ulysses met Tiresias. We must recall that "Death by Water" originally had the long passage leading to a shipwreck and ending with the adventurer's *death*—as Dante invented it, but without Dante's faith in "the will of Another." Once Eliot decided upon a different Part V (based on the *Upanisads*), he would have seen that "The Fire Sermon" could be made Part III, continuing the vision of degraded sexuality begun in "A Game of Chess," and that the sexually tormented Tiresias could both deliver the last word on lust and also merge with the Fisher King in his (anti-Grail legend) renunciation of hope for renewed life. This renunciation is, to my mind, the final stage of the poem's negative way.

Reading "The Fire Sermon" this way thus solves several problems, including the loss of the hopeful line "These are pearls that were his eyes!" which had first accompanied the dirge for Phlebas in "Dans le Restaurant." It was appropriate for Madame Sosostris to say it, for she makes a business of pandering to hope, while the message of "Death by Water" is that *this* corpse will suffer no better sea change than a ghastly recapitulation of "his age and youth." Pound wanted to excise the Ariel line from Madame Sosostris's speech, but Eliot insisted on retaining it.[22]

. . . .

Eliot's attitude at the time can be guessed from his last two notes for Part III, the one affirming a parallel between the Buddha's sermon and the Sermon on the Mount; the other clarifying that what interested him in the collocation of Augustine and the Buddha was their asceticism (rather than any common beliefs). It is hard to see any parallel between Jesus's sermon (leading up to the prayer to God, "for thine is the kingdom, and the power, and the glory, for ever") and the Buddha's sermon:

> All things, O priests, are on fire. . . . The eye, O priests, is on fire; forms are on fire: eye-consciousness is on fire; impressions received by the eye are on fire; and whatever sensation, pleasant, unpleasant, or indifferent . . . that also is on fire . . . With the fire of passion . . . with the fire of hatred, with the fire of infatuation; with birth, old age, death, sorrow, lamentation, misery, grief, and despair are they on fire. . . .[23]

This is *The Waste Land*'s message, as the last part (with all its negations) assures us:

> Here is no water but only rock
> Rock and no water and the sandy road
> The road winding above among the mountains
> Which are mountains of rock without water

The "red rock" of the poem's first stanza had at the outset signaled the burning rock (which in an early draft had been gray[24]), and nowhere in the poem (early or late) is there any burning with love such as Augustine describes throughout his *Confessions*. For instance, in the same book Eliot cites, Augustine describes the burning desire which Eliot reckons *without*: "how inwardly did even then the marrow of my soul pant after Thee" (III, 10). The "Lord" who "pluckest me out" in *The Waste Land* is surely more like the Lord Buddha of the "Fire Sermon," where there is only a tormenting fire. The poem's next section quenches this in the grimmest of ways.

"Death by Water" here comes in dramatically, not as a reminder of a resurrected god on the Nile but as a death without any desired sequel. The wheel, which is both Ixion's and the Buddha's *chakra*—that is, both the racking instrument of fortune and the law of escape from it through asceticism—is now the one link between the drowned sailor and the reader. No longer "hypocrite lecteur," as when the sailor himself addressed the reader, we are still his "semblable," but we are addressed in a far different mood than in part I. Now the poem's more philosophical voice speaks:

> O you who turn the wheel and look to windward,
> Consider Phlebas, who was once handsome and tall as you.

The voice, as I have said, is that of Tiresias (chastened by the Buddha's) merging with a modern Fisher King, the sailor who has no hope for cure but can only hope to control the wheel of torment, thus finding a condition of peace.

The hope of happiness is evidently one that must be stilled if the burning is to cease; and in the last part of the poem, "What the Thunder Said," the modern Fisher King explicitly renounces the Christian promise: "He who was living is now dead / We who were living are now dying / With a little patience." This is the poem's late reflection on the Sibyl's "I want to die." And the rhythmic negations we have come to associate with Eliot's more serious voice continue from the passage on patience:

> Here one can neither stand nor lie nor sit
> There is not even silence in the mountains
> But dry sterile thunder without rain
> There is not even solitude in the mountains
> But red sullen faces sneer and snarl
> From doors of mudcracked houses

The mythical mind of the past may have vanished, but the primitive instincts of violence and hate survive in force. And the way through this wilderness is mocked by delusions of a God who shared the unending human ordeal. "Who is the third who walks always beside you?" Readers are not wrong to latch on to the several associations with Christ in the poem's last part; they are only wrong in missing what Eliot's note clearly says: "the party of explorers, at the extremity of their strength, had the constant *delusion* that there was *one more member* than could actually be counted." (I have stressed "delusion" though it hardly seems necessary.) His first note for the part indeed says that "three themes are employed: the journey to Emmaus, the approach to the Chapel Perilous . . . and the present decay of eastern Europe." But the themes are treated from the standpoint of pure negation. The chapel is explicitly *not* haunted, as in the Grail legends, for the speaker assures us,

> There is the empty chapel, only the wind's home.
> It has no windows, and the door swings,
> Dry bones can harm no one.
> Only a cock stood on the rooftree

No cross. And the cock banishes all ghosts. "Then a damp gust / Bringing rain." But the rain brings no new life, which indeed the whole poem has urged would be only a renewal of destructive desires. Lines 394–396 clearly indicate that rain leads only to the waiting for more rain. The empty chapel reminds us that Eliot is just where he was when he wrote, in "Lune de Miel," of the church as "an old factory abandoned by God." But now the emptiness is the Buddha's *sūnyatā,* an emptiness that brings release from desires which are self-defeating. As one scholar describes this teaching found in Nāgārjuna,

The apprehension of emptiness was "enlightenment," the recognition of things as they really are . . . Ultimate release (*nirvāna*) was the nonreplenishing of fuel for the flames of hate and greed.

....

The soteriological importance of this negation is its attempt to divert the religious man from longing after or desiring an eternal, unchanging, self-existent Ultimate . . . To see [things] as "empty" is to see them in actuality . . . Thus, the expression of "emptiness" is *not* the manifestation of *Absolute Reality,* the revelation of the Divine, but the means for dissipating the desire for such an Absolute.[25]

After the words on the emptiness of the chapel, the thunder speaks, and the wisdom achieved in the poem is revealed. The voice in the waste land recognizes that if he could give more, sympathize more, control his life more, the fires would abate. The insight is the same as the Buddha's vision of enlightenment through compassion, surrender of selfish desires, and self-control. "These are small gains," says Rajan, speaking of *The Waste Land*'s ending, "but their very narrowness suggests their authenticity . . . The break-out from sterility is no more than that; it is not a movement into fruitfulness." Compared with Eliot's earlier poems, however, *The Waste Land* moves forward "to the fringe of a world which the poem can formulate but not enter."[26]

As the composite speaker now sits upon a nameless shore, "with the arid plain behind," a life of order and peace seems possible. Though London bridge is still falling down, the poet distractedly recalls other poets with comparable afflictions: Arnaut Daniel, who was refined but not destroyed by cleansing fire; and the lovelorn, disinherited poet Nerval. Also he recalls victims of lust turned into birds, suggesting the power of song to sustain love among the ruins of time. Fragments of poems telling their story are props against his own ruins. Finally a fragment of Kyd's *Spanish Tragedy* recalls Hieronymo's madness, deliberately put on to catch unwary villains. Hieronymo, like Eliot, when young gave his mind "to fruitless poetry," but now his apparent vanities have a deadly aim—at the world of the living dead.

The Waste Land ends repeating the words of the thunder in the *Bryhadaranyaka Upanisad:* "Datta. Dayadhvam. Damyata. [Give. Sympathize. Control.] / Shantih shantih shantih." Spoken in stark, impersonal severity, the words harmonize well with the Buddha's fire sermon (based on the wisdom on the *Upanisads*), but there is no reference as in the *Upanisads* to an ultimate union with Brahma. This concluding peace offering has been generally read as evidence that Eliot combined the highest hopes of Christianity with the Hindu vision, but his own words undercut any reading of an affirmatively Christian kind. His last note in the early editions of the poem (1922–1926) identify the last words of the poem as the "formal ending to an

Upanishad." He added rather brutally that the Christian " 'Peace which passeth understanding' is a feeble translation of the content of this word."[27]

With this remark, Eliot virtually dismissed the Christian's peace, announced by the angel of the Nativity and again by Jesus, parting from his disciples before the Crucifixion. Here Eliot again echoed Babbitt, who also saw the Buddha's peace as superior to the Christian's. In 1917 Babbitt had written, "One should grant the Buddhist his Nirvana if one is willing to grant the Christian his peace that passeth understanding. Peace, as Buddha conceives it, is an active and even an ecstatic thing, the reward not of passiveness, but of the utmost effort."[28] Eliot's note, ending *The Waste Land*, makes the same invidious comparison.

The poem's nightmare vision of Europe after the Peace Treaty of Versailles helps to explain why no Western formula for peace could satisfy Eliot at the time. Yet the poem is not a political diatribe. It is an expression of horror at the panorama of anarchy and futility within the poet's mind as well as outside in the modern world. In the face of such interior horror, the voice of *The Waste Land* asks relief from consciousness itself, and this is the peace promised by the *Upanisads*. As the *Brihadaranyaka Upanisad*, on which the poem's last stanza is based, expresses it: "Arising out of these elements, into them also one vanishes away. After death there is no consciousness"—for the deserving who have reached Nirvana.[29] Many years later, in *Four Quartets*, Eliot would have a very different view, seeing moments of perfect stillness as a liberation *into* consciousness:

> Time past and time future
> Allow but a little consciousness.
> To be conscious is not to be in time
> ("Burnt Norton," II)

Despite *The Waste Land*'s closing words on such positive virtues as generosity, sympathy, and control, the last line of the poem answers the Sibyl's opening to it: "I want to die." At some subliminal point, release from consciousness is what the poem seeks and finds. All the same, as *The Waste Land* ends, the seer's cage is opened, and the void is freely chosen.

. . . .

Notes

1. Martin Heidegger, *Nietzsche*, 2 vols. (Pfullingen: Neske, 1961), I, 73. I have been guided by J. L. Mehta's incisive commentary, *Martin Heidegger: The Way and the Vision* (Honolulu: University Press of Hawaii, 1976), in translating from the German. See Mehta, pp. 185 and 346, n. 9.

2. Heidegger, "What Is Metaphysics?," trans. R. F. C. Hull and Alan Crick, in Werner Brock, *Existence and Being* (Chicago: Regnery, 1949), p. 355.

3. Ibid., p. 354.

4. Heidegger, *Unterwegs zur Sprache* (Pfullingen: Neske, 1959), p. 98.

5. Heidegger, *Wegmarken* (Frankfurt: Klostermann, 1967), p. 319.

6. Heidegger, "The Onto-theo-logical Structure of Metaphysics," *Identity and Difference*, trans. Joan Stambaugh (New York: Harper & Row, 1969), p. 121.

7. Heidegger, "What Are Poets For?," *Poetry, Language, Thought*, trans. Albert Hofstadter (New York: Harper & Row, 1971), p. 138.

8. *Wegmarken*, p. 328.

9. *Poetry, Language, Thought*, pp. 105, 190. Translating the second passage, I follow Mehta, p. 47.

10. Douglas Bush, "T. S. Eliot," *Engaged and Disengaged* (Cambridge: Harvard University Press, 1966), p. 98.

11. Lyndall Gordon, *Eliot's Early Years* (New York: Oxford University Press, 1977), p. 95. See also pp. 23, 32, 35, and 69, where I should say Gordon reads the early poems as unduly positive in their religious significance.

12. I am indebted to John Margolis for setting Eliot's relation to the Action Française in the context of his intellectual development in *T. S. Eliot's Intellectual Development, 1922–1939* (Chicago: University of Chicago Press, 1972), pp. 87–99. As late as 1928, in *Criterion*, 7, Eliot supported Maurras even while acknowledging that he had ended with a different view. In this issue of *Criterion*, he described Maurras's attitude as "that of and unbeliever who cannot believe, and who is too honest to pretend to himself or to others that he does believe; if the others can believe, so much the better not only for them but for the world at large." In "Hommage à Charles Maurras" (1948), Eliot called Maurras "a kind of Virgil who led [some of us] to the doors of the temple." By 1930, however (as Margolis shows), Eliot distinguished more radically between his own view and Maurras's, saying that the latter held "grosser positive errors and far greater dangers" than, for instance, the fairly anti-Christian Irving Babbitt. (Letter to *The Bookman*, 31 March 1930—unpublished, as Margolis says, because *The Bookman* published no letters.) The next year, Eliot wrote against using Christian faith as a political credential—as Hitler and Mussolini both did. Thus in "Thoughts After Lambeth," he wrote, "One of the most deadening influences upon the Church in the past, ever since the eighteenth century, was its acceptance by the upper, upper middle, and aspiring classes, as a political necessity . . ." In the *Christian News-Letter* of 28 August 1940 he went still further: "My particular defense of the *Action Française* may or may not stand; but I believe now that the Pope understood its tendencies better."

13. T. S. Eliot, *After Strange Gods* (New York: Harcourt, Brace, 1934), p. 30.

14. Hugh Kenner, "The Urban Apocalypse," *Eliot in His Time*, ed. A. Walton Litz (Princeton: Princeton University Press, 1974), pp. 42–43. The persistence of the tendency to read *The Waste Land* as a "quest for regeneration," based on the Grail motif, is exemplified in the generally expert commentaries of the new *Norton Anthology of American Literature* (New York: 1979), II, 1215, 1242n.

15. Eleanor Cook, "T. S. Eliot and the Carthaginian Peace," *English Literary History*, 46, no. 2 (Summer 1979): 346 ff.

16. T. S. Eliot, *The Waste Land: A Facsimile of the Original Drafts Including the Annotations of Ezra Pound*, ed. Valerie Eliot (New York: Harcourt Brace Jovanovich, 1971), pp. 31 and 127–128. See also St. Augustine, *The City of God*, I, 35.

17. "*The Waste Land:* Critique of the Myth," in *A Collection of Critical Essays on "The Waste Land,"* ed. Jay Martin (Englewood Cliffs: Prentice-Hall, 1968), p. 60 Brooks's essay first appeared in his *Modern Poetry and the Tradition* (1939).

18. *Selected Essays* (New York: Harcourt, Brace & World, 1964), p. 324.

19. Conrad Aiken, "An Anatomy of Melancholy" (1923), in Martin, *Critical Essays on "The Waste Land."*

20. See Eliot's "Baudelaire" (*Selected Essays*, p. 379): "Indeed, in much romantic poetry

the sadness is due to the exploitation of the fact that no human relations are adequate to human desires, but also to the disbelief in any further object for human desires than that which, being human, fails to satisfy them." This was written in 1931, when Eliot could speak about a "further object for human desires," as he could not in *The Waste Land*. It seems worth noting that Eliot's antiromanticism had two phases (at least): one in which he derided a "mystical" yearning for satisfaction beyond those available to "human relations" (a "classical" attitude) and a later antiromanticism in which he criticized desires that sought satisfaction in merely human relations. As "Prufrock" and "Portrait of a Lady" represent the first phase, "The Dry Salvages" exemplifies the second (the "partial fallacy / Encouraged by superficial notions of evolution").

21. *The Waste Land: A Facsimile*, p. 126.

22. Ibid.

23. In his Notes, Eliot directs us to Henry Clark Warren's *Buddhism in Translation*. The passage is quoted as given here by Herbert Howarth, *Some Figures behind T. S. Eliot* (Boston: Houghton Mifflin, 1964), p. 204.

24. *The Waste Land: A Facsimile*, p. 95.

25. Frederick J. Streng, *Emptiness: A Study in Religious Meaning* (Nashville and New York: Abingdon Press, 1967), pp. 161–162.

26. B. Rajan, "The Overwhelming Question," rpt. in *Critical Essays on "The Waste Land,"* ed. Martin, p. 49.

27. *The Waste Land: A Facsimile*, p. 149. Eliot did not delete the word "feeble" until after his conversion to Christianity in 1927. Donald Gallup tells me that if the change had been made at any point before 1932, it would have been made in the 1926 edition of *Poems: 1909–25* (London: Faber & Gwyer, 1926), but the invidious comparison is retained in that edition.

28. Irving Babbitt, "Interpreting India to the West," *Spanish Character and Other Essays* (Boston: Houghton Mifflin, 1940), pp. 159–160. This essay originally appeared in the *Nation* in 1917. Again I am indebted to Carey Sassower's "T. S. Eliot: A Critical Disciple" (Bowdoin Prize Essay, Harvard University, 1979), for the reference.

29. Robert Ernest Hume, *The Thirteen Principal Upanishads* (London: Oxford University Press, 1931), p. 101.

Absence and Density in *The Waste Land*

HARRIET DAVIDSON

. . . *The Waste Land* is a poem full of strategic absences. Thematically, the poem gives us the absence of love, of life, of belief, and to some extent, of meaning. Formally, the absences are as interesting and as striking. The controlling rhetorical figure in the poem is allusion, a device which, I will argue, signifies in deference to certain kinds of absences. The grammar of the poem is heavily paratactic; logical and syntactical connections are often absent. The larger structure of the poem is also paratactic in its seemingly unrelated series of fragmented narratives and lyrics, connected only by allusive section titles and themes. Sometimes from word to word, often from line to line, and virtually always from episode to episode, our first experience as readers of *The Waste Land* is of the absence of expected connections or sources. Our second experience, if experience could be so catalogued, would surely be of the density of possibilities corresponding to these absences.

But the most important absence in the poem, the absence which underlies the formal and thematic absences, is the absence of a persona. This is a vexed issue in *The Waste Land,* and much energy has gone into finding the missing consciousness of the poem. Still, the many voices of the poem cannot be reconciled into anything we know of as a single self, while the extremely personal and unique sense of the poem belies the notion of some universal consciousness or collective unconscious. The poem simply does not have what we would identify as a controlling consciousness, and this absence is a powerful and disturbing one.

Absence is the primary communication of the poem, communicating, to paraphrase Eliot, before it is understood. Many of our best critics have pointed out that this poem can be meaningful to even the uninformed reader who does not know the Grail legend, or recognize the allusions, or have any of the secondary knowledge which we bring to the poem in seeking understanding.[1] Although the semantic content of the poem does communicate themes of loss and lack, absence is also communicated in two other, more primary ways. First, the poem makes the reader experience the absence of expected connections. This reader-response observation capitalizes on the existential confusion which readers may feel and does not necessarily lead us

Reprinted with permission of Louisiana State University Press from *T. S. Eliot and Hermeneutics* by Harriet Davidson. Copyright © 1985 by LSU Press.

beyond the state of subject confronting object. Secondly, and more profoundly, the poem discloses absence ontologically as a state of the world, not as the state of a consciousness trying to know a world. This second, crucial definition will be taken up at length in Chapter Two with an examination of the philosophy of Martin Heidegger in which absence (as always concealed Being) is a central dynamic force setting in motion a world which is interpretive—or, hermeneutic—in its very nature.

The terms *absence* and *hermeneutic* are central for my argument and will take some extensive discussion to define. For now, let me specify that by *absence* I mean the absence of a transcendent foundation, center, origin—whether subjective or objective—for our being. Because of this absence of transcendence, interpretation or *hermeneutics,* rather than empirical certainty or innate ideas, becomes the foundation for meaning in the world. This post-Heideggerian hermeneutics is the process of creating meaning in the absence of any ultimate foundation for truth, a process revealed, in part, in the diacritical function of language. The technique of *The Waste Land* discloses this ontological absence and this process of interpretation. The poem resists any attempt to encompass it by a coherent psychological, structural, or logical idea; the poem's existence, like the voice of the woman in the pub in "A Game of Chess," is real, meaningful and defiantly untranslatable. The poem reveals a world which is almost totally concealed from us in our desire for structures to explain it, but is also meaningful in itself. What Heidegger calls concealedness is the most powerful form of absence in the poem and the one which ties together linguistic and thematic absences.

Curiously, in experiencing this absence in *The Waste Land,* we are not experiencing the desolation of a wasteland. That theme of emptiness has been taken up by existentialists such as Camus, Sartre, and often Hemingway, who so powerfully manipulate language toward a minimum of referential and diacritical possibility and thus retain the dominance of the existential I AM over a meaningless and indifferent world. But no one has ever confused these landscapes with that of *The Waste Land.* Rather, Eliot's poem confronts us with a bewildering multiplicity caused not only by the fragmentation of the coherent world, but also by a fragmentation of the self. This fragmentation does not result in despair or emptiness or in the egocentric accrual of all meaning to the self as some existentialists have done. Rather, the fragmentation releases meaning into the play of a human world rich with possibilities, even if destitute of certainties. It is a peculiarly contemporary situation. In *The Waste Land* the disappearance of God is compounded by a disappearance of the self as an autonomous and unified whole, and the result is a poem radically new for its time and still not wholly assimilated today.

The poem's persistent lack of clear signification opens up the possibility of a metaphoric connection at every turn, leading to a multiplicity of interpretations. The brilliance of Eliot's formal experiments is that no amount of subsequent reading will totally remove the absences in the poem. The opacity remains stubbornly there, not dissolved by any interpretation. Instead, the poem seems to expose the conditions for the possibility of all interpretations of this text and any text. Prior to the essentialist's assertion of meaning, or to the existentialist's recognition of meaninglessness, is man's state within the world (being-in-the-world, if you will), which necessarily precedes these judgments.

The existentialists may make up for a lack of external authority with the controlling consciousness. Without either, the world changes entirely. We are left with a rather indiscriminate, though not necessarily meaningless, jumble of events, characters, thoughts, texts, memories, and desires out of which the self must be created and create. This state holds much fascination for Eliot, not only for the delicious oppression it offers the romantic Prufrockian consciousness, but also for the poetic and ontological possibilities it offers the anti-romantic consciousness of Eliot. Eliot had a lifelong intuition, most strongly stated in "Tradition and the Individual Talent," that poetry was dissociated from the poet. His most commonly known poetic dicta reveal his suspicion that the ego is not the source of creativity. For Eliot, poems communicate apart from rational understanding; the power of expression is carried by the "external facts," the objective correlative, not internal states; the poet's mind is only the catalyst—the shred of platinum which sets off a reaction it does not enter into. The substance of the poem is not interior any more than it is empirical; rather it is a gathering up of the tradition in a particular moment. The only authority rests in the unstable hands of culture, and culture is uniquely both subjective and objective in that it is created yet it creates, both temporal and timeless in that it retains everything in a state of continual change, both personal and universal in that it is both homogeneous and a unique horizon from every point within it. In short, the self becomes a locus of culture with no transcendental dominion over the cultural matrix.

. . . .

Critical theory has only recently absorbed the implications of a linguistic world which denies the romantic self, so that now we are in a position to interpret *The Waste Land* somewhat differently than has been done in the past by establishing a critical context in which a radical critique of the self is possible and absence and interpretation are central. This task will lean heavily upon the linguistic turn in twentieth-century philosophy for documentation, but the initial questions about absence, meaning, and the self remain rooted in the poem. The circularity of a hermeneutic is evident here. By taking absence seriously in *The Waste Land,* we must experience a shift, or indeed a revolution, in all of our assumptions about language and the world; the world reinterprets itself around a new insight. But the initial questions about the poem could never have been asked without using language in which these new assumptions are already inherent. So that a new interpretation involves an enormous, but involuntary, change, difficult to trace in rational discourse. Insight comes in a flash, we say, as a whole, with the

particular and universal defining each other, a message from the unpredict-
able Hermes himself.

. . . .

Hermeneutics has, of course, been with us for centuries, having arisen
from the desire to determine the truth of God as inscribed in the Bible. Until
the nineteenth century, hermeneutics remained a means to attain an absolute
and objective truth. But as thinkers began to turn their attention to the
human sciences such as history, psychology, sociology, and literary criticism,
they realized that the rigid rules of interpretation were not adequate for the
living character of human objects. In the best spirit of romanticism,
Schleiermacher and Dilthey added the subjective to the hermeneutic process,
making understanding a process of interaction between human subject and
human object based on their common participation in "the historical consciousness of the human."[2] But, as Hans-Georg Gadamer clearly shows in
Truth and Method (192–225), Dilthey's attempt to ground understanding in
life was in conflict with his need to combat relativism by positing the
possibility of an absolute historical consciousness. Likewise, Husserl's scientific attempt to begin with the life-world is undermined by the idealism
inherent in his process of transcendental reduction. While both Dilthey and
Husserl tried to go beyond dualism, they both finally give consciousness
priority over language. In each case the search for a ground for knowledge
returned to a dualist epistemology running counter to their attempts to
overturn traditional metaphysics.

Only with Heidegger's work is this conflict resolved into a seamless
expression of Being. For Heideggger defines human being (*Dasein* or There-
Being) as an event of understanding prior to the possibility of knowledge.
What was previously an object of knowledge for a subject is now "itself
ultimately of the essence of There-being" (TM, 232). As Heidegger's noted
commentator William Richardson explains,

> Heidegger saw that the problem had to be posed on a different level in terms of
> an intimate correlation between the Being-process and man, by reason of
> which the "sense" of beings was something more than mere entity, yet also
> more than the fabrication of consciousness. This would demand, however, an
> analysis of man in his relationship to Being that would shatter the realist-
> idealist dilemma by overcoming the subjectivism that lay at its roots.[3]

To repeat, Heidegger has changed the "sense" of beings or reality so that it is
rich with human interpretation but not subjective. In other words, the process
of interpretation is what *is*, not a way to reach what is. Interpretation achieves
ontological status, not as a subjective process but as the *being* process.

. . . .

. . . [T]he harshness and malaise in the opening lines of *The Waste Land*
are distinctly of a particular historical time of existential anxiety. The tradi-

tion takes up, is taken up by, the century defined by a devastating world war and a loss of faith in God and rationality, giving us angst about April, about growth, about time (that union of memory and desire in our present). But these declamatory lines will not provide any stability against this angst. Suddenly the syntax shifts *gestalts,* mutating into the incidental and chatty: "Summer surprised us, coming over the Starnbergersee / With a shower of rain . . ." (ll. 8–9). This narrative about Munich hardly seems connected to the opening seven lines. The portentous generality with which spring and winter are interpreted gives way to a particular and neutral interpretation of summer, breaking out of the control of the rhetoric, the logic, and the idea. There is no center here, only generation, which is the initial source of the anxiety. The shift of voice accomplished by a syntactical metonymy is both disturbing and liberating, confirming anxiety in the mechanism of displacement, but also diffusing it in the errancy of the particular.

By the end of the poem, the spring rain will undergo an interpretive metamorphosis from a cruel to a saving release, as generation and interpretation are chosen over sterility and rigidity. Then, the meaningless repetition of the spring thunder is interpreted in three ways and these three commands form an invitation to the give and take of hermeneutic experience—give, sympathize, control; and each command is further diffused into the opaque particularity of lyric interpretations. The anxiety caused by the lack of clarity throughout the poem is hermeneutically attached to the freedom from rigidity which this density affords. Could we find a situation that more wholly contains this union of fear and freedom than:

> And when we were children, staying at the archduke's,
> My cousin's, he took me out on a sled,
> And I was frightened. He said, Marie,
> Marie, hold on tight. And down we went.
> In the mountains, there you feel free. (ll. 13–17)

This is "precise emotion."

The Waste Land is the fruit of Eliot's early critical work. It is both more conscious of tradition than his first volume of poetry—*Prufrock and Other Observations* (1917)—and less conscious of the self than the satires of the second volume—*Poems* (1919). By presenting an historical cultural world, not a subjective world, *The Waste Land* presents neither undigested philosophy nor vague emotion. The lyric voice of the poem is only one among many narrative, dramatic, and prophetic voices. Here, the artifacts of modernity—the motorcars, gramophones, typists, crowds, nerves—exist alongside the artifacts of culture—Shakespeare, Dante, Spenser, the Bible. No one thing seems privileged in this world as a central meaning. In particular, the voices of culture do not provide any overall framework, since they, too, are woven into the texture of the world, not kept apart as a comment on this world. The culture is not in the past; as Eliot taught us, only because tradition is present is it part of our world. For no one in Spenser's day did the Thames contain the meaning, "Sweet Thames, run softly, till I end my song" (l. 177). Only since Spenser's "Prothalamion" is the world so enriched. The poem makes nostalgia impossible because of the blending of present and past. The world of the poem would not exist without the cultural allusions; and the meaning of the allusions is as completely dependent on the present as the present is on its cultural heritage. The poet is, indeed, wholly absorbed into his object, so that it is the cultural world which speaks and which provides the ideas and emotions, not a persona. The poem has *form* in Eliot's sense.

The density and complexity of the poem and the corresponding absence of finality are in some sense untranslatable into rational discourse because rational enclosure is precisely what the poem avoids. Still, I would like to suggest some avenues for interpretation of this difficult poem based on hermeneutic ideas. My reading is by no means a complete explication of the poem. Rather, I have chosen a few examples from the poem to display the larger principles of a hermeneutic view of world and self. First, I will give a brief overview of the poem as a presentation of hermeneutic existence. Then, I will examine some poetic techniques which do the work of presentation, specifically metonymy, narrative, and allusion. Then, in what may seem at first like a digression, I would like to explain the hermeneutic analysis of the psyche based on the theories of Jacques Lacan in order to account for the poem's persistent interest in relationships, particularly sexual relationships. The relationships between self and other and between love and death are crucial for the poem as a whole. Finally, I hope to gather up these interpretive strands in an analysis of the final section of the poem, "What the Thunder Said."

I do not plan to discuss the manuscript version of *The Waste Land,* which was published in 1971,[4] because I am more interested in the poem which has interacted with our culture, that is, the original 1922 version. For all of the arguments I have advanced about Eliot's aesthetic theory, I am not making an argument about Eliot's intentions, but about an historical *Zeitgeist.* The poem as first published said something to its own time and continues to be a presence in our time. That Pound could understand the force of Eliot's poem is only evidence for its cultural meaning. I do not, however, believe that Pound was responsible for the innovations in *The Waste Land.* An examination of the manuscript shows that, apart from a few minor revisions in diction, Pound's contributions were the removal of two long sections beginning "The Fire Sermon" and "Death by Water" and rather extensive revisions of the teatime episode in "The Fire Sermon." The long section at the beginning of the poem seems to have been excised by Eliot himself.

Pound certainly did the world a favor by removing the satiric Fresca episode and reworking the original teatime episode, both of which, like many of Eliot's satires, are grating and tasteless. Eliot seems to have abandoned this sort of satire in poetry after *The Waste Land,* whether under the influence of Pound or religion, and we can only be grateful. But the strategy of the poem and the most powerful passages in the poem are not disturbed by Pound. The cut passages give us more voices and more narrative, but no more logical connections than in the published version. Section V is untouched by Pound (according to the manuscript edition), as are the remaining stanzas of Section IV and the beginning and end of Section III. And many of Pound's minor suggestions in Sections I and II are rejected by Eliot. *The Waste Land* is, in my opinion, a better poem for Pound's advice (and, we must remember, for Eliot's understanding that the poem was not inviolably his own), but the draft version is not different in its entelechy from the published version.

By avoiding the onus of either idea or personality, *The Waste Land* is at once highly intellectual and purely emotional, because "precise emotion" is totally realized in the objects of the poem. That is, the world of the poem wholly contains any idea or emotion which could be inferred from the poem. We could even say that the density of the poem exceeds the limitation of idea or sensibility. Yet the poem is clearly informed by idea, even though one would be hard pressed to find a line of undigested philosophy in the poem, and by emotion, even though the emotion does not emanate from a personality. The poem presents a world defined by the absence of a central stabilizing force, whether God, logic, the self, or empirical certainty. Without this center, the world has no order or delimitation among objects, subjects, ideas, emotions, past, or present. The situation is one of being-in-the-world. In the absence of essence, self and world define each other diacritically; the self is made up of social, cultural, existential forces, while the world exists *for* us (even in its horrors) as the meaningful arrangement of human interpretations. Being-in-the-world is the ongoing process of interpretation in the face of change and finitude.

The Waste Land begins with the paradox most basic to human existence, the absolute interdependence of life and death. The first lines present the inevitability of generation in the movement of the seasons, where the projection of our desire to be sufficient gathers up the memory of our thrown, insufficient, finite state into the hermeneutic of time. But the poem tries to reject this hermeneutic foundation by separating desire from memory. The poem is full of anxiety about death and generation, and aching with desire for a separation from our limitation and finitude. But every separation from memory and a world (even a bad world) is sterile and barren, a fate worse than death. Like the Sibyl in her prison of immortality, with lack of death there remains no desire except for death: ". . . she would always respond: 'I yearn to die.' "[5] Throughout the poem, the worst horror is reserved for the barren, changeless environments devoid of a human life of pain and death. The human world is, in contrast, full of meaningful fragments, a vast sea in which no one survives.

This simple duality in the poem is not so simple, for the hermeneutic world resists and defeats this duality. The human world is created in the desire to escape the absence defining our existence. The symbols, myths, art, and all of society attempt, in the endless elaboration of a relational linguistic world, to cover the absence. Lacan identifies this human activity as the "metonymy of desire,"[6] which reveals our lack of wholeness and sufficiency even while it tries to hide this lack. Human life is a constant conjunction of death and desire to escape death. We are never purely toward death, without the errancy of our desire. *Errancy* is a key term from Heidegger which will serve to focus several issues here. Errancy is the inevitable human condition of being able to know only particular beings and never Being as a whole. Our desire to know Being as a whole—something changeless, eternal, and complete—and thus escape from change, finitude, and absence can only be manifest in beings which are themselves finite. In *The Waste Land* the attempt to achieve some metaphoric/symbolic enclosure (or presence) is undercut by metonymic particularity, allusive dispersion, and constant metamorphosis. While the poem desires presence, the desire produces only particularity and absence. We cannot escape our errancy; we can only recognize and accept the always fragmentary and hermeneutic nature of human being. The search for presence, which if achieved would bring only sterility and imprisonment in a fixed and isolated self, is possible only because of the freedom residing in the absence which allows beings to be. The poem, especially the end of the poem, presents a world imbued with our desire for changelessness, even while it shows our finitude. We cannot just reject the sterility of a quest for changelessness and embrace our finitude. The acceptance must be of a world of desire and death where questing is a way of life which continually discovers only the necessity for the quest.

II

This brief overview of issues in *The Waste Land* will serve to frame a more specific discussion of techniques of the poem that present the absence of essence underlying death and desire. Formally, the poem conspicuously lacks the features of language which limit and define meaning. The various episodes and passages in the poem appear to have no logical connection, syntax is often disjointed, constant allusion defers and diffuses meaning. If this overriding parataxis were not enough to dispel the illusion of a center, especially a controlling consciousness, the poem also speaks in various dramatic voices, and, in passages of description, predication is often given to the object rather than to an observing narrator.

. . . .

Throughout "The Fire Sermon," the tantalizing glimpses of beauty offered in moments of song are, in our errancy, taken as something other than manifestations of the same desire, which, as sexual, reduces the song to a dirty joke. Philomela can sing as a nightingale because she has been violated; that her song, too, is violated into the leering "Jug jug" shows the constancy and complexity of the force of desire. Each type of singing depends on the possibility of the other, and singing comes to represent the unresolved state of being human.

The song of Mrs. Porter is interrupted, not by the pure voices of the children singing for Parsifal, but by a reference to these voices singing in the distance: *"Et O ces voix d'enfants, chantant dans la coupole!"* The distancing effects of this reference and the fluidity of French after the sing-song English ballad suggest another world entirely than the British world of Sweeney. (Even in Verlaine we hear this difference from Parsifal's world of lust and bloody battle.) This momentary vision is mocked by the prosaic "Twit twit twit" of the much reduced nightingale's song.

The music returns at the end of the typist section, starting with a "record on the gramophone" (l. 256), becoming Ariel's mysterious music in an allusion to *The Tempest,* " 'This music crept by me upon the waters' " (l. 257), and then the more empirical "Pleasant whining of a mandoline" (l. 261). Each of these references—to the empty world of the typist, the magic world of Ariel, and the neutral, everyday world—tells of a different way of singing. This remarkable recurrence of music out of misery is gathered up in the magnificent line, "Inexplicable splendour of Ionian white and gold." The reference to religion and the wonder of divine redemption beyond this world of singing is, of course, clear. But the anapestic music of the line is also powerful. "Ionian" suggests not only architecture, but also the Ionics of Greek metrics, and the quantitative principle of classical verse is surely at work in the rhythm of this line.

This expansive burst of song seems to grow out of the first emotionally neutral and world-accepting passage in the poem since the scene of drinking coffee in the Hofgarten. The communal Hofgarten is now replaced by a "public bar" where "fishmen" meet for lunch. The "pleasant" and everyday nature of this scene displaces the indifference and loneliness of the typist as a way of breaking out of depression. But perhaps under the influence of the vibrating word "fishmen" (a vision of mermans?), the vision in the church violates the metonymic regularity of this normal, communal world. So even while the vision offers great beauty, it does so at great expense. And with the next lines of the poem, we feel that the singing of the Thames daughters is stifled. These lines are the shortest in the poem, breaking up the flow of syntax and emphasizing metaphoric substitutions rather than metonymic connections. Indeed, the centering of these very short lines on the page makes the long, Ionian line appear to rest upon the following stanzas like a capital on its column, as if the symbolic thrust of "Inexplicable splendour" rests upon the certainty of fragmentation and loss of meaningful connections: "I can connect / Nothing with nothing" (ll. 301–302). The "white and gold" become "oil and tar" and the river song is once again of sexual degradation.

This is an unbearable state, and as a response to this paradox the ending of "The Fire Sermon" is the greatest forgetting of errancy in the poem. The wish to be purged of desire is the vehement response to the sexuality which undermines the few fleeting glimpses of beauty. But you cannot cure the self by getting rid of desire, since the human is defined in its happiness and misery by that desire. The purging of desire and consequent loss of humanity are what lead us into the extended desert section opening "What the Thunder Said." But much of our agony may be spared if the self did not feel it had to fight the desire. We do not need to burn, but rather we need to disperse ourselves into the fecund and music-giving water. "Death by Water" is an alternative to burning. The solution is not to erase the desire and keep the self—that gives us the barren waste. The solution is to erase the self and keep the desire.

VI

This understanding leads us into the resolution of the poem. The beginning of "What the Thunder Said" returns us to the technique and tonality of the red rock section in "The Burial of the Dead." The metaphoric/symbolic syntax and diction again distance us from a meaningful world, but now there is an explicit recognition of the failure of symbolic escape from death and desire, the failure of a savior to save from death:

> He who was living is now dead
> We who were living are now dying
> With a little patience. (ll. 328–30)

The desire for water to relieve the inhuman sterility of the wasteland is explicit, but there seems to be no way to create water from the prison of symbolic enclosure. The attempt to transform the symbols of barrenness is doomed to failure within the confines of the symbolic world. The language cannot blossom into a fertile world:

>   If there were water
> And no rock
> If there were rock
> And also water
> And water
> A spring
> A pool among the rock
> If there were the sound of water only
> Not the cicada
> And dry grass singing
> But sound of water over a rock

> Where the hermit-thrush sings in the pine trees
> Drip drop drip drop drop drop drop
> But there is no water (ll. 346–59)

For a moment the hermit-thrush does sing in the pines. But the metaphoric fragmentation of language emphasizing the object—water—and ignoring the metonymic and syntactic relations which would complete the sentence indicates a failure of desire in its concealing/revealing function. The glimpse of the world brought forth with the hermit-thrush is fleeting and particular, concealing any vision of the whole. But the symbolic urge is to erase the fragmentary particularity and temporality in a whole. Thus, the categorical conclusion, "But there is no water." This imprisoned symbolic urge has forgotten errancy, forgotten that we can never escape the process of desire and memory which disallows essence and stability.

The rigid definition of the desert begins to dissolve under the reemergence of desire, manifested in a blurring of clear and categorical distinctions which provokes the *quest*ioning. Under stress, apparitions appear, denying the death of possibility, but offering only a haunted vision of the human world:

> —But who is that on the other side of you?
>
> What is that sound high in the air
> Murmur of maternal lamentation
> Who are these hooded hordes swarming
> ....
> What is the city over the mountains
> Cracks and reforms and bursts in the violet air
> (ll. 366–69, 372–73)

These visions have the quality of things glimpsed on the edge of vision, or illuminated in flash of lightning and then destroyed in darkness. They culminate in a passage unlike any other in the poem:

> A woman drew her long black hair out tight
> And fiddled whisper music on those strings
> And bats with baby faces in the violet light
> Whistled, and beat their wings
> And crawled head downward down a blackened wall
> (ll. 378–82)

These lines echo earlier images: the woman's hair in "A Game of Chess," the violet hour of "The Fire Sermon," the whisper of the sea in "Death by Water." With this series of surreal images, we are back in a realm of civilization and the other and out of the desert; it is a world of possibilities, though horrible possibilities. The mutations of the nightmare are a shock, existing on that twilight edge between the real and unreal. These surreal images show the particular taken up by a symbolic technique which does not respect metonymic relations. The surreal tries to create a fullness of meaning by manipulating symbols, even if the meaning is a nightmare vision. There is still an unwillingness to quit looking for symbolic wholeness.

But with that nightmare release we are brought to the traditional climax of the quest, the chapel perilous, where we find no peril. We have instead a return to the particular and the metonymic world, briefly attempted in the hermit-thrush vision. Again, the grass is singing and the bird sings. The chapel is empty, "only the wind's home. / It has no windows, and the door swings, / Dry bones can harm no one" (ll. 389–91). The portentous symbolism previously attached to the wind and the bones is now gone. Bones, like sagging doors, exist as the inevitable result of time. Death is finally accepted, but not as the peaceful descent of Phlebas. The cock crows "In a flash of lightning" (l. 394). This is a reawakening of desire, which now hears not the "dry sterile thunder" of the desert (l. 342) but a voice which must be understood: DA, a polysemic syllable which must be interpreted.

The extreme difficulty of these final lines of *The Waste Land*—of the interpretation of the thunder and the cultural fragments—lies in the deep paradox of our existence. We only learn to accept death, that absence at the center of our being, by attention to particulars which hold the mystery of time in their opaque being. But the particular only comes to its being through the metonymy of desire—desire which covers the absence and wishes to escape it. Therefore, the interpretation must lead into other interpretations, never dispelling the darkness, but always trying to dispel it. The thunder is interpreted as give, sympathize, and control—not explanations, but commands toward an activity of hermeneutic give and take. And each of these interpretations is further interpreted. In the Upanishads, the men interpret the meaning of DA as Give, the demons interpret the meaning as Sympathize, the gods interpret it as Control. What man gives is no-thing, but only "The awful daring of a moment's surrender" (l. 404), the gift of the other, or absence. The demons sympathize with our errancy; we are trapped in the prison of our desire for essence—yet at that violet hour, the mystery of the particular (here the enigmatic reference to "a broken Coriolanus") recurs, haunting us. The key confirms both the prison and the release; it is the absence or finitude which both traps us and gives us possibilities. The gods offer control, which brings exhilaration; our desire captures and is propelled by finite existence as the sails capture and are propelled by the wind. The only being is being-in-the-world.

Finally, "the arid plain" is no longer "my lands" (ll. 425–26); the "waste" and the "land" are sundered. But my land is not my self. The land is a world in which the other speaks, and this is a rich and full world speaking of childhood and adulthood, past and present, of myth, religion, art. The allusions speak where we could not speak, celebrating the absence which allows their joint existence. And yet, each fragment speaks of our ruin. London is crumbling. Arnaut Daniel must be purged of his lusts. Philomela wishes to flee her human degradation, and the Prince of Aquitaine is bereft in his abandoned tower. We are not to escape the ravages of time. But the satisfaction of the play will distract us from death—"Why then Ile fit you." Our true foundation is not death but is that ceaseless hermeneutic between desire and death in which finite existence always just escapes our efforts to capture it in the word.

Notes

1. Hugh Kenner and Ezra Pound are the major critics insisting that the poem is meaningful without knowledge of the secondary material.

2. David M. Rasmussen, *Mythic-Symbolic Language and Philosophical Anthropology: A Constructive Interpretation of the Thought of Paul Ricoeur* (The Hague, 1971), 12.

3. William J. Richardson, *Heidegger: Through Phenomenology to Thought* (The Hague, 1963), 28.

4. T. S. Eliot, *"The Waste Land": A Facsimile and Transcript of the Original Drafts Including the Annotations of Ezra Pound,* ed. Valerie Eliot (New York, 1971).

5. Epigraph to *The Waste Land* from Petronius, *Satyricon,* chapter 48, translated by George Williamson, *A Reader's Guide to T. S. Eliot* (New York, 1953), 129.

6. This phrase actually comes from the famous article on Lacan by Jean Laplanche and Serge Leclaire, "L'Inconscient," *Les Temps Modernes,* XVII (July, 1961), 81–129.

[From *T. S. Eliot and the Politics of Voice*]

John Xiros Cooper

"Undermining the foundations" meant, principally, winning the governing or directive elites back to a religious conception of society as the natural state of the social organism, that state where the divisions on the social ground are rooted to absolute authority and the signifiers that mark them to an absolute signified beyond historical contingency. The thinking and feeling of these elites, or the "governing classes," in the nineteenth century had been profoundly influenced by liberal ideas and the currents of European humanism that had shaped progressive thinking since the Renaissance. By the beginning of the twentieth century in Britain this humanism had taken root in the collective mentality of the middle classes and provided a philosophical basis for their political and economic programs when in power. And increasingly these tendencies not only won power, but maintained their control over longer periods of time with the attendant subsidiary penetration in depth of other institutions: the civil service, the judiciary, the professions, the managers, and education. Even when their opponents, the conserving classes, won power in Westminster, they often found themselves unable to halt the wave of liberalizing to which the successive administrations of leaders like Gladstone or Bright or Morley had given a political focus.[1]

It was the intellectual and emotional foundations of this new social equilibrium that Eliot, through his whole life, wished to shake. The liberal notion of society as a contractual balancing of clashing personal and collective interests and of the individual as the primary social unit[2] Eliot, and other conservative reactionaries, found offensive. This reaction had not taken long to crystalize as the new practical outlines of modern liberal society took shape. Instead Eliot came to desire, and increasingly said so, social coordination from above, spreading harmony, and a kind of feudal calm, from a supreme authority through intermediate hierarchies of obedience and control to the individual. He did not conceive of individual existence as the *terminus ad quem* of history, but only as the medium for the perpetuation of authority. Human subjects, in this view, are important only as occasions for supreme authority to glimpse the movement of its own shadow in history. Humanism errs, Eliot asserts, in misreading these shadows as the signs of human power, rather than as evidence of human frailty and incompleteness in the face of a greater potency (*CP* 45). Only a unified, catholic Church, functioning as the sign of the presence of God in history, and, correspondingly, individual subjectivity, valued according to its disposition to obedience, or faith, allows us to experience that greater power. Ignore these "truths," work to defeat them, and then watch the Sweeneys and the house agent's clerks and the social outsiders, like the Jews, swagger on the stage of history. And this, Eliot thought, led to the end of civilization as we know it.

The vision of a coordinated, organic society, first fully articulated in *The Idea of Christian Society* (1939), is evident everywhere in Eliot's work before that summary statement. Eliot used the word "Idea" to suggest its Platonic associations, that is, "Idea" as generative form or ideal conception.[3] The Idea was of a society "in which a finely conscious elite," exercising a monopoly over the master codes of that society, "transmits its values," not by transmission of the elaborated codes, but "through rhythm, habit, and resonance to the largely unconscious masses, infiltrating the nervous system rather than engaging the mind."[4] This is a vision, of course, transplanted to the twentieth century from Coleridge's late social and religious writings and his notion of the "clerisy" as the primary collective subject in the transmission and control of culture.[5] The major difference between Coleridge and Eliot lies in the social situation they both addressed, thus affecting their texts' mood and tone. Eliot had a clearer view, in the 1930s, precisely against what constellation of principles and social actions his Idea had to contend; after all, his text came at the end of the liberal era, whereas Coleridge's *On the Constitution of the Church and State . . .* (1830) was drowned in liberalism's rising tide.

Liberalism, however, in Eliot's time, was not an entirely lifeless sociopolitical force either. An important locus of "liberalizing" thought, feeling, and action with which Eliot has close contact was Bloomsbury.[6] Bloomsbury represented "a specific moment of the development of liberal thought," restating and extending "the classical values of the bourgeois enlightenment."[7] But what kind of "specific moment" in the history of British liberalism does Bloomsbury represent? First there is "the remarkable record of political and organizational involvement, between the wars, by Leonard Woolf, by Keynes, but also by others, including Virginia Woolf. . . ."[8] Public, engaged work stimulated by a specific sense of "social conscience" and, in another characteristic phrase, a "concern for the underdog" should color all our perspectives of Bloomsbury. But as Raymond Williams notes:

> . . . what has most carefully to be defined is the specific association of what are really quite unchanged class feelings—a persistent sense of a quite clear line between an upper and a lower class—with very strong and effective feelings of sympathy with the lower class as victims. Thus political action is directed towards systematic reform at a ruling-class level; contempt for the

stupidity of the dominant sectors of the ruling class survives, quite unchanged, from the earliest phase. The contradiction inherent in this—the
search for systematic reform at the level of a ruling class which is known to be,
in majority, short-sighted and stupid—is of course not ignored. It is a matter
of social conscience to go on explaining and proposing, at official levels, and at
the same time to help in organizing and educating the victims. The point is
not that this social conscience is unreal; it is very real indeed. But it is the
precise formulation of a particular social position, in which a fraction of an
upper class, breaking from its dominant majority, relates to a lower class *as a
matter of conscience:* not in solidarity, nor in affiliation, but as an extension of
what are still felt as personal or small-group obligations, at once against the
cruelty and stupidity of the system and towards its otherwise relatively help-
less victims.[9]

Eliot saw clearly the contradictory character of such commitments and
increasingly said so in the *Criterion,* in *For Lancelot Andrewes,* and in *After
Strange Gods,* although he never unequivocally challenged the political activities of his friends in Bloomsbury. *The Idea of a Christian Society* represents his
attempt to vitiate these contradictions by resolving the genuine commitment
of intellectual elites to the pursuit of truth and justice with their responsibilities for the governance of a society and to the wider governing class from
which such elites are normally drawn. The feelings of sympathy for the poor,
the downtrodden, the victims of a cruel and unresponsive socioeconomic
system were for Eliot a dangerous line for an influential fragment of the
governing class to take, whether members of Bloomsbury, liberal clerics, or
educators. In his prose he was quite clear about this issue and he grew
increasingly distant from the liberal-minded intelligentsia, symbolized by
Bloomsbury, as his hardening religious commitments in the twenties challenged in too uncompromising a manner the root values of these elites. In his
poetry the portraits of the so-called "victims" of British society among the
working class and the *petite bourgeoisie* more gibingly challenged and denied
what would have seemed to him the squishy romanticizing of such characters
by wet-eyed liberal dreamers. "Apeneck Sweeney" (*CP* 59), the broad-footed
"Doris" (*CP* 45), and the cast of low-life and *arriviste* character-types in *The
Waste Land* are his answer to such illusions.

> Sweeney addressed full length to shave
>   Broadbottomed, pink from nape to base,
> Knows the female temperament
>   And wipes the suds around his face.
>
> (The lengthened shadow of a man
>   Is history, said Emerson
> Who had not seen the silhouette
>   Of Sweeney straddled in the sun.) (*CP* 44–45)

If, as Williams argues, the liberalism of "the Bloomsbury fraction" represents the moment of social conscience and concern within the governing class itself, Eliot's portraits of "the silent vertebrate[s]" (*CP* 59) represent an uncompromising and even jeering response to that impulse.

Eliot's eye for exploitable contradictions in the rhetoric and behavior of liberals and humanists was always unerring. Thus, he saw that humanist claims about "the dignity of man," or liberal sentiments about man's limitless potential for improvement and progress, must deal with the problem of Sweeney.

> Gesture of orang-outang
> Rises from the sheets in steam.
>
> This withered root of knots of hair
> Slitted below and gashed with eyes,
> This oval O cropped out with teeth:
> The sickle motion from the thighs
>
> Jackknifes upward at the knees
> Then straightens out from heel to hip
> Pushing the framework of the bed
> And clawing at the pillow slip (*CP* 44)

Recent scholarship routinely accounts for the genesis of literary modernism either in aesthetic or philosophical terms: the formation of Mallarmé's poetics, for example, or the transformation of narrative by Flaubert and James, or the invention of phenomenology become generative events in the remaking of aesthetic perception and literary form on the way to the modernism of the first three decades of this century. But the literary modernism of the "men of 1914" in London encompassed more than a new poetics. It offered also a thoroughly antihumanist vision of life, especially of the "lower orders" who were beginning in that period, threateningly, to break out of the political and social constraints in which bourgeois society had sought to contain them.[10] The modernist's vision ran against the inherited humanist abstractions and ideals. This harsh antihumanism, always noticed by literary historians, but rarely examined, became an important and continuing theme in the work of the whole generation: Eliot, Lewis, Joyce, Pound. In Eliot's work his vision of humanity never changed in essentials though the rhetoric tended to lose its hard edge with time.

In the period of *The Waste Land* Eliot consistently characterized people from the lower classes and other marginalized groups either as subhumans or nonhumans. A survey of *Poems, 1920,* for example, reveals unrelenting revulsion towards people outside the middle- and upper middle-class norms in which he was bred. Jews, for instance, are "spawned" (*CP* 39) rather than born, and when they aren't squatting on window sills (*CP* 39), they are reduced to "protozoic slime" (*CP* 42) or symbolized as "rats" (*CP* 43); the proles are referred to as orang-outangs (*CP* 44), epileptics (*CP* 45), "red-eyed scavengers" (*CP* 47), "punaises" (*CP* 50); and they sometimes give off "une forte odeur de chienne" (*CP* 50) or "a feline smell" (*CP* 56), and they are always "en sueur" (*CP* 49, 50), when not "délabré" (*CP* 53), or being compared to zebras, giraffes (*CP* 59), and silent vertebrates (*CP* 59). Later as Eliot matured, or one might argue as his own social position grew more secure, he became more benign towards "the low." His comments on Marie Lloyd's working-class fans, though thoroughly condescending, are warm enough (*SE* 407). In *Idea* he imagined the Sweeneys in a more paternalistic spirit. They were simply limited intelligences in need of considerable guidance; the goodwill of the directive elite would guarantee that this control, though firm, was just.

Apart from what these attitudes tell us about Eliot himself, they serve a clear antiliberal purpose. As attitudes towards the "lower orders," none of this should startle us. There was nothing abnormal in such reaction. Eliot is here simply reproducing the conventional recoils of horror of his class at the sudden appearance of these new masses on the political and social scene. He is only making his readers, members of his own class, look into the unrefined, unprepared, inexperienced masks of the new upstarts from below with their new demands on the socioeconomic settlements of the nineteenth century. These new people were unvarnished, unmannered, unnameable, garish beyond belief, and holding alien and offensive political and social ideas inside their heads. The attitudes themselves are not surprising; such attitudes were the daily food of the popular press in England in *The Waste Land* period, none more so than Eliot's favorite newspaper of the time, the *Daily Mail*. What is interesting is the extent to which they sometimes led Eliot into the expression of an animus of considerable violence.

It is tempting to see in Eliot's excesses in this respect an open invitation to speculate on the state of his unconscious at this time. This is a temptation worth resisting. Poems, essays, or even private letters are not in themselves adequate bases for such speculation. After all if the individual unconscious were that easy to penetrate, we would all be open books from the minute we were able to speak and write. Also Eliot didn't then feel he needed to repress or deflect his opinions about the Sweeneys, the Jews, or the sexuality of women. He was confident, quite obviously, that his readers would understand the voice speaking to them, and know tacitly from what social place it was speaking. Here, again, it seems to me, is another example of that complicity between author and reader which the text urges. Rather than seeing Eliot's intemperate attitudes as telling us something about the inner man, about which we can know very little until the complete life-records at least are made available, we can measure to some extent their place and intended effect in the social context to which they refer. From this perspective I want to argue that their primary effect was to give his liberal and reform-minded bourgeois readers, including the Bloomsbury set, a vision, of the most horrible kind, of the social demons that their democratic and egalitarian rhetoric was beginning to unchain in their midst.[11]

A particularly complex example of this process at work occurs in "The Fire Sermon" section of *The Waste Land,* the fragment in which the seduction of the typist is presented. I would like to examine aspects of this fragment before looking at *The Waste Land* as a whole and before approaching the very difficult question of its "unity" because my observations on the larger issues depend on what the poem's details teach us about how the whole ought to be read. Questions of the "global" structure depend on how we deal with the poem's microstructure.

The "seduction" in "The Fire Sermon" is not enacted as a moment of lived experience, but rather as a complex attitude towards such a situation and such characters.[12] Firstly, we are urged by the text to be interested in the clerk and typist as social types, not as fully realized individuals. Tiresias constitutes the text's substantial experiencing subject; he is realized on the margins, by what he observes and suffers through. The social typing of clerk and typist is thus easier to communicate through this distancing of point of view. Tiresias's location in the text is above the events he witnesses, but his observing and suffering, carrying a major universalist charge, are hardly above it all, especially if he "sees" this scene in this way. What we want to retrieve in fact is the social ethos where "doing" the seduction in this way makes sense.

We should take note of the strategy (Eliot presents it as that in his notes to the poem) of mythologizing the experiencing subject. Whatever else Eliot intended, Tiresias actually functions to obscure the clarity of the social tone and thus its interpretability.[13] The note to Tiresias (*CP* 82) invites us to see through his eyes; the tone tells us *how* to see. As well, we hear, in the stilted diction and syntax of the description of the seduction, the hiss of sarcasm as an undertone, playing against the "Tiresian" foresufferance, rather than being asked to visualize or feel, even in all its sordid horror, the scene "Enacted on this same divan or bed . . ." (*CP* 72). The foresufferance, of course, by suggesting this specific feeling-state, controls the way of seeing the "substance of the poem" (Notes, *CP* 82). What the text teaches us to respond to is not the fact that beyond a line such as "Endeavors to engage her in caresses" something is actually happening; rather we acknowledge, perhaps not even fully consciously, the dismissive social gesture and the irony that the inflated language of the description ("The time is now propitious . . .") communicates, while, at the same time, this is the very language clerk and typist, or characters of *that* type, believe to be socially correct and literate.[14]

An article in the *Cornhill Magazine* in 1862 suggests the appropriate contemporary context for interpreting, in social terms, the diction of the seduction fragment. The article also helps to locate the particular place the aspiring commercial clerk occupied in the common intuitive life of his "betters."

A gentleman and a labouring man would tell the same story in nearly the same words, differently pronounced, of course, and arranged in the one case grammatically, and in the other not. In either case the words themselves would be plain, racy, and smacking of the soil from which they grow. The language of the commercial clerk, and the manner in which he brings it out, are both formed on quite a different model. He thinks about himself, and constantly tries to talk fine. He calls a school an academy, speaks of proceeding when he means going, and talks, in short, much in the style in which the members of his own class write police reports and accounts of appalling catastrophes for the newspapers.[15]

If, in the published *Waste Land,* there is any doubt about what social types Eliot had in mind and what attitudes the reader is implicitly urged to adopt towards them, then turning to the earlier drafts of the poem makes his intention perfectly clear. There Eliot elaborates the seduction more concretely (*Facsimile WL* 33 and 35, lines 129–88). Clerk and typist are situated socially by more clearly coded, typifying detail. As a reader of social codes— of manners, speech, dress—Eliot was inimitable.

He sketches not only the vacuousness of the typist's existence but emphasizes, in her fake Japanese art and costume, the falsity of her inwardness. Her slattern sprawl carries a double dismissal. She is fixed in the posture of the passive and mechanical consumer of fake cultural commodities, on the one hand, and, on the other, of sex. The male clerk is given literary and artistic pretensions to go along with the pimples, greasy hair, dandruff, predatory reflexes, and impertinent stare (mentioned three times— lines 153, 158, 161). In keeping with the diction of *Poems, 1920,* Eliot further particularizes the two participants in the seduction as crawling insects (line 143). In the passage, also, the London café to which the clerk refers is identified by Valerie Eliot as the Café Royal, a favorite haunt at that time of people active in the arts (*Facsimile WL* 128). The name Nevinson refers, of course, to the Royal Academician C. R. W. Nevinson (128), who was often found there and whose support, the clerk implies, could make or unmake one's career. The clerk's snobbish attention to fashion in knowing the "right" café marks him not simply as a typical *petit bourgeois* clerk on the make, but a *petit bourgeois* clerk who fancies himself something of an artist. The Japanese costume, the fake print, and the decorative sprawl signal that the typist is also as modishly up-to-date as the clerk, supposedly a fit artistic consort for the aspiring literary man staring boldly about the Café Royal.

Edwardian and Georgian literary life was not unfamiliar with this type of fringe character. George Gissing's *New Grub Street* (1891) had already contributed to an understanding of the socioeconomic mutations that had brought a new kind of practitioner into the literary world, much to the annoyance and contempt of the older generation and of those who felt themselves to be the principal guardians of truth, goodness, and beauty in literature. Indeed, the degree of contempt in which the pushy hack was held is well captured by Eliot in the passage. Pound's caricature of Arnold Bennett in *Hugh Selwyn Mauberley* (1920) remains, of course, the famous dismissal. Eliot's "young man carbuncular" is no Arnold Bennett.[16] But the social and literary conditions which make a Bennett possible at one end make possible, on the fringes, residual "scurf" that in its pretentious aspirations and its hunger for the "right" sponsorship (the reference to Nevinson) comes to cultivate an entirely ersatz existence, a life devoted to the consumption of public images as the vocabulary of a new conception of fame, the publicist's notion of celebrity. The styles, the gestures, the *objets d'art,* even inwardness itself can be commercially had as a conscious mimicry of the cultured and refined. The typist, no less than the young man, purchases the "props" of *la vie de bohème* on Oxford Street; Oxford Street, by the way, had already acquired its connotations of vulgar commercialism and popular taste in Eliot's time. Eliot makes us aware not only that the objects themselves have been purchased, but, more importantly, that they are supposed to signify a metropolitan sophistication. She has purchased her "sprawl" as surely as she has bought herself a piece of the public taste for "oriental" effects.[17] Such public consumption of imagery and "effects" raises up a system of fashion, whose codes are inculcated by the new journalism.[18] This system prescribes the outward, and inward, rituals of consumption by which the commodity fetish wishes to be worshipped.[19] Eliot's satire unmasks and vilifies not just the typical emptiness of such a life, but, very presciently, the psychological reality of a consumer-based capitalism which was beginning to take shape at the turn of the century.[20]

There can be no doubt that the blame for this state of affairs was placed not so much on the underlying mutations of British capitalism, very difficult to perceive in its midst, but more on such highly visible and contentious "liberalizing" activities as the Education Acts (London) of 1902 and 1903,[21] which gave greater access to secondary education to students from "the lower orders." The appearance in society of the "young man carbuncular" was Eliot's portrait of the typical product of such liberalizing. J. A. Hobson, an important and widely read Liberal ideologue in this period, had argued in *The Crisis of Liberalism* (1909) for extension of social and cultural equality to all: "It is a broad, easy stair, and not a narrow ladder, that is wanted, one which will entice everyone to rise, will make for general and not selected culture."[22] Eliot's young man and typist were not an answer to such thoughts; they were his furious rebuke. The literary pretensions of the young man and the attainments of a general culture in Hobson's terms are put on the same level as the typist's consumption of fashionable sprawls and cheap prints. In the era of accessibility, literature, its media and techniques are subject to the same commodity fetishism as the decorative styles of the Ballets Russes, to use another contemporary source of once fashionable and consumable imagery. The clumsily self-conscious "literary" language of the seduction enacted in *The Waste Land* has its origins in precisely these identifications.

The short seduction fragment enacts a recognizable discursive voice making the typical sounds (in phonics, diction, and syntax) of the strained literary language of late nineteenth- and early twentiety-century popular narratives.[23] It is a language of stylistic residues, those that signify the conventionally literary as it was received by the "low" ascending Hobson's broad and easy stair, a reception that Eliot always interpreted as entirely a matter of the uncomfortable assimilation of consumable effects. The more important elements of this debased literariness are the lexical and generic residues of Augustan literary practices, especially the stiffly laborious effect of a nonironic use of periphrasis; the clotted Miltonic syntax with its awkwardly positioned modifiers and obscure sentence agency; and, finally, the studied exploitation and simile (*CP* 72, lines 233–34), the trope most familiar to journalism.

It is the same voice Joyce parodies for its humor in the "Eumaeus" section of *Ulysses.* In *The Waste Land,* it is not the humor of such speech that stands out; here it functions as a social sign of cultural and moral destitution.[24] Thus the double irony when, after the typist "with automatic hand . . . puts a record on the gramophone," we hear, following a short pause in which the mixed tone of pity and contempt is allowed to take shape, the rare music of *The Tempest*—" 'This music crept by me upon the waters' " (*CP* 72)—instead of the kind of music the text leads us to believe this sort of woman is more likely to want to hear. The quotation picks up the "music" of the preceding scene, made explicit by the gramophone, a scene sounding its own kind of mechanical and stiff lyricism, and twists it, by ironic comparison, with the music of the enchanted isle, and then twists it again into the "pleasant whining of a mandoline" a few lines later, heard beside a "public bar in Lower Thames Street."[25] Although the music directs our attention to contrasting senses of what constitutes value (through the internal socially determined hierarchy of values in the paradigm from which they are drawn—the gramophone does not have value, *The Tempest* does), this is nowhere made explicit, except as we decipher the "music" of the tonal structure.[26]

To do that, *our* general attitudes toward society as a whole, towards *petit bourgeois* sexual relations in particular, and towards idealized, but socially distant, characters like the "fishmen" lounging at noon under the walls of Magnus Martyr, must coincide with those attitudes that the tonal structure of the passage consciously enacts. When that coincidence takes place, the potent transformation which takes us from the knowing dismissiveness of the gramophone to the acceptability of *The Tempest* as *social* reference occurs in the silence of the gap that separates them, occurs without having to be specified. This "seduction" syntagm reveals in its syntax, continuity, and its lexical choices a certain attitude towards the social and sexual relations of a particular class of people from another, quite distinct, social vantage. Although generally acknowledging the class identification of clerk and typist, criticism has largely ignored and repressed the fact that Eliot's tone *only* makes sense when another class position, Eliot's own, is heard as the place from which the voice of the poem comes, the voice (called "Tiresias") that produces the sound-shape of the parody in the language of the "seduction" itself. Most critics have chosen to hear the voice as coming from some place above or beyond society that measures conduct by a universal and natural authority. This is an ideological refraction that obscures the restricted code really being spoken in these lines. Sharing Eliot's social views about such events as are represented in the passage, critics quickly "raise" the text's class-specific attitude towards the "seduction" to universal status. Allen Tate: "The scene is a masterpiece, perhaps the most profound vision that we have of modern man." Anne Bolgan: "The joyless and dreary automatism of contemporary sexuality. . . ." Nancy Duvall Hargrove: "The dark stairs down which the young man gropes his way upon departing are symbolic, suggesting the blackness and vacancy of his soul as it descends into moral and spiritual blindness."[27]

What is interesting about these traditional judgments is the absolute terms in which they are formulated. They are made often in a matter-of-fact, it-goes-without-saying tone that can only be explained by the fact that the critics believe they are not controversial; thus they do not have to be formulated in another way, one sensitive to the relativity of Eliot's own placing judgment. Everyone, on this issue at least, speaks the same language. Stanley Fish's notion of "interpretive community" is relevant here, especially his sense of that sort of community as being essentially a *social* formation.[28]

As a social formation an interpretative community occupies a place in society, a place where, for example, a reference to Greek mythology carries a particular privilege and prestige that does not need specifying because it is a component of the restricted code which members of these particular social formations use to communicate their allegiance to the community to which they belong, by reinforcing one of its touchstones of value. The case of Cleanth Brooks is typical:

> The fact that Tiresias is made the commentator serves a further irony. In *Oedipus Rex,* it is Tiresias who recognizes that the curse which has come upon the Theban land has been caused by the sinful sexual relationship of Oedipus and Jocasta. But Oedipus' sin has been committed in ignorance, and knowledge of it brings horror and remorse. The essential horror of the act which Tiresias witnesses in the poem is that it is not regarded as a sin at all—is perfectly casual, is merely the copulation of beasts.[29]

Since the *specific* sinfulness of Oedipus's relationship with Jocasta is that it offends the incest taboo, the comparison Brooks decides to make with the clerk and typist becomes absurd: the clerk is not the typist's son. Clearly that is not what Brooks wants to say. What in fact he intends comes down to this: sexual relations should not be casual and if they are, they make the participants no better than beasts. Of course, that assumes that the sexual relations of beasts are "casual," an entirely illegitimate assumption. The word "casual" only activates meaning in the human world, and it is only to that world that the word refers. Its eccentric amplification by Brooks in the "copulation of beasts" makes no biological or logical sense; the phrase is simply a term of *social* abuse, which, in the context of Brooks's paragraph, is opposed by the courtesies paid Sophocles. The shade and shape of Brooks's "eccentric" amplification of the tone are controlled by the ideology the text silently activates, an ideology that valorizes the social position in which Brooks finds himself by a visible and, he must feel, acceptable contempt, not of fully realized participants in the "seduction," but the sort of people they represent metonymically, who, in fact, can only be thought of in class terms.

But who exactly are these people? The message of the voicing of the "seduction" itself is plain enough. The poem's restricted speech code suggests that this is the way people of this sort *textualize* their experience, that is, in terms of the stilted and clichéd formulations of the literary hack. Isn't it pathetic of them? From here the political point is not much further up; these are the people liberalism wants us to believe are our equals. Isn't it absurd? In Joyce's parody of this style, the point is: isn't it *comical* the way Bloom's voice apes the literary style he knows, adjusting to the situation of having to talk to a "literary man" in a language Bloom thinks this "literary man" will accept? The comedy lies in our knowledge that this literary man's— Stephen's—literariness is going through an identity crisis.

In the context of critical "argument," Brooks's use of *Oedipus Rex* clearly functions to sandbag the conclusion he wants to proffer, which is, in effect, arrived at by a *silent* reading of the poem's tone, a reading he cannot make explicit because the thought processes he has gone through, if that is what they are, have no empirical privilege, being simply and intimately bound up with the attitude of one class towards another.[30] In fact, it might be useful to interpret Brooks's responses to Eliot as the working out toward the reader of the intent of the poem, namely a cleansing of the egalitarian crud that has obscured the clarity and social obviousness of fundamental class distinctions. Moreover, his judgment is the result of the functioning of the restricted code which Brooks shares with Eliot and with other members of the interpretive community who understand and accept the implicit values, attitudes, opinions, privileges that characterize the code, in short, the common intuitive life of that community. What *Oedipus Rex* does in this context is work Eliot's social contempt free of its genesis in class feeling and raise it to a higher station in an elaborated form that rewrites it as a comment on the "decline of civilization."

And it was as a diagnosis of the malaise universally afflicting European civilization that Eliot's first readers chose to read *The Waste Land*.[31] That Eliot in later years attempted to deflect attention from this sort of reading by suggesting that the poem's genesis was wholly in private experience and that its intention was, at least partly, therapeutic[32] cannot efface the evidence of the poem itself, especially the evidence that can be derived from the way Eliot chose to enact his experience, private or public.

The point of this analysis is to suggest that Brooks's reading of *The Waste Land*, like Moody's of "Prufrock," is the kind of reading the poem itself has been designed to provoke. The particulars of the poem—the typist's "half-formed thought" (line 251) for example—do not simply name some narrative event but evoke the concrete social context in which such an event carries an important ideological message. Because I define a text as a signifying practice always entangled in an active, transformative relationship with the common intuitive life readers carry around in their heads, I have looked at one of Eliot's best readers, Cleanth Brooks, reading the seduction fragment of the poem. I mean by "best" in this context something like the kind of reader who brings the appropriate literary background, tacit social assumptions and beliefs to the poem which the poem itself requires in order that its transformative work proceed unhindered. In addition, such a reader brings, at a minimum, a tacit understanding of the way experiences—and ways of talking about them—are valued and hierarchized in bourgeois society. Thormählen's assumption, for instance, that sexuality which is "religiously significant" is more valuable than what she blandly dismisses as "the modern situation" exemplifies just such a mental reflex.

Eliot's readers were also on Ezra Pound's mind when he was reading *The Waste Land* for the first time. In the draft Eliot put before him, the finale of the seduction fragment describes the departure of the clerk in more detail than the published draft (*Facsimile WL* 35, lines 177–80). After the final kiss and the dark stairs, the clerk turns a corner by a stable (the animal reference here is deliberate) and stops to urinate and spit. Pound scored out the final two lines of the quatrain during his revisions of the text and commented marginally that the references to stable, urine, and saliva probably went too far (*Facsimile WL* 47, lines 179–80).

M. L. Rosenthal suggests that Pound's comment acknowledges that the "best available reading public for poetry" in 1922 would not have been ready for such descriptive candor.[33] Harvey Gross contends that the revisions gave *The Waste Land* "the right amount of aesthetic distance," thus eliminating Eliot's "kinky expressions of disgust with the human animal and its undignified functions." Like Rosenthal, Gross decides the revisions were done with a view to what the poem's readers might be able to stomach.[34]

In his comment Pound is clearly referring to the tone of the excised lines. There is an intensity of contempt, even hatred, of this sort of person that stands out too lividly, too immediately, as merely social abuse, the hatred of one class towards another. In the revision these feelings are pushed further back in the internal perspective and the Tiresian foresufferance allowed to muffle by just that right amount the free, but embarrassing, play of the speaker's feelings. This acts to blur the hard edges of these feelings within the mythological haven that, by definition, presents states of affairs in a form in which they are no longer within reach of reason. In short, what begins as typical social contempt is made palatable by linking it to a mythical framework that universalizes it. Cleanth Brooks certainly takes this step without a moment's hesitation. But palatable for whom? Certainly Eliot would not have cared for the sensitivities of the usual middle-class readers, for example, of the *Daily Mail* who were no doubt familiar with these kinds of feelings directed toward pushy clerks and "Bradford millionaires."[35] No, the revisions were not for readers who found accounts from Italy in 1922–23 of the castor oil torture of socialist civic officials by the new Fascist governors thoroughly amusing.[36] They were for people with more delicate sensibilities, those whom Eliot thought suffered from the "whiggery tendency," the ultrarefined liberals of the "Bloomsbury fraction," who up to this time, according to Hayward, were his principal audience. They needed to be shown the brutal face of the social world they had helped bring about. Protected, also, by their privileged positions within the bosom of the governing class, these midwives of demos ought to be shown the whole extent of their handiwork. But as Pound reminded Eliot, there were still limits to that to which such a reader, even one growing more sympathetic after the Great War, might be expected to assent.

From this critical perspective, then, the meaning and function of a style or poetic form cannot be captured adequately in literary terms, especially in Eliot's case, where the literary itself (in its late romantic forms) is remorselessly subverted and displaced. The choice of one locution over another in the characterization of a person or an event, within a modernism that has worked itself free of "literature" and the traditional generic or modal codes for the universalizing of moral experience, becomes a more overtly social act. Eliot calls the young man "carbuncular" and compares his assurance to a silk hat worn by a rich provincial *arriviste* (a source of regional power, one might add, of the Liberal party in Britain at this time)[37] in order not only to present the deplorable results of particular social developments, but, and this is the important point, to knock any taste for the ideas and feelings that bring about such conditions clean out of a reader's head.

What we traditionally mean by style and form requires considerable rethinking from this perspective. And also what we mean by unity. A reading such as I have proposed for the "seduction" fragment clearly pierces the seamless hide that a formalist or structuralist account stretches tightly over the text. In the critical reception of *The Waste Land* from F. R. Leavis (*New Bearings*) to our day the question of the poem's unity settles, at the end of the day, on the status of Eliot's use of myth. I will argue that the choices Eliot made to "unify" *The Waste Land* within a mythic framework do not represent a description of the poem's unity at all, but are an effect of a larger dialogical demand.

. . . .

The Waste Land does not merely reflect the breakdown of an historical, social, and cultural order battered by violent forces operating under the name of modernity. For Eliot the disaster that characterized modernity was not an overturning, but the unavoidable, and ironic, culmination of that very order so lovingly celebrated in Victoria's last decade on the throne. Unlike the older generation, who saw in events like the Great War the passing of a golden age, Eliot saw only that the golden age was itself a heap of absurd sociopolitical axioms and perverse misreadings of the cultural past that had proved in the last instance to be made of the meanest alloy. The poem's enactment of the contemporary social scene in "The Burial of the Dead," "A Game of Chess," and "The Fire Sermon" exhibits the "negative liberal society" in which such events and people are typical. Eliot's choice of these events and people—Madame Sosostris, the cast of characters in "A Game of Chess," and the typist—as *representative* of a particular society is susceptible, of course, to a political analysis, which is to say, their representativeness is not self-evident, though they are presented as if it is. The "one bold stare" of the house-agent's clerk, put back in the bourgeois context where staring is one of the major lapses in manners, does not hold up the mirror to a simple gesture, but illuminates the underlying conditions that make a mere clerk's swagger possible. What is exposed is the "fact" that clerks in general no longer know their place. What we are to make of this fact is pointedly signaled by the disgust that the specifics of the rendering provoke and the social distance generated by the Tiresian foresufferance. . . .

As its social critique was aimed negatively at the liberal ethos which Eliot felt had culminated in the War and its disorderly aftermath, *The Waste Land* could not visibly adopt some preliberal code of values. In the same way, the poem could not propose a postliberal, historicist or materialist ethic without an historicizing epistemology. The poem's authority rested instead on other bases that provided, not a system of ideas as the primary form of legitimation, but a new lyric synthesis as a kind of experiential authenticity in a world in which the sacred cosmologies, on the one hand, had fallen prey to astrologers and charlatans, while, on the other, the cosmology of everyday life, i.e. the financial system (the "City" in the poem), had fallen into the soiled hands of racially indeterminate and shady importers of currants and the like, among them, of course, the pushing Jews of the plunderbund. . . .

The poem attempts to penetrate below the level of rationalist consciousness, where the conceptual currencies of the liberal ethos have no formative and directive power. Below that level lay the real story about human nature, which "liberal thought" perversely worked to obscure, by obscuring the intersection of the human and the divine at the deepest levels of consciousness. That stratum did not respond to the small-scale and portable logics of Enlightenment scientism, but to the special "rationality" of mythic thought. Its "logic" and narrative forms furnish the idiom of subrationalist, conscious life. To repeat: if not on the conventional rationalist basis, where does Eliot locate the authority of *The Waste Land,* and authority that can save the poem from mere eccentric sputter and give it a more commanding aspect? I think it was important for Eliot himself to feel the poem's command, and not simply to make it convincing to skeptical readers; Lyndall Gordon's biography makes this inner need for strength in his own convictions a central theme in Eliot's early life. But to answer our question: the authority the poem claims has two dimensions.

The first is based on the aesthetics of French *symbolisme* and its extension into the Wagnerian music-drama.[38] Indeed the theoretical affinites of Baudelaire et al. and Wagner, which Eliot obviously intuited in the making of *The Waste Land,* can be seen now as nothing short of brilliant. Only in our own time are these important aesthetic and cultural connections being seriously explored. From *symbolisme* Eliot adopted the notion of the epistemological self-sufficiency of aesthetic consciousness, its independence from rationalist instrumentality, and thus its more efficacious contact with experience and, at the deeper levels, contact with the divine through its earthly language in myth. From his French and German forebears, Eliot formulated a new discourse of experience which in the 1920s was still very much the voice of the contemporary avant-garde in Britain and, in that sense, a voice on the margins, without institutional authority. But here the ironic, even sneering, dismissal of the liberal stewardship of culture and society reverses the semiotics of authority-claims by giving to the voice on the margins an authority the institutional voices can no longer assume since the world they are meant to sustain has finally been seen through in all those concrete ways the poem mercilessly enacts. *The Waste Land* is quite clear on that point. We are meant to see in "The Fire Sermon," for example, the "loitering heirs of City directors" weakly giving way to the hated *métèques,* so that the City, one of the "holy" places of mercantilism, has fallen to profane hands. The biting humor in this is inescapable. . . .

The second dimension of the authority on which *The Waste Land* rests involves the new discourse on myth that comes from the revolutionary advances in anthropology in Eliot's time associated with the names of Émile Durkheim, Marcel Mauss, and the Cambridge School led by Sir James Frazer and Jane Harrison. We know that Eliot was well acquainted with these developments at least as early as 1913–14. The importance of these new ideas involved rethinking the study of ancient and primitive societies. The impact of these renovations was swift and profound and corresponds, though much less publicly, to the impact of *On the Origin of Species* on the educated public of midcentury Victorian life. Modernist interest in primitive forms of art (Picasso, Lawrence, and many others), and, therefore, the idioms and structures of thought and feeling in primitive cultures, makes sense in several ways. Clearly the artistic practices of primitive peoples are interesting technically to other artists of any era. Interest in the affective world or the collective mentality of a primitive society is another question altogether. That interest, neutral, perhaps, in scholarship, becomes very easy to formulate as a critique of practices and structures in the present that one wants to represent as distortions and caricatures of some original state of nature from which modernity has catastrophically departed. Eliot's interest in the mythic thought of primitive cultures, beginning at Harvard, perhaps in the spirit of scientific inquiry, takes a different form in the argument of *The Waste Land*. There it functions pointedly as a negative critique of the liberal account of the origins of society in the institutions of contract, abstract political and civil rights, and mechanistic psychology.

The anthropologists rescued the major cultural production of primitive societies—myth—from the view that saw these ancient narratives either as the quaint decorative brio of simple folk or, if they were Greek, as the narrative mirrors of heroic society. Instead myth, and not just the myths of the Greeks, was reconceived as the narrative thematics of prerationalist cosmologies that provided an account of the relationship between the human and the divine. Myth was also interpreted psychologically, and Nietzsche is crucial in this development, as making visible the deeper strata of the mind. If the concept is the notional idiom of reason, myth is the language of unconsicous life. What Eliot intuited from this new understanding was that myth provided a totalizing structure that could make sense, equally, of the state of a whole culture and of the whole structure of an individual mind (*Notes* 25). In this intuition he found the idiom of an elaborated, universalizing code which was not entirely the product of rationalist thought. In addition, this totalizing structure preserved the sacred dimension of life by seeing it inextricably entwined with the profane. For the expression of this intuition in the context of an environment with a heavy stake in the elaborated codes of a rationalist and materialist world view which had subordinated the sacred to the profane, Eliot adapted for his own use the poetics of juxtaposition.

The textual discontinuity of *The Waste Land* has usually been read as the technical advance of a new aesthetic. The poetics of juxtaposition are often taken as providing the enabling rationale for the accomplishment of new aesthetic effects based on shock and surprise. And this view is easy enough to adopt when the poem is read in the narrow context of a purely literary history of mutated lyric forms. However, when the context is widened and the poem read as a motivated operation on an already always existing structure of significations, this technical advance is itself significant as a critique of settled forms of coherence. Discontinuity, from this perspective, is a symbolic form of "blasting and bombardiering." In the design of the whole poem, especially in its use of contemporary anthropology, the broken textual surface must be read as the sign of the eruptive power of subrational forces reasserting, seismically, the element totalities at the origins of culture and mind. The poem's finale is an orgy of social and elemental violence. The "Falling towers," lightning and thunder, unveil what Eliot, at that time, took to be the base where individual mind and culture are united in the redemptive ethical imperatives spoken by the thunder. What the poem attempts here, by ascribing these ethical principles to the voice of nature and by drawing on the epistemological autonomy posited by *symbolisme*, is the construction of an elaborated code in which an authoritative universalizing vision can be achieved using a "notional" (mythic) idiom uncontaminated by Enlightenment forms of rationalism.

Powerful as it is in the affective and tonal program of the poem, functioning as the conclusion to the poem's "argument," this closural construction is, at best, precarious when seen beyond the shaping force of the immediate social and cultural context. This construction, achieved rhetorically, in fact is neither acceptable anthropology, nor sound theology, nor incontestable history, but draws on all these areas in order to make the necessary point in a particular affective climate. The extent to which the poem still carries unsurpassable imaginative power indicates the extent to which our own time has not broken entirely with the common intuitive life that the poem addressed 60 years ago.

Eliot himself abandoned his creation as soon as it was formulated, migrating to a Christian orthodoxy in the Anglican church. This movement to an institutionally established authority displaced the special kinds of authority claimed for the perceptiveness and argument in *The Waste Land*. The same perceptions and the same argument were, in the mid-1920s, lodged in a social institution; the critique of "negative liberal society" continued without interruption, but no longer from the margins. The lyric voice, alloyed on the margins, was not abandoned however; it was adapted to the new situation within an historical institution and within the discursive and notional modes that institutional affiliation provided.

From this new social position Eliot's critique of the liberal orthodoxies of thought and feeling continued. The attack, as before, remains focused on the liberal-romantic account of experience. Important as immediate personal experience seems to be in *The Waste Land*, enacted in the lyric intensity of the metaphoric voice, it cannot be taken as final or absolute. The sharp focus on experience in *The Waste Land* is primarily strategic in the service of the dispersal of the liberal-romantic hegemony of thought and feeling. Eliot is more sensitive to the way men and women *talk* about experience, than to experience itself. The brilliantly achieved collocation of lyric consciousness, myth, and Indo-Christian scripturality embosomed by a sacramentalized nature, a synthesis that would have served lesser artists for a lifetime, was soon itself dispersed in Eliot's announcement of his final theme, the one that he would carry forward for the rest of his life.

The escape from his own brilliant creation coincides in fact with Eliot's own changing social position in England. By the late 1920s, he had closed socially on what he felt was the center of English life in its most important and guiding social faction. His earlier ambiguous position in an established and stratified society, a hierarchy in which he had no inherited privilege and thus no access to a voice "natural" to any one of its discriminated ranks, led him, as we have seen, to construct one. This new lyrical voice gave his middle-class audience a vision of the reality that embraced them, from a place (on the margins) that was not implicated in the psychoethical impotence of the reigning order.[39] But this composite voice was ultimately like Blake's, as Eliot described it in *The Sacred Wood,* adrift without an anchor in a "framework of accepted and traditional ideas," a voice "with a capacity for considerable understanding of human nature, with a remarkable and original sense of language and the music of language, and a gift of hallucinated vision" (*SW* 157–58), but without the historical nourishment of an institutionalized and cosmological tradition. Blake required respect for "impersonal reason . . . common sense . . . the objectivity of science" (*SW* 157). But the reason, common sense, and science that Eliot recommends here were not the orders of rationality that *The Waste Land* assaults. Eliot was not against reason, common sense, and science; he was simply against the way these were used in the liberal ethos. With the publication of *For Lancelot Andrewes* (1928) and "Ash Wednesday" (1930) Eliot moved decisively towards gaining the institutional authority he believed Dante to have had.

The name of Dante brings to a focus a final, philosophical point. One of the many revolutionary intellectual impulses of Enlightenment thought was the progressive alloying of reason and freedom as constituting the two elements of a single human essence informing each and every individual. The consequences of this identification have been profound in every area of human life. But for Eliot this union of reason and freedom in the individual represented the crucial seed of discord in modernity, planted at the beginning of the bourgeois era. *The Waste Land* presents the consequences of what seemed to him a misguided faith. From *The Waste Land* on, he more explicitly moved to reestablish the notion that reason is intrinsic to . . . historical institutions, not to the atomic individual, and that an apostolic and historical Church embodies to the profoundest degree Reason as such, or at least a Reason that carries a nonhuman, divine authority. From this perspective, the individual, as conceived in Christian doctrine as limited and fallen, approaches Reason the closer he is to its sacred source and, in that way, and in that way alone, can guarantee his freedom. Having come to this position, acknowledged in practice in 1927 by his acceptance of the Anglican confession, Eliot began to point his poetry in a different direction.

Notes

1. Richard Shannon, *The Crisis of Imperialism, 1865–1915.* The Paladin History of England (London: Paladin, 1976), 11–16, 76–77, 199–225. [Ed. note: References from T.S. Eliot's poems are taken from *The Complete Poems and Plays* (New York: Harcourt Brace, 1952);

and from "*The Waste Land*," *A Facsimile and Transcript of the Original Drafts Including the Annotations of Ezra Pound*, ed. and intro by Valerie Eliot (New York: Harcourt Brace Jovanovich, 1971).]

2. C. B. Macpherson, *The Political Theory of Possessive Individualism: Hobbes and Locke* (Oxford: Clarendon Press, 1973), 263–65; Steven Lukes, "The Meanings of 'Individualism,' " *Journal of the History of Ideas* 32 (Jan.–March, 1971): 45–66.

3. Roger Kojecky, *T. S. Eliot's Social Criticism* (London: Faber & Faber, 1971), 134–35.

4. Terry Eagleton, *Criticism and Ideology: A Study in Marxist Literary Theory* (London: NLB, 1976), 147.

5. Kojecky, 131–32.

6. Lyndall Gordon, *Eliot's Early Years* (Oxford: Oxford University Press, 1977), 85 and passim.

7. Raymond Williams, *Problems in Materialism and Culture: Selected Essays* (London: Verso/NLB, 1980), 165.

8. Ibid., 155.

9. Ibid.

10. For one of the many contemporary expressions of fear, one might even say terror, felt by the bourgeoisie at the surge from below, see Gustave Le Bon's *The World in Revolt*, which appeared in London in English translation in the spring of 1921 (159, 179).

11. C. F. G. Masterman (*The Condition of England* [1909]), who, as a liberal ideologue and reformer from the mid-1890s to the Great War, had sympathized with the condition of the underprivileged, began having second thoughts, as did most liberals, when the practical effects of the political emancipation of the proletariat began to transform English society after the war (C. F. G. Masterman, *England After War: A Study* [London: Hodder and Stoughton, n.d.], 70–72).

12. C. K. Stead, *The New Poetics: Yeats to Eliot* (Harmondsworth: Penguin, 1967), 165–66, provides the typical treatment of these lines, making a convenient distinction between "a detached account of an event" and "an enactment" of it. How the status of enacted contents, or the processes of selection and combination, change because a text "enacts" rather than "reports" is not specified. Stead rightly senses that the passage does not merely report, but by saying it enacts an event, without specifying *how* the enactment works and how we recognize the difference, he does not clarify matters. What exactly *is* being enacted in these lines? It is certainly not a self-evident and universal "image of human life" (165).

13. Terry Eagleton, "T. S. Eliot and the Uses of Myth," *Exiles and Emigres: Studies in Modern Literature* (London: Chatto and Windus, 1970), 161: "The objection which can be registered to this is then the criticism which can be made of much of the poem: in so far as the limits of the mythology remain unquestioned, the whole projection (as its automatic rhythms tend to imply) is 'natural,' and Tiresias's detachment the impotence of an observer of how life 'really' is; in so far as that social mythology is questioned, his detachment becomes, not a quality of response, but a quality of the tendentious mind out of which the incident is created." See also Ian Hamilton, "*The Waste Land*," *Eliot in Perspective: A Symposium*, Ed. Graham Martin (London: Macmillan, 1970) on Tiresias: "Old, blind, bisexual. Why should we take these characteristics to denote unusual wisdom (especially about sex) when they can more easily be taken to confess unusual ignorance" (109).

14. Hugh Kenner, *The Invisible Poet: T. S. Eliot* (London: Methuen, 1966), 145; David Trotter, *The Making of the Reader: Language and Subjectivity in Modern American English and Irish Poetry* (London: Macmillan, 1984), 51–53.

15. Quoted in Trotter, 51.

16. This identification is not as far-fetched as it sounds. It occurred to Clive Bell in his review of *The Waste Land* in the *Nation and Athenaeum* 33 (22 September 1923), 772–73.

17. The *Daily Mail*, under Northcliffe, pioneered daily journalism targeted at women. Women seem to have been seen primarily as consumers of clothes, cosmetics, decorative

furnishings, pulp romances, and pictures. Oddly enough, the *Mail*'s general attitude towards the "modern" woman in its editorial pages was usually scornful, when it wasn't openly misogynist, although the *Mail*'s advertising strategy largely depended on women and was a major contributor in the social construction of the image of the "modern" woman. The naturalizing of this cynical contradiction makes for an interesting ideological episode in the further construction of the gender stereotype—women as insatiable consumers—to suit a new mutation of capitalism.

In the period when Eliot was a regular, even avid, reader of the *Mail*, the back pages of the paper were devoted to women. On those pages, also, one finds the pulp fiction and, on the very back page, the new photojournalism. Apart from the occasional newsphoto, the back photo page normally pictured social and show business celebrities, human interest subjects, and the antics of picturesque eccentrics.

In the women's pages news features and advertising were often coordinated. The fashions and furnishings writers would highlight a particular style and the merchandisers would supplement these features with the necessary props. Women were encouraged to think in terms of purchasing what we would now call a "look" for themselves and their immediate domestic surroundings. For example, the *Mail* on 1 Sept. 1920 ran a spread on "le style japonais" in cosmetics, clothes, furniture, and complementary decorations, like the typist's "bright kimono" and "false Japanese print."

The advertisements for women's underwear were also very interesting. The typist's "drying combinations," an early type of body-stocking, are prominently featured in drawings of girlish-looking, but buxom, women. The combination of the primly innocent glance and the voluptuously ripened body quite obviously appealed to some erotic fashion of the time. Whether the drawings were made with male or female readers in mind is an open question.

18. The commercial consumption of mechanically reproducible cultural commodities in the twentieth century was first described and analyzed in detail by the Frankfurt School. Walter Benjamin's "The Work of Art in the Age of Mechanical Reproduction" (*Illuminations*, trans. Harry Zohn [New York: Harcourt, Brace & World, 1968], 219–53) remains the definitive starting point in the analysis of this process. Max Horkheimer and Theodor W. Adorno, in *Dialectic of Enlightenment*, trans. John Cumming (New York: Seabury Press, 1972), developed and extended Benjamin's insights in the service of a critique of an industrially mature, profit-ruled "culture industry" as one of the limits of the Enlightenment, namely, the limit at which the emancipatory, antifeudal project at the heart of the Enlightenment is turned by the "culture industry" in on itself and ironically defeats its own deepest purposes and aspirations. "Freedom to choose . . . proves to be freedom to choose what is always the same" (166–67).

19. Walter Benjamin, *Reflections: Essays, Aphorisms, Autobiographical Writings*, trans. Edmund Jephcott (New York: Harcourt Brace Jovanovich, 1978), 153.

20. E. J. Hobsbawm, *Industry and Empire: From 1750 to the Present Day*, Vol. 3 of *The Pelican Economic History of Britain* (Harmondsworth: Penguin Books, 1970), 192–93.

21. Donald Read, *England 1868–1914: The Age of Urban Democracy* (London: Longman, 1979), 436.

22. Quoted in Read, 250.

23. With the expansion of the popular media, Grub Street hacks came into their own. They often produced pulp romance and adventure fiction serialized in the daily press. On 28 October 1922, for example, the *Daily Mail* began a new serial called "Helen of London: A Romance of Modern Babylon." The verbal style of this and other such serials is cut from the same cloth as the stylistic mannerisms of the seduction. Eliot must have been amused at being able to make such devilishly ironic use of this familiar style. As for "Helen of London," it was a sort of downmarket *Waste Land* for shop assistants and chars.

24. Bernard Bergonzi, *T. S. Eliot* (New York: Macmillan, 1972), 101, finds that the language of the seduction has "a peculiar austere beauty," a response aimed at discomfiting Ian

Hamilton's sense of these lines as unsatisfactorily prissy and fastidious. Hamilton has not recognized that the effect is intentional (Hamilton, 109).

25. Nancy Duvall Hargrove, *Landscape as Symbol in the Poetry of T. S. Eliot* (Jackson: University Press of Mississippi, 1978), 76 ignores the linking function of the "music" and connects the syntagmatic chain by reference to the geography of the City of London, the direction, in short, in which someone called "the protagonist" heads in order to end up in Lower Thames Street. A. D. Moody, *Thomas Stearns Eliot, Poet* (Cambridge U. Press, 1979), 92–93 acknowledges the music's connective function.

26. David Craig, "The Defeatism of *The Waste Land*," *Critical Quarterly* 2 (1960): 241–52.

27. Allen Tate, untitled essay, in *T. S. Eliot: A Selected Critique,* ed. Leonard Unger (New York: Russell & Russell, 1966), 292; Anne C. Bolgan, *What the Thunder Really Said: A Retrospective Essay on the Making of* The Waste Land (Montreal: McGill-Queen's University Press, 1973), 87; Nancy Duvall Hargrove, *Landscape as Symbol in the Poetry of T. S. Eliot* (Jackson: University Press of Mississippi, 1978), 76.

28. Stanley Fish, *Is There a Text in This Class? The Authority of Interpretive Communities* (Cambridge: Harvard University Press, 1980), 318.

29. Cleanth Brooks, *Modern Poetry and the Tradition* (Chapel Hill: University of North Carolina Press, 1939), 156. Cf. Marianne Thormählen, The Waste Land: *A Fragmentary Wholeness.* Lund Studies in English 52 (Lund: G. W. K. Gleerup, 1978), 113.

30. Graham Martin, ed. and intro, *Eliot in Perspective: A Symposium* (London: Macmillan, 1970), 20.

31. *SE* 324. "As Stephen Spender sees it, what Eliot took to Pound was 'a series of sketches in a modernist manner about the breakdown of everything. There were a great many ideas about breakdown around at the time—Spengler's *Decline of the West,* for instance, and writers were concerned aoubt the breakdown of public life and individual lives.' " Spender quoted in Hugh Herbert, "An Ode to Old Possum," *Manchester Guardian Weekly,* 29 (August 1982), 20; see also John Press, *The Fire and the Fountain: An Essay on Poetry* (London: Methuen, 1966), 29; F. W. Bateson, "Criticism's Lost Leader," *Literary Criticism of T. S. Eliot: New Essays,* Ed. David Newton-De Molina (London: Athlone Press, 1977), 8–9.

32. T. S. Eliot, quoted by Theodore Spenser during a lecture at Harvard University (*Facsimile WL* 1) and James E. Miller (152–59).

33. M. L. Rosenthal, "The Waste Land as an Open Structure," *Mosaic* 6 (Fall 1972): 189.

34. Harvey Gross, "Metoikos in London," *Mosaic* 6 (Fall 1972): 145.

35. All through May 1919 the *Daily Mail* and other Conservative papers published reports on the theme of England's "new owners," generally identified with war profiteers.

36. Percival Phillips, "The Castor Oil Weapon," *Daily Mail,* 27 December 1922, pp. 7–8.

37. Read, *England 1868–1914,* 160, 322–23.

38. Michael Black, "The Literary Background," *The Wagner Companion,* ed. Peter Burbridge and Richard Sutton (New York: Cambridge University Press, 1979), 81–84.

39. Bergonzi, 100.

The Defeat of Symbolism in "Death by Water"

JEWEL SPEARS BROOKER AND JOSEPH BENTLEY

> We shall not cease from exploration
> And the end of all our exploring
> Will be to arrive where we started
> And know the place for the first time.
> —"Little Gidding," V

T. S. Eliot brought to his early poetry a sophisticated awareness of the nature and limits of language and symbolism.[1] He studied language theory at Harvard and Oxford universities, and he wrote a doctoral dissertation that is concerned in part with the nature of language. In his early philosophical papers, in a seminar paper on interpretation written for Josiah Royce at Harvard in 1913–14, and in the dissertation itself, he revealed a number of convictions about interpretation,[2] convictions of permanent importance in his poetry. In these and other studies, he argued that all knowledge is interpretation, that all meaning is constructed through interpretation, that all interpretation is fragmentary because filtered through a limited point of view, and that any notion of ultimate meaning is ultimately meaningless.

Eliot's early focus on the nature of interpretation became a part of his work as an artist, and many of his poems from 1909 to 1942 are in one of their aspects commentaries on language and its limits. In *Four Quartets*, a series of meditations on language and time, he refers to ceaseless journeys which have as their end (destination and purpose) a return to the starting place with an enhanced ability to know that starting point. Such journeys, common in Eliot's life and work, are spiritual on one level and hermeneutic on another, a parallelism consistent with the poet's running analogy between life and text. The hermeneutic exploration and return to home base that Eliot refers to in "Little Gidding" provides a helpful model for readers of his poetry. He often includes images encrusted with symbols and weighted by allusions, images which force the reader to undertake hermeneutic forays of great complexity, but which finally reveal the inadequacy of all interpretation and thus return the reader to the text as text. Most of the interpretative

This essay was written specifically for this volume and is published here for the first time by permission of the authors. For further elaboration on the ideas presented here, see Jewel Spears Brooker and Joseph Bentley, *Reading "The Waste Land": Modernism and the Limits of Interpretation* (Amherst: University of Massachusetts Press, 1989), copyright © 1989 by The University of Massachusetts Press.

journeys initiated by Eliot's texts lead finally to a defeat of symbolism. In illustrating the inadequacy of symbols, Eliot is making a striking point about the limits of interpretation. His practice of leading his readers through interpretative exercises before circling them back to a newly demythologized text that they will be able to know "for the first time" can be illustrated by reference to his use of water references, particularly in *The Waste Land*.

From "The Love Song of J. Alfred Prufrock" to "The Dry Salvages," Eliot's work contains complicated and ambiguous references to water. In the early poems, he often imagines mindless existence beneath the sea as an attractive alternative to existence in civilized society. J. Alfred Prufrock's "I should have been a pair of ragged claws / Scuttling across the floors of silent seas," for example, reveals the persona's need to escape both the fashionable intellectuality of Bostonian society and his own highly intellectual consciousness. Prufrock's preoccupation with submarine life continues, culminating in "Till human voices wake us, and we drown," an image in which a return to consciousness is associated with death. In "Mr. Apollinax," the narrator imagines the old man of the sea laughing as fingers of surf drop worried bodies into the green silence. The puns on "profound," "worried," and "drift" play with the ideas of laughter that is mindless but profound and worry as a mental phenomenon replaced by the physical action of the waves on a drifting body:

> His laughter was submarine and profound
> Like the old man of the sea's
> Hidden under coral islands
> Where worried bodies of drowned men drift down in the green silence,
> Dropping from fingers of surf.

Eliot's prose also abounds with metaphorical uses of water, the most common being his recurrent use of "melting" as a metaphor for merging into unity.

The most powerful instance of Eliot's interest in water imagery is in "Death by Water," Part IV of *The Waste Land:*

> Phlebas the Phoenician, a fortnight dead,
> Forgot the cry of gulls, and the deep sea swell
> And the profit and loss.
>
>   A current under sea
> Picked his bones in whispers. As he rose and fell
> He passed the stages of his age and youth
> Entering the whirlpool.
>
>   Gentile or Jew
> O you who turn the wheel and look to windward,
> Consider Phlebas, who was once handsome and tall as you.

This is Eliot's most formal treatment of an image of disturbing ambivalence associated with overwhelming questions of the meaning of life and death. Many critics have commented on this section of *The Waste Land*.[3] Most note that it is a slightly revised version of a stanza from "Dans le Restaurant," an earlier poem by Eliot in French; some comment on the longer manuscript draft version; and all try to make sense of the text itself, with special attention to the several patterns of water references. In the drafts shown to Ezra Pound, preserved in *The Waste Land Facsimile,* this part of the poem includes a narrative of a sea voyage and shipwreck and is almost ten times as long as the final version published in 1922.[4] Pound suggested that Eliot delete the lines about the voyage and shipwreck. Somewhat reluctant to drop them, Eliot countered by saying that perhaps he should drop all of Part IV. Quite rightly, Pound protested. "I DO advise keeping Phlebas. In fact, I more'n advise. Phlebas is an integral part of the poem; the card pack introduces him, the drowned phoen. sailor. . . . Phlebas is "needed ABSOlootly where he is.' "[5]

As part of a poem called *The Waste Land,* the title "Death by Water" automatically takes on certain symbolic values. It evokes, for example, the relation between lack of water and deserts, between presence of water and fruitfulness. The title also brings powerful suggestions from the myths Eliot drew on for his poem, myths in which water is explicitly associated with rituals designed to remove the curse from the land and its people. Jessie Weston's *From Ritual to Romance,* which Eliot claims as a major source for his underlying myth, traces the relation between freeing the waters and lifting the curse from the land. Frazer's *Golden Bough,* similarly, includes innumerable literal and symbolic connections between wastelands and the presence or absence of water. In Weston and Frazer, and also in Eliot's Indic sources and the Bible, "death" by water is more than death; as the focal point of rituals of rebirth and salvation, it is a powerful symbol of life.

Water is central from the beginning to the end of *The Waste Land.* "The Burial of the Dead" begins with April mixing "Memory and desire, stirring / Dull roots with spring rain" and summer surprising characters "With a shower of rain." This section of the poem also contains the famous fortune-telling episode in which Madame Sosostris consults her Tarot cards, finds the drowned Phoenician Sailor, and warns a character inside the poem to "Fear death by water." "A Game of Chess" begins with an allusion to Cleopatra in her river barge and ends with Ophelia's sad valedictory—"good night, sweet ladies, good night"—a poignant allusion to death by water. The ironically titled third section, "The Fire Sermon," takes water as a major symbolic element. Its depiction of life on and beside various rivers suggests that this life by water is in a figurative sense death by water, and that literal death would be preferable. "Death by Water," the penultimate part of the poem, collects and intensifies the earlier references to water. "What the Thunder Said," finally, continues the complex sequence of references to rain, rivers, boats, wetness, and dryness, but the emphasis changes from death by water to desire for water. In the so-called water dropping song, this desire for water is pushed to an extreme before the reader encounters the anticlimactic line—"then a damp gust, bringing rain"—and in the last lines, another river, another boat, and more fishing.

Eliot's use of water references is in part a commentary on the nature of interpretation, a commentary that can be clarified by a few observations on his understanding of the way language works. Some philosophers use the word *interpretation* as a synonym for perception. They would maintain that to perceive is to interpret, by definition. But Eliot in his dissertation and early philosophical writings uses the word to refer to an activity that comes after and builds upon perception.[6] He distinguishes between "facts" as primary points of attention and the "interpretation" of those facts as a movement to something beyond the facts themselves. Interpretation is a first-order process of transcendence, a mental movement beyond the object focused on in a given moment. Fact perception can be confined to a single instant or, conceptually, to a position outside time altogether; interpretation, on the other hand, implies a time sequence.

Put another way, perception involves two terms, the perceiver and the thing perceived. Interpretation adds a third term, the meaning assigned to the thing perceived. In the process of adding that third term, relations are multiplied. At one instant of time, only the mind with nothing to take note of exists. This instant, part of an interval between perceptions, is somewhat analogous to the blank moment between frames of a film. At another instant, the mind centers an object, isolates it from both other points of attention and the blank instants between them. The act of placing an object at the center of attention, to follow the definition Eliot gives in his dissertation, makes it a fact and thus requires a sense of that mind's relation to the centered object. The subsequent act of assigning significance to the object turns the fact into a means to an end (the interpretation), thus decentering it.

In interpreting poetic texts, especially dramatic ones such as *The Waste Land,* it is useful to distinguish between internal and external interpretations, that is, between interpretations occurring within the text and interpretations made by the reader of the text. *The Waste Land,* including "Death by Water," consists to a large extent of voices stating interpretations. For example, "April is the cruellest month" can be read as an assignment of meaning by a figure in the poem, possibly named Marie. The statement first isolates a time of year by naming it, then decenters it by shifting attention to its meaning, "cruellest month." This assignment of meaning by Marie is an internal interpretation. Having understood that Marie has conveyed an interpretation, the reader can then go on to interpret Marie's interpretation, to decide the significance of her assignment of meaning. This is external interpretation. The reader, of course, has the option of refusing to interpret the textual fact, but most readers are not so detached. They will be curious about why the internal interpretation is made and then will move on through successive utterances to more and more interpretations. If the internal interpretation is a single statement, readers can progress with relative ease to external interpretation, but if internal meanings proliferate, readers tend to become entangled in the text and to reach increasingly various external meanings. As internal significations increase in quantity and complexity, in other words, the likelihood of common external significations decreases. It becomes less likely that readers will agree on meanings to be assigned from outside to the aggregate of meanings stated inside the text by characters. Neither the internal nor the external interpretations should be equated with the author's interpretation. For example, Eliot the poet does not announce that "April is the cruellest month"; rather, he presents a heterocosm in which a character says this. Interpreting Marie's interpretation is one activity; interpreting Eliot's is another activity altogether. To return to "Death by Water": it would be inaccurate to attribute "Consider Phlebas, who was once handsome and tall as you" to Eliot; this solemn warning comes from a narrator within the text.

External interpretative activity, or reading, often produces a circular experience that we call a "hermeneutical loop."[7] When a text is decentered through the assignment of meaning (that is, through the process of interpretation), the text is pushed aside by that meaning and an external thought, the reader's thought, takes its place. After considering the thought, the reader can and often does decide that it is insufficient or aesthetically less desirable than the initial textual fact. As a result, the interpretation dissolves, and the original item in the poem returns to the center of focus. The reader has moved outside the text, found a meaning, considered it, and returned to the text; in a sense, the reader has returned to the moment before interpretation. But it is a return with a difference, a difference made by the process of trying to interpret. The hermeneutical loop effect acknowledges that there is a posthermeneutical stage, a stage that is in a sense *after* meaning. It is a way of referring to what happens when serious readers struggle with a complex text like *The Waste Land* (or with a simple text like a nursery rhyme).

Attention to the nature of reading is particularly helpful in reading Eliot's poetry. In reading the notoriously polyphonic text of *The Waste Land,* for example, the distinction between internal and external interpretation is crucial. Internal interpretation is obviously of the essence, and external interpretation, though difficult, is unavoidable. The process of attributing meaning to the water references takes one into many fields, some of them remote from the text. Most readers will begin with the fact that the wasteland is the controlling or privileged term, and with Eliot's explicit note to the reader on the relevance of *The Golden Bough.* These considerations force water to refer in some way to a rejuvenating element, and death by water to refer in some way to ritual. The reader may think of Christian baptism, Frazerian archetypes of death and rebirth, Freudian return to the womb, or even of fish as a traditional fertility symbol, to name only a few possible meanings. The "death" in

"Death by Water" can mean the negation that precedes affirmation; or it can mean that old archetypes are themselves dead and that water is only water for drinking or drowning.

At some stage of the reading process, the reader will probably notice the worrisome fact that the pointers toward redemption which typically accompany these archetypes are missing from "Death by Water." The absence of sacramental promises, actually, is conspicuous and would be noticed instantly except for the fact that the archetypes themselves automatically suggest such promises. But in this brief elegy, redemptive presence is insinuated only to be mocked. Phlebas does not seem to be preparing for rebirth. On the contrary, he is described as quietly decomposing and entering the whirlpool. The water cleanses his bones, not symbolically, but literally: the death by water is death by water. "Putting off the filth of the flesh" (as St. Paul describes the new birth) is physical. The elegy ends with a voice warning someone to be mindful of Phlebas as one who died at sea. He was handsome and tall, and he could sail as well as Ulysses himself. But now he is merely dead.

Or is he? In the context of the Frazerian myths, Phlebas is related to Osiris, the god whose body was placed in a current that carried it from the place of his death to the place from which it would be taken from the water as a symbol of rebirth. In "Dans le Restaurant," a current simply carries Phlebas far away, destination unspecified. In "Death by Water," the function of the current changes. Instead of carrying the body to the place of resurrection, "A current under sea / Picked his bones in whispers." This revision undermines any suggestion of resurrection; instead of floating downstream to be plucked out, the body decomposes en route and is pulled into a whirlpool. The most striking word in the new line, however, is "whispers"; the statement that the bones were picked in whispers inevitably recalls the earlier line "shall these bones live?" but does not suggest any answer.

In Jules Laforgue's "L'Aquarium," one of the shadow texts in "Death by Water," drowning is imagined as positive because it symbolizes existence without mind, pure vegetative happiness. The tone of Eliot's elegy carries the same suggestion, a kind and easy exit into a "condition of complete simplicity" costing (to use the language of Four Quartets) "not less than everything." Perhaps Madame Sosostris was simply a false prophet to warn her client to fear death by water. "Annihilation and utter night," to borrow a phrase from Eliot's dissertation, have seldom been so attractive. This reading is complicated, however, by a number of hints that this death by water may be more than simple annihilation. There are definite indications that the mind of the persona survives his death. These hints could be ironic, or could be just a part of linguistic entanglement, but they are clearly present: "Phlebas the Phoenician, a fortnight dead, / Forgot the cry of gulls, and the deep sea swell / And the profit and loss." The odd detail here is that this "forgetting" takes place two weeks after his death. In "Dans le Restaurant,"

Eliot's French poem from which these lines were taken, the suggestion of the survival of consciousness is even stronger. "Forgot" is in the imperfect (*oubliait*), emphasizing continuing rather than completed action. In addition, the narrator in the French poem remarks that it was "painful" for Phlebas to have to pass through the stages of his former life, suggesting perhaps the physical pain of the death itself, but also the psychological pain or spiritual anguish of witnessing a postmortem descent through the stages of his former life. Recalling the drowned men's "worried bodies" in "Mr. Apollinax," the reader notes that Phlebas' descent to mindless nonexistence is complicated by a postmortem forgetting, by a suggestion that Phlebas survives and witnesses his own descent into the whirlpool.

The complexities related to Phlebas's decomposition require an acknowledgment that the narrator's warning is more complicated than it seems to be. Is it merely a warning, for example, that all shall die? Or is it a statement that death is all? Do the classical allusions and the classical tone indicate that this address to the reader is an updating of Aristotle's exercise in logic, a restatement using Phlebas instead of Socrates as an example? And what of the context of this warning within the poem itself? Does the perception that the warning is an internal interpretation change its significance for the reader who is trying to assess external significance? It is, after all, a line in a poem about a wasteland, in a special sense a poem about the twentieth century, a demythologized age in which water is for most people no more than H_2O. And what about the reader's awareness that Eliot is a master of irony, the awareness that irony, like water, is everywhere? In the last analysis, these questions are unanswerable, forcing the reader to discard them and return to the text as text. This return, generated by the fact that all readings that suggest themselves end by pointing to their own inadequacy, is in our terminology a hermeneutical loop.

Whatever may be said of "Death by Water," then, cannot be said with any finality. The tale of Phlebas refuses allegorization, refuses to be caught in final statements of meaning. This intransigence is not only clear from a close reading of the text, but also from attention to the form. In this section of *The Waste Land,* water is the primary metaphor, but because of the poem's title, water as metaphor is framed by dry and barren land. The title privileges the metaphor of the dead land, but the text tends to cause water as symbol to dominate the reader's picture of the poem. In a sense, land is a frame for water in the poem, but the dominance of the frame and the competition between the frame and the picture generate an oscillation which prevents any stable or privileged focusing. The oscillation produced is a crucial aspect of the presentation—a movement more than a meaning. If Eliot had permitted a conventional understanding of these two metaphors, the reader would have been unable to evade the sense that water is a signifier pointing in the direction of salvation, for, after all, irrigation is an obvious way of making wastelands bloom again. The reader is returned to the text but, having looped through tortuous interpretive exercises, now experiences the text in a new way.

"Death by Water" forces the reader to interpret, but fails in the end to permit the reader to grasp any satisfactory meaning. This refusal to concede adequate meanings outside itself brings the reader back to the text. This movement beyond interpretation can only be characterized as postherme-neutical. The reader's experience beyond meaning includes the experience of interpretation, an experience that does not yield satisfactory meanings but that cannot fail to enrich subsequent experience with the text. The water pattern will not be the same when the reader recenters it after giving up on external interpretations. The reading process invents and reinvents borders, and this process makes a difference. For example, water imagery is bordered at first by contrasting imagery and by internal interpretations. Later it receives all the borders, containers, or frames that come with various interpre-tations. Finally, it is bordered by the interpretative activity itself when it returns to being only water imagery again. The movement beyond hermeneu-tics is a return to the starting place, the text, but in the posthermeneutical state the text is changed (or the reader is changed).

In strictly literary terms, the hermeneutical loop can only be accurately noted as a defeat of symbolism, as a refusal of the text to become a means to an end. It is hard to imagine water in a context of dryness, lovelessness, anomie, and disorder failing to be a symbol of hope. Its defeat as a symbol, its status as antisymbol, is a remarkable achievement. A nonsymbol is a nonsignifier, a centered fact defined as such by it refusal to be permanently cast into the supporting role of pointer toward something other than itself. The reader may be tempted to suppose that nonsymbols are symbols of the failure of symbols in the modern chaos the poem evokes. But that supposi-tion leads to an infinite regression that is conspicuously unsatisfying. At some point, there must be a return to water as water, the beginning and the end of meaning.

"Death by Water" is a crucial point in the reader's experience of *The Waste Land.* If Eliot had omitted this brief elegy on Phlebas the Phoenician, the conventional expectations created by the use of water in a poem about a desert would have produced an entirely different work. The longing for water in "What the Thunder Said" would have signaled the possible presence of a healing, sacramental element in a spiritually dry realm. As the poem stands, however, it is difficult to attach any sacramental value to water. "Death by Water" desymbolizes it by treating it literally as an element in which to drown. There is a change, but no "sea-change / Into something rich and strange"; his body rises and falls, but both rising and falling are literal, an effect of the tides. In the final analysis, there is a descent but no ascent, a death but no rebirth, no archetypal womb that Phlebas can return to for maternal comfort. The world within the poem is one in which symbols fail, one in which mythologies collapse in a heap of broken images. This literalization of ancient symbols (from water as symbol to water as H_2O), this demythologizing and desacramentalizing of language, is a central aspect of Eliot's representation of the wasteland.

Notes

1. All quotations from T. S. Eliot's poems are taken from *The Complete Poems and Plays* (New York: Harcourt Brace & World, Inc., 1952).

2. The seminar is described in *Josiah Royce's Seminar, 1913–1914 as Recorded in the Notebooks of Harry T. Costello,* ed. Grover Smith (New Brunswick, N.J.: Rutgers University Press, 1963). Eliot's dissertation was published as *Knowledge and Experience in the Philosophy of F. H. Bradley* (New York: Farrar Straus, 1964). Eliot's early philosophical papers have not been published, but they are described in Jeffrey Perl's "The Language of Theory and the Language of Poetry," *Southern Review* 21 (1985): 1012–23.

3. Remarks on "Death by Water" by the following critics are representative: Grover Smith, *The Waste Land* (London: George Allen & Unwin, 1983), 106–10; Helen Williams, *T. S. Eliot: The Waste Land* (London: Edward Arnold, 1968), 41–44; and Marianne Thormählen, *"The Waste Land": A Fragmentary Wholeness* (Lund: C. W. K. Gleerup, 1978), 154–66.

4. T. S. Eliot, *The Waste Land: A Facsimile and Transcript of the Original Drafts Including the Annotations of Ezra Pound,* ed. Valerie Eliot (New York: Harcourt Brace Jovanovich, 1971), 55–69.

5. *The Waste Land: A Facsimile,* 61.

6. Eliot, *Knowledge and Experience,* 60.

7. The term "hermeneutical loop" is our own coinage, with our own special meanings. It should not be confused with Wilhelm Dilthey's "hermeneutical circle."

Considering Phlebas: The Poetry of
The Waste Land

RUSSELL ELLIOTT MURPHY

If it is presumptuous to speak for a generation, which is what I am about to do, then I nevertheless have for my precedent none other than one of the subjects of this essay—the poet of *The Waste Land,* T. S. Eliot. The only difference, though a major one, is that Eliot very quickly disclaimed that role as forming any part of his intentions and as quickly eschewed even the role of Lost Leader, which equally rapidly fell to him.

The claims I make to being a spokesman for my generation are modest nevertheless, for I willingly admit that mine is a personal view and therefore one open to neither confirmation nor refutation by others. My aim is to put *The Waste Land* in perspective not in terms of how it affected by generation but in terms of how it affected me during that awful decade we call the sixties. Still, that I also happen to be of that generation born in the 1940s and just coming of age as John F. Kennedy was entering the White House gives me that most peculiar of slants, the *à la mode.* If I must appeal to any authority, it is that I was there.

Despite the subjective limitation on my point of view, however, I will not protest all innocence of larger intentions. A scholar and teacher of modern literature by profession, I have given the matter of Eliot's *The Waste Land* much thought over the years, so much has it been a continuing part of our lives, and I have never failed to notice, even while the events were transpiring, the similarities between my generation and his, my epoch and his.

The most obvious is that we too were naysayers, quite willing to tell our elders just where to get off. Joyce and Eliot and Pound, Hemingway and Fitzgerald, the pantheon of the twenties from our point of view (with Yeats standing above and beyond) and unquestionably from their own, had never entertained the idea of pulling any punches, or so it seemed to us, and neither would we. Otherwise, one-for-one correlations will not work. We of the authentic sixties generation were still in our childhood or late adolescence when the sixties began, for example, while the authentic twenties generation were into ("well into," when we think of Joyce and Pound and Yeats) their

This essay was written specifically for this volume and is published here for the first time by permission of the author.

adulthood during that celebrated decade. The most startling affinity between the so-called generation of the sixties and Eliot's generation, who were the first to embrace his great poem as their tragic anthem, is that each generation came into its own during a similarly unstable period ill-suited to the expression of common values and to focused collective endeavors. For in both periods an old order was yielding way to a new with nothing of grace and something less of hope. In Eliot's, imperial Europe, so lately flowered, died. A dream no older than Napoleon, nationalism succumbed to its own spiritual inertia, taking much of Euorpe's pride and bearing with it and leaving Eliot and his contemporaries to survive the aftermath of such a great fall like the shell-shocked refugees of a botched civilization that they were. In ours, with something more of speed though little more of wisdom, imperial America floundered on her own sons and daughters' daring to tell their parents that a lie was a lie, no matter how or by whom it was mouthed.

But a major difference existed, and will always exist. For their imaginative guidance Eliot and others of his age had nothing and no one to turn to. All vision, like the prophecies of Israel, had ended for the West with Shelley and Keats and Goethe, whose grandsons and great-grandsons were swallowed up by the nuances and dalliances of Wagner and Swinburne (hawking rank nationalism or swilling about in escapist fantasies, or both) while the geopolitical, industrial-military world the epoch had also fostered went to hell in a handbasket. Whereas we had T. S. Eliot's *The Waste Land* to turn to for our metaphorical reference points. As I hope to show, Eliot's poem provided us with many, so many in fact that *The Waste Land,* along with poems like *Gerontion* and *The Hollow Men,* seemed to us to be more a poetry prophesying the New Age attitudes of the sixties than an echoing of their own contemporary scene and decaying ethos.

*The Waste Land'*s power as poetry and myth is greater than its power as a celebrated literary artifact, which is also considerable, if not as important. *The Waste Land* is deservedly a great poem, but that is—or should be—because it is unquestionably great poetry first. Exactly why it is great poetry, as well as why it is a great poem, has been—and will continue to be—the topic of serious critical debate; but that matters little to those of us who have already experienced it as poetry, which is, I believe, exactly what many of us of the generation of the sixties did. To be truly "with it" then, whoever one was, involved knowing something about Eliot, and that ultimately involved knowing something about *The Waste Land,* and knowing something about *The Waste Land* meant knowing that it was a stinging indictment of all the values the West in the twentieth century had come to represent and propagate.

For us (speaking for myself), Eliot's poem was finally the one great naysayer to all that was foul and evil in the strange-bedfellows worlds that commerce and culture had become, a naysaying we then merely imitated. I know that viewing *The Waste Land* as a cultural critique is no longer fashionable, but I also know that it was Eliot's generation's view of his great poem, and that it certainly was mine, for it had become, during my formative years, something of a popular commonplace, as familiar a catchphrase as the "Lost Generation" (which we wrongly attributed to Hemingway). Even we schoolboys and schoolgirls knew the story. Some great poet named Eliot had told the most withering truth. Culturally, he said, we had become a wasteland.

If we did not know exactly what that meant, we at least knew that it was not attractive or ennobling. Yet when Eisenhower's FCC chairman, Newton Minnow, called television a vast wasteland, we all seemed to know exactly what he meant.

We were just children then, but how wonderful that a government official would make a literary allusion to illustrate how vacuous television, that nemesis of reading and intelligence, was. How strange, too, that everyone recognized the illusion. What a marvelous comment on the impact Eliot's poem had had on his society, not for its poetry or for its critical reputation, but for the way it could provide the many with an image that instantaneously portrayed the malady of their age in all its paralyzing reality.

As a working-class kid growing up in East Providence, Rhode Island, and attending public schools there, I knew enough about *The Waste Land* as poetry—or maybe it was already only as literary history—to know that a man named T. S. Eliot had written it; that no one really understood it (and so it was also used as a metaphor for the difficult as well as the most modern); that he had in addition written lines prophesying that our world would end— shortly, it seemed, to us Nuclear Age children—not with a bang but a whimper; and that, like Picasso's weird-faced women, he typified all that was new and rare about the modern way of seeing things. And everyone wanted to do that—to see in the best modern way. No one—not a soul—wanted to appear old-fashioned anymore, so Eliot's view was still all the rage in the outside world, where it mattered. In fact, his strange poetry gave shape to our uniquely distorted vision of things, our sense of alienation from everything that had gone before us, our forebodings over what might come after. For *The Waste Land* offered a vision that our history seemed somehow to be justifying with its violence and war, hatred and coldness. We *were* the dead land, the cactus land.

This was the people's *Waste Land,* the popular view, you must understand. We did not know that in the academy the poem had already become firmly entrenched in a half dozen or more traditions and trends by the lights of critics like Cleanth Brooks and Elizabeth Drew, Helen Gardner and Hugh Kenner, F. R. Leavis and I. A. Richards, Edmund Wilson and Richard P. Blackmur, Yvor Winters and Allen Tate, and Grover Smith and F. O. Matthiessen. If the poem had originally been something in the nature of the Hiroshima bomb, laying waste several millennia of inherited culture and wisdom, the poem's erudite critics were all acting now rather like those Nuclear Age visionaries who insisted that there were peaceful uses for nuclear power. Read rightly, they were saying, *The Waste Land* endorsed human endeavor and celebrated our achievements as much as it encouraged—yea, welcomed—our continuing struggle against the dying of the light.

First, however, it had said its piece for itself, and its piece had a devastating effect. For Eliot's generation, his poem had said that the game was up. Not everyone agreed with the point of view, but they did all believe that that was what the Eliot poem "said." Witness Hart Crane's frantic efforts to counter what he perceived to be its negativism, its refusal to affirm, with a long poem of his own, *The Bridge.*

But I get ahead of my story, for the views that prevailed in the academy had not yet reached the streets. Out on the streets, *The Waste Land,* icon that it had become, remained for most of us a pretty awful prospect as the postwar world went about sprucing itself up with two-tone cars and ballpoint pens. It was not quite the sixties yet, and all was not lost, after all. There was still Milton Berle and Lucy and Jackie Gleason's "The Honeymooners," but there, like the cadaverous incarnation of a lost gentility, from time to time we'd see in the pages of *Time* or on the evening news T. S. Eliot, his limpid smile speaking volumes about the sorry state of the world and the emptiness of our lives just beneath the surface of our humdrum prosperity. With the sort of pride in our technology that not even Sputnik could shake, only challenge, we knew that we were moving faster, flying higher, communicating better and more quickly than in any other epoch of human history, but poets like Eliot pointed to the dark side of our common reality. Like some Ur-Rod Serling, he seemed to know that all our progress and self-congratulatory promotion were nothing compared to the hollowness we felt when the lights went off.

And then there was a new decade to traverse. If the poem had any continuing meaning for me as I entered my later teens, it was that *The Waste Land* summed up the world beyond my father's walls—inchoate, uncertain, unfriendly, impersonal, and vast. The sixties would change all that. It would be a time when events would so catch up with the mythic that there could no longer be any time but the present, no longer any history but the news. Kennedy was in the White House. There was the Bay of Pigs, but there was also the successful naval blockade of Soviet missile shipments to Cuba. There was the Berlin Wall, but there were Kennedy's rousing words to West Berliners. There was the growing threat of nuclear war, but there was also the Nuclear Non-Proliferation Treaty. There was Selma, but there were sit-ins. Even the spirit of modernism, with its dilemmas and uncertainties, ambiguities and ironies, seemed caught up in and overcome by the wave of new enthusiasms. Eliot was not forgotten, but the contemporary world was too alive for his vision of a dead land to appeal to the young as a suitable image. When we wanted to imagine that we were feeling creatures, there was Bob Dylan; Eliot spoke of another era, our grandfathers', which had given up all hope. Our fathers had won the war against fascism, and we knew that we would inherit the stars.

So when I first actually encountered Eliot's poetry in a sophomore literature class at the University of Massachusetts, I remember being impressed by what was obviously an incredible work of literature, for, like any student, I identified greatness with difficulty; but Eliot did not speak to me and my sense of social reality as well as, say, Pete Seeger or Joan Baez did. The poem was "The Love Song of J. Alfred Prufrock." I don't think that I understood it or that it was even taught particularly well. I thought it an awfully sad poem about very bored, confused people, told by a man who somehow wanted to feel something again but knew, or had convinced himself, he could not any longer. I thought that man was T. S. Eliot, the poet who had written *The Waste Land,* but was told that it was actually J. Alfred Prufrock himself. I bought it, for I was being introduced to literature. It was a subject being taught me, so it made sense that literature was something I did not yet understand; I still had things to learn, and I was now being taught that sometimes the poet might not be the speaker of a poem. Now it all seemed easy to understand: the poet created characters who sounded just the way you would expect him to sound. Otherwise, this sort of literature simply did not connect with the lives of young people for whom the major question of a public nature was whether or not the Soviets were going to bury us, or we them.

Then suddenly even that didn't matter anymore. Kennedy was dead, there was rioting in our major cities, and more and more horror stories began to come out of Southeast Asia. In the jungles the fighting was getting bad, and once more the tide was turning, our enemies were winning. We were going to have to do something. We were going to have to get involved. We do, more and more. There is Student Power, there is Black Power, there is Flower Power. There are drugs, and reports of bad trips become as common as the trench confessions of Pound and Eliot's day. There are the Beatles and the Rolling Stones, Janis Joplin, Jimi Hendrix. Tet. Eugene McCarthy. Someone shoots Martin Luther King, Jr. Soon another Kennedy is dead, and the police riot at the summer's Democratic National Convention in Chicago. In Miami, the Republicans have already nominated Richard Nixon. And somewhere in the midst of all this, T. S. Eliot passed quietly away.

We spent the last few minutes of a class in modern poetry discussing *The Waste Land,* I recall, and that was it. Any questions? There were none. Who would dare? By then the poem was the Stalin of graduate studies, so formidably entrenched in the canon, what was there left to say, let alone ask? As a descriptive work, it had become a literary artifact; certainly it no longer provided a fictive paradigm for the state of the contemporary world or our view of modern history. In fact, it was not too difficult to find oneself longing for those simpler days of yesteryear when everything was chaotic in a manageable kind of way; and I can recall a teaching assistants' meeting at which someone quoted Erich Segal saying that Bob Dylan had inherited

Eliot's mantle. And Eliot did seem—*all* the moderns did seem, if I may say so—dated. I had already seen *Intolerance,* and had studied it and Eisenstein enough to know that, beyond its considerable literary value, *The Waste Land* had become something of a commonplace model for the structural ideals of modernism, its use of fragment and juxtaposition, counterpoint and irony, rather old hat, although we respected Eliot for having done it first. What the poetry said of the past and *its* present we hardly cared to know anymore, having come at last, as a culture, to admit that we admired the classics only because they were dead things by dead people.

The Waste Land, we now know, will never appear so dated again. It survived that assault on the validity of its vision, and it survived for the very reason that it is an accurate vision. In the wildest moments of the sixties, we thought that we had outsped *The Waste Land*'s most annoying tale, its firm insistence that we are slaves neither to memory or desire so much as to *ennui,* boredom pure and simple. *The Waste Land* with its games of chess and hours at one's toilet, its crowded pubs and sleazy assignations, passions and frustrations, bewildering allures, horoscopes and drownings and mind-blowing quests, and "O O O O that Shakespeherian Rag—" said finally that it was boredom from which all art and philosophy, religion and industry—all that we call culture—spring as merely momentary escapes and/or escapades. We thought in the sixties that we had outsped the vapid life-style *The Waste Land* had tried to eternize and were approaching instead the magical, the mystic, about to enclose it, expose it, become it. *The Waste Land* was wrong, we thought, because it accurately depicted *their* world—the old, dead world of the Wall Street and Madison Avenue lizards, now dinosaurs on the way out— but Eliot had failed even to imagine *ours,* had only hinted at it with the enigmatic "Shantih shantih shantih" with which the now-dead poet's work ended.

The Waste Land continued to play well with us in its depictions of the failures of the culture we were now countering with our rag-mop tops and our bell bottoms, experiments with drugs and loose sexuality. Rats' alley was not some lowlife hangout but the rat race, the Bradford millionaire allusion, like Mrs. Porter and her daughter, further embodiments of the Hollow Men and their spouses and children who, vacuously comported, comprised the Establishment. Those images of a sterile earth ("stirring / Dull roots with spring rain . . . feeding / A little life with dried tubers"), of faceless crowds and listless lovemaking in the midst of meaningless activity; of rivers fouled with garbage; of sun-baked nightmare landscapes—all seemed to be prefigurings of the crisis of values we were now facing, wherein the forces of death were arrayed not against life but against the zest of youth. We could even read our ecological concerns and the ravages of urban blight into Eliot's lines, for what else was there to hear in Spenser's lyric refrain, juxtaposed as it was with a description of the river as an open sewer, but a lament for a natural order that had been subverted, like the ideal of a City of Man, to the basest of human designs, the needs of commerce for the quick buck. Mr. Eugenides was our Nero, wheeling his deals while our cities died and Phlebas, ephebe, symbol of youth and its beauties, drowned—in a sea of blood called Vietnam.

The fact remained, however, that for us there were now others saying all this much more forcefully because they were saying it in the words and images of our own day rather than through the elusive tools of erudition and irony. Bob Dylan summed it all up: You didn't need to be a weatherman to know which way the wind was blowing. In late 1969, I was looking around for a suitable graduate course for the coming spring 1970 semester, over and above the ones we had to take. A young professor who had already published a well-received book on Hopkins, Paul Mariani, was offering a seminar in Christocentricity in four modern poets—Hopkins, Crane, Lowell, and Eliot. Good lapsed Catholic that I was, I signed up. We had just finished studying the *Four Quartets* when, in early May, Kent State occurred.

It should not seem odd that an essay dealing with the impact *The Waste Land* had on a generation should conclude not only with *Four Quartets* but with the last of them, "Little Gidding." As we well know, Eliot himself saw the continuing relationship between all his subsequent poetry and *The Waste Land,* not the least in his continuing to be an explorer. It would not have occurred to me then, but it has many times since, that one of the great lessons of *The Waste Land* is that it urges the quest and stresses its private nature: "Shall I at least set my lands in order? . . . These fragments I have shored against my ruins." I and my generation saw a land, a nation, in disorder, but not for the reason everyone else assigned. Not for the reason that the young were rebelling. No, we saw the disorder in our elders' inability (which was a kinder way to put it than to imagine that it was reluctance) to set the land in order again, to recognize priorities and reorganize them so as to do honor to our common humanity. It did indeed strike us as sinfully wrongheaded that billions were being spent on warfare and moon walks while in our own cities, to say nothing of the slums of India and dozens of other Third World nations, children starved, minds were wasted, hearts were broken, and dreams were blasted. What we could not have known—what Eliot did not know either until he got older—was that everyone thinks the truth is his, whereas it is no one's. That is a frightening prospect, but *The Waste Land* led me to Eliot, and Eliot led me to that freedom costing not less than everything, that freedom called tolerance and forbearance.

I cannot describe now the horror that filled us all when, on that day in May 1970, we heard that young American soldiers had shot and killed four young American students protesting the war. It is not rhetoric to say that America—the dream it represented—teetered for a moment over the void; it seemed as if some great internal cataclysm was about to burst and history would sweep us, the young, and our elders, the enemy, up into one vast and impersonal storm until blood washed this land clean of thought and cause.

> We cannot revive old factions
> We cannot restore old policies
> ....
> These men, and those who opposed them
> And those whom they opposed
> Accept the constitution of silence
> And are folded in a single party.

Classes were canceled, campuses across this country closed down, and students and faculty milled around before spray-painted libraries wondering what was going to happen next. At a nighttime rally on the Amherst common, a speaker announced that there was rioting in downtown Madison, that students had stolen a plane and bombed a nearby Army base. Now we can be circumspect, perhaps even smile. Then my heart feared for the fate of my nation and the future of my children.

> Who then devised the torment? Love.
> Love is the unfamiliar Name
> Behind the hands that wove
> The intolerable shirt of flame
> Which human power cannot remove.

I cannot say that I will ever forget those days, but I can say that Eliot's words in "Little Gidding," that history is here and is now and is redeemed by the intersection of the timeless with time and through the will of a God who does not recognize our banners or sympathize with our causes, and yet whose hand, with Love, weaves the broadcloth as well as the shirt of fire—

> With the drawing of this Love and the voice of this Calling

—that these words of Eliot and other words like them sustained me by convincing me that it indeed is so.

And so I came to understand, too, that Eliot's smile, coming as it did in pictures taken years after his penning *The Waste Land,* was not the limpid smile of the cynic hardly bothering to sneer at a race too stupid to recognize the source of its doom, but the blissful smile of benevolent sage who has realized the source of our salvation.

But first he had taught us (undoubtedly without intending to) that to come to such an understanding ("shantih shantih shantih"), one must undertake the quest, one must confront *The Waste Land* and find there, in its cacophony and almost choking abundance, how one can starve in the midst of plenty, become deaf from too much hearing, go blind from too much vision, until we learn the Buddha's lesson in the Fire Sermon and free ourselves not from the cycles of nature but from the cycles of hatred and anger and blame. We learn to give, to sympathize, and to control ourselves: "Datta, Dayadhvam, Damyata. Shantih shantih shantih." We learn, in other words, what it is to be human, and that that is to accept the lonely burden of one's responsibility to respect the things of a world one did not make but must yet abide in. The most religious poetry in the Eliot canon is to be found, in my view, not in "Little Gidding" or *Ash-Wednesday* but in *The Waste Land*, where all faiths are tested and none is found wanting in its expression of our most common and essential desire, and that it is not, like the Cumaean Sibyl's, the desire to die but rather the desire to be at peace with ourselves, with each other, and with the world around us. To be, as it were, on "the shore / Fishing, with the arid plain behind" us.

The Waste Land: Cousin Harriet and
the Poetry Critic

GEORGE MONTEIRO

During his time at Oxford University in 1915, T. S. Eliot wrote three poems that he promptly placed in Harriet Monroe's new magazine. In that first year's October issue of *Poetry* appeared "Aunt Helen," "Cousin Nancy," and "The *Boston Evening Transcript*." The last of this trio of satiric poems reads:

> The readers of the *Boston Evening Transcript*
> Sway in the wind like a field of ripe corn.
>   When evening quickens faintly in the street,
> Wakening the appetites of life in some
> And to others bringing the *Boston Evening Transcript*,
> I mount the steps and ring the bell, turning
> Wearily, as one would turn to nod good-bye to Rochefoucauld,
> If the street were time and he at the end of the street,
> And I say, "Cousin Harriet, here is the *Boston Evening Transcript*."[1]

It is difficult to recognize in Cousin Harriet's delivery "boy" the prophetic poet who would soon astonish the literary world with his expiatory poem *The Waste Land,* so swiftly did Eliot move, in those few years, away from his callow Harvard youth, marked as it was by poetry of rather brittle social satire of a decidedly local cast.

Whether or not one agrees that in its day the *Boston Evening Transcript* enjoyed "a status not unlike that of today's *New York Times*," it is indisputable that it was the newspaper read by Bostonians (and Cantabridgians).[2] Of particular interest to a young man from St. Louis, one who had had his Harvard University Class "Ode" published in the newspaper's pages and who wished to make a reputation as a poet, was the space the *Transcript* made available for reviews and discussions of poetry.[3] These columns were always open to William Stanley Braithwaite (1878–1962). Reviews and essays on the state of American and English poetry flowed steadily from the pen of this Afro-American, who rather quickly earned a reputation as a maker of poets'

This essay was written specifically for this volume and is published here for the first time by permission of the author.

257

reputations. He had no intention of making Eliot's. When Eliot's *Poems* appeared in 1920, Braithwaite reviewed the book but had nothing good to say about it. "He is one of your young poetic bucks of the present era who happens to be born in St. Louis, but who now lives in England and writes poems in French," he begins. Then he continues: "He has a scorn for the ordinary substance of human nature, a scorn streaked more with vanity than understanding, and strikes a posture that might be magnificent with jest if it were not so much the attitude of a monkey in a cage." To illustrate his point he quotes several lines from the poems "Sweeney Erect" and "Mr. Appolinax." And these poems are not atypical of Eliot's work, he finds; there are "many more lines of like inanity." He then points out that Eliot is "the author of 'The Love Song of J. Alfred Prufrock,' a powerful portrait in which the 'new' poetry takes pride." "Let Alfred have his say before oblivion descends upon his strut and his leer," predicts Braithwaite, quoting the concluding twenty-one lines of the poem beginning with the Prince Hamlet passage. He ends his review in this way: "Reading these poems (?) is like being in a closed room full of foul air; not a room in an empty house that is sanctified with mould and dust, but a room in which the stale perfume of exotics is poisoned with the memory of lusts. Open the window and let the fresh air clear and invigorate the imagination!"[4] Interestingly enough, Eliot directed his complaint about Braithwaite's review to his friend, protector, and promoter, Ezra Pound: "*Boston Ev. Transcript* says I am an Exotic Poet. ('Closed room . . . stale perfumes . . . memories of lust . . . open the window'."[5] We do not have Pound's reply on this occasion, but we do know that Pound knew full well who "W. S. B." was. Five years earlier in a letter to the *Transcript* Pound had referred to him disingenuously as the newspaper's "(negro?) reviewer," and to Harriet Monroe, later in the same year in a letter in which he also talks about Eliot's "Portrait of a lady" and "The Love Song of J. Alfred Prufrock," he refers sneeringly to Braithwaite as a "coon."[6]

Pound's racial overreactions to Braithwaite, as well as Eliot's sensitivity to the *Transcript's* reviewer's comments on his poetry, reveal less, perhaps, about the *Transcript's* importance to American poetry than about what was generally perceived to be Braithwaite's personal but real influence on the public reception and continuing reputation of American poets. That influence derived from another of Braithwaite's ventures on behalf of American poetry. Starting with the first such collection in 1913, Braithwaite's *Anthology of Magazine Verse* appeared annually, on schedule, until 1929. Over those years Braithwaite would champion the cause of many poets, including, among the more familiar names, Edwin Arlington Robinson, Edgar Lee Masters, Amy Lowell, Ridgely Torrence, and Robert Frost. He was also the first to anthologize, in 1915, Wallace Stevens's "rare and perfect" poem (as he called it) "Peter Quince at the Clavier."[7] The same anthology reprinted E. A. Robinson's "Flammonde," Amy Lowell's "Patterns," and Robert Frost's "Birches," "The Road Not Taken," and "The Death of the Hired Man."

Astonishingly, given our perspective, no poem of T. S. Eliot's was ever included in Braithwaite's annual anthologies. In the same year, then, that the *Transcript*'s literary journalist spotted Stevens's "Peter Quince" as well as the other poems just listed, he passed up "The Love Song of J. Alfred Prufrock," which had appeared in the June 1915 issue of *Poetry*.

Such was the perceived power of Braithwaite's good word (in time Harriet Monroe would refer to him unkindly and derisively as "Sir Oracle" and the "Boston Dictator")[8] that for years poets such as Frost and Louis Untermeyer, to name only two, went out of their way to curry favor with this man, who was himself only a minor poet but who had discovered a vehicle for the promotion of English-language poetry. Assessing his efforts for poetry, he admitted, "My labors have not been perfect, but they have been heavy, faithful and enduring,—and I hope not in vain."[9] One of those "imperfections" must have been his obviously systematic ignoring of Eliot in his annual anthologies. Even in 1923, when in his table of poetry prizes and awards he was compelled to list Eliot as the winner of the $2000 awarded by the *Dial* to *The Waste Land*, he did not include the poem in his anthology (or even bother to mention it in his introduction), choosing rather to reprint "The Sowing," a 106–line poem which attempts its own definition of the month of April.[10] In fact, the one time that Braithwaite found need to refer in one of his introductions (1927) to Eliot's work he made reference not to his poetry but to his criticism. Of *The Sacred Wood*, which "reflects one representative quality of the contemporary poetic mind and character," he decided: "This work . . . has been set up as a sort of Bible by followers of the contemporary metaphysical manner, and though the book had a scant circulation, its influence has been wide and impressive."[11] Oddly (but characteristically), he did not give the name of the author of the essays collected in *The Sacred Wood*. By that time, five years after the appearance of *The Waste Land*, Eliot could not have much minded the slight. His literary reputation as critic as well as poet was well established and still growing.

In 1915, however, things were different. Eliot's poetry was just beginning to appear, thanks to Ezra Pound, in Harriet Monroe's new journal. While Braithwaite was planning for the first issues of his periodical *The Poetry Journal* (it was short-lived: May 1916 through February 1917) and writing his columns for the *Transcript*, he was also preparing a statement about the state of poetry, in the context of the "magic" that is wrought always by good poetry, that could be seen as a reply to the "enemies of Imagism." To Amy Lowell, he wrote at the time:

> The enemies of Imagism are all about our heads. I shall be in for the shock of attacks when the Anthology comes out. I want to make myself sure in the introduction. I've been begged to leave it alone. In considering this matter it's not a case of merely looking at appearances, there is something deeper that both the public and the critics have got to realize. I think I've got them on that

one question of 'Magic.' I had a test of it the other day. A friend debated the opposition with me, and I held that in reserve until after we had exhausted nearly all the arguments on both sides. On that point he surrendered. 'Work that has that,' I said, 'is poetry, and if you concede that you concede all your other objections which are non-essential.' It was surprising how it worked.[12]

In its entirety this introduction for the 1915 *Anthology* constitutes Braithwaite's most passionately lyrical defense of the kind of romantic poetry he so dearly loved. To the twenty-seven-year-old Eliot, whose few poems were characterized by imagery of sordid things in a squalid world, Braithwaite's introduction must have spoken about contemporary poetry in exactly the wrong terms. Moreover, not only did the *Transcript*'s critic advocate the writing of a kind of emotional poetry that Eliot would soon oppose in his critical and theoretical writings but he chose to begin his apology for such romantic poetry with a paean to the month of April, a decision that would ultimately have more to do with the opening lines of *The Waste Land* (as published) than did Shakespeare or Robert Browning or even, as so many critics have asserted, Geoffrey Chaucer.[13] Braithwaite's introduction begins:

> The very name of *April* has a quiet mystery when spoken: as if at the sound of those soft and liquid letters some haunting *memory* begins to glow with indefinable ecstasies. The name leads one to sense a curious kind of secrecy, wherein some *stirring* and changing miracles are happening. It lures one into harmony with something intangibly but delightfully and poignantly strange. No *month* is named so appropriately. A-P-R-I-L, is sound and color of the spirit and substance of *earth*. There is a pagan sensitiveness to grace and beauty in the naming. There is a vigorous moral courtesy in the reliance upon a name that is physically so frail. Yet it is the one *month* of the year to which we apply the word Eternal. It is a Breath, a Vision, a Realization of Immortality. In its constant fleetingness of moods, it symbolizes Permanence. It is a spiritual flame, burning with prophecies and declarations. And its one message is *Life!*[14] (italics added)

If April's message is "Life" and if, moreover, "the serene intensity of April dawns and twilights prepare the sacraments, and Poetry with her habiliment of dreams and visions, carries the blessed bread and wine of life for the communion of supplicant humanity" (as Braithwaite says later on), then consider the opening lines of *The Waste Land,* the first section of which is entitled "The Burial of the Dead." (I have italicized the words in Eliot that first appear in Braithwaite's opening paragraph.)

> *April* is the cruellest *month,* breeding
> Lilacs out of the dead land, mixing
> *Memory* and desire, *stirring*
> Dull roots with spring rain.

> Winter kept us warm, covering
> *Earth* in the forgetful snow, feeding
> A little *Life* with dried tubers.[15]

It may be, incidentally, that these lines are "a denial of Chaucer," as Hugh Kenner asserts,[16] but if so, they deny him not in Chaucer's own language, but in William Stanley Braithwaite's very words.

We can now return, after quoting these lines that extol the workings of the "cruellest" month, whose name Braithwaite found "physically so frail"— a month that brings about "recurrence" and not "resurrection"—to Braithwaite's next two paragraphs.

> That is why the spirit of Poetry is so akin to the spirit of April. The April mood sanctifies the poet's dreams. He has come, through them, to realize the eternal grace that beats in the pulse of life. April typifies, not so much Resurrection, as Recurrence. The great Rhythm with its discords is also a Rhythm with its increasing harmonies, and it is this Divine Accent which April strikes, that opens the vistas of an infinite and eternal conviction of life.
>
> This touch of mystery that comes creeping out of the shadow into the sunlight, transfiguring all with a motionless alchemy of breath, and color, and odor, evokes from poetry a similar touch of mystery that comes out of the shadows of human sorrow and pain into the joyousness of aspiration, a transfiguring power of Faith, Hope, and Love, quickening the nature of man.[17]

Surely Eliot would not quarrel with Braithwaite's observation that April brings about recurrence and not resurrection, but, unlike Braithwaite, he finds this fact less a matter for celebration or even neutral acceptance than the occasion of voicing a complaint. Braithwaite's promise, moreover, that the three traditional virtues—Faith, Hope, and Love—will "quicken" man gets transformed in *The Waste Land,* in the final section "What the Thunder Said," into *Da—Datta, Dayadhvam,* and *Damyata*—that is to say, as the poet explains in his notes to the poem, Give, Sympathize, and Control. Eliot's prophetic words, unlike Briathwaite's buoyant ones, are meant to castigate and chastise rather than console.

Yet Braithwaite and Eliot are not always completely at odds. It might even be said that in some ways *The Waste Land* is in accord with Braithwaite's views of what poetry would be like in the "era of new poetry" emerging in 1915:

> The life of the "people" or the life of the aristocracy, the life that is vulgar and oppressed, that is criminal or ignorant, as well as the life that idealizes virtue and morality, that is cultivated and noble, life that is past in antiquity and history, as well as the life we experience in our rapidly changing modern world, have all an equal chance to be made vivid and real, vital and actually manifest by the eternal embodiments of Truth and Beauty.[18]

Braithwaite's Whitmanian democratic impulse or his final Keatsian plea notwithstanding, it can be said that in its range over historical/ mythical time and its movement through levels of society, *The Waste Land* reflects each of the extremes and contraries listed by Braithwaite. It is also true, however, that Eliot sees in what is "vulgar" and "ignorant" disturbing spiritual truths that Braithwaite's more generous impulses did not allow him to recognize as such.

As for Eliot's use of a mythic method in *The Waste Land,* there again the poet parts company with Braithwaite. It will be recalled that of James Joyce's practice in *Ulysses,* Eliot wrote: "Myth is simply a way of controlling, or ordering, of giving a shape and a significance to the immense panorama of futility and anarchy which is contemporary history."[19] In his similar employment of the mythic method in *The Waste Land* Eliot flies directly in the face of Braithwaite's warnings:

> If . . . a poet is attracted to the idealisms of Greek and Roman myths, and uses the symbols of their characters, with their passions and language, instead of a direct utterance of the language of modern democracy, he may be given every credit for poetical perfection: he will be said, by the passionate lovers of modernity, to have truth and beauty in his work—but no pulse of life. It must be understood that the pulse of life beats in poetry not from the theme but through the abstract realities of the poet's soul, breathing into the theme the inexplicable sentiency of being.[20]

The truths of the old myths, for Eliot, were certainly not always those of beauty in the sense in which Braithwaite always employs the term, though the truths they embody, Eliot would argue, would make them always beautiful, even when they inspire horror and terrify. If Braithwaite would praise the beauty of Keats's poem and the urn it celebrates, Eliot, in the period of *The Waste Land* at least, would see the terrifying beauty (because of its truth) of Tereu's rape of Philomela.

Braithwaite also appeals to something he calls "the inexplicable sentiency of being." What I take to be the meaning of this phrase is something like the writer's capacity for poetry-making emotion. It is related to the poet's peculiar personality in its particulars. "All poetry comes out of feeling," Braithwaite says with great assurance; "the degree to which feeling is personalized in images determines not the logic of form but the measure of emotion and imagination which gets into the substance."[21] Compare Eliot, writing a few years later: "Poetry is not a turning loose of emotion, but an escape from emotion; it is not the expression of personality, but an escape from personality."[22] That is not to say, of course, that the personalities of others—not the poet's—might not be expressed, for they can be: as they are, say, in "A Game of Chess." There and elsewhere the creator of the couple who crackle at one another over their little games (as well as Prufrock) encourages us to react skeptically to Braithwaite's statement: "The final test of poetry is its magic. It is not the feeling of contemplative anxiety aroused by the philosophic or moral imagination that gives to poetry its highest value as an art, but the agitated wonder awakened in the spirit of the reader by the sudden evocation of magic."[23] Braithwaite had of course got it exactly wrong—when his position is seen in the context of Eliot's burgeoning "modernism." In this sense *The Waste Land* can be viewed as a prophetic answer to Braithwaite's standard form of romantic theorizing about poetry circa 1915. How odd it is that the words of the well-meaning poetry reviewer of the *Boston Evening Transcript,* Cousin Harriet's newspaper of preference, should have so directly challenged the young poet who was to write the great showpiece poem of American modernism and that Braithwaite should never have acknowledged the fact. Even when he had the opportunity to do so, in a letter to Marianne Moore when she was awarded the Bollingen Prize in 1952, he wrote with no knowledge, apparently, of his own catalytic role in the making of Eliot's poem. It was her part he extolled. "How much, I wonder, does the present generation realize the part you played in introducing Eliot's 'The Waste Land' to the public, an act that had a profound bearing upon the tendencies and development of the imagination and technique of a whole generation of poets."[24]

Notes

1. T. S. Eliot, "The *Boston Evening Transcript,"* in *The Complete Poems and Plays* (New York: Harcourt Brace, 1952), 16–17.

2. Philip Butcher, "Introduction" to *The William Stanley Braithwaite Reader,* ed. Philip Butcher (Ann Arbor: University of Michigan Press, 1972), 3.

3. See Donald Gallup, *T. S. Eliot: A Bibliography* (London: Faber & Faber, 1969), 196.

4. W. S. B., "An Exotic Poet: A Scorner of the Ordinary Substance of Human Nature," *Boston Evening Transcript,* 14 April 1920, part 2, p. 6.

5. *The Letters of T. S. Eliot, Vol. 1, 1898–1922,* ed. Valerie Eliot (San Diego: Harcourt Brace Jovanovich, 1988), 384.

6. *The Letters of Ezra Pound 1907–1941,* ed. D. D. Paige (New York: Harcourt, Brace & World, 1950), 62, 66.

7. William Stanley Braithwaite, "Introduction" to *Anthology of Magazine Verse for 1915 and Year Book of American Poetry,* ed. William Stanley Braithwaite (New York: Laurence J. Gomme, 1915), xviii.

8. Kenny J. Williams, "William Stanley Braithwaite," *Dictionary of Literary Biography,* vol. 50: *Afro-American Writers Before the Harlem Renaissance,* ed. Trudier Harris and Thadious M. Davis (Detroit: Gale Research, 1986), 15 and 17.

9. Braithwaite, *Anthology for 1915,* xxv.

10. The author of "Sowing" is Frederick R. McCreary. The poem begins "April is a man" (*Anthology of Magazine Verse for 1923,* ed. William Stanley Braithwaite [Boston: B. J. Brimmer, 1923], 238–41).

11. Braithwaite, " 'Introduction' to *Anthology of Magazine Verse for 1927,"* in *Braithwaite Reader,* 87.

12. *Braithwaite Reader,* 256.

13. For the persistence of this putative connection to Chaucer, see, for example, Elizabeth Drew, *T. S. Eliot: The Design of His Poetry* (New York: Scribners, 1949), 68; Hugh Kenner, *The Invisible Poet: T. S. Eliot* (New York: McDowell, Obolensky, 1959), 157; and Burton Raffel, *T. S. Eliot* (New York: Frederick Ungar, 1982), 72.

14. Braithwaite, "Introduction" to *Anthology for 1915,* xi.

15. T. S. Eliot, "The Waste Land," in *Complete Poems and Plays,* 37.

16. Kenner, *Invisible Poet,* 157.

17. Braithwaite, "Introduction" to *Anthology for 1915,* xi–xii.

18. Ibid., xv.

19. T. S. Eliot, "Ulysses, Order, and Myth," *Dial,* November 1923, pp. 480–83.

20. Braithwaite, "Introduction" to *Anthology for 1915,* xv.

21. Ibid., xxi.

22. T. S. Eliot, "Tradition and the Individual Talent," in *The Sacred Wood* (London: Methuen, 1953), 58.

23. Braithwaite, "Introduction" to *Anthology for 1915,* xxiii.

24. *Braithwaite Reader,* 298.

The Waste Land: Eliot's Play of Voices

John T. Mayer

Almost as soon as it appeared in print, *The Waste Land*'s integrity was questioned. Contemporary reviewers wondered whether its "bright-coloured pieces" formed an "integrated design"[1] or simply a "kaleidoscopic confusion," what Conrad Aiken called an "emotional ensemble" with "a kind of forced unity."[2] Eliot was uneasy enough about whether the pieces cohered that he spoke reassuringly in the Notes about a "plan" and referred readers to Jessie Weston and *The Golden Bough;* it was Eliot himself who thus inspired a half century of misdirected efforts to unify the poem through the wasteland myth. The failure to do so, however, is no argument against the integrity of the poem whose source is to be found elsewhere. Its parts are shaped, not forced, into an "ensemble" by the tensions and resolution of an inward quest that transforms the individual and his relation to the world; this shaping occurs especially through the play of voices, whose central role in the poem is clearly indicated by Eliot's original title, "He do the police in different voices." The published title shifted the emphasis from the voices to the quest, and distorted its direction. For this quest is not from death to life but from life to death; it is away from the life cults of *The Golden Bough* toward the death enjoined in the Buddha's Fire Sermon and the wisdom traditions of the East.[3]

The quest conducted in the poem is as elemental as the forces associated with the fertility cults; it has to do with disclosing the nature of life in this world, and the horror of living in a certain way. Its catalyst is the return of spring, an event which, in its repetition, universality, timelessness, and immersion in time, overwhelms the resigned voice that observes it with the sudden force of a revelation. For the recognition of spring as a return, a recurrence, repels through its suggestion of entrapment in a world of repetition and forces the examination of the meaning of life in this world. This initial reluctance to reenter the life of memory, desire, and breeding disposes the individual to bury the dead not, as in the fertility rites, so that life will repeat its cycle (night to day, winter to spring) but so that, as in the Christian ritual of "The Burial of the Dead," which Eliot used to point his theme here,

This essay was written specifically for this volume and is published here for the first time by permission of the author. For further elaboration on some of the concepts presented here, see John T. Mayer, *T. S. Eliot's Silent Voices* (New York: Oxford University Press, 1989).

life may be changed, transcended. The observer of spring's return, a return that evokes the Eastern world of the endless cycles of life, sees himself immersed in this world, and gradually recognizes that its life is death, its city unreal. This is the burden of his witness to the Unreal City and to the "hypocrite lecteur," who are images of himself bound upon the wheel and thus bonded to him by the need to be transformed. His experience is their experience, his vision may become their vision.

The spectacle and voices of his vision transform his attitude toward life in this world and this alters his sense of himself. Seeing life in a new way implies reshaping himself to live in a new way: epiphany invites self-transformation, and finally, self-transcendence. In this sense *The Waste Land* is the culmination of a continuous quest implied in all Eliot's early poetry, which is largely a poetry of the questing consciousness, the record of a highly self-conscious seeker's search for the meaning of life and of himself in his own tangled feelings and his relations with an often hostile world. Behind Eliot's recurring quester-figure is the Prufrockian ambition to assume the prophet role and disturb the universe. Though Prufrock the would-be prophet is trapped by his own self-consciousness—he will not speak and fears to live—for Eliot, consciousness holds the potential for entrapment or release, and these alternatives, like the other claims and possibilities of experience, most compellingly realize themselves as a play of voices in consciousness. Eliot's provisional title "He do the police in different voices" acknowledges the intensification of this paradigm into the radical and pervasive strategy of *The Waste Land.*[4]

It is through the play of voices, then, that the protagonist, the "he" of "He do the police," learns to see life in a new way and to shape a new identity. This poem of voices enacts its quest over a psychic landscape whose features are the scenes and especially the voices from which the seeker gradually uncovers meaning. This sense of the poem is clear in Eliot's original epigraph from Conrad's *Heart of Darkness,* which shows us what he conceived the poem to be, as Pound's Petronian epigraph does not, and explains why he was so emphatic to Pound about its accuracy: "it is *much* the *most appropriate* I can find" (my emphasis). The poem is to be the retrospective of a life, the moment of truth that clarifies the meaning of life: "Did he live his life again in every detail of desire, temptation, and surrender during that supreme moment of complete knowledge?" *The Waste Land* is such a reliving of the "details" which, taken together, constitute a supreme epiphany that redefines the meaning of life and death.

Retrospection and epiphany occur in the poem in the manner of *Heart of Darkness:* Kurtz first "presented himself [to Marlow] as a voice . . . that carried with it a sense of real presence" (119).[5] Indeed, voices are such presences in *The Waste Land* that they usurp the protagonist's role and displace him as a presence; like Kurtz possessed and transformed by the voice of the wilderness that "whispered to him things about himself which he did not know" (133), the protagonist is possessed—and the surface of the poem is dominated by—his own voices, which tell him things about life in this world he did not know. Kurtz is led to a horrific metamorphosis; by the time Marlow sees him, he is a darkly shining "apparition" (135), "an animated image of death carved out of old ivory" (135). This "shadow" (136) still seems to Marlow "a voice! a voice!" (136) but now through struggle transformed, extraordinary: "common everyday words . . . had behind them . . . the terrific suggestiveness of words heard in dreams, of phrases spoken in nightmares" (143–44). This sense of voice and of language as possessed, as empowered with the "terrific suggestiveness" of "phrases spoken in nightmares,"[6] gradually transforms the protagonist's voices of memory and experience, of myth and literature, of poets and prophets, into his vision. Through the act of attending to these voices, that is, by the act of the mind that is the poem, the discovering seeker gradually buries his dead, uncovers the meaning of life, takes on the prophet role, and utters his witness.

The details of this extended act of retrospective epiphany expand in reference partly through the archetypal, mythic, and intersecting implications of the experience. Like the fortune-teller's cards that hold simultaneously the cup and lance of the medieval Grail legend, of Christ's sacrifice, and of the ancient fertility rituals, as well as the protagonist's fortune and an index of the poem's characters and events, its details are multivalent signifiers, tokens of differing levels of awareness and initiation. If Jessie Weston gave Eliot any "plan" for the poem, it was as a way of seeing connections, through the layered meanings in things; this explains how her book "will elucidate the difficulties of the poem," as the wasteland myth does not.

Through making connections, revealed in the sequencing of its details and voices, the protagonist moves from the condition of connecting nothing with nothing in his "heap of broken images" to the achievement of shoring "fragments" against his "ruins." The process transforms his personal experience into prophetic witness, so that the act of mind that begins as personal seeking becomes a vision that describes simultaneouusly his state of soul and the state of the world. His vision expands its implications particularly as he takes on the voices of poets and prophets; when he thinks their words, he sees through their eyes; out of such fused seeing, he gradually produces a new thing, a "third" thing, his own vision.[7]

This simultaneity through which his retrospective, overlapping, and fusing experience builds the poem's vision has eluded readers and cirtics, as it eluded Pound, who systematically eliminated references that turn events prophetic.[8] Yet the mythic resonances of the poem's published title urge the universality of its personal details, and the Petronian epigraph sets this in a public, prophetic context, even if one of rejection and mockery; the Sibyl was particularly consulted concerning the life of the City. The published epigraph with its alien Latin and Greek also points up the need to translate in order to retrieve meaning, a point further emphasized at the end of Part I when Eliot appropriates Baudelaire's "You! hypocrite lecteur!" to involve the reader intimately and necessarily in the task of completing the poem's meaning through a personal translating of its voices and vision.

The context of the Conrad epigraph emphasizes both the universality of Kurtz's vision and the need to move, like the prophet, beyond appearances: "his stare . . . could not see the flame of the candle, but was wide enough to embrace the whole universe, piercing enough to penetrate all the hearts that beat in the darkness" (149). Kurtz discovers the horror of his way of living; this is what the protagonist discovers, and what Eliot invites us to discover. The voice of the Sibyl in her cage suggests that prophets find their visions "in the cage" of their own lives. Like the Sibyl, the protagonist awaits a death that will release him from bondage to this life, and his release comes, as did Kurtz's, from looking within: "alone in the wilderness, [his soul] had looked within itself, and, by heavens! I tell you, it had gone mad" (144). To look within to this depth involves a kind of madness, shown most obviously in the poem's obsessive, often neurotic imagery (especially Parts I and III), distortive fantasies (Part II), hallucinogenic passages (Part V), and closing reference to Hieronymo's madness. The protagonist knows that he will be shown "something different" than the shadow life of his daily experience. As with Marlow, who sees "as though a veil had been removed from my eyes" (117), the experience casts a sometimes terrifying light on such "shadows."

This process shapes *The Waste Land* into Eliot's most radically presentational poetic work. The retrospective reliving is immediate, and its details, as events and voices, displace the self in the foreground of consciousness so that, in effect, the self becomes a spectator to its experience; it is the way Tiresias sees as seer. But Tiresias is not the self experiencing, but only one of many voices, a "mere spectator" because this is not his experience but the protagonist's. Nor is he a "character" but a "personage," "uniting all the rest" of the characters because he alone has universal sexual knowledge ("the two sexes meet in Tiresias") as well as prophetic vision. Entering the poem when he does, he climaxes the protagonist's discovery of his own prophet identity first begun when the voices of Ezekiel and Ecclesiastes sound in his mind, and continued as he thinks in the words of poet-prophets such as Dante and Spenser, Milton and Baudelaire, John the Divine and Jeremiah.

The prophet is first a spectator, a *seer;* when Eliot in his note on Tiresias distinguishes him from a "character," he invites us through his quotation marks to read character figuratively, as the figures and shapes through which the prophet reads the condition of the world, partly through the "character," the attitudes and values, that individuals display. The seer differs from these "actors" in the world of appearances: they do things that he watches; they enact roles on a stage they cannot comprehend, whereas he penetrates appearance, time, and motives. They are like Oedipus, who sees and thinks he knows, and scorns his prophet's witness. The poem's characters see with the appearance-eyes of Oedipus, and so at the outset does the protagonist, who gradually takes on through the voices he hears the reality-vision of the prophet that brings release from the world of appearance.

The poem's mode, then, is double-visioned: on one level is the two-dimensional flat world of ordinary experience and quotidian routines in the Unreal City of "characters" walking around in a ring bound on the turning Wheel; on another is the prophet's vision, an enlarged way of seeing that makes Tiresias a "personage," one of power and presence, a norm for judging the meaning of "the rest" in that, living in two worlds, knowing both sexes, and comprehending all times, he sees the "third" dimension that "walks always beside" events, the "that" or meaning ("But who is that on the other side of you?") on the other side of this world. A personage is one worthy of imitating, and the protagonist fully enters into his prophet-identity when he takes on the reality-vision of Tiresias, the comprehensive perspective that transcends time, sex, and the life of this world. As his earlier voices prepared him for this central moment of the poem, later voices confirm this identity and enlarge his experience. St. Augustine and the Buddha reveal more completely the nature of the life of appearances, and the Voice of the Thunder offers the possibility of release.

This process of uncovering the prophet's call in these voices parallels his discovery that his own experience is "wide enough to embrace the whole universe"; it is the stuff of prophecy. The cycle of repetition suggested by the return of spring is quickly confirmed by other voices: the sunny innocence of life in the Hofgarten is subverted by the testimony of sleepless nights and the boring round of society's seasons. The Lithuanian who, speaking German, disavows her heritage is a naive voice of cultural confusion, so that what follows, "And down we went," takes on cultural as well as personal resonances which tell the seeker that he dwells in a confused world of divided loyalties not different from Ezekiel's, and which remind him that ancient instances of chaos formed the ground of prophecy. The context of the Lord's epithet for Ezekiel, "Son of Man," emphasizes that the prophet needs mainly courage before his own fear and the indifference of others: "Stand on your feet and I will speak to you. . . . Whether [others] hear [you] or refuse to hear . . . they will know that there has been a prophet among them" (Ezekiel 2:1, 5).

Still, the protagonist distrusts his call: do words addressed to earlier prophets call him to their task? The voice of his own skepticism argues the unlikeliness that what he knows, "a heap of broken images," will yield vision. However, another voice beckons to a world of shadows, as the source of "something different" from the quotidian shadows of his own comings and goings. The promised revelation comes through new voices, from the Hyacinth Garden *and Tristan und Isolde.* The opera's voices reinforce the promise-frustration pattern developed in the earlier April, Hofgarten, and Marie episodes, for the sailor's fresh wind that takes him from his love symbolizes the deceptive force of romantic passion that carries Tristan and Isolde to their fateful destiny and all lovers in the poem to theirs. The outcome of such encounters is death, and not the life promised by the fertility cults. Lovers' meetings lead to *Liebestod,* death brought by love. For Eliot, the fertility rites are entrapping, ensuring bondage to the Wheel of nature's cycles without leading to a higher life. The Hyacinth Garden is not the site of ecstasy experience but of ambiguity, frustration, and, as the mythic Hyacinth discovered, death.

Shaken, the seeker consults Madame Sosostris, the prophet trivialized to the fortune-teller; his "horoscope" (Greek, *hora* [hour] or *horos* [year] and *skopein* [to look at]) outlines his situation at this time, in this world. In his own card, the drowned Phoenician sailor, he discovers something extraordinary ("Look!"), the possibility of transformation: "Those are pearls that were his eyes." Like Hyacinth transformed by Apollo into a flower associated with spring and rebirth (and thus with the Great Wheel), with remembrance in art, and, through Easter hyacinths, with resurrection and eternal life, the protagonist through death may experience transformation, though whether by literal or symbolic death is unclear. Other cards relate to his present situation: Belladonna, a contrariety figure (beautiful lady; poisonous drug, used to enlarge the pupil of the eye), suggests that a woman who is poison to him may also enlarge his vision; the man with the phallic staves points up his sexual allegiance. The Wheel is the Wheel of Fortune, a sign that this world is not to be trusted, but particularly it is the Eastern Wheel of repetition, of entrapment in the cycles of this life. The seeker's reluctance to enter into April's renewal prefigures his turning from the life of the Wheel. Together, the cards profile one living in the world of the fertility cults, but who with knowledge may be transformed and delivered from his place upon the Wheel. The remaining cards pose the barriers to transformation. The one-eyed merchant transacts this world's business only; as Mr. Eugenides, he is a debased version of the Phoenician sailors and Syrian merchants who spread the cult mysteries, reminding us of the power of these life-rites. The walking crowds move in a "ring" of repetitive routines, trapped in the rounds of naturalistic life in this world.

Reading the cards' code, the protagonist in the original version now sees the world with enlarged eyes, taking on through the words of John the Divine ("I John saw these things") his vision. Pound canceled the line and Eliot acceded, recognizing that the skeptical protagonist must work through the "details" of his past to confirm his prophet identity. In the published poem he now begins this process, not through sudden but gradual enlargement of perception gained by assimilating his experience to others' visions. He *sees* through the voices of Dante and Baudelaire that his city, the Unreal City, is their city. Its people are Dante's walking dead, with vision "fixed" to the ground, narrowed to earth, to this world only. They are also Baudelaire's spectral figures who accost our conventional sense of things. The fusion of visions releases his own vision, of a world without past or present, but only reprtition. He has moved beyond these voices' individual visions and seen a new thing; he has enlarged his sense of things.

As a result he recognizes "one he knew" in a new way, and himself as well. He calls to Stetson over the ages and through personal and cultural intersections that evoke Eliot's American background, the mythic Western cowboy, and lonely figures on many frontiers; that fuse men in battles ancient and modern, in "Great" wars and Punic wars, all of which endlessly repeat the same pattern—the life and death of individuals, nations, and empires. From this higher perspective he sees that all wars are one war, all cities one city, all times one time for those bound upon the Wheel. Rituals too fuse as he sardonically asks this returning veteran of the Wheel whether the corpse he planted in his garden has sprouted, ensuring another year of life and death. Stetson is one of the ignorant crowd trapped in the ring of repetition, and his corpse is the ritual figure of the fertility cult, but the protagonist's dead encompass those deadened to life or ignorant of the Wheel, as well as the ghosts of his own past, just as his garden includes the personal and symbolic gardens of readers now forced into the poem to participate in what we think we merely observe, to "see" fully by reading with the seer's enlarged eyes.

By the end of Part I the protagonist, by "doing" the "different voices" of his experience, has begun to bury his dead in a way different from Stetson, and to see beyond the life of this world. He has moved decisively from his point of departure, resignation before another April and another turn upon the Wheel. In Part II, he sees in the emptiness of his own marriage and those of others that even relationships begun with commitment bind individuals to the Wheel.

The original title "In the Cage," in alluding to the Sibyl as caged prophet, suggests that the would-be prophet is caged by a marriage that turns his eye from the vision to his own anguish; yet this cage may release the prophet within the husband. He looks at his marriage and sees parody lovers who sing a parody *Liebestod,* confirming that love is death. The wife at her "vanity" is desperate to be acknowledged; he sees in her the fire, the misplaced passion, of the life cults, and his overwrought fantasy of their bedroom as a synthetic Temple of Venus reduces her to a parody temptress who arouses him to nothing but burlesque. Through a collage of literary voices he mocks her through association with a procession of legendary temptresses—Eve, Cleopatra, Dido, Pope's Belinda—who distract heroes from their tasks. Her desire is clear, but the only sexual exchange in the scene is recorded in a picture of the "change of Philomel," a rape. For the protagonist, marriage is a cage of animality, his wife is a parody-lover, and sex is dirty, "Jug Jug."

As she tries to communicate, his lack of voice parodies their failure to relate and his absorption in his inner voices. Succeeding "exchanges" emphasize the emptiness of their life together, but the obsessive repetition of "nothing" and of O's associated with him project his disposition to accept the nothingness of human relationship, and of his personal life in this world. To the insistent question, does he remember nothing, he responds to himself with the leitmotif of metamorphosis, "Those are pearls that were his eyes," a norm through which to clarify his nothingness. This Shakespeherian "rag," a kind of raga or holy line, intimates the metamorphosis of the fleshly eye into a pearl, a jewel of vision (prophecy) or of art (the poem), and, in the higher sense, the pearl of great price, faith, something strange to earthly vision. The exchange ends with the desperate questions, "What shall I do now . . . tomorrow . . . ever?" Life on the Wheel brings the seeker to the ultimate question, how to escape the turning and meet the void of "ever."

The conventional reading of the pub scene that follows, to extend the emptiness of marriage to all classes—upper-class neurotic lovelessness and infertility give way to lower-class mechanical fertility and abortion for a "good time"—does not account for the scene as part of the protagonist's experience. Yet it is a crucial part of his progressive enlightenment, indeed, a turning point, the catalyst that determines him to change his life. Its import is carried in the upper-case "transformation" of the pubkeeper's last call into the Last Trump, a call to Final Judgment. Resigned to playing out the game of marriage until death, he sees in the pub that Judgment, "its time," cannot be stayed. He must seek transformation now, not in the outer world that he may not be able to alter, but in his inner world of attitude, the world that matters because it is the world that, by attitude, can be freed from the Wheel. Having buried his dead in Part I, he hears in the pubsters slurred "goonights" that he must bid farewell to the ladies; thinking of Ophelia's "Good night, sweet ladies" and the popular song's "Good night, ladies, we're going to leave you now," he hears his own goodbye to sex and love. The ladies of Part II confirm that love is death: vampish allure and death (Cleopatra), rape and death (Philomel), desertion and death (Dido), fertility and death (Lil/Lilith). He is now prepared to be enlightened.

In Part III, the seeker sees his personal vision of life in this world confirmed by general human experience; this prepares him to say farewell not only to love but to life in this world. He sees enough to accept the message of the Buddha's Fire Sermon, to turn radically from this world. As with his other revelations, this occurs in stages. In a nightmarish meditation he first sees in the empty river and the barren land a vision of the world according to the empiricists, the world as matter and forces, and he experiences a horrific sense of death and corruption; this is followed by a parade of unholy lovers whose sexual conjunctions are the meetings of bodies only, the behavior of instinctual automatons. Interspersed, however, are voices of a higher vision that gradually reveal a way of enlightenment.

The Thames meditation that begins "The Fire Sermon" emphasizes the loss of the sacral in nature; the "nymphs," mythic signs of its presence, have "departed." What remains is empiricist nature, the result of the play of evolutionary forces now sustained through instinctive drives. Like the brown land, empiricist nature is bleak and reduced; humans revert to an earlier stage of evolution and behave rather than act, like animals. The voice of Spenser, the poet-prophet, recalls a different vision, of the "Sweet Thames" whose prothalamial "nymphes" are bonded to nature as "Daughters of the Flood" and whose stately procession celebrates marriage, continuity, and nobility as institutional means of rationalizing instinct and nature. The protagonist is so far removed from such a world that he sees himself as Jeremiah in exile, exiled from meaning in this life and from any higher life, for his river runs on and on to the end predicted by the play of empiricist forces, the void of grinning death. Obsessed, he can only think of death, sex, and naked bodies, maddened images that announce the procession of deathly lovers who now overpower him with evidence of the pervasive emptiness of the life of this world. He hears in the sounds of the city its behaviorist sexual drive, the "horns" and "motors" of automatons bound upon the Wheel.

The series of conjunctions, a parody of the medieval parade of the seven deadly sins, reduce the sexual act to various kinds of animal copulation in a pageant of sex in the empiricist world. The emptiness of the public crowds of Part I and of private lives in Part II is now the emptiness of a whole people trapped in the sexual round. He reenacts Augustine's experience in Carthage, whose caudron of unholy lusts failed to satisfy. At this point in the original *Waste Land,* the protagonist projects a Buddhist address to London, whose life is said to swarm and breed like a biological mechanism and whose people are "bound upon the wheel"; Eliot deleted it as perhaps a too obvious indicator, in view of the "Fire Sermon" title, of the "burning" which possesses this world. The seven deadly encounters are those of Sweeney and Mrs. Porter (sex as brutish and whorish), the rape of Philomel (sex as brutal rape), Mr. Eugenides (sex as commercial and casual), the clerk and typist (sex as mechanical and boring), and the three Thames daughters (sex as trivial and debasing). Together they project Eliot's world of birth, copulation, and death, whose bodily meetings are of throbbing human engines, instinctive, predictable, robotic.

These variations on the theme of sex as deathly life are particularly disturbing in their lack of feeling. Although full of brutality and appetite, this is a world without passion. Its sexual archetype is that of the clerk and typist, robots of Metropolis dominated by automatic mechanism—eyes and back that involuntarily "turn upward" at quitting time, automatic breakfast and teatime routines, the clerk's mechanics of assault, the typist's final indifference. The protagonist has seen enough of such coupling by this time to know that he is Tiresias, whose voice he takes on at this point in his experience because such sex has been the "substance" of his experience, revealing the bound condition of all in the Unreal City (literally confirmed by identifying the three Thames daughters with the *places* of their undoing, as if they are physically bound to the Wheel). The poem is now a fire sermon built of instances meant to pluck seers out of the burning.

The protagonist-prophet approaches illumination by preparing to enter into the conversion experience of Augustine, who turns from the things of this world, which do not satisfy, to the God who does. He also repeats the pattern of Aeneas, who found love in Carthage but no peace, until he turned from Dido to his higher calling. Dido's sacrifice upon the burning pyre, as well as Brunnhilde's immolation (evoked by the Thames daughters' complaisant songs) are fire sermons calling for a radical turning from sex, love, and the things of this world through the ultimate act of detachment, death. This is, of course, the whole point of the Buddha's Fire Sermon, whose fire is not that of lust or passion but of attachment. To be engaged by the things of this world is to be burning, and the way of release is "to be no more for this world." The way of detachment brings eventual release from the cycles of attraction and repulsion, and from their pattern of desire and frustration. In this sense the burning also refers to the purifying process by which attachment is overcome.

Thus illuminated by the words of Augustine and the Buddha, the protagonist ends Part III by beginning the process of detachment. The final lines indicate a process similar to Buddhist "emptying" through which individuals void themselves of personal identity, and even of dependence upon a personal deity or savior. The truncated lines remove first the "me," then the "Lord," to leave only the process, "burning."[9] The seeker has reached a *stage* of enlightenment: he knows what he must do, and accepts that *he* must do it, on his own. The end fragments mark as well the submergence of his personal identity in the higher role of prophet: the Lord plucks out his "me"; he assents to the power that the Lord bestows; as a result he becomes the burning vessel of the Lord, an inspired voice, a fire sermon.

In Part IV, "Death by Water," the protagonist contemplates a death different from the deathly lives he has seen that may image a way of release. In Part V, he undergoes the prophet's trial of faith that prepares him to hear the voice of release. When he interprets "what the thunder said," he ends his quest with a new beginning. In "Death by Water," what is "expected," to use Eliot's term, may be the personal self figured in the drowned Phoenician sailor, the poem's recurring signature of metamorphosis. As Phlebas the Phoenician, he typifies those who live by the life cult of the vegetation god that his forebears disseminated; as the drowned Phoenician sailor, he symbolizes those who by the waters of death turn from this world's life. Forgetting the gulls' crying and the profits and losses of this life, he reaches beyond the things of this world. Although still rising and falling in its currents, he is released from its cycles; his whirlpool is different from that of endlessly whirling time, which all who "turn the wheel" and look to "windward" keep in motion: it is the apocalyptic vortex, "something different" from the Wheel.

Phlebas is an example that all who turn the wheel are asked to "consider." He is a type of the protagonist who, by reliving the details of his life, replicates Phlebas's experience of passing the stages of age and youth during decomposition. This takes the protagonist's earlier images of corrupting flesh to a higher level: by literally detaching his matter from him, the self is emptied in a purifying action that brings a release such as that posited by Buddhist detachment and, in the Christian faith, by purgatory and the afterlife. Phlebas's death is a type of the transformation implied in the protagonist's horoscope, the revelation of "something different" from his immersion in this world's shadow life.

In Part V, having entered deeply into his prophet identity and its revelation, the protagonist endures the desert of trial that now tests the prophet as the prelude to final revelation. It takes the form of a crisis of belief, in the validity of his own vision and the possibility of deliverance. His despair is imaged as a nightmare journey in a wasted and ruined land; he thirsts so fiercely that merely the sound of water makes it real, until the mind recognizes the deception. Here is his final trial, that he has urged his own vision into being, and it is unreal. Has he seen the "third" dimension of reality, or is there only the flat world of shadows, of appearances?

He approaches the Chapel that Jessie Weston found to be the site of "an adventure in which supernatural, and evil, forces are engaged,"[10] but it is empty of horrors and, more pertinently, of the supernatural. It seems to exist solely on the natural level, with "only a cock" on its rooftree. "Only" seems to strip the cock of its traditional symbolism as the resurrected Christ, and to strip reality of any transcendence. But "only" read as "however" expands the natural object in significance, and this sign proves to be real, so that its crowing instantly—in a "flash of lightning" that is a flash of revelation to the protagonist—releases the longed-for rain that brings relief on the natural level and on the higher level cures the prophet's sterility of spirit. Weston notes that the ordeal at the Chapel is an initiation ritual carried out on a double level, the lower, into the mysteries of generation, the higher, into spiritual divine life.[11] In the poem, this higher initiation occurs when the rain-bearing "gust," an aspect of the lower initiation, releases the voice of the thunder of Hindu fable, the agent of the protagonist's higher initiation. In the fable, the thunder *is* the voice of the divine lord of the creatures, and the title of this part, "What the Thunder Said," affirms that the divine has communicated with the world. By responding, the protagonist acknowledges the divine principle in the universe: he has passed his crisis of belief.

In the fable, what this voice says is simply *Da,* on the lower level a noise, an appearance, but on the higher level a sound, a sign to be interpreted. The hearers—gods, humans, demons—interpret it in their own way. The three groups suggest its universal import, as addressed to the whole world of "souls," but it sounds differently in the ears and hearts of each, as (in Eliot's translation in the Notes) Give, Sympathise, Control. The protagonist hears three Das, accepts the groups' interpretations, and in turn interprets the interpretations in images that largely acknowledge his, and others', failure to respond to these injunctions. We have not given our selves in the Buddhist or in the Christian sense of "surrender"; our own self-obsessed "thinking" further imprisons us; yet giving and sympathy seem to be disciplines that, if cultivated, would yield a controlled life.

The protagonist admits, in effect, that he has failed to love, not in an earthly way, but in the high way intimated by the sacrifices, the fire sermons, of figures such as Dido and Brunnhilde, and by the water-death of Phlebas. This confession releases him from bondage to his past, so that he sits now with the wasteland "behind" him. Guided by his voices, he has seen the "horror" of this heart of darkness and determines to amend his life, by setting "at least" his own lands in order. He has arrived at a new beginning, though sobered by the magnitude of his task. As his final voices speak to him, they are not so much "broken" as saving fragments through which to avoid ruin. The child's chant of falling London Bridge reminds him of the collapse of this world's cities and this world's loves ("Take the key and lock her up, my fair lady"), and the Dantesque fragment that follows recalls the need to hide the self in the refining fire of suffering.

The next voices point a way of release from this world while he remains in this world. Recalling the deceptive quality of the nightingale's song (whose beauty hides sexual pain) and a poet's yearning to sing like the swallow, they invite the protagonist to end his own silence as poet and prophet by transformation and active commitment to vocation. He and others have suffered through sexuality and love; by singing his experience, he dies to the life of nature to serve art, and through art utters his witness to others, so that they may see, and he be purged. Thinking of the "dispossessed" prince by the ruined tower, he perhaps recognizes that he must be emptied of his self and his worldly attachments for his own good, to live authentically and to serve as a model for others.

The use of these fragments is finally clarified through Hieronymo's voice, which asserts the value of role-playing and indirection as a kind of madness through which to restore order to the individual and the world. In Hieronymo's play, art becomes life and roles become real; not "characters" but players are killed, who enact their own deaths by playing their roles. By playing fully the roles of poet and prophet, the protagonist continues the process of self-emptying begun at the end of "The Fire Sermon." This is perhaps Eliot's final point in the poem, that we live—or die—best by the way we play the roles we are called to, roles that can bring us peace. This discovery comes through the kind of painful process-quest enacted in the poem. When the three commands are heard again, they are spoken not by the thunder but by the protagonist, who repeats them ritualistically, a sign of his commitment. This releases the thrice-repeated "shantih" that closes the poem through a voice of blessing, a sign of the peace that the long struggle bestows.

But this most extravagant of Eliot's poems finally has no ending: the process of ending it is itself endless, requiring all readers, who have been incorporated into the poem and its quest almost from the outset, to "end" it for themselves. We complete it by discovering in the "details" of our own experience the equivalents of the protagonist's stages of enlightenment. He reaches understanding through his successive voices; through the process of the poem he puts the wasteland behind him and says "shantih." Readers who put *The Waste Land* behind them may join in this benediction, now in their own voices.

Notes

1. Louis Untermeyer, *Freeman*, 6 (17 January 1923): 453; rpt. in *T. S. Eliot: The Critical Heritage, vol. 1*, ed. Michael Grant (London: Routledge & Kegan Paul, 1982), 151.

2. *New Republic*, 33 (7 February 1923): 294–95; rpt. in *T. S. Eliot: The Critical Heritage, vol. 1*, 158, 160.

3. The presence of Eastern thought, and particularly of Buddhist thought, in *The Waste Land* is widely acknowledged but not deeply absorbed. Eliot studied Indic texts and traditions as a graduate student at Harvard, but their profound import for the poem reflects the fact that, as Stephen Spender reports, at the time of writing *The Waste Land,* Eliot was thinking seriously of becoming a Buddhist. See *T. S. Eliot* (New York: Penguin, 1976), 20.

4. For a full discussion of the nature of Eliot's early poetry as a poetry of consciousness and of the role of voice in this poetry, see John T. Mayer, *T. S. Eliot's Silent Voices* (New York: Oxford University Press, 1989).

5. All quotations are from *Heart of Darkness* (New York: New American Library, 1950). Page references follow each quotation.

6. This quality of language reminds us that *The Waste Land*'s voices and images often reflect what Ronald Bush, using a revealing phrase of Eliot's, calls "the poet's inner world of nightmare." In the poem, access to this world frequently occurs, as it did in Marlow's case, through "accidental" images drawn from everyday life which function like the accidental details of disturbing dreams that enable the mind to confront what it dare not in its waking state. At their most extreme, the voices and images drawn from this inward heart of darkness force ordinary life, what Eliot calls "the quotidian experience of the brain," into "seldom explored extremities of torture." See Ronald Bush, *T. S. Eliot: A Study in Character and Style* (New York: Oxford University Press, 1983), 50–52.

7. This sense of vision as a kind of third dimension that gives depth to "seeing" is consistent with Eliot's persistent concern with third figures and ideas in *The Waste Land,* in other poems, and in his own life. In the modern instance of the Antarctic expedition that was his source in Part V of *The Waste Land,* the third figure is a delusion; in the ancient instance at Emmaus, it is Christ, the third who is unknown to the disciples but later recognized by the eyes of faith. In poems associated with Eliot's marriage, a recurrent third figure complicates relationships; in Eliot's reading of Bradley's thought, a third, "higher" position is said to reconcile oppositions between two apparently contradictory positions.

8. Pound deleted the line "I John saw these things . . ." in Part I, deleted the "your" that turned the Unreal City passages into addresses to the city itself ("Unreal City, under the brown fog of *your* winter morn") in Parts I and III, questioned the use of the vocative in these passages and elsewhere, and deleted the London passage of "The Fire Sermon" that described the prophetic mind and ended with a reference to "another world."

9. Cleo McNelly Kearns, *T. S. Eliot and Indic Traditions* (Cambridge: Cambridge University Press, 1987), 76.

10. *From Ritual to Romance* (Cambridge: Cambridge University Press, 1920; rpt. Garden City, N.Y.: Doubleday, 1957), 175.

11. *From Ritual to Romance,* 182.

Index

abortion, 129, 197, 272
absence, 20, 205–17
Action Française, 194
Adonis, 27, 76, 141; *see also* fertility cults
After Strange Gods, 19, 220
"After the turning," 181
Aiken, Conrad, 2, 46, 172, 173, 177, 184, 196, 265
Aldington, Richard, 173
Anderson, Julia Quinn, 62
Anderson, Mary Quinn, 62
angst, 208–9
anthropologists, 188, 232–33; *see also* Frazer; Weston
Apollinaire, Guillaume: *Les Mamelles de Tirésias,* 126
April, 260–61
Ara Vos Prec, 149
"archetype," 113
Ariel Poems, 7, 194
Ariel's song, 96, 98, 102, 105, 109–10, 141
Arnaut, Daniel, 107, 148–50, 201, 217
Arnold, Matthew, 137; "Dover Beach," 136
artist, 113–14
asceticism, 102, 133, 134, 166n14, 198–99
Ash-Wednesday, 6, 7, 85–86, 102–3, 114, 141, 146, 147, 149, 151, 176, 185, 191, 194, 235
Attis, 27, 134, 141; *see also* fertility cults
"Aunt Helen," 257

Babbitt, Irving, 202
Babylonian Captivity, 90, 98–99, 130, 159

baptism, 105, 134, 146, 148, 243; *see also* rebirth; water imagery
Battenhouse, Roy, 150
"Baudelaire," 88
Baudelaire, Charles, 84, 92, 93, 94, 96, 194, 232, 268, 270; *Les Fleurs du Mal,* 128; "Les Sept Viellards," 127
Beare, Robert L., 45
Beaumont and Fletcher: *Philaster,* 123
"Bel Esprit," 45–46
Bell, Clive, 50
Belladonna, 91, 116, 126, 128, 136, 141, 270
Benét, William Rose, 3
Bennett, Arnold, 40, 225
Berg Collection, 61, 64, 173
Bergonzi, Bernard, 13
Berlin Wall, 251
Bishop, Jonathan, 16
Blackmur, R. P., 4
Blake, William, 235
blindness, 128, 129
Bloomsbury, 219, 222, 230; *see also* Woolf, Leonard and Virginia
Bolgan, Anne, 227
boredom, 253, 269
Boston Evening Transcript, 257–58, 263
"*Boston Evening Transcript,* The," 257
Bouilet, Louis, 173
Bradley, F. H.: *Appearance and Reality,* 169, 188
Brady, Ann P., 15
Braithwaite, William Stanley, 257–63: *Anthology of Magazine Verse,* 258–59
Braybrooke, Neville, 9